David Hirst

The Gun and the Olive Branch

The Roots of Violence in the Middle East

Futura
Macdonald & Co
London & Sydney

A Futura Book

First published in Great Britain by
Faber & Faber Limited in 1977

First Futura Publications edition 1978
Reprinted 1983

Copyright © David Hirst 1977

ISBN 0 7088 1401 8

Printed in Great Britain by
Hazell Watson & Viney Ltd
Aylesbury, Bucks

Futura Publications
A Division of
Macdonald & Co (Publishers) Ltd
Maxwell House
74 Worship Street
London EC2A 2EN

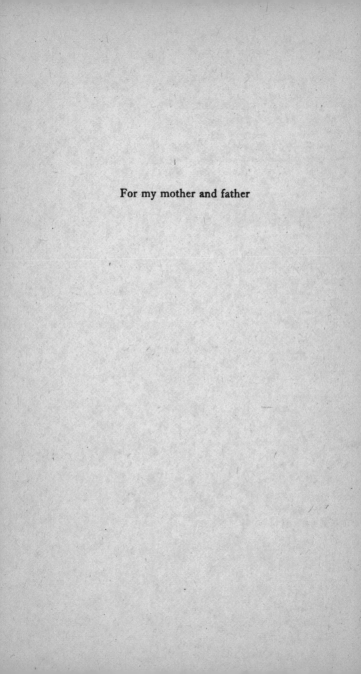

For my mother and father

Contents

Preface

In November 1974 Yasar Arafat, Chairman of the Palestine Liberation Organization, stood on the rostrum of the United Nations General Assembly and told the world: 'I have come bearing an olive branch and a freedom fighter's gun. Do not let the olive branch fall from my hand.' The Israelis promptly hurled it to the ground; it was, they said, a grotesquely stunted foliage. Arafat's peace offer was made in unusually theatrical circumstances, but it got essentially the same reception as all those—from either side—which had preceded it. The gun, not the olive branch, rules in the Middle East. It always has.

There have been four full-scale wars between the Arabs and the Israelis—in 1948, when the Jewish State came into being, in 1956, 1967, and 1973—but the history of one of the world's most implacable and dangerous conflicts reaches way back into the 1880s, when the earliest Zionist pioneers began to settle in Palestine, and from the very outset it has been shot through with continuous violence. The full-scale wars, once they are under way, tend to have a mindless character of their own, in which the single obsession of achieving victory or avoiding defeat masters all else; the lesser forms of violence often furnish more interesting insights into the nature of the conflict and the minds and motives of the protagonists.

The forms which this violence have taken are diverse. It has been both Arab and Jewish. It has been individual and spontaneous, or large-scale and state-sponsored; a selective assassination or an indiscriminate massacre of innocents; a clumsy protest of illiterate peasants or the ruthless exploits of 'revolutionary' zealots; frontier raids and reprisals, mobs on the rampage, or the deliberate uprooting, through terror, of whole communities. It has included some very conventional uses of violence and some weirdly unexpected and ingenious ones.

Diverse though it has been, the violence has had its own internal logic and patterns, its characteristic phases and episodes, and these, though sometimes intertwined with the larger cataclysms of the last quarter century, are clearly distinguishable from them. *The Gun and the Olive Branch* is an attempt to identify them in a straightforward chronological narrative. There have been several books on aspects of the subject—and a spate of them on the Palestinian guerillas who are its most spectacular contemporary manifestation—but historical surveys of Jewish or Arab violence, let alone the two together, are rare. Thus a mere chronicle of the events as they have occurred can lay claim to a certain originality in itself. It does not, of course, claim to be comprehensive—that would make an interminable catalogue. Nor does it dwell exclusively on the events themselves—it also encompasses the moral, political and psychological climate in which they take place.

In the author's opinion, only by tracing it stage by stage from its origins is it possible to expose the true nature of a conflict which has been unusually prone to prejudice and propaganda. Doubtless the first impulse of many readers, friends of Israel, will be to cry that if ever there were prejudice and propaganda it is here. But upon maturer reflection they will, he hopes, come to another conclusion: that the literature hitherto available to them, particularly if they are Americans, has been overwhelmingly Zionist in sympathy or inspiration. It is therefore only right and proper that the balance be redressed, the other side of the story told. It is also very important. For the acts of violence here described are no more than episodes in an inexorably unfolding drama which, more than any other conflict of our times, raises passions among ordinary people—in the West, the Soviet bloc and Asia—far beyond the arena in which it is enacted; a drama, almost Lilliputian in origin, whose ever-widening dimensions could eventually plunge mankind into World War Three.

THE GUN AND THE OLIVE BRANCH

One

The Seeds of Conflict, 1882–1920

'IN the name of God, leave Palestine in peace.' The recipient of this plea was Zadoc Khan, Chief Rabbi of France. Its author was Yusuf Zia al-Khalidi, the Mayor of Jerusalem and former deputy in the Ottoman parliament. It was sent from Constantinople in March 1899. And it came at the end of a long and carefully argued letter which, the seventy-year-old scholar explained, a 'sacred call of conscience' had bade him write. Theoretically, he told his friend in Paris, the Zionist ideal was 'completely natural, fine and just'. 'Who can contest the rights of the Jews to Palestine? God knows, historically it is indeed your country!' In practice, however, the ideal was unworkable. The 'brutal force' of reality had to be taken into account. Al-Khalidi pointed out that Palestine was now an inseparable part of the Ottoman Empire; it was already inhabited; and he warned that if the Zionists persisted in their ambitions, they would face a popular uprising which even the Turks, however well disposed towards them, would not be able to put down. They should therefore look for a homeland elsewhere.[1]

Zadoc Khan immediately conveyed the letter to a personal friend of his, Theodor Herzl. Herzl, a Jewish journalist and playwright, was the father of Zionism as we know it today and his book, *The Jewish State*, is its bible. The 'political Zionism' he preached was to be the solution to the so-called Jewish Question which had bedevilled Christian civilization for centuries. It was his answer to the age-old curse of anti-Semitism, with which he had come face to face in all its ugliness in his native Hungary where pogroms and ritual-murder trials still persisted. Although things were not so bad in Vienna, the metropolis of the ailing Austro-Hungarian empire where he began his career, to be a Jew was still a grave disadvantage for an ambitious and brilliant young

man like Herzl. Had it not been for the offence to his father, he
would gladly have converted to Christianity. But in 1891, after
several years of struggle, he was appointed Paris correspondent
of the famous Vienna newspaper *Neue Freie Presse*. In the French
capital, he covered the notorious Dreyfus affair, the frame-up,
rigged trial and conviction of the Jewish officer accused of passing
secrets to the Germans, and he saw how deep was the prejudice
still to be found even in the land of Liberty, Equality and Frater-
nity. He also knew that in those traditional bastions of anti-
Semitism, Russia and Eastern Europe, the Jews were suffering
renewed and terrible persecution. The Herzl who had previously
toyed with the idea of complete assimilation into gentile society
as the answer to the universal Jewish Question now reverted to
the belief that anti-Semitism was an incurable gentile pathology.
He determined to lead his people out of 'perpetual enemy territory'. The Jews should have a nation-state of their own.

Herzl himself would have been ready to contemplate any
territory for this purpose, but most Zionists felt that Palestine
was the only possible one. Palestine was the Land of Their
Ancestors; the idea of the Return to Zion, of Next Year in
Jerusalem, had been kept alive through long centuries of exile
and suffering; only 'the mighty legend' of Palestine had the
power to stir the Jewish masses. True, the idea of return had
become essentially spiritual in significance; it meant redemption,
a recovery of grace in God's sight; moreover, the ethnic connection between nineteenth-century European Jewry and the
Ancient Hebrews was a myth. But Palestine was so deeply rooted
in the Jewish cultural and sentimental heritage that it was not
difficult for the 'political Zionists' to invest the return with a
secular, physical meaning. So in 1897, at their first congress in
Basle, they adopted a formal programme whose object was the
'establishment for the Jewish people of a home in Palestine
secured by public law'. The first, and most important, item on the
programme was to be the 'promotion, on suitable lines, of the
colonization of Palestine by Jewish agricultural and industrial
workers'.

It was a very meek and reassuring reply which al-Khalidi received from the founder of Zionism. There was 'absolutely nothing to fear' from Jewish immigration, he insisted, for 'the Jews
have no belligerent Power behind them, neither are they them-

selves of a warlike nature. They are a completely peaceful ele-
ment, and very content if they are left in peace.' As for the Arabs
of Palestine, 'who would think of sending them away? It is their
well-being, their individual wealth, which we will increase by
bringing in our own. Do you think that an Arab who owns land
will be very angry to see the price of his land rise in a short time,
to see it rise five and ten times in value perhaps in a few months?'
No, the Arabs would gain 'excellent brothers' in the Jews, and
the Turkish Sultan 'faithful and good subjects'; Palestine,
benefiting from Jewish intelligence, enterprise and financial
acumen, would prosper for the good of all.² A few months later
Herzl began to write a novel, *Altneuland* ('Old-Newland'), his
vision of Palestine as it might be, through Zionist colonization,
in a mere twenty years' time. At one point in the story, delighted
visitors to this Jewish utopia are introduced to a distinguished
Arab who, showing them round a prosperous and contented
village, speaks of the love which his compatriots feel for the
Jewish brethren to whom they owe so much.

Yet al-Khalidi was right, and Herzl knew it. One should remember, in looking for extenuating circumstances, that Herzl
was a child of his age. It was the heyday of European imperialism; an advanced and dynamic continent competed in the
conquest and penetration of backward lands. Force, in the service
of civilization, did not seem as reprehensible as it does today.
And what was Palestine, in Herzl's view, if not a 'plague-ridden,
blighted corner of the Orient?' to which the Jews, 'as representatives of Western civilization', would 'bring cleanliness, order, and
the well-distilled customs of the Occident'?³ Yet, in adopting the
Basle programme, Herzl knew that the 'brutal force' of reality
would make nonsense of the *Altneuland* idyll and provoke the
uprising of which al-Khalidi warned. He knew—indeed, he had
written—that immigration into an already populated country
would soon turn the natives against the newcomers, breeding, as
he saw it, that very anti-Semitism which it was his purpose to
combat. 'An infiltration is bound to end badly. It continues till
the inevitable moment when the native population feels itself
threatened, and forces the government to stop a further influx of
Jews. Immigration is consequently futile unless based on an
assured supremacy.' And that could only come through state-
hood.⁴

Violence, then, was implicit in Zionism from the outset. The prophet of Zionism foresaw that coercion and physical force were inevitable; they were not unfortunate necessities thrust, unforeseen, on his followers. To his diaries, not published until twenty-six years after his death in 1904, Herzl confided the beliefs which, in his public utterances, he had been careful to omit: that military power was an essential component of his strategy and that, ideally, the Zionists should acquire the land of their choice by armed conquest.[5] True, the Jews had had no military means of their own, but Herzl sought to enlist, among the imperial powers of the age, a sponsor which did. The methods which he recommended to achieve this included the trading of Jewish influence in press and finance, the promotion of antagonisms and the exploitation of rival colonial ambitions. He sought to instil in non-Jews fear of the Jews, their influence and particularly their revolutionary mentality. He portrayed his co-religionists as ten million secret agents. He tried to confront European statesmen with a dilemma: Zionism or Jew-fomented revolution. All who did not desire that 'the Jews corrupt everything' should support Zionism. A new European war, he contended, could not harm Zionism, but only urge it forward.

As for the natives of Palestine, the new settlers should 'gently' expropriate their property and 'try to spirit the penniless population across the border by procuring employment for it in the transit countries, while denying it any employment in our own country. The property-owners will come over to our side. Both the process of expropriation and the removal of the poor must be carried out discreetly and circumspectly. Let the owners of immovable property believe that they are cheating us, selling us things for more than they are worth. But we are not going to sell them anything back.'[6] Before they left, however, the natives should be put to work exterminating wild animals, such as snakes, to which the Jews were not accustomed. The settlers would pay 'high premiums for snake skins, etc., as well as their spawn.'[7]

In 1901, Herzl arrived in Constantinople in an unsuccessful attempt to obtain a charter for the establishment of a Jewish–Ottoman Colonization Association in Palestine. Article Three of the draft charter would have granted the Jews the right to deport the native population.[8]

'Qui veut la fin, veut les moyens' ('he who desires the end

desires the means') is a saying which Herzl cited with approval.[9] But in proposing such an end—a Jewish State in Palestine—and such means he was proposing a great deception, and laying open his whole movement to the subsequent charge that in any true historical perspective the Zionists were the original aggressors in the Middle East, the real pioneers of violence, and that Arab violence, however cruel and fanatical it might eventually become, was an inevitable reaction to theirs. Some, perhaps, of his followers really did not know what awaited them in Palestine, really did believe that it was more or less uninhabited, that—in the mischievous epigram of Israel Zwangwill, a contemporary of Herzl's—it really was a 'land without a people, waiting for a people without a land'.[10] The truth, when they learned it, might at first have disconcerted them. When Max Nordau, one of Herzl's earliest disciples, did so, he came running to his master crying: 'I didn't know that—but then we are committing an injustice.' But it did not seem to disconcert them for long. Nordau himself helped develop two strains of Zionist thought—the need for physical force and dissimulation—which Herzl had first propounded. Doubtless he was reflecting the German *Zeitgeist*, in which many early Zionists were deeply steeped, when he called for a 'muscular Judaism' of the kind that had been lost through eighteen centuries of exile and wandering. Zionism, he taught, was to awaken Jewry to new life, 'morally through renewal of the National Ideal, materially through physical rearing'.[11] The modern Jewish youth should model themselves on Jewish heroes of old, on Bar Kokhba, the last incarnation of a Judaism that maintained itself by the sword—Bar Kokhba, 'who refused to accept defeat and, when victory deserted him, knew how to die'.[12] Nordau was echoed by other poets and theorists who, in their idealization of martial virtues, were rising in revolt against two millennia of Judaic pacifism.

Like Herzl, whom he survived by nineteen years, Nordau tried to reassure the natives of Palestine—while privately claiming credit for the systematic duplicity which this entailed. Instead of a Jewish State, the Basle programme had introduced the expression 'a home secured by public law'. This expression was deliberately ambiguous. Twenty-three years later Nordau wrote that it was he who had thought up the term 'homeland' (*Heimstätte*):

> I did my best to persuade the advocates of the Jewish State in
> Palestine that we might find a circumlocution that would express
> all we meant, but would say it in a way that would avoid provoking
> the Turkish rulers of the coveted land. I suggested 'Heimstätte'
> as a synonym for 'state'. . . . this is the history of the much com-
> mented expression. It was equivocal but we all understood what
> it meant . . . to us it signified 'Judenstaat' (Jewish State) and it
> signifies the same now . . .[13]

From Basle onwards, it became deliberate policy to deny that
there was, or ever had been, any intention of establishing a Jewish
State. For example, fourteen years later the President of the
Zionist movement opened the tenth Congress with a speech in
which he indignantly declared that 'only those suffering from
gross ignorance, or actuated by malice, could accuse us of the
desire of establishing an independent Jewish kingdom'.[14] And
yet, on 3 September 1898, after that first congress, Herzl had
confided in his diary:

> Were I to sum up the Basle Congress in a word—which I shall
> guard against pronouncing publicly—it would be this: at Basle
> I founded the Jewish state. . . . If I said this out loud today, I
> would be answered by universal laughter. Perhaps in five years
> and certainly in fifty everyone will know it.[15]

It was hardly an inspired prophecy which al-Khalidi made.
The omens of eventual revolt were already easily discernible. If
it is possible to designate a year in which, on the earliest possible
reckoning, the great Zionist adventure began it would be 1882.
Obviously that antedates Herzl's political Zionism proper. But it
is the year to which Zionist historians now assign the first *Aliyah*,
the first 'going up', or wave of immigration, to the Land of
Israel. At that time there were already about 24,000 Jews, mostly
immigrants, in Palestine. For much of the nineteenth century the
character of the *Yishuv*, as the community was called, had remained the same. They had come mainly to Jerusalem, as to
Hebron, Safed and Tiberias, with a religious aim: to end their
days in one of these holy cities. They were often old, and many
spent their time in perpetual study of the Talmud. Most lived in
great poverty. The newcomers were different; they called themselves the 'Lovers of Zion'; they emigrated to Palestine to establish agricultural settlements there. But their political ideas were

still vague: they had no clearly formulated, Herzlian grand designs for Jewish statehood. They sought a refuge from East European and Russian anti-Semitism, the dignity of toil, cultural —as much as national—regeneration. Their numbers were small; in thirty-two years, by 1914, they—and their post-Herzl successors—raised the Jewish population to 85,000. As a result of World War I, the total fell to a mere 56,000 in 1918. By that time the immigrants had managed to acquire some 162,500 acres, or about 2 per cent of the land area of Palestine.[16]

Their numbers may have been small, and their political ambitions limited, but from the very beginning there was an Arab reaction commensurate with the threat which the Lovers of Zion did seem to represent. It came not so much from the élite, from the political leadership, as from the humblest segment of Palestinian society, the peasantry, who were the first really to feel the threat. At the time a good 75 per cent of the Palestinians were peasants, deeply attached to their land. Contemporary European travellers spoke of the skill and diligence with which, in spite of primitive resources and political and social oppression, they tended their fields and orchards.[17] The fame of the Jaffa orange had spread throughout Europe. The peasants were the first to lose land and livelihood to the settlers from overseas. They intuitively sensed the ultimate dimensions of the threat. 'Is it true that the Jews want to retake this country?' This naïve questioning of illiterate villagers was recorded by Albert Antebi, an official of the Jewish Colonial Association, before the turn of the century.[18]

THE PEASANTS RESIST

It was only a few years after the first *Aliyah* of 1882 that the peasants resorted to physical violence against the settlers. Their resistance, spontaneous and clumsy as it was, nevertheless followed a pattern. They did not resist the actual sale of the land from which they were to be expelled. That was frequently completed without their knowing anything about it, for they were tenants working plots whose owner they might never see. They did resist the ensuing takeover process. This happened in 1901 when peasants from villages near Tiberias fell upon the estate agents who had come to stake out land bought from the Sursock

family of Beirut.[19] They naturally resisted the eviction itself.
Sometimes Turkish troops had to be brought in to enforce it;
this happened in 1910 when, in another Sursock sale, the dispossessed tenants from Lower Galilee were arrested and thrown
into prison.[20] Then, defeated, they, or other threatened neighbours, might make a single planned assault on a new colony or
keep up a sporadic harassment of it in a variety of ways, plundering cattle or produce, ambushing, robbing and occasionally
killing farmers.[21]

Contemporary accounts of Jewish-Arab relations in these early
pioneering days are rare, but one, which describes the founding
of the Jewish township of Hadera, illustrates with piquant irony
the disdain in which the newcomers frequently held the natives,
and their indifference to any hardship which they inflicted upon
them. The settlement dates from 1891, and the author of the
account, Moshe Smilansky, a well-known Jewish orange-grower
and writer, was one of the original settlers, being at the time a
boy of sixteen. One day that winter, recalls Mr Smilansky, immigrants freshly disembarked at Jaffa learned that 30,000 dunums
of land had been acquired in the north of the coastal plain. A
group of enthusiasts, some middle-aged men with families, some
still boys, volunteered to take part of this land. An experienced
settler asked them if they knew why the village in the neighbourhood was called Hadera.

> Our host looked somewhat confused. 'Unless I err, it means
> green.' 'H'm a bad sign! Isn't there some connexion between the
> name and the blackwater fever which the Arabs claim prevails in
> that district?' 'Possibly, but surely we're not going to let ourselves
> be frightened off by Arab tales of fever? We're not Arabs, and
> we'll find some way of putting an end to malaria . . .'

When the first settlers arrived at Hadera, their driver smiled
wryly on observing their delight at the green appearance of their
land.

> 'These green valleys are swamps. . . . That's where the malaria
> comes from. . . . Look around you. In all this broad valley you
> see not a single village! There's a Circassian village on the edge
> of your land, but almost all its inhabitants are dead. The few who
> are left are cripples!' 'We needn't take our cue from barbarians!'
> replied the settlers.

The pioneers set to work, planted a vineyard, and sowed wheat. With the summer came the fever, and soon the colonists were dying off. Sometimes an entire family, such as the Reverend Jacob Idelsohn, his wife and two sons, were wiped out. The enthusiasm of the settlers carried them through five years. But there came a moment when, defeated by disease, it seemed they must abandon the colony. At this moment, however, the millionaire philanthropist Baron de Rothschild intervened from Paris with a promise of funds for draining the swamps. Accordingly in the summer of 1896 'hundreds of black labourers came from Egypt to dig the broad and deep trenches required for the drainage'. These men also 'died in scores'. But in time the drainage was completed and Hadera eventually became a prosperous colony. Besides the Circassians, Smilansky recalls, there used to be bedouins living in the vicinity, who sometimes stole the settlers' horses. 'The Bedouin neighbours, the Damireh and the Infiat tribes, rose up in protest. . . . Where would they pasture their cattle and sheep? But the [Turkish] mudir came from Caesarea with a detachment of police and dispersed them. From that time on the work proceeded without disturbance.'[22]

Commenting on this account, the British historian Neville Barbour points out that while the enthusiasm of the colonists was admirable, their arrogance was at least equally conspicuous. The draining of the swamps was not accomplished through their superior skill, as compared with that of the native 'barbarians', but through the aid of superior funds. Characteristic, too, was the reliance of the settlers on the Turkish police for driving off neighbours whose livelihood they had put in jeopardy.[23]

It was about this time that Ahad Aham, the conscience of early Zionism, first raised his stern and eloquent voice against the aberrations of a movement which he conceived of in a very different way from Herzl. Zionism, for this moralist cast in the prophetic mould, was to be a means for the Jews to recover their spiritual and cultural greatness, to become once again, in the noblest sense, 'a light unto the nations'. Zionism in its narrow political form, land-obsessed and predatory, the Zionism of force, diplomatic manipulation, the facile Messianic short-cut—this Zionism was anathema to him. There was no more fundamental and obvious test by which the Zionists should be judged than the way they treated their Palestinian neighbours—and no

test, in his opinion, by which they failed so badly. Jewish history,
he insisted, proved the need for the befriending and respecting
of neighbours.

> Yet what do our brethren do in Palestine? Just the opposite!
> Servants they were in the land of their exile. Suddenly they find
> themselves in a state of freedom without limits, an unbridled
> freedom such as exists only in Turkey, and the sudden transfor-
> mation has produced in them that inclination to despotism that
> always occurs when the servant becomes the master! They treat
> the Arabs with hostility and cruelty, unscrupulously deprive
> them of their rights, insult them without cause, and even boast of
> such deeds; and none opposes this despicable and dangerous
> inclination.[24]

That was in 1891. Already, in these earliest, embryonic days of
Zionism, the settlers were earning harsh judgements from the
man who, for the next thirty years, was to lament the misdeeds
done in its name. Nevertheless, the settlers were less imbued
with that myopic egoism of later, more doctrinaire Zionists, and
on the surface at least they frequently managed to establish
profitable and even friendly relations with their Arab neighbours. According to H. M. Kalvariski, Arabs and Jews

> ... met both in their houses and in their fields and got to know
> each other intimately. When the Jewish colonies were first started
> there was a great demand for labour ... and there were no Jewish
> labourers in the country. It was therefore necessary to engage
> Arab labour, and thus Jewish farmers and Arab labourers had an
> opportunity of knowing each other. The fellahin from neigh-
> bouring villages worked in the Jewish colonies, returning at night
> to their own homes. There they related that the 'Yahudi' (the
> Jew) and the 'Hawaja' (owner) were good men who paid well.
> At the same time close relations were gradually established be-
> tween the Jewish colonists and the Arab land-owners. Jewish
> farmers bought horses for breeding and riding in partnership
> with Arab Sheikhs and often owned flocks of sheep and cattle in
> common.[25]

Mr Kalvariski was a Jewish publicist and administrator of the
Palestine Jewish Colonization Association, but his impressions,
though doubtless too sanguine, seem to be basically honest ones.
The newcomers did have much to offer. They used new methods

and machinery, they could provide remunerative employment, a market for produce, medical care and the loan of equipment. Most colonies actually employed five to ten times as many Arabs as Jews. Naturally the peasants violently resented the initial intrusion by which they were ousted from their lands, but once they had come to the conclusion that a colony was permanent, a *modus vivendi* could often be struck up. This pattern—initial resentment, suppressed or open hostility giving way in time to resignation and outward reconciliation—repeated itself almost every time a colony was founded.[26]

THE CONQUEST OF LABOUR

With the turn of the century, Jewish attitudes hardened. The second *Aliyah* brought to Palestine a tougher breed of settlers armed with the ideological apparatus that Herzl and his disciples had developed. They were bent, in the words of Leviticus, on 'redeeming the land'; the Jewish National Fund, established in 1901, laid down that all land which it acquired was to remain inalienable Jewish property that could not be sold or leased to others. They were bent on the 'conquest of labour'; only Jews should work the land that Jews acquired. It was of course from the Arabs that the land was redeemed, from them the labour conquered. The Jews often took this ideology to absurd lengths. Zionist historians speak with great pride about what happened in 1908 at Ben Shemen near Lydda. A forest was founded there in memory of Theodor Herzl. But when they learned that the saplings had been planted by Arabs, Jewish labourers came and replanted them, and only then were they satisfied. Such purism was not always practicable. Dr Ruppin, the first head of the Zionist Bureau in Palestine, records in his memoirs that he tried to build Tel Aviv with 'Hebrew Labour' only, but he soon had to turn to the Arabs on account of their experience (and low wages); the first house built by Jewish labourers had collapsed under construction.[27] The settlers were socialists, deeply committed to the communal ideal, but the deeper their commitment the narrower its application seemed to be. Their socialism did not extend to their non-Jewish fellow-men. True, it repudiated conventional European colonialism, frequently regarded as morally reprehensible, but it was heavily impregnated with a colonial mentality which, in effect if not in intent, was worse. It did not deliberately set out to exploit the natives, but it blithely deprived them of their livelihood—and eventually of their country. 'The international brotherhood of workers', they would argue, 'applied only to workers who were already secure in their employment; it did not apply to a potential proletariat that had to struggle to find employment and could not refrain from conflict with workers whose places of work they must take for themselves.'[28] From this philosophy grew the celebrated *kibbutzim*, agricultural communes founded on exclusively Jewish labour; it also led to the expulsion of Arab labour, which one Zionist theoretician described as a 'painful leprosy',[29] from existing Jewish colonies, and eventually to the boycott of Arab goods as soon as the Jews could produce enough of their own.

The zealots of the second *Aliyah* were actually given to arguing that in the long run Arabs as well as Jews stood to benefit from Hebrew Labour. Some of them were doubtless quite sincere in this extraordinary belief, which was rooted in the Marxist theorizing of the period. Sophisticated European socialists were saying, on the eve of the biggest bloodletting in history, that war was becoming improbable because the workers of one nation would refuse to shoot at those of another. The Zionist pioneers, Marxists of a rugged and intellectually simplistic kind, contended that this must apply to Palestine too. They professed to see no contradiction between their proletarian enterprise and the interests of the local population. This was composed mainly of peasants and workers, exploited by a corrupt élite of feudal landowners, who, they felt sure, would soon make common cause with their toiling Jewish brethren. If there were no 'exploitation' of Arab labour, Arab labour could not 'objectively' oppose the Zionists. There is a deep and tragic irony, writes the Israeli historian Amos Elon, in the fact that Hebrew Labour, advocated as a means of allaying conflict, actually led to that total cleavage between the two peoples which made it inevitable. It began a process of economic, political, cultural and psychological self-segregation, which the Arabs reciprocated with a vengeance. Since its foundation, the State of Israel has been trying to break out of the rigorous quarantine which the entire Arab world has thrown round it; the scale is immeasurably different, of course, but by all the laws of heredity the Arab blockade is but a lineal descendant of the first expulsion of an Arab labourer from a Jewish farm.

MILITARIZATION BEGINS

The 'conquest of labour', as the expression itself implies, could not be accomplished without violence. Indeed, a Zionist poet like Saul Tchernichowski could not conceive of one without the other: 'We shall put forth our hands in urging labour, the work that is holy, while grasping the sword. Raise the banners of Zion, warriors of Judah.'[30] By 1903, the more perceptive older immigrants had come to the conclusion that 'these Russian Jewish labourers together with the principle of exclusive Jewish Hebrew labour', constituted 'a major factor in arousing the hostility of the Palestinian Arabs'.[31] The process of militarization foreseen by Herzl gradually got underway. In 1907 an organization calling itself *Hashomer* ('The Guardian') came into being with the task of replacing Arab with Jewish guards on the ground that Jewish property must be protected by Jews. The name *Hashomer*, favoured by many Jewish youth organizations at this time, epitomized the pugnacious spirit in which they were formed. So too did the names which many of the new settlers, anxious to make a complete break with the abasements of their Diaspora past, took for themselves: Yariv ('antagonist'), Oz ('strength'), Tamir ('towering'), Hod ('splendour'), Barak ('lightning'), or Tsur ('rock').[32]

The *Hashomer* constituted the first nucleus of a military force. In 1909 a secret defence organization was organized. Yitzhak Ben Zvi, a future President of Israel, was among the founders. His description of the organization's first meeting, which took place in his rooms, is full of forebodings about the future. 'Mats, spread out on the floor, and a few wooden crates served as armchairs and desks . . . one feeling seized all those present . . . they gathered up courage [and they knew] that not by word of mouth shall the nation be saved, nor shall a country be rebuilt by speeches. "In blood and fire Judea fell, in blood and fire it shall rise again".'[33] In the same year the Kaimakam (District Officer) of Tiberias authorized the formation of a Jewish armed guard for fear of a massacre.[34] The militarization had been preceded by a discussion between two young pioneers in the colony of Sejera.

One of them, David, wished to establish a Jewish 'self-defence' organization. The other, Shlomo, opposed this. They had re-turned, he argued, to the Promised Land in order to lead a peace-ful life. If they stirred up the Arabs, there would be no *shalom*, no peace, ever. David persisted. This was a world in which force and force alone won respect. Shlomo left for Paris. David—David Bengurion—remained.[35]

Arab attitudes were hardening too. It was a slow and halting process. For the Palestinian leaders had a less developed ideo-logical propensity towards the use of force than their Zionist counterparts. It was alien to their whole outlook as the re-presentatives of a subject people. When, in 1890, the Palestinian élite, in the shape of a group of Jerusalem 'notables', took their first formal initiative in the struggle that was beginning, they did the only lawful thing they could. They protested to their im-perial masters, the Sublime Porte in Constantinople. They were thereby exhibiting a deferential instinct which remained with them, in gradually diminishing strength, through the remaining years of Ottoman rule, thirty years of the British Mandate, and twenty-five years of their post-1948 diaspora. They protested at the appointment of a Turkish governor who manifestly favoured the Zionists. The next year, they submitted another petition which contained two demands: the ending of Jewish immigration and land purchases. Then, in 1898, Yusuf Zia al-Khalidi made his direct approach to the Zionists. Appeals of this kind had little effect. The Zionists only pretended to listen. The Turks listened —but only fitfully. The Porte would periodically impose restric-tions on immigration, only to lift them again under European pressure, or to allow venal officials on the spot to turn a blind eye to the continued defiance of them.

Inevitably, therefore, as time passed and the Zionists continued to make slow, but steady, headway, the Palestinian élite gradually lost that popular respect which, for the conduct of a national struggle, a leadership must have. If more men of influence and authority had behaved as a Jewish observer described the Kaimakam of Tiberias as behaving things would have been different. Of the eviction of peasants from the estates in Lower Galilee he wrote:

It was then that, for the first time, I came in contact with Arab nationalism. Rashid Bey the Vali (Governor), who was a Turk, cared very little whether the Tiberias District was inhabited by Arabs or Jews, and was thus prepared to order the eviction of the tenants. But Emir Amin Arslan, the Kaimakam of Tiberias, who was an Arab Druze, not only insisted on the payment of compensation to the evicted Arabs, but also as I was later informed, resisted the de-Arabization of the district . . .[36]

THE LANDSELLERS

Few of the élite were like the Kaimakam of Tiberias. Their chief offence, in the eyes of their critics, was the readiness of too many of them, as individuals, to make their fortunes out of those very Zionist land acquisitions in which, as citizens, they perceived the omens of national calamity. The great bulk of the land that the Zionists acquired came from large, predominantly absentee, landowners. As resistance built up, the area relinquished by small farmers, 42·7 per cent of the total from 1891 to 1900, fell to a mere 4·3 per cent from 1900 to 1914.[37]

The name Sursock occupies an invidious and recurrent place in this story. The Sursocks were a Levantine family of high breeding and immense wealth who spent much of their time in Western Europe. They also owned some of the richest land in Palestine. In a series of transactions from 1891 to 1920 they sold it all to the Zionists, as unmoved by high appeals to their sense of Arab history as by workaday calls on their conscience. In 1910 they sold the region of Foule, with its Crusader castle made famous by Saladin, in the fertile Vale of Esdraelon; in 1920 they disposed of the rest of their holdings, along with 8,000 peasants in twenty-two villages who made a living from them. They had acquired the whole area in 1872 from corrupt Ottoman officials for the derisory sum of £18,000 to £20,000.[38] It brought in a revenue of £12,000 to £40,000 a year. They sold it for ten times the price they had paid for it, but subsequently complained bitterly that they had let it go so cheap—as indeed they had.[39] The fate of the 8,000 peasants was never determined; the tenants among them—but not the labourers—received 'compensation' of £28,000—precisely £3·5 per head for the lot. The Sursock sale was a famous and much-deplored transaction. But there were many others.

Patriotic voices soon began to rise in protest. *Carmel*, a newspaper published in Haifa, never ceased to reproach the *zaims* and *effendis* and their business agents.

> 'Today with your own hands, and your own seals, you are wasting your own substance, thinning your own ranks, increasing the substance of others and swelling their ranks . . . what are we to think of a people whose leaders, many of them champions of reform and self-styled guardians of the nation's security, sell out to the Zionists and act as their agents . . '; leaders 'who sate their appetites and pursue their quarrels indifferent to the dangers that surround them', and 'enter Zionists' service to fritter away the homeland.'[40]

ANTI-ZIONISM S ADS

How should the Palestinian leaders—and everyone else—have behaved? Like the Zionists themselves, of course. It did not take the Palestinians long to feel that the Zionists were an enemy. And it did not take much longer for those who felt it most strongly to conclude that the best way to fight the enemy was to learn from him. Najib Nassar, the Christian from Haifa who established his newspaper *Carmel* to urge this idea on his countrymen and other campaigners did not hide their admiration for the Zionists. It marked a striking change of attitude. For the Palestinians had tended to despise those Jews, mostly meek, devout and impoverished, who came to Palestine before the first *Aliyah* of 1882. They even taunted cowards among their own ranks with the insult *isiknag*, a distortion of Askenazi. 'The Jewish people', wrote Nassar, 'was scattered for two thousand years until Herzl appeared and convened the [Basle] conference; the Zionist Organization came into being with all its ramifications and in fifteen years it spread its doctrine to the whole nation, purchased the best land in Palestine, gave the Jews a united voice, and opened banks to finance the farmers; if we do likewise we shall succeed . . .'[41] He and others found the Jews to be a 'purposeful people, hardworking, energetic . . . anyone who sees the villages they have colonized will realise that a struggle for existence lies before the people of this country . . . the people must be aroused to compete with the Jews . . . otherwise they will fall prey to their neighbours.'[42] They listed the manifold ways in which the Arabs could profit from the Zionist example: in holding conferences, organizing communal projects, helping peasants, education, social reform, and generally catching up with the modern world the Zionists brought with them. They even foreshadowed the famous claim of the Zionists that they, unlike the Arabs they displaced, at least 'made the desert bloom'. 'Let us be their equal in toil and devotion . . . it is a general law of civilization that the land is for him who works it.'[43]

By the eve of the Great War, anti-Zionism, from being the essentially non-political, spontaneous eruptions of the peasantry it was at the outset, had broadened into the central issue of Palestinian politics. After the peasants, it was the small class of urban traders and professional men who reacted most strongly against Jewish immigration. They were behind that first protest which, in 1891, the Jerusalem notables despatched to the Sublime Porte. They feared the economic competition that the continued growth of an alien community, as aggressive as it was ingrown, would indubitably bring. This class was largely Christian. In fact, the Zionists were at first inclined to believe that they had less to fear from Moslems than Christians; 'the one and only source of hatred of the Jews that raises its voice against Jewish immigration is the Christian establishment'.[44] The Christians' opposition was perhaps reinforced by a certain doctrinal prejudice and by the fact that, better educated and more widely travelled than their Moslem compatriots, they were influenced by typical European attitudes towards the Jews. Levantine minorities, second-class citizens themselves, had often derived satisfaction from the discomfiture of the Moslem majority, but—though this sentiment has not been entirely absent—an unusual degree of Moslem–Christian solidarity, engendered by the gravity of the 'Zionist peril', has been one of the permanent features of the Palestine struggle. Along with the traders and professional men, the intellectual élite, substantially Christian too, could not remain deaf to what European Zionists revealed of their plans in frequent indiscretions that were not intended for Arab ears. With the overthrow of Sultan Abdul Hamid in 1908 Palestinian publishers took advantage of the relative new freedoms. In *Carmel* Najib Nassar published a series of lengthy treatises, later reproduced as a book, entitled *Zionism: Its History, Aims and Importance*. It was rudimentary, evidently little more than a

cleverly slanted translation from a section of the Jewish Ency-
clopaedia Nassar had acquired from an English friend. But it was
the first of its kind in Arabic. After *Carmel*, other, more in-
fluential newspapers in Beirut and Damascus took up anti-
Zionism. Arab leaders were invited to express their opinions.
Gross caricatures of Jews began to appear in humorous weeklies.
Carmel subscriptions were donated to school libraries in Haifa.
Anti-Zionist societies were formed in several Palestinian towns,
Constantinople, Cairo and Beirut. In Jaffa a political organization,
'The Homeland Party', made anti-Zionism its *raison d'être*. Anti-
Zionism became an important vote-winning gambit in elections
to the Ottoman parliament. All the while the peasants were growing more turbulent, and outsiders like Najib Nassar began to
play a part in egging them on. He also formed a vigilante group
to see that restrictions on Jewish immigrants were strictly applied
at Haifa port. Zionist representatives would be molested on their
way to official gatherings; they had to arm themselves with sticks
and guns. By 1913, observed Albert Antebi, there was no
Jerusalem notable who would dare compromise his political
position by openly favouring Zionism.[45]

ABORTIVE ATTEMPTS AT ARAB-ZIONIST UNDERSTANDING

It was becoming clear that the Palestinians faced two basic
choices; either to reach some kind of accommodation with the
Zionists, who, in return for certain concessions, would be obliged
to place definite limits on their ambitions, or to fight them tooth
and nail. At all events, the failure of the leadership to demonstrate its ability, or even its desire, to contain the menace meant,
in the end, that the people would try to do it for them—in their
own way. Those first rural convulsions were harbingers of an
inchoate, popular violence to come. In 1914, Rashid Rida, the
leading Moslem thinker of his time, formulated the choice as
follows:

> It is incumbent upon the leaders of the Arabs—the local popula-
> tion—to do one of two things. Either they must reach an agree-
> ment with leaders of the Zionists to settle the differences between
> the interests of both parties . . . or they must gather all their
> forces to oppose the Zionists in every way, first by forming
> societies and companies, and finally by forming armed gangs

which oppose them by force. Some [Arabs] say this is the first thing to be done because cauterization is the only way—and cauterization is the ultimate remedy, as it is said [in an Arabic proverb].[46]

In 1913 and 1914 the Palestinians did attempt to reach an accommodation with the Zionists—although it is stretching a point to call it a representative Palestinian initiative at all. For its main impetus came from emergent Arab Nationalist parties of Syria who were seeking autonomy or independence for the Arab provinces of the moribund Ottoman empire. The Decentralization Party, *al-Fatah* and *al-Ahd* were numerically insignificant; according to one estimate, they numbered a mere ninety-six to 126 members all told, of whom a mere twelve or twenty-two were Palestinians.[47] As—for the most part—young, Western-oriented patriots, they were keen to profit from the capital, expertise and equipment which they thought the Zionists would inject into the Arab economy; as—for the most part—non-Palestinians, they had little direct experience of Zionism in practice. They did not realize how self-centred it was. Rashid Rida, a founder-member of the Decentralization Party, believed that, provided the Zionists could be induced to abandon their political ambitions, the Arabs should make a compact with them. In 1913 the party, through its Cairo Committee, did indeed reach an *entente verbale* with the Zionist representative in Constantinople. 'Being in principle favourable to Jewish immigration into Syria and Palestine,' the text of it read, 'the Cairo Committee undertakes to work for a rapprochement between the Arab and Jewish worlds, and, through the Arab press and by word of mouth, to dissipate the prejudices which prevail in the Arab world concerning Jewish immigration and which hinder Arab-Jewish rapprochement.'[48] The *entente verbale* was to be superseded by an *accord complet*. The First Arab Congress, held in Paris in June 1913, passed a resolution favouring such Jewish immigration as was capable of benefiting Syria economically.

In the end no final agreement was ever reached. In truth the Zionists did not really want one. For, though it offered them short-term tactical advantages, it would have involved grave strategic disadvantages: they were to be asked to come clean, to state what they really wanted in Palestine. This was the dilemma which confronted them when, in 1914, under the auspices of the

Decentralization Party, Palestinians took a more representative
part in renewed efforts to reach an accommodation. For a meeting
they were to hold with Zionist representatives in Brummana,
Lebanon, the Arab side submitted an agenda which read in part:
'The Zionists should explain, as far as possible by producing
documentary evidence, the aims and methods of Zionism and of
the colonization of Palestine connected therewith.'[49] The Zionists
were loth to accept this agenda. For their aims were in fact un-
limited; in the light of fundamental Zionist doctrine they could
not be otherwise. The Zionists were only too well aware that
there was precious little room for compromise on precisely those
points—immigration and land purchase—about which the Arabs
wished to be reassured. They procrastinated. And in the event
they never had to come clean. The Great War broke out. It
rendered a meeting impossible.

This, for the Palestinians, was a historic opportunity lost. For,
however obvious the Zionists' lack of interest in an agreement
might be, the Palestinians have always stood to win an immense
moral and political advantage by irrefutably proving it in the
only way they could—by challenging them to reach one. Of
course, they might not have taken the opportunity, even if great
events had not snatched it from them, because the very idea of an
agreement has always generated fierce resistance in their own
ranks. And this was true, even in these early days, when the
'Zionist peril' was embryonic and the concessions they would
have had to make in return for a clear delimitation of the settlers'
rights and obligations, could hardly have been far-reaching. Thus,
when the Decentralizationists reached their *entente verbale* with
the Zionists they ran into fierce criticism from publicists like
Nassar, who proposed the holding of another congress at Nablus,
a traditional bastion of nationalist feeling, to discuss a harder
line. And when, the following year, the Palestinian–Zionist
meeting in Lebanon was mooted, its Decentralizationist sponsor
had to include Nassar and four other well-known anti-Zionists
among the ten Arab delegates. And after that it was not long
before the Decentralizationists themselves began to have second
thoughts. Taking issue with his colleagues who still favoured
entente, Haqqi Bey al-Azm wrote to a friend:

Understand, dear brother, that these people are moving towards

their object at a rapid pace. . . . I am sure that if we do nothing to
affect the status quo the Zionists will attain their object in a few
years (in Palestine) where they will found a Jewish state. . . . But,
by employing means of threats and persecutions—and it is this
last method we must employ—by pushing the Arab population
into destroying their farms and setting fire to their colonies, by
forming gangs to execute these projects—then perhaps they will
emigrate to save their skins.[50]

He had come to the conclusion that, an agreement being impossible, 'cauterization'—that is, violence—was the only answer.

JEWISH WARRIORS

As for the Zionists, they now deemed that conciliation was unnecessary. War in Europe, as Herzl had foreseen, could be turned
to their advantage. It opened up dazzling opportunities, both
in Palestine itself and outside it. Early in the war, two young
men, Joseph Trumpeldor and Vladimir Jabotinsky, created a
Jewish fighting unit, the Zion Mule Corps, which served with
British forces in Gallipoli. During the war, too, a third, Aaron
Aaronsohn, organized an espionage network, the *Nili* (acronym
for *Netzakh Israel Lo Yeshaker*—The Eternal Jewish Shall Not
Fail), which collaborated with British intelligence. And as the
war drew to a close, Jabotinsky succeeded in forming 'The
Jewish Legion', four battalions of Royal Fusiliers, 5,000 men in
all, who fought with the British under their own flag. The three
men were celebrated militants. To Trumpeldor, said to have been
the only Jewish officer in the Czarist army, is attributed this
chilling description of the ideal Zionist:

> We need men prepared to do everything . . . we must raise a
> generation of men who have no interests and no habits. . . . Bars
> of iron, elastic but of iron. Metal that can be forged to whatever is
> needed for the national machine. A wheel? I am the wheel. If a
> nail or a flying wheel are needed—take me! Is there a need to dig
> earth? I dig. Is there need to shoot, to be a soldier? . . . I am a
> soldier. . . . I am the pure ideal of service prepared for everything.

For him, fighting against the Arabs demolished the gentile
conception of the Jew:

If only the Gogols, the Dostoevskis, and other Russian writers could have seen these brave, determined lads, their Jewish types would certainly have been portrayed differently . . . forty brave lads standing fearlessly at their post, facing an angry sea of [Arab] rebels.[51]

Trumpeldor furnished the *Yishuv*—and Zionists everywhere —with their first heroic legend. He fell in battle against Arab insurgents in Galilee. Of course, he was not the first to die this way. But he was the kind of awe-inspiring figure of whom national myths are made—and he rounded off a short life of blind dedication and unflinching valour with famous last words. These were: 'It is good to die for our country.' Some say, however, that this prosaic exit line was a jest, and that his last utterance was actually a hefty Russian curse.[52]

Aaron Aaronsohn took a seigneurial attitude towards the Arabs,[53] and no doubt shared this opinion of his brother, Alexander, with whom he lived: 'The Arab is a cunning fellow, whose only respect is for brute force. He exercises it himself for every possible victim and expects the same treatment from his superiors.'[54]

As for Jabotinsky, his aim—in the words of his biographer— was 'realistic and stern: the establishment of a Jewish majority in Palestine will have to be achieved *against the wish* of the country's present Arab majority; an "iron wall" of Jewish armed force would have to protect the process of achieving a majority.'[55] His Jewish Legion was formed with the avowed aim of occupying Palestine after its conquest by the British, and, in the minds of its founders, it was to serve as the military backbone of the future Jewish State. A contemporary historian noted the arrogance of the legionaries and the intoxicating effect which the sight of them had on certain Zionist leaders, one of whom 'came out with the fantastic idea of resettling Palestine Arabs back in the regions from which their forefathers had allegedly come to Palestine centuries ago'.[56]

It did seem fantastic and—officially at least—reprehensible too. The most influential Zionist of the time, Chaim Weizmann, disparagingly described Jabotinsky as 'our own D'Annunzio'.[57] And indeed, at this stage, he did believe that the main thrust of the struggle should be diplomatic; it would stand or fall by the leverage which it could exert in the contemporary centres of world power. It was there, more than in Palestine itself, that the European cataclysm furnished Zionism with its real opportunity —and there that this consummate diplomat seized the opportunity. What Weizmann needed was the kind of international charter for which, two decades before, Herzl had toured European chancelleries in vain. His skilful and untiring persuasions eventually conjured it out of the British wartime leaders in the shape of the Balfour Declaration. That famous document, which, from 1917 on, incorporated Zionism into the imperial designs of the dominant power of the age, revolutionized its prospects overnight and rendered agreement with the Arabs entirely superfluous.

THE BALFOUR DECLARATION

The Balfour Declaration was one of the two key documents that have shaped the modern history of the Middle East. The other was the Sykes-Picot agreement of 1916. This secret deal was part of an understanding in which the three major allies, Britain, France and Czarist Russia, defined each other's interests in the post-war Middle East. Sir Mark Sykes, Secretary to the British Cabinet, and the French plenipotentiary, M. Georges Picot, agreed that, after the break-up of the Ottoman empire, Britain and France would divide its former Arab provinces between them. Ironically, the most backward parts of the Arab world— what is now Saudi Arabia and Yemen—were to be permitted independent statehood, while the more advanced and mature were to come under 'direct or indirect' foreign rule. France was to take over Lebanon and Syria, Britain would get Iraq and Transjordan. Palestine was to be placed under an 'international administration' of a kind to be decided on later. This document, made public, much to Britain's embarrassment, by the newly installed Bolshevik government, violated the promises which it had earlier made to the Arabs. In return for the Arab contribution to the allied war effort, it had undertaken to 'recognize and support' the independence of the Arabs in the Arabian Peninsula, Palestine, Transjordan, Syria and Iraq.

The Balfour Declaration grew out of Sykes-Picot, but, in retrospect, its importance far outweighs it. Indeed, it is difficult to recall a document which has so arbitrarily changed the course of history as this one. The Arab-Israeli struggle is the likeliest of contemporary world problems to precipitate the nuclear doomsday; if it does, surviving historians will surely record that it all began with the brief and seemingly innocuous letter, consisting of 117 words, which Arthur Balfour, the British Secretary of State for Foreign Affairs, addressed to Lord Rothschild on 2 November 1917. Poetic licence will enable them to point out that though Palestine, with which the letter dealt, seemed at the time a rather benighted patch of the earth's surface, hardly destined for such a cataclysmic role, it is a country steeped in poignant symbolism, at whose centre lie the barren hills of Armageddon. The letter ran as follows:

> Dear Lord Rothschild,
>
> I have much pleasure in conveying to you, on behalf of His Majesty's Government, the following declaration of sympathy with Jewish Zionist aspirations which has been submitted to, and approved by the Cabinet:
>
> 'His Majesty's Government view with favour the establishment in Palestine of a national home for the Jewish people, and will use their best endeavours to facilitate the achievement of this object, it being clearly understood that nothing shall be done which may prejudice the civil and religious rights of the existing non-Jewish communities in Palestine, or the rights and political status enjoyed by Jews in any other country.'
>
> I should be grateful if you would bring this declaration to the knowledge of the Zionist Federation.
>
> Yours sincerely,
>
>   Arthur Balfour

It seemed, on the face of it, to be a purely British initiative, sprung wholly from the good will and wise purposes of His Majesty's Government. The Zionists certainly have reason to remember Balfour as one of the great benefactors of the Jewish people. But it was hardly love of the Jews that inspired a charity far from home. In the last years of the nineteenth century, Britain had been flooded with Jewish refugees from Eastern Europe; there were riots and demonstrations against them in the streets of London. An Aliens Act was passed which restricted Jewish immigration. None other than Balfour, Prime Minister at the time, defended the legislation in language which the

Zionists denounced as 'open anti-Semitism against the whole Jewish people':

> A state of things could easily be imagined in which it would not be to the advantage of the civilization of the country that there should be an immense body of persons who, however patriotic, able and industrious, however much they threw themselves into the national life, still, by their own action, remained a people apart, and not merely held a religion differing from the vast majority of their fellow-countrymen, but only inter-married among themselves.[58]

The document bears Balfour's name, but in reality it was the Zionists themselves who, in very large measure, both inspired the Declaration and framed its text. It must be reckoned the finest flower of Zionist diplomacy at its most sophisticatedly ambivalent. A whole chapter would be required to do justice to the genesis and real import of those few words. Whole chapters have indeed been devoted to the task, and suffice it to say here, on the strength of others' researches, that the Zionists who framed the Declaration saw in it the charter of a future Jewish State and that, in appearing to care for the rights of the 'non-Jewish communities in Palestine', they were actually laying a legal foundation, through the ingenious deployment of the words 'civil', 'religious', and 'political', for taking these rights away.[59]

The Zionists were not entirely unmasked by their triumph. It was still too early for that. They continued to deny the ultimate ambition, Jewish statehood, which friends and enemies attributed to them. Weizmann warned more extreme Zionists than himself that 'Palestine must be built up without violating the legitimate rights of the Arabs—not a hair of their heads shall be touched'.[60] He went to Palestine to assure the Arabs that it was not 'our objective to seize control of the higher policy of the province of Palestine. Nor has it ever been our objective to turn anyone out of his property.'[61] Yet even as he was there, dispensing these assurances to the natives, he was conveying what he really thought about them in his correspondence with Balfour:

> The Arabs, who are superficially clever and quickwitted, worship one thing, and one thing only—power and success. . . . The British authorities . . . knowing as they do the treacherous nature of the Arab, have to watch carefully and constantly that nothing

should happen which might give the Arabs the slightest grievance or lest they should stab the Army in the back. The Arab, quick as he is to gauge such a situation, tries to make the most of it. He screams as often as he can and blackmails as much as he can. The first scream was heard when your Declaration was announced. All sorts of misinterpretations and misconceptions were put on the declaration. The English, they said, are going to hand over the poor Arabs to the wealthy Jews, who are all waiting in the wake of General Allenby's army, ready to swoop down like vultures on an easy prey and to oust everybody from the land. . . .[62]

Yet even in public Weizmann could often only cloak his real hopes in the thinnest disguise of discretion and sweet reason. And occasionally this most eloquent of speakers seemed quite to forget himself, as when he told a London audience a mere two years after the Declaration:

I trust to God that a Jewish state will come about; but it will come about not through political declarations, but by the sweat and blood of the Jewish people. . . . [The Balfour Declaration] is the golden key which unlocks the doors of Palestine and gives you the possibility to put all your efforts into the country. . . . We were asked to formulate our wishes. We said we desired to create in Palestine such conditions, political, economic and administrative, that as the country is developed, we can pour in a considerable number of immigrants, and finally establish such a society in Palestine that Palestine shall be as Jewish as England is English, or America is American . . . I hope that the Jewish frontiers of Palestine will be as great as Jewish energy for getting Palestine.[63]

It appears that Zionist historians have been more discreet than Weizmann. These revealing passages were omitted from later editions of the book in which they appear.

As for the mechanics of the thing, the *modus operandi*, Weizmann pioneered two basic concepts that have underlain Zionist policies ever since. One was the concept of the empty framework. As he subsequently explained in his autobiography, 'the Balfour Declaration was no more than a framework, which had to be filled in by our own efforts. It would mean exactly what we would make it mean—neither more nor less. On what we could make it mean through slow, costly and laborious work would depend whether and when we should deserve or attain statehood.'[64] The other was the concept of stages. In a speech to the English

Zionist Union, a few months before the issue of the declaration, he put discretion aside to explain it.

> States must be built up slowly, gradually, systematically and patiently. We, therefore, say that while the creation of a Jewish Commonwealth in Palestine is our final ideal . . . the way to achieve it lies through a series of intermediary stages. And one of those intermediary stages, which I hope is going to come about as a result of the war, is that the fair country of Palestine will be protected by such a mighty and just Power as Great Britain. Under the wing of this Power, Jews will be able to develop, and to set up the administrative machinery which . . . would enable us to carry out the Zionist scheme.[65]

What the Zionists were to do in the fair land of Palestine they could only do in the teeth of increasingly vigorous opposition from the Arabs who lived there and in violation of those terms of the Balfour Declaration which, properly interpreted, would have safeguarded their interests. But that they could rely on mighty and just Britain to help them do it was not, for those in the know, a wildly optimistic interpretation of the British intent. Indeed, what more reassuring than the interpretation which the author of the famous declaration himself put upon it? Weizmann had been confidentially assured by the Prime Minister, in Balfour's presence, that 'national home' was a euphemism for Jewish State.[66] He may also have read a candid secret memorandum which Balfour submitted to the British cabinet. In this memorandum Balfour discussed the League of Nations Covenant, its championship of the principle of self-determination of peoples and its insistence that 'the wishes of these communities ("independent nations" like Syria and Palestine requiring administrative advice and assistance until they are able to "stand alone") must be a principal consideration in the selection of a mandatory.' Lord Balfour wrote:

> Do we mean, in the case of Syria, to consult principally the wishes of the inhabitants? We mean nothing of the kind. . . . The contradiction between the letter of the Covenant and the policy of the Allies is even more flagrant in the case of the 'independent nation' of Palestine than in that of the 'independent nation' of Syria. For in Palestine we do not propose even to go through the form of consulting the wishes of the present inhabitants of the country. . . . The Four Great Powers are committed to Zionism.

And Zionism, be it right or wrong, good or bad, is rooted in age-long traditions, in present needs, in future hopes, of far profounder import than the desires and prejudices of the 700,000 Arabs who now inhabit that ancient land. . . . In short, so far as Palestine is concerned, the Powers have made no statement of fact which is not admittedly wrong, and no declaration of policy which, at least in the letter, they have not always intended to violate.[67]

NOTES

1. Central Zionist Archives, Jerusalem, H111 d 14, 1 March 1899; see Mandel, Neville, 'Turks, Arabs and Jewish Immigration into Palestine, 1882–1914', St Antony's Papers, *Middle Eastern Affairs*, ed. Hourani, Albert, Oxford University Press, 1965, p. 89.
2. UN General Assembly, 2nd Session, 9 September, 1947, *Report of the Special Committee on Palestine*, Vol. II, A/364, Add., I, pp. 39–40.
3. *The Complete Diaries of Theodor Herzl*, Herzl Press and Thomas Yoseloff, New York, 1960, Vol. I, p. 343.
4. Herzl, *The Jewish State*, Rita Searle, London, 1946, p. 29.
5. Herzl, *Besammelte Zionistische Schriften*, Jüdischer Verlag, Berlin, 1934–5, Vol. I, p. 114; Vol. II, pp. 50, 58, 78, 102; Vol. III, p. 526. This and the following list of Herzl's recommended techniques is largely taken from L.M.C. Van der Hoeven, 'Het Palestina-Vragstak in Zijn Ware gedaante', *Libertas* (Holland), Lustrum, 1960; republished in English in Khalidi, Walid, *From Haven to Conquest*, Institute for Palestine Studies, Beirut, 1971, p. 115.
6. *The Complete Diaries, op. cit.*, Vol. I, p. 88.
7. *Ibid.*, p. 98.
8. Böhm, Adolf, *Die Zionistische Bewegung*, Berlin, 1935, Vol. I, p. 706.
9. Herzl, *Besammelte Zioniste Schriften, op. cit.*, Vol. III, p. 77.
10. Zwangwill, Israel, 'The Return to Palestine', *New Liberal Review II*, December 1901, p. 627.
11. Nordau, Max, *Zionistische Schriften*, Jüdischer Verlag, Berlin, 1923, p. 72.
12. *Ibid.*, p. 425.
13. Sykes, Christopher, *Two Studies in Virtue*, Collins, London, 1953, p. 160.
14. Barbour, Neville, *Nisi Dominus*, Harrap, London, 1946, p. 52.
15. *The Complete Diaries, op. cit.*, Vol. II, p. 581.
16. Hadawi, Sami, *Bitter Harvest*, The New World Press, New York, 1967, p. 11.
17. Oliphant, L., *Haifa or Life in Modern Palestine*, William Blackwood, Edinburgh, 1887, p. 60; Newton, Frances E., *Fifty Years in Palestine*, Coldharbour Press, Wrotham, England, 1948, p. 97.

18. Mandel, *op. cit.*, p. 90.
19. Al-Kayyali, Abdul al-Wahhab, *A History of Modern Palestine* (Arabic), Beirut, 1971, p. 50.
20. Barbour, *op. cit.*, p. 116.
21. Mandel, *op. cit.*, p. 85; see also Ro'i, Yaacov, 'The Zionist Attitude to the Arabs, 1908–14', *Middle Eastern Studies*, London, Vol. 4, No. 3, April 1968, pp. 198–242.
22. *Hadera*, Jewish National Fund Library No. 2, Tel Aviv, 1935, cited in Barbour, *op. cit.*, pp. 115, 116.
23. Barbour, *op. cit.*, p. 116.
24. Aham, Ahad, *Am Scheideweg*, Berlin, 1923, Vol. I, p. 107.
25. *Jewish-Arab Affairs*, Jerusalem, 1931, p. 11, cited in Barbour, *op. cit.*, p. 124.
26. Mandel, *op. cit.*, p. 86.
27. Jiryis, Sabri, 'Recent Knesset Legislation', *Journal of Palestine Studies*, Institute for Palestine Studies, Beirut, Vol. I, No. 1, Autumn 1971, pp. 57–8.
28. Ro'i, *op. cit.*, p. 233.
29. Ussishkin, Menachim, see Avneri, Uri, *Israel Without Zionists: A Plea for Peace in the Middle East*, Macmillan, New York, 1968, p. 86.
30. Snowman, Leonard Victor, *Tchernichowski and his Poetry*, Hasefer Agency for Literature, London, 1929, p. 26. See Taylor, Alan R., *The Zionist Mind, The Origins and Development of Zionist Thought*, Institute for Palestine Studies, Beirut, 1974, pp. 47–80.
31. Ro'i, *op. cit.*, p. 223.
32. Elon, Amos, *The Israelis, Founders and Sons*, Sphere Books, London, 1972, p. 131.
33. *Ibid.*, p. 124.
34. Mandel, *op. cit.*, p. 93.
35. St John, Robert, *Bengurion*, New York, 1959, pp. 31–2.
36. Barbour, *op. cit.*, p. 117.
37. Grannott, Abraham, *The Land System in Palestine*, Eyre and Spottiswoode, London, 1952, p. 280.
38. *Ibid.*, p. 80.
39. Weizmann, Chaim, *Trial and Error*, Hamish Hamilton, London, 1949, p. 457.
40. Qasimiyah, Khairiyah, 'Najib Nassar and *Carmel* Newspaper, One of the Pioneer Opponents of Zionism', *Palestine Affairs* (Arabic), Beirut monthly, July 1973, p. 111, citing *Carmel*, 11 January, 22 and 26 August 1913.
41. *Ibid.*, p. 114, citing *Carmel*, 1 July 1914.
42. *Ibid.*, citing *al-Muqtabas* (Damascus newspaper), 11 January 1911.
43. *Ibid.*, citing *al-Muqattam* (Cairo newspaper), 1 May 1914, and *Carmel*, 5 May 1914.
44. Ro'i, *op. cit.*, p. 225.
45. Mandel, Neville, 'Attempts at an Arab-Zionist Entente: 1913–1914', *Middle Eastern Studies*, London, Vol. I, No. 3, April 1965, p. 263.
46. *Ibid.*, p. 256, citing *al-Manar* newspaper, Vol. 27, 1914, p. 320.

47. *Ibid.*, p. 340.
48. *Ibid.*, p. 246.
49. *Ibid.*, p. 260.
50. *Ibid.*, p. 265; translation from *Journal de Beyrouth* 413, 1 September 1915.
51. Elon, *op. cit.*, p. 143.
52. *Ibid.*, p. 143.
53. Tabenkin, Yitzhak, *Chemins et Détours de la Renaissance Juive*, Paris, 1948, pp. 120–3.
54. Aaronsohn, Alexander, *With the Turks in Palestine*, Constable, London, 1917, p. 25.
55. Schechtman, Joseph, *Fighter and Prophet, The Vladimir Jabotinsky Story*, Thomas Yoseloff, New York, 1961, p. 324.
56. Revusky, Abraham, *Jews in Palestine*, P. S. King, London, 1935, pp. 286 and 317–18.
57. Elon, *op. cit.*, p. 163.
58. See Rabinowicz, Oskar K., *Winston Churchill on Jewish Problems*, Thomas Yoseloff, New York, 1960, p. 167.
59. See Jeffreys, J. M. N., *Palestine: the Reality*, Longmans, Green and Co., London, 1939, Chapter II.
60. Speech to Fourteenth Zionist Congress, Vienna, 1925.
61. Khalidi, *op. cit.*, p. 189.
62. Ingrams, Doreen, *Palestine Papers 1917–1922, Seeds of Conflict*, John Murray, London, 1972, p. 31.
63. *Chaim Weizmann: Excerpts from his Historic Statements, Writings and Addresses*, The Jewish Agency for Palestine, New York, 1952, p. 48.
64. Weizmann, *op. cit.*, p. 302.
65. *Palestine, A Study of Jewish, Arab and British Policies*, ESCO Zionist Institute, Yale University Press, New Haven, Vol. I, pp. 98–9.
66. Ingrams, *op. cit.*, p. 146.
67. *Ibid.*, p. 73.

Two

No Peace in Zion, 1921–1935

THE SLAUGHTER OF 1921

IN 1921 there was little to distinguish the town of Jaffa from the other seaports—Haifa, Tyre or Sidon—that lay along the eastern shores of the Mediterranean. It was a picturesque labyrinth of narrow alleys packed against the quay. Its dominant spirit was still conservative; it was touched, but not badly disrupted, by the intensifying contact with the modern world of Europe. Its merchant class was favourably disposed towards Britain, an important market for the famous orange to which Jaffa had given its name. It had its water-front world of boatmen, porters, artisans and labourers. They were sociable, credulous, excitable in the Levantine way and, when anything unusual occurred, they would quickly form a crowd. They included, as in any port, a number of toughs and bad characters. But in general the citizens of Jaffa were law-abiding and, if anything, more respectful of authority than vigorous Western societies would consider normal.

On 1 May of that year unprecedented violence erupted in Palestine. May Day traditionally raised uneasy expectations in many European countries. But the proletarian struggle meant very little to the Arabs of Palestine. There was little reason to expect trouble from them. Trouble came, however, and although it struck in a number of places, its focus was Jaffa. For the one thing which had, in recent years, distinguished this otherwise unexceptional Arab coastal town was a profoundly unsettling one. It had become the principal point of Jewish immigration into Palestine. It was there that the refugees from the ghettoes of Eastern Europe first set foot on the Promised Land. And just to the north the new city of Tel Aviv, the biggest concentration of Jews in the country, was taking shape.

The violence had small, indeed foolish, beginnings. The Jews came to Palestine armed with the social and political doctrines of their East European Diaspora, and since it was a time of revolutionary upheaval they naturally had their share of Bolshevik extremists. Since 1909 the Socialist Revolutionary Party—or *Mopsi*, the German for pug, as its rivals derisively called it—had been trying to win Jewish Labour groups to the principles of the Third International; but it never made much headway in these efforts to 'prepare the soil of Palestine for the Social Revolution'. In 1920 it was reinforced by newcomers from the Soviet Union; but at its height it never numbered more than 300 members. It was on May Day that *Mopsi*, in accordance with proletarian tradition, chose to make a show of its puny strength. Led mainly by illegal immigrants, it was determined to make up in noise and provocation for what it lacked in numbers. In the morning of 1 May, the militants assembled at their headquarters in the Borochoff Club in a mixed Arab-Jewish quarter of Jaffa. Then, in defiance of an official ban, they issued into the streets, eluded a police barrier and marched on Tel Aviv. They wore red rosettes and raised cardboard slogans stencilled in red: 'Long Live 1 May; Down with English Coercive Power; Long Live Socialist Revolution; Long Live Socialist Soviet Palestine.' In violent language they invited Jewish and Arab workers to join in overthrowing their oppressors and 'beating down the torturers and tyrants among you'. It was a clarion call to class warfare— but the very oppressed they were trying to save, their hapless co-religionists, were the main victims of the warfare, or, rather, the mindless slaughter which it provoked.

The violence began as an inter-Jewish clash. *Mopsi* ran into the much bigger, officially authorized demonstration staged by *Ahdot ha Avodah*, a social democratic party. The two sides came to blows; there were some injuries and one woman was knocked down with a bad head wound. Hitherto, Jewish labour disturbances had produced little more than Arab curiosity. This time, however, it was different. Quite suddenly the Arabs seemed to go berserk. Normally law-abiding citizens perpetrated acts of savagery that lasted a week and spread deep into the surrounding countryside. A crowd had gathered to watch the quarrelling Jewish demonstrators. British-controlled policemen stood between the two groups at opposite ends of a sandy open space. They glowered at each other. Tension rose. Neither side would disperse. Somebody began breaking Jewish shop windows in the adjoining quarter of Menshieh. The crowd deserted the sandy space and, armed with sticks, iron bars, knives and anything that came to hand, they began a general hunt of the Jews. The civil police, overcome by partisan emotions, were completely ineffectual. Three Arab notables offered their services to quieten the populace. In Menshieh they found the Jewish market entirely looted, and pillage in progress elsewhere. They stilled the tumult only where they were; it resumed as soon as their backs were turned. The army was called in, but the rioting kept breaking out afresh, and by the time it finally subsided nearly 200 Jews and 120 Arabs were dead or wounded. The Arabs had been the first to turn it into a racial conflict, but the Jews retaliated with equal savagery. After examining the dead bodies on this first day, Dr Beadles, the Medical Officer in Jaffa, recalled that he was 'struck most with the number of wounds on each body, and the ferocity of the wounds. I am speaking particularly of broken skulls. Some of the victims had dozens of wounds.'[1] Some of the worst atrocities were premeditated.

On the second day groups of Jews went out seeking cold-blooded vengeance. One of them, apparently led by a policeman from Tel Aviv, broke down the door of a house; they shot a man in the stomach and when his little daughter ran to her father her head was cleft with the blow of an axe. The Arabs were no less methodical. On the same day six Jews who lived in an isolated house were found dead nearby; five of them had been beaten or stabbed to death; the sixth, some distance apart from the others, had died with his hands tied behind his back. But the symbolic climax had already come on the first day, when the Arab mob stormed the Zionist immigration hostel in the middle of the town. Arab constables, caught up in the general frenzy, actually led the assault. The official British committee of inquiry, led by Sir Thomas Haycraft, concluded:

We are satisfied from the evidence of the Reverend A. C. Martin, of the London Jews' Society, who saw much of what happened from a window on the opposite side of the main street, that the police in the street broke through the door and led a part of the mob into the yard. They broke into the ground floor of the main building and into the other buildings. Men who sought refuge by running into the street were beaten to death by the crowd. Others were killed inside the courtyard. The invaders came in from all the entrances when the defence had broken down. Only one woman was killed, namely by a shot fired through a window. Those women who escaped into the street were roughly handled by the crowd, but not killed. They were wounded, but not dangerously, and were sheltered from further harm by an Arab neighbour. Perhaps the most revolting incident was the conduct of one of the Arab policemen. He was at first regarded by the women as a protector, but he took advantage of the prevailing terror to rob them of their small possessions, and to two he made indecent advances, telling them that he was a Jew, with threats of violence if they refused to comply with his demands. They appear to have avoided this crowning act of brutality by escape. This man was convicted by a special court for the trial of offences committed during the riots, and was sentenced to 13 years' imprisonment. It must not be supposed that no resistance was made by the Jews. The toll of dead and wounded in the gruesome episode of the Immigration House was as follows: 13 Jews killed or mortally wounded and 24 wounded; one Arab killed and four wounded.[2]

Coming three years after the greatest carnage in history, what Bengurion called 'the slaughter of 1921' might seem an insignificant affair. But it was not so for the Jews. They might regard anti-Semitic outbreaks in Eastern Europe as a kind of seasonal misfortune, but that a pogrom could occur in Palestine, and under the enlightened rule of Great Britain, many of them found shocking and incomprehensible.

HAYCRAFT VINDICATES THE ARABS

Yet the pogrom had a specific and a general cause, and Sir Thomas Haycraft had no difficulty in identifying them. The *Mopsi* demonstration, he concluded, was the specific cause, the immediate trigger of the Arab rampage, while the fear and hatred of the Jewish immigrant, and all he stood for, was the general one. *Mopsi* amounted to little in themselves; they were a complete failure, despised by most of their own community as much as by the Arabs. But, owing to the deeper inter-communal antagonisms, they produced an effect far out of proportion to their numbers. For the Arabs, they were not fundamentally different from their fellow-Zionists; they merely typified, at its most offensive, an alien invasion which, by its very nature, they

found intolerable. Not only were the foreigners invading their
country, here they were desecrating it with their repugnant, subversive creeds, their quarrels and their violence. Repudiated by
their own people, here they were trying to convert them, the
natives, and importing Communist literature in Arabic from
Vienna for the purpose. The Arabs saw 'the beginnings of industrial strife, previously unknown in the country; they saw
strikes and labour demonstrations, which filled their conservative minds with alarm; they read leaflets . . . in which the people
were invited to participate in class war, and to promote anarchy
and social upheaval.'[3]

Labour unrest was only part of a whole complex of alien and
insulting ways. The Arabs felt that in all they did the newcomers were arrogant and aggressive. They also found them indecent. 'Several witnesses have referred to the manner in which
strings of these young men and women, in free and easy attire,
would perambulate the streets arm in arm, singing songs, holding
up traffic and generally conducting themselves in a manner at
variance with Arab ideas of decorum.'[4] Other contemporary
reports speak of the shock which the straitlaced Arabs felt at such
extremes of modernism as mixed bathing in the nude. The Jews
had come, they felt, to corrupt their society and whole way of life.

The animosity was frequently reinforced by outright prejudices. Through Westernization, the Arabs had acquired some
of these. Communism, revolution and anarchy, they claimed,
were rooted in the Jews' very being. In many countries they were
'sowers of controversy and ruin'. In their view Jews were like
bacteria; if Britain and America were unable to contain them,
how could Palestine? The Arabs also had some inherited prejudices of their own. Even a leading scholar wrote that it was
forbidden to believe the Jews, who claimed that their intentions
were good, since 'they are scoundrels and the Koran itself is full
of stories of their fraudulent acts'.[5]

It was a favourite Zionist argument that in coming to Palestine
the Jews would help to develop it for the benefit of all its inhabitants. The Arabs were never impressed, particularly when
they saw what kind of people these would-be developers were.
They were not, they said, the wealthy, the merchants, the men
of property, but a disparate multitude, 'vagabonds and outcasts',
from all over the world.[6]

It was a fundamental clash of culture, yet the Arabs would
have absorbed it but for the one totally inadmissible premise that
underlay the whole Zionist enterprise. The Jews were not only
introducing an alien culture, they planned to make it the only one
in the country. Nor was the takeover bid only cultural; it was
political, economic and demographic too. To this deep-rooted
fear the Haycraft Commission—like many that were to succeed
it over the years—devoted much sympathetic attention:

> It is important that it should be realized that what is written on
> the subject of Zionism by Zionists and their sympathizers in
> Europe is read and discussed by Palestinian Arabs, not only in
> the towns but in the country districts. Thus a witness from
> Tulkaram . . . quoted as an instance of provocative writing the
> following passage from a book entitled 'England and Palestine',
> by H. Sidebotham: 'It is desired to encourage Jewish immigration
> by every means, and at the same time to discourage the immigra-
> tion of Arabs . . .' The book was published as far back as 1918;
> but our attention has been called to other not less provocative
> statements appearing in Zionist publications since the disturban-
> ces, whilst we were sitting. Thus the *Jewish Chronicle*, No. 2,720,
> of the 20th May, 1921, makes the following statement in the course
> of its leading article: 'Hence the real key to the Palestine situation
> is to be found in giving to Jews as such, those rights and privi-
> leges in Palestine which shall enable Jews to make it as Jewish as
> England is English, or as Canada is Canadian. That is the only
> reasonable or, indeed, feasible meaning of a Jewish National
> Home, and it is impossible for Jews to construct it without being
> accorded a National status for Jews.'
>
> Again, *Palestine*, the official organ of the British Palestine
> Committee in its issue of the 4th June, 1921, in discussing the
> question of Jewish immigration, describes Palestine as a 'de-
> serted, derelict land'. This description hardly tallies with the
> fact that the density of the present population of Palestine, accord-
> ing to Zionist figures, is something like 75 to the square mile.
> On the 14th May there appeared in *The Times* a letter from Mr.
> V. Jabotinsky . . . in which he urged that, in view of the Jaffa
> disturbances, Jews alone should have the privilege of military
> service in Palestine, Arabs being excluded from the right to bear
> arms . . .
>
> Until the Commission came to examine Dr. Eder, acting
> Chairman of the Zionist Commission, they were unaware to what
> extent such expressions of opinion as those we have quoted above

were authorized by responsible Zionists. Dr. Eder was a most enlightening witness. He was quite unaggressive in manner and free from any desire to push forward opinions which might be offensive to the Arabs. But when questioned on certain vital matters he was perfectly frank in expressing his view of the Zionist ideal. He gave no quarter to the view of the National Home as put forward by the Secretary of State and the High Commissioner. In his opinion there can only be one National Home in Palestine, and that a Jewish one, and no equality in the partnership between Jews and Arabs, but a Jewish predominance as soon as the numbers of that race are sufficiently increased . . . As acting Chairman of the Zionist Commission, Dr. Eder presumably expresses in all points the official Zionist creed, if such there be, and his statements are, therefore, most important. There is no sophistry about Dr. Eder; he was quite clear that the Jews should, and the Arabs should not, have the right to bear arms, and he stated his belief that this discrimination would tend to improve Arab-Jewish relations . . .[7]

The Arabs were genuinely persuaded, Haycraft went on, that the Palestine government was under Zionist influence and therefore led to favour a minority at the expense of the vast majority of the population. And in the light of all this he exonerated Arab leaders:

We are convinced that the charge constantly brought by Jews against the Arabs, that this outbreak had been planned by them, or by their leaders, and was pre-arranged for the 1st May, is unfounded. It appears in evidence that on more than one occasion Arabs in European dress incited the crowd; but the notables on both sides, whatever their feelings may have been, were always ready to help the authorities in their restoration of order, and we think that without their assistance the outbreak would have resulted in even worse excesses. A good deal has been alleged by Jewish witnesses about the instigation of the Arab mob to violence by their leaders. If this means no more than that while educated people talk and write, the mob acts, then there is truth in the allegation. But if it means that had it not been for incitement by the notables, effendis, and sheikhs, there would have been no riots, the allegation cannot be substantiated. . . . All that can be truly said in favour of the Jewish view is that the leaders of Arab opinion not only make no secret of what they think, but carry on a political campaign. In this campaign, however, the people participate with the leaders, because they feel that their political

and material interests are identical. There is no evidence worth
considering, to show that the outbreak was planned and organised.
Had that been the case, we hesitate to conjecture what the consequences would have been.[8]

British government papers of the period are replete with
similar opinions expressed by officials on the spot. The Jaffa
location of the outbreak—said the monthly political report from
Jerusalem—'can cause no surprise' because discontent is most
acute in places 'where the irritant which causes it is most in evidence'.[9] And immigration, said the Chief Secretary of the
Palestine government, is 'the tangible, visible evidence of
Zionism. It is a measure which they [the Arabs] can judge by.'[10]
For the temporary inmates of the immigration hostel, defenceless
newcomers to the Promised Land, it was a cruelly ironic fate.
But for those who cared to see it, the Arabs could scarcely have
chosen a starker way of making their point: there would be no
peace in such a Zion.

THE ZIONISTS BLAME THE ARAB 'POLITICIANS'

The Zionists did not care to see it. Dr Eder's opinions were
standard. Jabotinsky's were merely an immoderate version of
them. It is one of the many peculiarities of a movement born of
resistance to injustice and persecution that it should have been
so insensitive to the self-same resistance that it bred in others.
Yet it is not very surprising. The Zionists came to Palestine with
such a passionate determination to succeed that they could not
bring themselves to acknowledge the seemingly insurmountable
obstacles—both moral and physical—which they found in their
way when they got there. They preferred to maintain the Diaspora
illusion that the Promised Land, if not actually uninhabited,
could easily accommodate them and all their aspirations. Or,
finding that it could not, they preferred the deception—which
was also a conscience-salving self-deception—that no harm
would ever come to those all-too-numerous inhabitants.
    In short, they invented a world of make-believe in which there
could be no resistance for there was nothing to resist. From the
turn of the century to this day, the Zionists, so sure of their own
high motives, have resolutely blinded themselves to the motives
of their enemies. It is scarcely going too far to say that, con-

fronted with Arab resistance, they have found explanations for
it which, to those who have unprejudiced eyes with which to see,
are not merely wrong, but often quite the opposite of the real
ones. And on the strength of their false diagnosis they have with
unfailing perversity proceeded to advocate remedies which
simply aggravate the malady which they were supposed to cure.
The trouble, they almost invariably said, lay with the 'politicians'
and not with the 'people'. In the Palestine of the Mandate, it was
local notables, the *zaims* and the *effendis*, who supposedly incited
the anti-Jewish riots—just as, after 1948, it was to be President
Nasser and other 'revolutionary' leaders who supposedly spread
hatred of the newly-born state of Israel throughout the Arab
world. The best way to handle rabble-rousing politicians, they
said, was implacably to oppose them—in other words, to press
on, more resolutely than ever, with the great Zionist enterprise.
Discrimination against the Arabs would improve the situation
for everyone—including, of course, the Arabs themselves. And
the more the Arabs disliked the discrimination, the more of it
they should suffer.

True, there were a few Zionists for whom this was an extraordinary contortion of logic. In the opinion of Chaim Arlosoroff,
'the slaughter of 1921' meant that 'an Arab movement really
exists and—no matter what sort it is—it will be calamitous if we
negate its importance or rely on bayonets, British or Jewish.
Such support is valid for an hour but not for decades . . . the
"strong-arm" policy never attained its aim.'[11] This was completely at odds with the usual diagnosis, of which Gershon
Agronsky, founder of the *Jerusalem Post*, furnished a typical
example: 'The Jaffa riots this year', he argued, 'and the Easter
outbreak in Jerusalem last year were not the result of a popular
uprising. They were caused by Arab politicians who, in their
campaign against the announced British Zionist policy, have used
the good-natured, uneducated Arab as a dupe. These politicians
. . . are of two classes: there are the superior natives of Palestine,
members of the landed class, who have had a much better time
of it under the Turkish regime, and who feel that their interests
are endangered by a Western government with Western ideas of
justice. They also fear Jewish immigration because of the effect
of the Jews' higher standard of living upon the exploited culti-
vator.' He concedes that the riots and other overt acts do seem to

point to hostility on the part of a section of the native population towards Zionist immigration. But he goes on: 'It is based, however, on a misconception of the Zionist aims, and could be overcome. Those who have spent any time in the country know, as the Arabs directly affected by Zionist work know, that Palestine has much to gain and nothing to lose from a large Zionist immigration. Where Arab villages cluster about Jewish colonies, said Winston Churchill, "the Arab houses are tiled instead of being built of mud, so that the culture from this centre has been spread out into the surrounding district". Low as the standard of wages is in Palestine, it is infinitely higher where Arabs are employed by Jews. Jewish labour has given an impetus to the organization of Arab labour.' And then comes the paradoxical remedy. 'Peace will be secured when the League of Nations puts the formal stamp of approval on the mandate, and when the Zionist organization obtains the means for carrying out its program. Those earnestly wishing to see peace in Palestine . . . want the Mandate to be ratified, the Keren Hayesod (Jewish National Fund) to succeed, and, as a result of the two, the Arab to be reconciled.'[12]

If this Zionist journalist on the spot could perhaps be excused for failing to see the wood for the trees, what about the world-renowned British scientist Redcliffe Salman? He was confident that 'the Jew and the Arab would get on perfectly well if the politicians would but leave them alone. There is more than enough room for both. The Arab is utterly incapable of developing the land alone. The Jew is the only one who will bring capital and the Arab knows it; even as one writes comes information of letters from village chiefs all over the country . . . praying for Jewish immigration.' He had no time for 'an Administration which has truckled to the noisy pan-Arabic party for the sake of peace and quiet, which has allowed party sedition to grow under its nose, which has removed the few arms from the hands of the voluntary Jewish police of the colonies and has suffered the wholesale pilfering of arms and ammunition by the Arabs.' And he too came to the unscientific conclusion that the more forcefully Britain adopted the Zionist programme—a programme which, he insisted, should lead to Jewish majority rule in Palestine—the happier the Arabs would be: 'As one writes one hears of conflicts and bloodshed in Jerusalem and a noisy Press campaign, which informs the world that the Arab *fellah* dreads the incoming rush of Jews. It would be idle to say that there is no opposition, but this much can be said without hesitation: had Britain assumed the Mandate immediately after the Armistice and carried out its promise contained in the Balfour Declaration, there would have been little or no opposition on the part of the *fellahin*.'[13]

It is of course questionable whether all those who expressed such unrealistic opinions sincerely believed them. There is no record of Bengurion stating publicly at the time what he was to write forty years later: 'I believed—and still do—that Jewish-Arab cooperation holds enormous benefit for both peoples. But at the same time I realized that the battle of Tel Hai in 1920, the slaughter of 1921, were as nothing compared to the blood-letting that was to come.'[14]

There is a tendency on the Arab side, especially among contemporary left-wing historians, to overstate the opposite thesis—namely, that the 'people', in their immediate and intuitive hostility to Zionism, were all irreproachable patriots, while the 'politicians' were quislings almost to a man. It is certain, however, that resistance derived its main impetus from the people; it was they who enforced it on the politicians, not the other way round.

THE ARAB POLITICIANS CHOOSE NON-VIOLENCE

The dilemma that the Palestinian leaders faced was a grave one. It was enshrined in the Balfour Declaration. It has been seen what this meant for the Zionists. They could rely on the British to help them fill in the 'framework' which—in Weizmann's phrase—it represented. They had not been disappointed. They secured sufficient imperial backing to tip an otherwise highly adverse balance of power in their favour. For the Arabs there had always been a choice between conciliation and resistance. In earlier pre-Balfour days, as we have seen, they had toyed with the idea of conciliation as a means of containing the embryonic 'Zionist peril'. But now that peril had assumed far more alarming proportions. Conciliation meant coming to terms with the British; resistance meant fighting them. It was a very difficult choice. It was, said the Palestinians, quite 'impossible to set up a Jewish homeland without prejudicing the civil and religious rights of the existing non-Jewish communities of Palestine'.[15]

How, then, could they cooperate with an alien rule which, by its very nature, trampled the national interest underfoot? On the other hand, how could they take on a leading military power of the age? They chose conciliation.

Naturally, the Palestinians did not like their new quasi-colonial status. Like other Arabs they regarded it as a breach of faith. But their immediate concern was not to get rid of it—they would manage that in due course—it was to ensure that, before they eventually did, the national interest would not be damaged beyond repair. They did try to cooperate with their new masters in the hope of persuading them to drop the whole idea of establishing a Jewish National Home. In 1921, Musa Kazim al-Husseini, President of the Arab Executive, which represented the Palestine community in dealings with the British authorities, appealed to his compatriots 'to put their hope in the government of Great Britain, which is famous for its justice, its concern for the well-being of the inhabitants, its safeguarding of their rights, and consent to their lawful demands.'[16] Basically, they had two approaches. One, the direct one, was to work for a formal renunciation of the Balfour Declaration, or at least the quiet non-implementation of its operative provisions; the other, the indirect one, was to work for the establishment of representative government in Palestine, thereby enabling them, the vast majority, to block the designs of the Zionist minority. After all, in accordance with the Covenant of the League of Nations, Britain had assumed the Mandate as a 'sacred trust of civilization', and the development of self-governing institutions was one of its basic obligations. Had it not already granted self-rule to far more backward areas of the Middle East?

They did not get very far with either approach. When Winston Churchill, the Colonial Secretary, visited the Middle East in 1921, he effectively foreclosed both. A delegation of Palestinian leaders petitioned him to rescind the Balfour Declaration, end all Jewish immigration and agree to the formation of a national government answerable to a popularly elected assembly. 'You ask me', Churchill replied, 'to repudiate the Balfour Declaration and to stop immigration. This is not in my power, and it is not my wish.' After extolling the idea of a Jewish national centre in Palestine, he turned to the second, 'safeguard' clause in the Declaration and what he described as 'the sacredness of Arab and religious rights'. 'I am sorry', he told his petitioners, 'that you regard the second part as valueless. It is vital to you and you should hold and claim it firmly. If one promise stands so does the other. We shall faithfully fulfil both.' As for a Palestinian parliament, he was at least frank: 'The present form of government will continue for many years. Step by step we shall develop representative institutions leading to full self-government, but our children's children will have passed away before that is accomplished.'[17]

Here, in Churchill's reply, lay the dilemma that was to face the Palestinians for most of the Mandate. They were trapped in a constitutional blind alley. It was no good their going direct to the heart of the matter—the basic unworkability of the Mandate—for Britain had neither the 'wish' nor the 'power' to give it up. It did not wish to do so, for such was British policy, and it did not have the power because, it claimed, it was merely performing the 'sacred trust' which the League of Nations had conferred upon it. That august body had early ruled that 'the two obligations imposed on the Mandatory are in no sense irreconcilable'. Armed with this verdict, Britain countered Arab assertions that they were. The Arabs could of course take their case over Britain's head to the League itself—only to find that the Permanent Mandates Commission was not competent to question the basic provisions of the Mandate.

They got no further with the indirect approach, for, even when due allowance was made for Churchillian rhetoric, it was clearly the British government's intention that they should wait a very long time for truly self-governing institutions. All they could do, then, was to put their faith in the safeguard clause and in Britain's promise that it would faithfully fulfil its obligations to both Jews and Arabs. Those obligations *were* irreconcilable, and in 1937 a British Royal Commission formally acknowledged it. But since, in the meantime, Britain had been consistently fulfilling the first obligation at the expense of the second, the Arabs had indeed come to regard the safeguard clause as 'value-less'.

It took sixteen years for the British officially to acknowledge it, but 'the slaughter of 1921' should have been warning enough: if a society has no means of expressing itself by legitimate constitutional means, it resorts to other means which, if it did have them, it would certainly condemn. Indeed, in the opinion of a British intelligence officer in Palestine, Churchill's visit and his outright insistence that he intended to deny to the Arabs the democratic privileges which he regarded as the birthright of every Englishman, lit the fuse of the Jaffa explosion. 'He upheld the Zionist cause and treated the Arab demands like those of a negligible opposition to be put off by a few polite phrases and treated like bad children . . . if policy is not modified the outbreak of today may become a revolution tomorrow.'[18]

In fact, Churchill appeared to have second thoughts. In June 1922, eight months after the Haycraft Commission published its findings, he laid before the Zionist and Palestinian representatives in London proposals for a legislative council. This, surely, would provide a constitutional alternative to violence. The proposals came in the form of a White Paper which made certain concessions to the Arab point of view. It reaffirmed the Balfour Declaration and insisted that a Jewish National Home would be founded in Palestine as of right and not of sufferance; it claimed that Arab apprehensions were 'partly' based on 'exaggerated interpretations' of the Declaration. But there was definitely to be no Jewish State. There was to be no subordination of the Arab population, language or culture. But what kind of legislative council was it to be? Clearly, the last thing the Zionists really wanted was that all the inhabitants of Palestine should have an equal say in running the country. This was embarrassing for them because they were supposedly coming to Palestine as the standard-bearers of Western civilization. To be sure, they did not reject self-governing institutions outright. They persuaded their imperial sponsor to offer a very limited form of them. With the backing of Lloyd George, the Prime Minister, and Lord Balfour, Weizmann had impressed on Churchill that representative government would have spelled the end of the National Home in Palestine. So, together with its twelve elected members—eight Moslems, two Christians and two Jews—the council was to include eleven appointed officials. The Palestinians rejected the offer. In their view—and leaving aside the fundamental objections of principle—this combination was likely to produce a permanent majority in favour of government policies which, in spite of the White Paper's reassurances, they considered completely unacceptable. All it would mean, they thought, was that

the 'Zionist policy of the government will be carried out under a
constitutional guise, whereas at present it is illegal, against the
rights and wishes of the people and maintained by force of arms
alone'.[19]

This was the first important instance of an attitude of mind
which is often held, even by sympathetic outsiders, to have contributed more than anything else to the disasters that eventually
overtook the Palestinian people. This standing on principle—
however just the principle—this rejection of compromise, this
forever saying 'no', has been judged the most purblind intransigence. 'Appalling blunder', says British historian Christopher
Sykes, who argues that the Palestinians' 'pathetic obstinacy' ensured that they never got representative government even in a
crude form and as a result could not avoid the evils of arbitrary
rule.[20] A contemporary Israeli scholar, General Yehoshafat
Harkabi, goes further. He believes that 'had the Arabs accepted
what the Legislative Council offered in the 1920's Israel would not
have existed. . . . Arab instransigence', he goes on, 'forced partition and Jewish statehood. It is an irony of history that the Arabs
should be counted among the founding fathers of the Jewish
state.'[21] It is certainly arguable that had the Palestinian leadership accepted the Council they might have fared better; there
was much hostility to Zionism in the ranks of the British administration, and some, at least, of the eleven officials might have
taken the Arab part. The argument cannot be disproved. But, in
its harsher forms, it is certainly unfair. The Palestinians were not
to know at the time—though their intuitions were accurate
enough—that subsequent events would furnish an impressive
counter-argument. When, in 1935, the British government did
offer a limited measure of self-government which, though by no
no means wholly impartial, was much less weighted in the
Zionists' favour, it was they, not the Arabs, who rushed to bury
this timid experiment in democracy. The Zionist Congress announced its 'categorical rejection'[22] of the offer, and when, at
Westminster, the Mother of Parliaments rejected it too, the
Zionist press hailed this as 'a great Jewish victory'.[23] The Arabs
had at least been ready to consider the offer. In fact, the celebrated 'Arab refusal' has always been welcomed by the Zionists,
for it has given them their most effective moral alibi—their *ein
brera*, their 'no-choice' but to fight the Arabs, fight them again

and again. And if, in the process, they gained more than they
planned or hoped for, that was their good fortune. The Arabs,
they contended, only had themselves to blame. General Harkabi
seems to be hoist with his own petard when, fifty-two years after
this early Arab rejection, and in the wake of the fourth Arab-
Israeli war in a generation, he could still advise against a settlement of the ever-expanding Middle East conflict:

> We must define our position and lay down basic principles
> for a settlement. Our demands should be moderate and balanced,
> and appear to be reasonable. But in fact they must involve such
> conditions as to ensure that the enemy rejects them. Then we
> should manoeuvre and allow him to define his own position, and
> reject a settlement on the basis of a compromise solution. We
> should then publish his demands as embodying unreasonable
> extremism.[24]

In rejecting the council, the Palestinians were not rejecting
conciliation. Resistance—merely civil disobedience or outright
violence—did not seem to them to be a serious alternative. This
is not to say that they had not considered it. The Palestinians
never managed to throw up the kind of leadership in which they
could place much confidence, but, before he became Mufti and
the most influential of the leaders they did have, Haj Amin
Husseini had in 1920 been sentenced by the British for incitement to violence. There were those who argued that violence did
pay. Before the Jaffa riots, Shaikh Arslan, a Syrian leader in
exile, wrote to his friends in the town to tell them that just such
an eruption in Palestine would be far more effective than sending
a delegation to the West.[25] The Arab Executive, semi-official
spokesman for the Palestinian community, condemned the riots
—but exploited them, for publicity purposes, as a manifestation
of the hatred which Zionism inspired among the people. There
was an attempt, albeit embryonic and short-lived, to set up a
guerilla movement. The Palestinians were deeply impressed by
Kemal Ataturk's triumphant repudiation—in so far as it affected
Turkey—of the same post-war allied *diktat* under which they
laboured: 'learn from Kemal, and follow in his footsteps', his
admirers urged.[26] And it cannot have been lost on anyone that,
though it was to be abused and unworkable in practice, an
official policy of limiting immigration in accordance with so-

called 'economic absorptive capacity' was a direct result of the
Jaffa explosion.

At the Fourth Arab Congress in 1921, it was resolved that
political, not violent, means should be used for pressing Palestinian demands. Young militants opposed this, but the Arab
Executive and the traditional leadership called for law and order
and promised the government that they would work for it. They
listened to the advice, among others, of a group of pro-Arab
British politicians who achieved prominence in 1921. Their
advice, which commanded great influence, was that violence
would make the Palestinians odious to the outside world and
therefore unworthy of the self-rule they were asking Britain to
grant them. Haj Amin, once he had become Mufti and President
of the Supreme Moslem Council, completely changed his stand
on violence. And on the whole, the rest of the ruling élite, for all
their bitter rivalries and militant attitudinizing, put their faith in
their own powers of persuasion, in their personal dealings with
the Mandatory authorities. Their faith was misplaced. By 1923
they had ample evidence of that. Whenever resistance did manifest itself, they usually intervened in a bid to restrain it. The
Jaffa riots were but the first of several occasions on which the
notables went out with the security forces to appeal for calm.
They also undermined various forms of organized passive resistance—strikes, the boycott of Jewish goods, the non-payment
of taxes or a ban on accepting government employment—which
the majority of the people tended to favour.[27] They would put
their case to a sympathetic British quarter in what—according to
the first High Commissioner—they saw as a calculated alternative to the violence favoured by the lower classes.[28] In 1923,
Jamal Husseini, secretary of the Arab Executive, told a British
official that there were two ways to secure Palestinian political
rights: 'either by constitutional means or by revolution; that the
first was to be preferred though the second would give them
what they justly claimed in six months'.[29] Even in the growing
tensions of the early thirties the High Commissioner, Sir Arthur
Wauchope, warmly praised the Mufti for the moderation he
showed in spite of his 'fears that the criticisms of his many
opponents that he is too British may weaken his influence in the
country'.[30]

Not only did they oppose violence, but—partly encouraged by

the difficulties Zionism faced in the late twenties—they actually
grew more conciliatory, and seemed ready to accept proposals for
limited self-government of the kind which they had so firmly
rejected in 1922. In early 1929, impressed by this moderation,
the High Commissioner advised London that it would be difficult to resist demands for a legislative council. The Arabs, he
said, were no longer demanding the abrogation of the Balfour
Declaration and the Mandate, and their fear of Zionism had
abated.[31] From a representational and democratic standpoint,
the legislature he proposed was even less attractive than the 1922
version. But the Arab Executive acquiesced in it and, in pro-
tracted negotiations with him, discussed the delicate business of
bringing it into being.

THE PEOPLE CHOOSE VIOLENCE

Violence erupted all the same. It destroyed the negotiations. It
came in August 1929 and, like the Jaffa explosion of eight years
before, it was the sudden, blind fury of the mob. It erupted in
spite of the politicians. It was the people's instinctive response to
what they saw as the violence of the other side. For was not the
Zionist programme, relentlessly pressed forward under the
British régime, a form of violence? True, the Zionists did not
rely on armed strength. They relied on the British; their persuasions worked where the Arabs' did not. Nevertheless, they
were already developing military organizations. Jabotinsky's
Jewish Legion had been disbanded by the British; but in
the early Mandate years, he set up a militia for the defence
of Jewish settlements; this was the *Haganah*, out of which the
Israeli army eventually grew. The ideals of the *Betar* also
flourished. The *Betar*—the name of the fortress in which Bar
Kokhba made his last stand against the Romans—was another of
Jabotinsky's creations. It was a youth organization intended to
set an example of *hadar* (a Zionist concept of honour and
chivalry) and it made a deep impression on the younger generation. One of its leaders wrote a newspaper column called 'Journal
of a Fascist'.

But if, at this stage, there was no outright violence, no actual
fighting, there was a ceaseless Judaization of Palestine by every
other means. The classic techniques of earlier days were broad-

ened, intensified and refined. Immigration, the cornerstone of the whole edifice, had in effect slipped out of control of the British administration and into the hands of the Zionist Labour Federation. The Federation represented 3 per cent of the people of Palestine—creating an anomaly of which a visiting British expert said that 'power has been, more or less completely, divorced from responsibility'.[32] At 156,000 in 1929, the *Yishuv* had doubled in ten years. A relatively crowded little country had the highest rate of population increase in the world, outstripping even pioneering countries like Australia and the Argentine. The 4 per cent, or thereabouts, of Palestine which the Jews had acquired represented about 14 per cent of its cultivable area.[33] It was not just the achievements of the newcomers that so alarmed the Arabs, it was the steadily unfolding evidence of the fully-fledged statehood they planned: their 'conquest' of land and labour, their insistence on Hebrew, their separate schools and hospitals, their self-segregation—residential, economic, social and cultural —and their expulsion of the Arabs from every institution they established. This is a veteran's vivid recollection of the atmosphere of the early Mandate years:

> I remember being one of the first of our comrades to go to London after the First World War . . . There I became a socialist. . . . When I joined the socialist students—English, Irish, Jewish, Chinese, Indian, African—we found that we were all under English domination or rule. And even here, in these intimate surroundings, I had to fight my friends on the issue of Jewish socialism, to defend the fact that I would not accept Arabs in my trade union, the Histadrut; to defend preaching to housewives that they not buy at Arab stores; to defend the fact that we stood guard at orchards to prevent Arab workers from getting jobs there. . . . To pour kerosene on Arab tomatoes; to attack Jewish housewives in the markets and smash the Arab eggs they had bought; to praise to the skies the Keren Kayemet (Jewish National Fund) that sent Hankin to Beirut to buy land from absentee effendis and to throw the *fellahin* (peasants) off the land—to buy dozens of dunums from an Arab is permitted, but to sell, God forbid, one Jewish dunum to an Arab is prohibited; to take Rothschild, the incarnation of capitalism, as a socialist and to name him the 'benefactor'—to do all that was not easy. And despite the fact that we did it—maybe we had no choice—I wasn't happy about it.[34]

Such were the general, underlying causes of the violence that
erupted. They were essentially the same as those which had
produced 'the slaughter of 1921'. The specific cause, the immediate trigger, was different.

The Wailing Wall, the last remnant of the Temple, is the most
sacred of Jewish shrines. But the Wall is a symbol for the Arabs
too. It could not be otherwise, for the massive platform on which
Herod raised the temple destroyed by the Romans in A.D. 70 is
the same on which the two great mosques of al-Aqsa and the
Dome of the Rock stand. The Wailing Wall is actually sacred to
Moslems; they call it the Burak, the name of the Prophet's
horse, and believe that it was from there that he embarked on his
night journey to heaven. The whole Wailing Wall compound is
also Moslem property.

Jewish devotional rights at the Wall had since time immemorial
been governed by the so-called status quo, a repertoire of agreements and reciprocal adjustments between the three great faiths
established in the city. The status quo had been supervised by
the Moslem temporal authorities. As the Jewish population increased, there developed at the Wall devotions of a more formal
and communal kind. The worshippers sought to chip away at the
status quo. They introduced innovations there, bringing benches,
chairs and other appurtenances, or tried to secure the right, sug-
gestive of ownership, to pave the passageway below the Wall.
But it was only with the rise of Zionism that they began to press,
quite openly, for a complete takeover. For the Zionists, the Wall
was to become less and less the reminder, essentially religious in
significance, of past glories and past sufferings, and more and
more the political symbol of the new Jewish nation-in-the-making
—or, as the *Jewish Chronicle* put it, 'a gauge of Jewish prestige in
Palestine'.[35] Inevitably, the Arabs came to vest in the preservation of the status quo all their passionate determination to keep
Palestine for themselves, while the Jews saw in its erosion evidence of their progress in wresting it from them.

When British forces entered Palestine in 1917, General
Allenby, their commander, solemnly declared that in matters of
religion the status quo was all. But the Zionists were quick to
challenge his proclamation. One of the first acts of a Jewish detachment with the British army was to hold a 'public service' at
the Wall. Weizmann wrote to Lord Balfour asking for the

'handing over of the Wailing Wall', asserting that 'our most
sacred monument, in our most sacred city, is in the hands of
some doubtful Maghreb religious community'.[36] But all the
stepped-up efforts which the Zionists now made to acquire land
and houses near the Wall came to nothing. No *Waqf* (religious
foundation) property, let alone this one, linked as it was to the
third most holy place in Islam, could be sold to the Jews, who
had designs on the western wall of the Haram al-Sharif, the
Noble Sanctuary. The Zionists were not deterred. On the first
anniversary of the Balfour Declaration, they insisted on a public
demonstration in Jerusalem. The Jewish detachment with the
British army behaved so provocatively during its visit to the Wall
that the British military authorities eventually forbade them
entry. When some Jewish soldiers disobeyed the order and
marched in the direction of the Wall, they were court-martialled
and the entire detachment was disbanded. In April 1920 Arabs
and Jews were killed in the first major clash in Jerusalem. Not
long after that Sir Alfred Mond (later Lord Melchett) declared
that he would 'concentrate the remainder of his energies on
building a great edifice where once stood the Temple of Solo-
mon'.[37] The statement gained notoriety among the Arabs, who
found in it confirmation of their fears that, fantastic though it
might seem, this really was the ultimate Zionist ambition. There
followed an endless series of incidents, childish in themselves,
with each side trying to assert itself in the Wailing Wall compound at the expense of the other. In general, the underlying
issue was ownership. The Jews were essentially on the offensive,
trying to establish the possession which they did not have; the
Arabs retaliated with various initiatives, deeply annoying to the
Jews, designed to emphasize that possession was, and would remain, theirs. Britain, faithful to the status quo, backed the Arabs
and when, on the Day of Atonement, 1928, Jewish worshippers
attempted to introduce a partition screen they did so in express
defiance of the Mandatory authorities. After this incident,
Jewish exasperation grew fast; the whole community was
aroused, and, characteristically, it was from the unbelieving
majority, especially the young, that the loudest clamour came.
Jabotinsky and his right-wing militants led the field. Their
mouthpiece, *Doar Hayom*, the Hebrew newspaper with the
widest circulation, called for 'revolt and insubordination'.[38] The

Arab press was just as inflammatory. Throughout the summer of
1929 the tension rose alarmingly. Vincent Sheehan, an American
journalist living in the city at the time, said that 'you could stick
your hand out in the air and feel it rising'. In his book, *Personal
History*, he records what happened when it finally reached
boiling-point. He begins with his diary entry for Thursday, 15
August:

> Yesterday was the Eve of Tisha'ba'Av. . . . Today is the actual
> fast itself: commemoration of the destruction of the Temple.
> The day is particularly associated with the Wailing Wall; and
> with the new Jewish Agency just formed, all the Wailing Wall
> propaganda going full tilt, the Arabs in a rare state of anxiety,
> the situation was ripe for anything. Trouble, trouble, and more
> trouble. There will be plenty. I knew nothing about it all—didn't
> even know Tisha ba'Av was so near—when Miss X (a young
> Jewish-American journalist) arrived at the Hospice at three in the
> afternoon. . . . Said she had to go to the Wailing Wall and write a
> telegram about it for *The Times* . . . would I go with her and help?
> I couldn't understand why, but she said there was going to be a
> 'bust-up'. . . . she said the word had been passed round and
> hundreds of Haluzim (rugged pioneer youth from the agricultural
> settlements) were coming in during the afternoon and evening
> from the colonies and Tel-Aviv, ready to fight. I simply couldn't
> believe all this. She said the Haluzim would be armed—'three
> quarters of them'—and it would be a good thing if there was a row
> at the Wall to 'show that we are here.' I didn't believe a damned
> word of it; too fantastic; but I told her I'd be ready to go along at
> five o'clock if she would come back. She was inconceivably cynical
> and flippant about the whole thing; said a row would be a very
> good thing for the Zionist cause, arouse world Jews and increase
> contributions to the new Agency. Before we reached the Wall it
> was evident that the police were well prepared. . . . There was no
> excitement whatever, only about half a dozen religious Jews and
> Jewesses (Oriental) praying and weeping against the Wall.
> Towards six, a little before, we went away to the Hotel St John
> for a glass of beer. Sat there a bit, talking; I couldn't understand
> her point of view at all, and tried to find out. When we returned
> to the Wall, a little before seven, everything had changed. There
> was a dense crowd, made up chiefly of Haluzim, in the little area
> in the front of the Wall. A Yemenite Jew was chanting the
> lamentations, from the Book, while four other Yemenites sat
> around him, weeping and rocking themselves back and forth.

These seemed to be the most sincerely religious manifestants present—they paid no attention to their surroundings, but only to their lament. The rest of that crowd was spoiling for a fight. The crowd I was in, that is, farther off, at the end of the Wall before the Grand Mufti's house, the service was being read by a Cantor (Sephardic, I believe) who stopped and looked around angrily at the slightest noise. Since noises were continually being made, he was continually stopping, but always had to begin again, as he discovered that the sounds came from zealous but irreverent Haluzim. . . . All the people who choked the area seemed to be either people like myself, who had come out of curiosity or interest, and Haluzim who were—as Miss X said— 'rarin' to go.' The Yemenites went on weeping and praying throughout; they noticed nobody and nobody noticed them. Strange scene.

Saw Halkin, the poet: very excited. So was everybody I spoke to (Warschawer was there, the most peaceful of people, and even he was angry). What seems to have upset them so is the new door in the Wall. I actually saw one revolver, but don't know who the man was who had it (hip pocket). There were only two actual 'incidents'. In the first a Christian Arab whom I did not see was accused of mocking at the services: I heard cries of 'Notzri!' (Nazarene) and saw the Haluzim shoving, but the police took the man out safely. Then there was an Arab in white clothes who walked through the place three times—did nothing, simply walked. I believe he was unmolested the first time, although there were angry murmurs. The second time he came through without difficulty. The third time he appeared, the police wouldn't let him go on—made him turn back. Very wise of them, for that crowd was in no mood to stand any kind of 'incident' without serious trouble. But in this incident the shouts of the Haluzim must certainly have been far more disturbing to the prayers of the religious Jews than the Arab's progress through the street would have been.

. . . Jews parading again today. Extreme provocation, but the Arabs are doing nothing. Small army of Haluzim—these precious Maccabees—passed half an hour ago, on their way to the Wall, with a flag, the Zionist national flag, I suppose, but I couldn't see it: it was furled. Shouts and cheers come from down there; the whole thing makes me very nervous. . . . The young heroes who passed a while ago were guarded heavily by the police; mounted police officers in front of them and behind them, with policemen on foot marching alongside them. The material for an awful

three-cornered fight. What an exhibition of imbecility the whole
thing is!

Saturday, Aug. 17th. The Jewish holy day passed off without
disaster, but now we are in the midst of a Moslem one, the
Prophet's Birthday. Yesterday a big crowd of Moslems came into
the Wailing Wall area and tore up the sacred books, pulled
petitions out of the stones of the Wall, etc. Might have been
expected; was, in fact, inevitable. No Jews there; nobody hurt.
Jews will be in terrible state of excitement, just the same.

Sunday, Aug 18th. Jewish boy hurt in a row between Jews and
Arabs yesterday; feeling gets worse all the time. . . .

Wednesday, Aug. 21st. The Mizrachi boy . . . died yesterday.
They are going to make a martyr of him, as sure as fate . . .

Friday, Aug. 23rd. The situation here is awful. Everyday I
expect the worst. It can't go on like this without an outbreak. The
Mizrachi boy . . . who was stabbed by an Arab after a row in the
football field (it seems to have been a row started by the Jewish
boys, or so they tell me), died on Tuesday. Wednesday morning
was the funeral. Of course, the precious Maccabees had to
seize the opportunity; fine chance to link up everything with the
Wailing Wall and the general agitation. Two or three thousand of
these heroes gathered with flags and tried to head their march
through the Jaffa Gate into the Arab city. Feeling has been
running so high among the Arabs since these fools raised their
flag at the wall of the mosque that anything might have happened.
Police barred the way, therefore, and the Jews made a rush at
their cordon. Police beat them back with clubs. About twenty-
five Jews were injured, none very seriously.

After I had finished the last entry in my diary I went down-
stairs to lunch and heard a new crop of disquieting rumours.
At about half-past one I went out to get some cigarettes, and the
old Arab porter at the Hospice told me the Grand Mufti had
passed a short time before, going out to speak to the crowds
around the city walls. Since the Mufti was not given to public
appearance—I had never once seen him, although I lived within
five minutes' walk of the Haram and his house—this seemed
serious. I ran back into the Hospice for my hat, found a friend
of mine (a British official), and went out with him to see what was
to be seen. We walked up the narrow street, through excited or
terrified groups of people, to the Damascus Gate. There we
found ourselves in the midst of a mob of country Arabs, who
seemed to be in a frenzy of excitement. Long yells of 'Islamiya!'
were going up. We got through these people without trouble—

my companion spoke Arabic well—and reached the corner of the
street called, I believe, the Street of the Prophet. The mob was
gathering directly in front of us, and it was certain that somebody,
somewhere, would soon be shedding blood. The houses on the
other side of the mob, opposite us, belonged to a group of
Georgian Jews, as I afterwards learned; the attention of the crowd
was directed towards them. In front of the Jewish houses were
ranged six policemen, armed only with short truncheons. The
mob gathered with incredible speed—it could not have taken
more than two or three minutes for them to get dense in front of
us. The long yells that filled the air were enough to curdle one's
blood.

A man dressed as a city Arab noticed us standing there and
thrust us almost by force into a doorway. 'Stand here, stand here
for God's sake,' he said. 'These fellahin will kill you.' We stood
in the doorway, and he took his place in front of us, shouting
hoarsely at the mob, telling them to go back, that all was well.
They paid no attention to him. They rushed towards the police,
who laid about them valiantly with their truncheons; but what
good were truncheons at such a time? The fellahin were flourishing
sticks, clubs and knives, and, as is the way of mobs, they rushed on
regardless of the efforts to stop them. Some rushed under horses'
bellies, others squirmed through between the inadequate six;
in another moment we heard smashing and a long scream. There
was nothing we could do but run, which we did . . .

I returned to the Damascus Gate about a quarter of an hour
after I had left it. When I got there the Arab mob had vanished
(so little time is required to accomplish the most irrevocable acts);
there were shattered glass and torn-up wood, débris of all sorts
in the street, and before the Georgian Jewish houses and on their
stone doorsteps there was blood.

The Jews of Jerusalem outnumbered the Arabs two to one.
It was a matter of common knowledge that the Jews possessed
firearms; the Arabs did not. Under these conditions it seemed
likely that the Jewish superiority in numbers and equipment, as
well as their organization and centralization, would enable them
to do great damage among the Arabs for a day or two if they so
desired, and from what I had seen and heard the previous week
I thought this was probably the wish of a good many among
them . . .

. . . The disorders of Friday resulted in many deaths among
both Jews and Arabs . . . and the impulse of murder continued
for a week. At the end of the terror the official roll for Jerusalem

was: 29 Jews and 38 Arabs killed, 43 Jews and 51 Arabs wounded. Here, as in Haifa, the Arabs got considerably the worst of it, but it seems clear . . . that the casualties inflicted by Jews were chiefly in self-defence . . .

The horrors of Friday in Jerusalem were followed by something much worse: the ghastly outbreak at Hebron, where sixty-four Jews of the old-fashioned religious community were slaughtered and fifty-four of them wounded. Hebron was one of the four holy cities of Judaism, and had had a small, constant Jewish population since medieval days. These were not Zionists at all; a more innocent and harmless group of people could not have been found in Palestine; many of them were Oriental Jews, and all were religious. They had had nothing to do with the Zionist excesses, and had lived in amity with their Arab neighbours up to that day. But when the Arabs of Hebron—an unruly lot, at best—heard that Arabs were being killed by Jews in Jerusalem, and that the Mosque of Omar was in danger, they went mad. The British police force at Hebron was inadequate—indeed, it could scarcely be said to have existed, for there was but one British officer there with a tiny native staff. In spite of the remarkable exertions and courage of this one officer (Mr. R. O. Cafferata), the Jewish houses were rushed by the mob, and there was an hour of slashing, killing, stabbing, burning and looting. Among the Jewish victims were some American boys who had arrived only a short time before to study at the rabbinical college. Eight or nine of them died at Hebron, and an equal number suffered severe wounds.

I cannot, at this late date, go through all the story of that week; it has been told over and over again. The horrors of Hebron were not repeated elsewhere, but an Arab mob attack on the religious Jews of Safad, on the following Thursday, was sufficiently terrible to be classified as another massacre. In Haifa, where the Jews were predominantly of the modern Zionist type and occupied an excellent strategic position at the top of the hill, the Arabs had much the worst of it. The same was true in some of the colonies; others were almost wiped out. At the end of the disturbances the official British casualty lists showed 207 dead and 279 wounded among the population of Palestine, of which the dead included 87 Arabs (Christian and Moslem) and 120 Jews, the wounded 181 Arabs and 198 Jews.

The effort to be an efficient, unemotional newspaper correspondent was difficult to the point of impossibility. Living as I did, without sleep and without rest, eating little, and that at the weirdest hours, I should probably have collapsed in time simply from physical exhaustion. But there was a great deal more to it than that. I was bitterly indignant with the Zionists for having, as I believed, brought on this disaster; I was shocked into hysteria by the ferocity of the Arab anger; and I was aghast at the inadequacy of the British government. I knew that the Moslem authorities were trying to quell the storm, and that the British officials were doing their best against appalling difficulties; I also assumed that the responsible Zionist leaders (none of whom were in Palestine then) had done what they could. But all around me were the visible evidences of their failure. Although I had spent a good part of my life amid scenes of violence and was no stranger to the sight of blood and dying men, I had never overcome my loathing for the spectacle even when it seemed, as in some of the conflicts I had witnessed, compelled by historical necessity. But here, in this miserable little country no bigger, in relation to the rest of the world, than the tip of your finger in relation to your body, I could see no historical necessity whatever. The country was tiny and was already inhabited; why couldn't the Zionists leave it alone? It would never hold enough Jews to make even a beginning towards the solution of the Jewish problem; it would always be a prey to such ghastly horrors as those I saw every day and every night: religion, the eternal intransigence of religion, ensured that the problem could never be solved. The Holy Land seemed as near an approximation of hell on earth as I had ever seen.[39]

BRITAIN SURRENDERS TO THE ZIONISTS

Britain reacted to the outbreak in the time-honoured way—with the despatch of a commission of inquiry. Sir Walter Shaw, like Sir Thomas Haycraft before him, ruled essentially in the Arabs' favour. There had been nothing planned or premeditated about the massacres. The Mufti had indeed rallied Arab and Moslem opinion in defence of the Wall. That was legitimate. True, he could and should have restrained some of the extremer forms of Arab emotionalism which accompanied his campaign, but it was not he who set the mob on the Jews. It was the custom for the peasants to come into Jerusalem every Friday and if, on that fatal 25 August, they came armed with clubs, knives and sticks, it had not been at his urging. There were agitators at work in the country, but they acted independently of him. One of them had

delivered a message to the headmen of the village of Kabalan
near Nablus. It read: 'Fighting will take place on Friday next,
the 18 Rabia, between the Jews and Moslems. All who are of the
Moslem religion should come to Jerusalem to help. Peace be on
you and your young men.' The message bore the Mufti's signature—but it turned out to be a forgery. The bloodiest outbreaks occurred in just those parts of Palestine where his influence was the weakest. In Jerusalem itself, the speeches which
he and other religious dignitaries made during and after the
Friday prayers had a distinctly pacifying character—so much so,
in fact, that some of their hearers felt moved to ascend the platform and exhort the crowd to take no notice of the speakers, who
were unfaithful to the Moslem cause. 'An appeal by the Mufti,'
Shaw averred, 'issued on this date to his co-religionists, to arm
themselves "with mercy, wisdom and patience for verily God is
with those who bear themselves in patience", was, in our view,
having regard to the outbreaks which had already taken place, to
the highly dangerous temper of the people, and to the rumours of
designs upon the Holy Places which at that time were flying from
lip to lip, a timely and courageous appeal and one which, on the
whole, had its effect in checking further outbreaks.'[40]

If the Commission had to single out one immediate and specific
cause of the violence, it said, that would be the Jewish demonstration at the Wailing Wall; as for the general causes, it concluded that, without the political and economic grievances of the
Arabs against the Mandate as a whole, 'the outbreak would not
have occurred, or had it occurred at all, would not have attained
the proportions which in fact it did reach'.[41]

The Zionists were stunned by Shaw's findings. But nine
months later the verdict of a second commission, led by Sir John
Hope-Simpson, angered them even more. His task had been to
investigate those deeper sources of Arab unrest, immigration
and land settlement, and his opinion, even more forcefully expressed than Shaw's, was that they should be drastically curtailed. And a legislative council should be set up.

Arab violence did seem to pay. But there was uproar in the
Zionist camp, on both sides of the Atlantic, and through the
application of heavy pressure at the metropolitan centre of
power it managed to induce the British government to repudiate
everything which its two distinguished emissaries had urged

upon it. In a letter to Dr Weizmann—the Black Letter, the Arabs called it—the Prime Minister, Ramsay MacDonald, surrendered to Zionist demands. Immigration and land settlement would continue unabated; negotiations for a legislative council, suspended with the riots, were not to be seriously resumed for years.

Weizmann's diplomacy was still Zionism's main weapon. Arab violence was no match for it after all. Yet, more systematically and purposefully used, it might have been. 'It is difficult to determine', writes the Israeli historian Yehoshua Porath of the Jaffa explosion, 'what would have happened had the violent outbreaks not ceased, but one cannot escape the impression that certain developments, favourable from the Arab point of view, might well have come about ten years earlier than they did.'[42] After 'the slaughter of 1921' the attempt to redress the balance of British policy in the Arabs' favour had failed, but at least the Zionists had been obliged to acquiesce in the attempt. After 1929 they were able to crush the attempt in embryo; for by then they had the strength and self-confidence to do it, and, through successive governments, British policy was increasingly taking on that sanctity of precedent and tradition which was so difficult to disavow.

In the 1920s, conciliation by the politicians got nowhere. The resistance of the people, fanatic but unsustained, massive but aimless, merely raised hopes that were quickly dashed. Germinating in the mind of an itinerant preacher was the idea that there should be new leaders, and radical new methods.

NOTES

1. Haycraft, Sir Thomas, *Commission of Inquiry into the Palestine Disturbances of May 1921*, Cmd. 1540, p. 44. This whole account of the violence is drawn from the Haycraft report.
2. *Ibid.*, p. 27.
3. *Ibid.*, p. 54.
4. *Ibid.*, p. 53.
5. Porath, Yehoshua, *The Emergence of the Palestine-Arab National Movement 1918-1929*, Frank Cass, London, 1974.
6. *Ibid.*, p. 56.
7. *Ibid.*, pp. 56-7.
8. *Ibid.*, p. 45.

9. Ingrams, *Palestine Papers 1917–1922, Seeds of Conflict*, op. cit., p. 122.
10. *Ibid.*, p. 122.
11. See Cohen, Aharon, *Israel and the Arab World*, Funk and Wagnalls, New York, 1970, p. 60.
12. *Current History*, New York, October 1921, Vol. XV.
13. *The Contemporary Review*, London, May 1920, No. 653.
14. *Jewish Observer and Middle East Review*, London, 8 May 1959.
15. See Porath, op. cit., p. 53.
16. *Ibid.*, p. 125.
17. See Jeffreys, *Palestine: The Reality*, op. cit., p. 456.
18. See Ingrams, op. cit., pp. 123–4.
19. Barbour, *Nisi Dominus*, op. cit., p. 111.
20. Sykes, Christopher, *Crossroads to Israel*, Collins, London, 1965, pp. 83, 124.
21. Harkabi, Yehoshafat, *Time Bomb in the Middle East*, Friendship Press, New York, 1969, p. 19.
22. *Report on the Conditions in Palestine, 1935*, H.M.S.O., London, 1935, p. 19.
23. Lord Peel, *Royal Commission Report*, 22 June 1937, Cmd. 5479, p. 92.
24. *Maariv* (Israeli newspaper), 2 November 1973.
25. Porath, op. cit., p. 131.
26. *Ibid.*, p. 159.
27. Al-Kayyali, *A History of Modern Palestine* (Arabic), op. cit., pp. 178, 195, 210, 273; Allush, Naji, *Arab Resistance in Palestine* (Arabic), Vanguard House, Beirut, 1969, p. 113.
28. Al-Kayyali, op. cit., p. 195.
29. *Ibid.*, p. 208.
30. *Ibid.*, p. 285.
31. Porath, op. cit., p. 255.
32. Campbell, Sir John, see Shaw, Sir Walter, *Commission on the Palestine Disturbances of August 1929*, Cmd. 3530, p. 104.
33. Hope-Simpson, Sir John, *Report to the British Government*, 20 October 1930, Cmd. 3686, p. 19.
34. Hacohen, David, *Haaretz* (Israeli newspaper), 15 November 1969.
35. See Sheehan, Vincent, *Personal History*, Doubleday, Doran and Co., Inc., New York, 1935, p. 390.
36. Tibawi, A. L., *Jerusalem, Its Place in Islam and Arab History*, Institute for Palestine Studies, Beirut, 1969, p. 32.
37. Porath, op. cit., p. 259.
38. Shaw Commission, op. cit., p. 45.
39. Sheehan, op. cit., pp. 392–408.
40. Shaw Commission, op. cit., p. 78.
41. *Ibid.*, pp. 96, 155.
42. Porath, op. cit., p. 13.

Three

The Arab Rebellion, 1935–1939

ON 12 November 1935 a grey-bearded sexagenarian, wearing the turban and cloak of the Moslem cleric, presided over a secret meeting in the old slum quarter of Haifa. Shaikh Izzeddin Qassam realized that he could delay no longer: his hour had come. The British had been in Palestine eighteen years; their rule, resented from the outset, had become quite intolerable in its disregard of Arab interests. Legal—not to mention illegal— Jewish immigration had reached the record figure of 61,844 a year. Land sales were increasing; in 1933 there had been 673 of them, 1,178 in 1934. More and more peasants were losing their livelihood; yet already, in 1931, it had been estimated that 30,000 peasant families, 22 per cent of the rural population, were landless.[1] Their average *per capita* income was £7 a year, compared with £34 for the Jewish farmers who replaced them. And the peasant family's average indebtedness—£25 to £30—was about the same as its average earnings.[2] Driven from the land, the peasants flocked to the rapidly growing cities in search of work. Many of them ended up as labourers building houses for the immigrants they loathed and feared. They lived in squalor. In old Haifa there were 11,000 of them crammed into hovels built of petrol-tins, which had neither water-supply nor rudimentary sanitation. Others, without families, slept in the open. Such conditions contrasted humiliatingly with the handsome dwellings the peasants were putting up for the well-to-do newcomers, or even with the Jewish working men's quarters furnished by Jewish building societies.[3] They earned half, or just a quarter, the wage of their Jewish counterparts, and Hebrew Labour exclusivism was gradually depriving them of even that. By 1935, an economic crisis, partly the result of uncontrolled immigration, produced Arab unemployment on a catastrophic scale. There could be no

more fertile ground than this dispossessed urban peasantry for
the ideals that Shaikh Qassam had assiduously sown—ideals for
which, that November evening, he and his followers resolved to
fight and die, and would do so within a week.

His whole life had seemed a preparation for this supreme self-
sacrifice. A Syrian of devout and cultured parentage, he studied
at al-Azhar, Cairo's great centre of Moslem learning; he sat at
the feet of Muhammad Abdu, the famous scholar who preached
that, through a reformed and reinvigorated Islam, the Arabs
could rise to the challenge of the modern world. On his return to
Syria, he did not confine himself only to teaching at the religious
college of Ibrahim bin Adham, he also took part in various
patriotic movements. He was a military leader in one of the up-
risings against French rule in Syria. Condemned to death in that
country, he fled to Haifa in 1922. There he taught, preached, did
charitable work and set up a night school for the illiterate.
Appointed 'marriage steward' for the Haifa Moslem court, he
attended wedding festivals in the surrounding countryside. He
moved easily among peasants and workers; he knew their intimate thoughts. Everywhere he warned of the gravity of the
Zionist invasion, he urged a true spirit of patriotism, the ending
of petty feuds and divisions, the emulation of the heroes of early
Islam. Verses from the Koran, particularly those which called for
struggle and sacrifice, were constantly on his lips. And everywhere, but especially in the mosques, he looked for disciples
among the pious and God-fearing. Over the years, with great
care and patience, he gathered about himself a band of followers.
There were about 800 of them altogether; 200 of them received
military training. They pledged to give their lives for Palestine.
They were expected to supply their own arms, and to contribute
all else they could to the cause. Their training was done by
stealth at night.

After the meeting in Haifa, Qassam and a group of his closest
comrades, almost all of them peasants, made their way inland to
the wooded hills of Janin. They had sold their wives' jewellery
and some of their household furnishings to buy rifles and
ammunition. They spent the daytime in caves, near the village of
Ya'id, praying and reciting the Koran. At night they attacked the
Jews and the British. At least that was their intention, for they
barely had time for action. The authorities, perhaps tipped off

by an informer, lost no time in sending out a mixed force of
British and Arab troops, aided by reconnaissance planes, to hunt
them down. Surprised and overwhelmed, Shaikh Qassam was
forced into premature battle. Called upon to surrender, he
shouted back: 'Never, this is a *jihad* for God and country.' He
exhorted his followers to 'die as martyrs'. When he saw the
Arab troops, he ordered his men to attack the British and to fire
on their compatriots only in self-defence. After a battle lasting
several hours, Qassam and three or four companions were killed,
the rest were captured.

It had been a brief and—from a military point of view—futile
rebellion. But it stirred up the Palestinian masses. It pointed the
insurrectional way ahead. And that was all Shaikh Qassam had
hoped for. The Jews failed to grasp its significance. For them
Shaikh Qassam was a kind of freak, the product of unnatural
fanaticism, a mad dervish. They could not see that, fifteen years
after their own hero's exemplary death, the Palestinians in their
turn now had the legend they needed, their own Joseph Trumpeldor. There had been a few who died, gun in hand, before
Shaikh Qassam, and there would be many thousands who were
to do so after him. But in his deep piety, in his unswerving sense
of mission and the deliberateness of its death-seeking climax, he
was the archetypal *fedayi*—'one who sacrifices himself'—of the
Palestinian struggle. He placed himself in a tradition that began
with an earlier Western invasion of Palestine. For it was the
Crusaders who had faced the first *fedayeen*—the militants of the
revolutionary Ismaili sect—who came down from their mountain
strongholds in northern Syria to terrorize the Frankish chieftains
or rival Moslem princes, the original 'assassins'—*hashishiin*—
who are popularly believed to have carried out their suicidal
missions under the influence of drugs. In the struggle against the
twentieth-century invader, Shaikh Qassam is the outstanding
example in a tradition of heroism, usually reckless, sometimes
high-minded and purposeful, sometimes pointless and ignoble,
but generally unavailing, which the Palestinians have been prac-
tising to this day. From a distance of forty years, during which
the Palestinians have suffered defeat and dispersal on a scale that
even Shaikh Qassam could scarcely have imagined possible, his
altruism has about it all the pathos of people who never quite
give up the struggle, but have so far been doomed, through their

own shortcomings as well as their enemy's superiority, always to lose, and subconsciously seem to know it.

A huge throng attended Shaikh Qassam's funeral in Haifa. He was buried ten kilometres away in the village of Yajour; the mourners bore his coffin all the way on foot. They shouted slogans against the British and the Jewish National Home; they stoned the police, and their procession was defiantly decked out in the flags of various Arab states. In Cairo, the newspaper *al-Ahram* wrote: 'Dear friend and martyr, I heard you preaching from pulpits, calling us to arms, but today, preaching from the Bosom of God, you were more eloquent in death than in life.'

It was a truly national event. But the nation's official leaders were absent. Their absence was characteristic. They were afraid of the passions Qassam had unleashed. In his martyrdom they sensed a reproach and a threat to themselves. They were right to do so, for although there have been many and often fortuitous circumstances to which the Zionists owe their astonishing success, by no means the least have been the incompetence and irresponsibility of the Arab leaders, the frivolity and egoism of the privileged classes. The frailties which the Haifa newspaper *Carmel* had first denounced a quarter of a century earlier were all the greater now. About nine-tenths of all land acquired by the Jews up to 1929 was sold by absentee landlords. But after that, the ever-growing 'Zionist peril' notwithstanding, the main culprits were resident landlords. It was at this time, too, that Arab usurers came most offensively into their own; smallholders were forced to borrow at interest rates of up to 50 per cent; they would cling desperately to their little plots of land, but in the end, under a crushing burden of debt, were forced to abandon them to the land-hungry Jews.[4] There were mouth-watering profits to be made: the price of a dunum near Rishon-le-Zion, originally eight shillings, had reached £10 to £25 by the early thirties.[5] Officially, of course, the willing squanderers of the Arab heritage were becoming the pariahs of society. They were ritually condemned on every suitable occasion—at conferences convened to consider the 'Zionist peril', in the campaign statements of rival political parties, in the anathemas issued by religious authorities. Thus in 1932, the Independence Party issued a proclamation declaring that 'there is no future for the nation unless the gates are closed on immigration, and the sale of land prohibited; the delegates reaffirm their dissatisfaction at the middlemen and the landsellers, and consider that the time has come to punish and oppose them . . .'[6] In Palestinian vocabulary *simsar*—'middleman'—has established itself ever since as a word of abuse. In 1935, when immigration and land sales were surpassing all limits, Haj Amin Husseini, the Mufti, assembled some 400 men of God, imams, qadis, muftis, preachers and teachers, who issued a *fatwa*, or religious edict, outlawing the sale of land to Jewish immigrants and denouncing its perpetrators as apostates to be denied burial in Moslem cemeteries.

However—and here is the real measure of the Palestinian leadership—although the landsellers and agents might suffer all manner of verbal abuse, they rarely suffered much worse. Landselling, branded as 'treason', was a characteristic accusation which one faction of notables hurled at another. It made for an immense hypocrisy. There was no real social ostracism, let alone any condign punishment. The very people who most vociferously condemned the practice were not infrequently the ones who most indulged in it. In 1928, the delegates to the Seventh Palestine Congress were described by a contemporary as a very odd assortment who included 'spies and middlemen selling land to the Jews'.[7] In 1932, the newspaper *al-Arab* found it strange indeed that the Arab Executive should wax so indignant about the sale of Arab land when some of its own members were doing the selling. No wonder a British fact-finding team's efforts to uncover the full extent of these odious transactions met with resistance from the Arab as well as the Jewish leadership.[8] If, by 1948, the landsellers had only allowed some 6·6 per cent of physical Palestine to fall into Jewish hands—though that represented a much higher proportion of its cultivable area[9]—the damage they inflicted on the Palestinian psyche is less easy to calculate. But it was undoubtedly great. The landsellers typified the Palestinians' response to Zionism at its most self-destructive. They were the most unhealthy part of a body politic so diseased that, instead of achieving that self-renewal which, under strain, an even slightly healthier one might have achieved, it degenerated still further. It did not immunize itself against the sickness which the landsellers represented; it let the sickness spread. The disloyalty of a few, rather than fortifying the constructive patriotism of the majority, aggravated the factionalism, recrimination and mistrust which poisoned the whole Palestinian struggle, and the behaviour of the politicians in particular.

When Shaikh Qassam stirred the people with his martyr's death, the politicians were still opposing violence—but failing to provide any alternative. Instead of marching behind the coffin, they sent lukewarm messages of sympathy—and ran to the High Commissioner to tell him that if he did not grant them some timely concessions they would lose what influence they still possessed and the situation would get quite out of hand.[10]

THE REBELLION BEGINS

That is precisely what happened. The events of 1936 to 1939 go down, in most Zionist history books, as mere 'disturbances'; but, for the Palestinians, Shaikh Qassam's self-immolation ushered in the Great Rebellion. One side saw an eruption of banditry, murder and robbery, a reversion to what Weizmann called the 'barbarism of the desert',[11] in which a primitive people, urged on by unscrupulous politicians, a fanatical clergy and international Fascism, hurled themselves against the higher civilization they did not want or understand. The other side saw a glorious patriotic struggle, which naturally sought outside help where it could find it, against the foreign invader.

There was indeed, in the 'disturbances', something of what the Zionists saw in them. But, as the British historian John Marlowe, by no means a partisan observer, suggests, their essential character was quite otherwise:

> Somehow or other, whether as a result of the propaganda of Haj Amin and his minions, or of more complex and less identifiable forces, the last dying embers of the spirit of jihad were being fanned into a flame which was, for a few short years, to grow brightly and heroically before being extinguished for ever. Although instigated, to some extent guided, and certainly used, by the political leaders of Arab Palestine, the Arab Rebellion was in fact a peasant revolt, drawing its enthusiasm, its heroism, its organization and its persistence from sources within itself which have never been properly understood and which will never be known. Like Faisal's revolt in the desert (the movement which, in alliance with Britain, liberated Arabia from Ottoman rule), it was one of the blind alleys of Arab nationalism doomed, like the desert revolt, to failure, and destined, unlike the desert

revolt, to oblivion for lack of a Lawrence to immortalize it. One
is reminded of G. M. Trevelyan's words about another peasant
revolt: 'the readiness of the rural population to turn out and
die for their faith was a new thing . . . The record of this brief
campaign is as the lifting of a curtain; behind it we can see for
a moment into the old peasant life. In that one glance we see not
rustic torpor, but faith, idealism, vigour, love of liberty, and
scorn of death. Were the yeomen and farm servants in other
parts of England like these men of Somerset or were they everywhere else of a lower type? The curtain falls and knowledge is
hidden for ever.'[12]

The Palestinian leadership did not plan this revolt any more
than it did the riots and massacres of the 1920s. Nevertheless, in
order to maintain its own supremacy, it accepted an involvement
—though just how much is controversial—which was thrust upon
it. The revolt was largely spontaneous in origin; its main impetus
came from below, from the largest, lowliest segment of the population, from the peasantry who had suffered most from the
Zionist invasion. It was a people's war, though not in the modern
ideological sense, for it did not have, as a principal or even in-
cidental aim, the overthrow of the existing social order. It represented a new stage in the Arab resistance that had begun, with
those clumsy localized outbreaks, some fifty years before: the use
of armed violence, in a sustained, organized and purposeful way,
not only against the Jews but against the British who had brought
them there. After their politicians had for twenty years vainly
tried, through constitutional means, to win a sympathetic hearing
from an indifferent or hostile Britain, the people had been goaded
—as one of them put it —into 'speaking with rifles instead of with
their lips'.[13] It was the product of a mysterious, but thoroughly
natural, evolution.

Such was its essential nature, though it was accompanied by
other forms of resistance. On the side of violence, there were
more urban riots carried over from the previous era—plus a new
strain of delinquency which was directed at least as much against
Arabs as Jews. On the side of non-violence, there was a six-
month, country-wide strike. And with the despatch of money,
arms and volunteers from neighbouring countries, the Palestinian
struggle first acquired a truly pan-Arab dimension that would
never cease to grow in the years to come.

The rebellion had two phases.

It all began incoherently enough. On 15 April 1936, Arabs held
up a number of cars on the Tulkaram-Nablus road. They only
robbed the Arabs and Europeans, but two Jewish travellers they
shot, killing one outright and fatally wounding the other. The next
night two Arabs living in a hut near a Jewish settlement met the
same fate. Before dying, one of the victims described his attackers
as Jews; in all probability the murder was a reprisal for the previous day's killing. The day after that, mourners turned the
funeral of one of the murdered Jews into a demonstration. They
stoned the police, made inflammatory speeches and shouted:
'We don't want this government, we want a Jewish army.' Meanwhile, Arabs were beaten up, stoned or otherwise molested. On
19 April, rumours spread in Jaffa that two Arabs had been killed
in adjoining Tel Aviv. Arab mobs in the neighbourhood turned
on Jews, several of whom were killed. Three more days of rioting
followed. In all, sixteen Jews were done to death, and five Arabs
were killed by the police.

On 20 April a National Committee was formed in Nablus, and
before the end of the month similar bodies had sprung to life in
all the towns and larger villages of Palestine. In origin, the committees were largely independent of the traditional leadership,
which had been bitterly criticized for its apathy. 'Rise to rid
yourself of Jewish and British slavery . . .', one newspaper had
urged. 'The leaders in Egypt have awakened. Where are our
leaders hiding?'[14] But now this leadership joined the Nablus
militants in calling for a general strike. An Arab Higher Committee was established under the Mufti, and the entire non-
Jewish population, Christian and Moslem, moderate and extremist, came together, with an unprecedented show of unity, in
a firm resolve to continue the strike until the British government
changed its policy 'in a fundamental manner, the beginning of
which is the stoppage of Jewish immigration'. A few days later,
the committees decreed a nation-wide non-payment of taxes.
Then lorry, bus and taxi owners, most of whom were relying on
their monthly earnings to pay their instalments, laid up their
vehicles. In June, senior civil servants, the judiciary among
them, submitted a memorandum to the High Commissioner
which insisted that Arab mistrust of the government was justified.
Although successive investigators had vindicated Arab grievances,

they complained, little had been done to remedy them. 'The Arabs have been driven into a state verging on despair; and the present unrest is no more than an expression of that despair.' The memorandum, described as unique in the history of British colonial administration, seemed to impress the authorities with its note of deep conviction moderately expressed.

The government did not stop immigration. On the contrary, when the so-called 'economic absorptive capacity' for the next six months came up for review, it authorized the Jewish Agency to bring in 10 per cent more newcomers than in the previous six. It did not want to give the Zionists the chance to accuse it of 'yielding to violence and terror'. This munificence was balanced by one of those reassuring statements that were apt to accompany pro-Zionist acts: it was announced that another Commission of Inquiry would be sent to Palestine. Unimpressed by a repetition of what they had seen so often before, the Arabs reiterated that they would only call off their strike if immigration were suspended until the Commission had delivered its report. And other official actions reinforced their resolve. With the strike as a pretext, the administration sanctioned the creation of an all-Jewish port at Tel Aviv; although, given the existence of a port at Jaffa, a mere two miles down the coast, this project had no economic justification, it had been a Zionist ambition since the days of Herzl. It meant that for the Jaffa boatmen there was to be no going back to work—ever. The administration also blew up 237 houses in down-town Jaffa. Ostensibly, the object was the 'beautification' of the town; in reality it was a peculiarly harsh security measure. The 6,000 victims helped swell the shanty town of old petrol tins which—like the one in Haifa where Shaikh Qassam had recruited his followers—was taking shape in the vicinity.

In the strategy of the National Committees, the strike action was to be confined to passive resistance and civil disobedience on the Gandhi model. That the leadership was still exerting a moderating influence long after the strike began was emphasized in a report which the High Commissioner addressed to the Colonial Secretary: 'It is a remarkable fact that the religious cry has not been raised during the last six weeks, that the Friday sermons have been far more moderate than I could have hoped during a period when feelings of the people are so deeply stirred, and for this the Mufti is mainly responsible.'[15] But, as in India,

unofficial violence did continue, and developed new forms. Its
perpetrators burned crops and maimed trees, mined and barri-
caded roads, derailed trains, cut telegraph wires and sabotaged
the pipeline that carried Iraqi oil across northern Palestine to the
terminal at Haifa. Arson was rife, and there was much hooli-
ganism, with youths roaming the towns, beating up strike-
breakers and puncturing the tyres of blackleg drivers. Many
Jews were killed, sometimes in brutal and cynical ways. So were
Arabs; gunmen would visit prominent personalities suspected of
lukewarm sympathy for the cause; they would extort contributions from businessmen or wealthy landowners; often they did not
stop at mere intimidation. But the mainspring of unofficial violence
and of the Great Rebellion into which it quickly grew, was the
armed bands that began to operate in hilly regions of the country.

These bands were joined by volunteers from the rest of the
Arab world. The best known of them was Fawzi Kawekji. He
later married a German woman and, like many of his contemporaries, he had seen the rise of Hitler as a development from
which the Arabs could profit in their struggle against Britain.
But neither this, nor the pro-Arab propaganda emanating from
Italy and Germany, meant, as Zionists and their Western sympathizers put it about, that the rebellion was merely an arm of
international Fascism.

Foreign support the uprising may have had, but its heart lay
firmly in Palestine—above all in that peasantry on whom, as it
grew, British aeroplanes showered leaflets urging them to
abandon violence and put their trust in the Royal Commission.
They had their local leaders. The best known was Abd al-Rahim
Haj al-Muhammad, a merchant of solid yeomen stock. He lacked
the professional skills or training of a Kawekji. But he was
described, even by the men who hunted him down, as a straightforward, home-grown patriot. He observed his own moral code,
insisting that his followers show a proper consideration for the
people on whose behalf they were fighting. Other leaders, like
Shaikh Qassam, were religiously motivated; just as the Zionists
took ancient Hebrew names, so they called themselves after the
heroes of early, militant Islam. Others, in varying proportions,
were part freedom-fighter, part-brigand, cloaking ill-gotten gains
in the glamour of revolution. In the first phase of the rebellion
there were about 5,000 altogether. Their organization was rudi-

mentary. They operated without centralized control. They were
divided, broadly speaking, into two kinds. There were the full-
timers in the hills; these constituted the hard core which bore the
brunt of the fighting. There were the part-time confederates;
these would join up for short periods when reinforcements were
needed, but most of the time they would stay in their villages,
keeping the rebels supplied with food, as well as with information about the movements of the police and troops, and about
villagers who worked against them. Their training was also
primitive. When they took to the hills, many of them had never
borne arms before. And their arms, when captured, proved to be
a jumble of antiquated stock abandoned in the Middle East at the
end of World War I; they boasted no such thing as mortar or
artillery. But what they lacked in equipment and expertise they
made up for in determination. According to a Palestinian parti-
cipant, Kawekji was amazed at the 'heroism, gallantry and self-
sacrifice' he found at his service; he would assign ten men to a
mission and 'scores would present themselves as if they were
being invited, not to risk their lives, but to attend a wedding or a
banquet'.[16] A British observer records that they would often see
their comrades killed, a dozen at a time, by machine-gun fire or
aerial bombardment, and yet return to fight a day or two later.[17]
A delegation of Moslem religious dignitaries told the High Commissioner that 'by attacking His Majesty's troops they commit
suicide, but, as Your Excellency is aware, a desperate man often
commits suicide'.[18] Furthermore, the British authorities, or
some of them, were well aware of these motives. Vice-Marshal
Pierce wrote from Palestine: 'The bands were not out for loot.
They were fighting what they believed to be a patriotic war in
defence of their country against injustice and the threat of
Jewish domination.'[19]

   Nineteen years before, the peasants had been flogged or im-
prisoned by the Turkish authorities for picking up the pro-
clamations dropped by British planes urging them to 'come
and join us' who are fighting 'for the liberation of all Arabs
from Turkish rule so that the Arab Kingdom may again become what it was during the time of your fathers'.[20] By now,
however, they had grown tired of the unfulfilled pledges of their
one-time ally and they wanted that positive demonstration of
goodwill—the suspension of immigration during the Royal

Commission's investigations—which the government was not prepared to give. There is little doubt that, with such a suspension, the disorders would have ended in twenty-four hours. During the summer, Arab rulers sought to mediate between the British and the Palestinians—but all to no avail until, in September, the government announced its intention of sending a fresh division of troops to Palestine. From then on the insurgents would obviously have had a much tougher time. Moreover, in the towns, the strain of the six-month strike was beginning to tell; and to have extended the stoppage into the citrus shipping season, thus depriving the country of its most important export earning, would have strained unanimity beyond breaking point. Once again, the Arab states intervened; three kings jointly appealed to the Palestinians to call off their protest and rely upon the good intentions of 'our friend' the British government. The Arab Higher Committee in its turn called on the people 'to put an end to the strike and disorders . . . and to ask all members of the nation to proceed, in the early morning, to their places of worship, in order to hold services for the martyrs and to thank God for the power of patience and fortitude with which he has endowed them'. The response was immediate; work was resumed throughout the country, and the violence ceased. The first phase of the rebellion was over. Some thirty-seven British had died, and sixty-nine Jews—for anything up to a thousand Arabs. The latter had achieved nothing more than they began with—the despatch of yet another Royal Commission. And the very day it left for Palestine, the government announced an unusually generous labour schedule for Jewish immigrants. Indignant, the Arabs decided to boycott the Commission—a boycott which they lifted only a week before the end of its three-month stay.

BRITAIN RECOMMENDS PARTITION

In July 1937, the Commission published its findings. To the amazement of the Arabs, it recommended precisely the kind of solution which, for years, they had fought against, and which finally proved the 'safeguard' clause of the Balfour Declaration to be as valueless as they had always claimed it was. It recommended the vivisection of their native land, the partition of Palestine into a Jewish and an Arab state.

One might have expected an immediate resumption of violence. But this did not happen; for despite its recommendations
there was much in the report's analysis of the workings of the
Mandate that vindicated Arab claims. Here, for the first time,
was authoritative acknowledgement that the Mandate was in
effect *un*workable and that the achievement of Jewish aims was of
necessity prejudicial to the rights of the natives. It roundly
asserted that only through 'the dark path of repression' could the
present policies be maintained. Yet since the alternative which
the Commission proposed in its stead was, in the eyes of the
Arabs, even less feasible, they were content, initially, to let the
logic of facts do their fighting for them.

The partition was not being implemented, it is true, but all
those things which had driven the Arabs to revolt in the first
place—immigration, land sales and signal acts of favouritism like
the creation of an all-Jewish port at Tel-Aviv—continued unabated. The peasants of relatively fertile and prosperous Galilee
were particularly impatient. For under partition this district was
to be allotted to the Jewish State, and partition was to be enforced, if necessary, by a 'compulsory' exchange of population.[21]
The Galileans—reported local British officials—received the
proposals with 'shock bordering on incredulity'. For they assumed that they would be the first to be dispossessed of their
lands and—as they pictured it—'left to perish somewhere in the
desert'.[22] Thus, when Mr L. Y. Andrews was appointed District
Commissioner for Galilee, those familiar with the temper of the
peasantry openly expressed anxiety for his life. Galilee was the
home of some of those politico-religious secret societies that
Shaikh Qassam had inspired. In Jewish eyes, Andrews, who had
been closely associated with the Royal Commission, was the only
official who administered the Mandate as it should be administered; not surprisingly, therefore, he was for the Arabs the very
symbol of their impending misfortune. At the end of September
he and two companions emerged from the Anglican church in
Nazareth. As they ascended the steep narrow land that led from
it, four armed men stepped out of the shadows. 'Run for your'
lives,' Andrews shouted. It would have been better had they
attempted to fight their way out, for as they ran another group
intercepted them from a side lane. Andrews was shot dead and a
police constable was also mortally wounded.

THE REBELLION REACHES ITS CLIMAX

The second phase of the rebellion had begun. This time, more clearly than before, the traditional leadership, or at least the Mufti, was embroiled in it from the outset. To what extent he chose this role himself, is a controversy best left to specialist historians, but certainly it was now much more difficult for him to advocate conciliation if he wished to retain his leadership of the Palestinian people. Moderation was no longer politically realistic; the moderates had been treated with contempt. Before the Royal Commission published its report, the conciliatory wing of the leadership, the Nashashibis, bitter rivals of the Mufti's Husseini clan, had seceded from the Arab Higher Committee, in order to take an independent line should the report prove acceptable to Arab opinion. It had proved so unacceptable that the moderates were totally eclipsed and their lives threatened by extremists' bullets. The administration had been under fierce pressure from the Zionists, the British press and parliament to hold the Arab Higher Committee, especially the Mufti, responsible for the violence. It is true that while the politicians disclaimed any part in it, describing it as a spontaneous manifestation of popular discontent, they did not denounce or seek to curb it. Yet there was no reason to attribute the Andrews murder to the Arab Higher Committee—indeed, this was one occasion when it did deplore the crime—but it was followed, a few days later, by the arrest and detention of two or three hundred notables. The Committee was dissolved, its members deported to the Seychelles; it was held 'morally responsible' for the violence. The Mufti himself was officially deposed, but no attempt was made to arrest him—evidently for fear of bloodshed in the Holy Places where he had taken refuge—and he managed, perhaps with official connivance, to escape to Lebanon. This high-handed action was a provocation to the entire Arab community. The traditional leadership may not have enjoyed much respect, but it was the only leadership the Arabs had; deservedly or not, it was symbolic of their aspirations; there was a sullen determination everywhere, and large deputations flocked into Jerusalem from all over the country to lodge a protest with the administration.

On the night of 14 October 1937, disorders erupted throughout Palestine; obviously, in its second phase, the rebellion had acquired a greater degree of coordination; to say that the Mufti was the evil genius behind the disturbances was at long last becoming a credible assertion, for he had finally been driven, largely through the influence on British policies of those who most insistently said it, into a conspiratorial exile. By the summer of 1938 the rebellion had reached a new climax, far surpassing that of 1936. In a despatch from Palestine, the correspondent of the London *Times* painted a grim picture of the 'murder, guerrilla warfare, rapine, brigandage, theft and arson' that prevailed there.[23] He recalled what the Peel Commission had reported a year before: that it was 'ludicrous' to suppose that Britain had not the resources 'to deal with a rebellion on so small a scale or so ill-equipped for modern warfare'. But the way things were going, he said in another melancholy despatch, it would soon be necessary 'to reconquer Palestine'.[24]

At the height of their power, when they numbered anything up to 15,000 men, the rebels' writ ran in most of the central mountain area, in Galilee, Hebron, Beersheba and Gaza; there they reduced the Mandatory authority to a fiction. The rebel 'government' collected its own taxes and established its own courts, in which it tried brigands who exploited their cause or spies and 'agents' who worked against it. The rebels won—or enforced—the cooperation of community leaders, schoolteachers and the Arab constabulary. Their encounters with the British took two forms: their own small-scale offensives—ambushing, sniping, bomb-throwing, or the mining of roads—or, in the later stages, the pitched defensive battles against pursuing forces. Their tactics were much the same against the Jews, although in that other characteristic form of warfare, waged against the fruits of Jewish labour, they also scored some heartbreaking successes: a settlement would wake up one morning to find that raiders had cut down a thousand orange trees in a single night.

It was a conquest of the towns by the countryside. This time the rebels came down from the hills into the plains; they moved out of their local fiefs to secure a much broader, interlocking hegemony; they dominated not just the villages, sympathetic from the outset, but some of the principal cities of Palestine. And everywhere, they drove the townsman's tasselled tarbush from

the streets, replacing it with the *kefiyyeh*, the countryman's flow-
ing headdress. This was a camouflage—for it made rebel infiltrators harder to detect—but it was also a symbolic self-assertion.
Young zealots engaged in campaigns of tarbush-smashing.
Members of the upper class, top civil servants, took to wearing
hats; Armenians and the religious minorities fell into line too.
Underlying it all, in the Qassam tradition, there was an Islami-
cally inspired intolerance of decadent, westernizing ways.
Christian women had to abandon their fashionable European
headgear in favour of the veil; church-goers would have offend-
ing apparel torn from their heads; short sleeves and lipstick were
outlawed.

The rebels would physically invest the towns. Several hundred
of them descended on Bethlehem, disarmed the police, sang
patriotic songs and withdrew, before the arrival of security forces,
in their own good time. In Nablus they twice raided Barclays
Bank under the noses of British soldiers. In Beersheba they
seized seventy-five rifles and 10,000 rounds of ammunition from
the unresisting police station. They took their defiance to the
temporal and spiritual heart of the conflict; within the walls of
the Old City of Jerusalem, with its Islamo-Judaic complex of
great mosques and the Wailing Wall, its medieval warren of
twisting alleyways, their control was absolute. Even in Jaffa,
down on the coast, the administration enjoyed only a semblance
of authority. The 3,000 Jewish citizens had to be evacuated;
Arab 'enemies' of the revolt were forced to flee. Police stations
were raided. There were almost daily assassinations whose perpetrators, slipping back into the anonymous mass, were practically never caught. Stores were looted in broad daylight. The
inhabitants were obliged to forego the use of electricity, because
it was a Jewish company which supplied it; street lights were
smashed, and oil lamps were selling at a premium.

Once, in Tiberias, the rebels came down to find and kill as
many Jews as they could. This was retaliation for bombs—pre-
sumed Jewish—which had slaughtered scores of Arabs in various
public places. At nine o'clock one October evening, a large band
entered the town; they had earlier cut all its telephone communications with the rest of the country; five minutes later, on a
whistled signal from the adjoining hills, the massacre began. As
one group attacked British and Arab police barracks, others set

fire to the synagogue and houses in the Jewish quarter and killed
their inmates. In all, nineteen Jews, including three women and
ten children, some of them mere babies, died. It took two hours
for the police, eventually reinforced, to drive the raiders out. It
was not the largest, but it was certainly the most deliberate
massacre since Palestinian violence began.[25]

BRITAIN 'RECONQUERS PALESTINE'

The British did, in effect, have to 'reconquer Palestine'. By the
autumn of 1938, they had more than 20,000 troops in the country.
They had already, a year earlier, introduced emergency regulations under which the discharge or the mere carrying of firearms
became a capital offence. Military commanders took charge of
several districts, with the civil authorities acting as political
advisers. The rebels, till then the attackers, became the attacked;
the tide turned relentlessly against them. It was old muskets
against aeroplanes and armoured cars; tactics out of Robin Hood's
day against the logistics, mobility and weaponry of one of the
leading military powers of the age. The infiltrators might abandon
the towns—such as the Old City of Jerusalem—almost as unobtrusively as they had entered them. But in the exposed countryside they sustained terrible losses. 'A British police officer was
killed, two British soldiers were wounded and a number of Arabs
—officially estimated at 40 but unofficially at 60—were killed
during an engagement at Ramallah yesterday.' So ran the dead-
pan despatch from Jerusalem in The Times of 3 October 1938. It
was typical of this unequal combat. The rebels suffered veritable
massacres from the air. The Times again:

> About 150 casualties, it is believed, were inflicted on rebels by
> aircraft late yesterday in the most important engagement of the
> year. An R.A.F. aeroplane making a reconnaissance flight observed
> a large band near Deirghassana, a village in the foothills east of
> Jaffa. The machine summoned assistance from Ramleh, where
> four aeroplanes are always ready to start at two minutes' notice.
> Twelve additional aircraft arrived, and the force engaged the
> band until nightfall. The planes were hit a number of times but
> there were no casualties among R.A.F. personnel and all the
> machines returned safely. Today the Air Force and troops
> thoroughly searched the area, where they saw signs of the burning

of bodies during the night. Fifteen dead horses were found, showing that the band were partly mounted. During the search various
remnants of the band were discovered. The R.A.F. killed four,
and the Irish Guards met a party, of which they killed three . . .
and wounded several others . . .[26]

The military courts set up to enforce the emergency regulations were as thorough and expeditious as the troops. Under
Moslem tradition no man over the age of seventy is executed and
no man is executed during Ramadan, the holy month of fasting.
But the first death sentence passed violated tradition on both
counts. Shaikh Farhan al-Saadi was found hiding in a barn
following a local skirmish between British forces and the rebels.
Asked whether he possessed any firearms, he replied that he did
have an old rifle hanging on the wall of his home. After a three-
hour trial, during which he calmly refused to answer any questions, he was summarily hanged. His judges evidently convicted
him less for this specific offence than for worse crimes—such as
the murder of Andrews—which he was alleged to have committed. It was Ramadan, and he was at least seventy-five years
old. For the Arabs, his was a martyrdom equal to that of Shaikh
Qassam. Altogether the British hanged 112 Arabs, as against one
Jew, in a ritual which made one commander, Sir Alec Kirkbride,
who had to witness it, feel 'guilty and mean'.[27] Condemned men
were reported to have uttered patriotic slogans on the way to the
scaffold, or to have tried to jump the queue.

Then there were the collective fines and demolitions. The fines
were paid in cash or in kind—and they were frequently imposed
without sufficient inquiry or proof of guilt. When one Squadron-
Leader Alderton was murdered, troops concluded, with the help
of tracker dogs, that the killers had found shelter in the village of
Igzim. It underwent a 'search' by a detachment of the South
Kents infantry. The British missionary Frances Newton visited
Igzim two days later. She found two houses at the entrance of the
village blown up and some sixty others where 'the havoc which
had been wrought was indescribable, and, unless seen with one's
own eyes, unbelievable'.[28] She found shutters and cupboards
smashed in, mirrors shattered, upholstered armchairs gutted,
sewing-machines battered to bits, clothing and beds soaked in
olive oil, and even a Koran ripped apart. Individual soldiers had
stolen money and jewellery. One unfortunate was shot when,

escaping with £25 he wanted for himself, he broke the security cordon round the village. All sheep and goats were seized as security for the collective fine. Those who could afford to buy them back at the price of eight shillings a head did so; those who could not lost them. Then, just to complete the ordeal, the government forced the villagers to foot the bill—nearly £700— for billeting forty supernumerary police in their midst for three months. Aware that if they did not pay up, all their possessions would be seized, they preferred to emigrate *en masse*, taking their property with them. Some of them, of course, ended up in Shaikh Qassam's Haifa shanty town. 'True refugees,' commented Miss Newton, 'but from *British* barbarism.' And it turned out in the end that Squadron-Leader Alderton's killers actually came from another village altogether.

When an Arab was killed laying ambush to a military patrol, the authorities ordered the demolition 'without compensation' of the house of a big landowner from the village of Endor. Their justification was that the dead man had been seen 'recently serving coffee' in the house—a justification that took no account of the fact that, in accordance with Arab traditions of hospitality, a part of the rich man's establishment had been set aside as a more or less public meeting place open to villagers and strangers alike. When the airport at Lydda was damaged by sabotage, a row of houses in the vicinity was dynamited in reprisal.

In March 1939, Abdul Rahim al-Haj Muhammad, the rebellion's outstanding commander, was killed, after prayers in a mosque, amid general Palestinian grief—and reluctant tributes from the British. Most other commanders fled the country. The uprising was virtually at an end. As a military force, the Palestinians had been broken. Official British figures for the number of Arab casualties during the 1936-9 disturbances have never been made fully known, but, according to the careful calculations of the Palestinian scholar, Walid Khalidi, the dead must have exceeded 5,000 and the wounded 14,000. These figures, translated into contemporary British or American terms, would have meant some 200,000 British killed and 600,000 wounded, or 1,000,000 Americans killed and 3,000,000 wounded.[29] Some 101 British died, and 463 Jews.[30]

The rebellion had its own internal defects and these, under the British onslaught, accelerated its collapse. There is much debate

among contemporary Palestinian historians, spurred by the new
phase of armed resistance, about just what the defects were.[31]
They are inclined to lay heavy blame on the *zaims* and *effendis*.
It was in origin, they contend, a truly spontaneous uprising;
its very spontaneity was a measure of its authenticity; but it
found no leadership to channel that spontaneity into organized,
truly purposeful revolution. It was only when the urban élite
had no choice that they tried to bring it under their wing—
or at least some of them, led by the Mufti, tried, while the more
conciliatory ones, led by the Nashashibis, fell into deeper dis-
credit than ever. Yet it never really worked; the gulf between
politician and fighter, between town and country, was never
bridged. While the rebellion, as the Palestinians' first attempt at
general armed violence, represented a qualitative growth in
resistance to the Zionist invasion, it was not matched by the
comparable social, political and organizational aptitudes that
were needed to sustain this high challenge. The fighters were not
encouraged to transcend regional, religious or family loyalties;
many refused to join bands in other areas; those who did might
be turned back as intruders. *Faz'a*, 'rallying to one's neighbour'
—and no one else—impeded rational strategy. Warlordism
flourished. But worse still was the debilitating effect of inherited
clan rivalries, of old blood-feuds mixed up with new and half-
understood political controversies. These could not only set
village against village, but could divide a single one upon itself;
it would sometimes happen that because one influential personage supported the uprising his rival automatically collaborated with the authorities. And occasionally rebel courts were
debased into instruments for the bloody settling of scores. What
possible justification could there have been for the 'execution'
not merely of the Mukhtar of the village of Deir al-Shaikh, but
of his wife, three sons, aged fourteen, twelve and ten, and a
servant too?[32] And even the hated enemy justice could be exploited for sordid vengeance. A firearm would be 'planted' in
the family domain of the intended victim and word passed to the
military authorities; thus a man could send his neighbour to the
gallows.[33] It was the same with the urban political leadership.
Fragmentation there meant open war between the Husseinis and
the Nashashibis. For the Mufti, champion of the Husseinis, the
personal ascendancy he had achieved was not enough: he had to

exploit the rebellion to reinforce it. It was mainly to his perni-
cious influence, his lust for power, that the 'opposition' attributed the wave of terror that enveloped them. When Fakhri Bey
Nashashibi survived, with serious wounds, an assassination
attempt, his resentment was so great that—in the judgement of
the High Commissioner—he began to collaborate with local
Jewish politicians.[34] He and his followers set up 'peace squads' to
revenge themselves on Haj Amin's supposed victims. Armed
violence against the common enemy, far from extinguishing the
sterile feuding of the *zaims* and *effendis*, ignited a minor civil war,
in which the opponents of the Mufti were driven to oppose the
Great Rebellion itself.

BRITAIN RELENTS: THE 1939 WHITE PAPER

Yet even as 20,000 British troops were 'reconquering Palestine',
the politicians back home were beginning to have serious misgivings about the whole rationale of a policy that required such
harsh and costly methods to sustain. The misgivings arose from
the belated recognition, in some influential quarters, that so
desperate a Palestinian resistance, even if ultimately unavailing,
must have profounder causes than hitherto understood. Malcolm
MacDonald, the Colonial Secretary, told the House of Commons
that most of the rebels were inspired by patriotic motives and
suggested that, had he been an Arab, he would have felt the
same as they did. A 'strong' policy, he said, could restore order,
but not peace. At the same time, Britain had a higher self-
interest to consider. With war clouds gathering over Europe, it
could spare neither troops nor funds on unnecessary colonial
conflicts that diplomacy could end; nor could it antagonize the
entire Arab and Moslem world, strategically vital areas increasingly exposed to the blandishments of the Axis powers, for the
sake of its importunate Zionist protégé. In 1937, Lord Peel had
declared the Mandate unworkable and proposed partition instead; but at the height of the rebellion, yet another commission
of inquiry, headed by Sir John Woodward, reported that partition was not workable either. At the same time the government
invited Arab and Jewish leaders to a round-table conference in
London. All that this gathering did, in a month of reciprocal
obstructionism, was to demonstrate the immensity of the gulf

between the two sides. Representatives of the Arab states—who
were also invited—did meet Weizmann, but the Palestinians did
not. Whereas, in 1914, the fathers would have been ready—had
not global war prevented it—to meet with the enemy over the
the dimensions of the struggle were such that, to have done so,
negotiating table,[35] the sons were not. After a quarter of a century
would have been a conferring of legitimacy on the whole Zionist
enterprise almost as unthinkable as 'recognizing' Israel was to be
for the generation to come.

In a prefigurement of 'indirect negotiations', of 'proximity
talks', of jet-age 'shuttle-diplomacy'—and all the procedural
ingenuities that peace-makers of the future would dream up—the
conference took the form of separate discussions between British
and Arabs, then British and Jews. When the inevitable deadlock
was reached, Britain issued a 'statement of policy', the Mac-
Donald White Paper, on its own. The government now asserted
that it was 'not part of their policy that Palestine should become
a Jewish state'; that 75,000 Jewish immigrants should be admitted over the next five years, but no more after that without
the approval of the Arabs; that land sales should be strictly
regulated; and that self-governing institutions should be developed with a view to the establishment, within ten years, of an
independent Palestine State. There were aspects of the White
Paper which caused the Palestinian delegation, on the instructions of the Mufti, to reject it; nevertheless, Palestinian opinion
was impressed by its main provisions. At last, it was felt, the
Arabs were getting a measure of justice; so much so, in fact, that
the Mufti's rivals, the Nashashibis, announced that they would
cooperate with Britain in enforcing the White Paper. Arab violence, which British arms had first drastically curtailed, British
diplomacy now stilled altogether.

Britain 'Betrays' the Zionists

The Zionists' response to the publication of the White Paper was
instantaneous and violent. Indeed, in Palestine itself, it could not
be formally proclaimed at the appointed hour because the trans-
mission lines of the broadcasting station were cut and its studios
bombed. The next day Dr Herzog, the Chief Rabbi, stood in the
pulpit of the great Yeshurim Synagogue in Jerusalem and before

the weeping congregation tore up a copy of the infamous document. The headquarters of the Department of Migration was set on fire, and government offices in Haifa and Tel Aviv were stormed by crowds bent on destroying all files on illegal Jewish immigration. In Jerusalem Arab shops were looted. A British constable was shot dead during a demonstration. A general Jewish strike was proclaimed. Throughout the country, mass meetings of Jews took an oath declaring that Britain's new and 'treacherous' policy would not be tolerated, that 'the Jewish population will fight it to the uttermost, and will spare no sacrifice to defeat it'. A few days later, activists initiated a campaign of sabotage and terror, directed against both British and Arabs. They blew up the Rex Cinema in Jerusalem; five Arabs were killed and eighteen wounded; two days later, they killed five more in an attack on the village of Adas. David Bengurion, acknowledged leader of the *Yishuv*, wrote after a day of demonstrations that these marked 'the beginning of Jewish resistance to the disastrous policy now proposed by His Majesty's Government. The Jews will not be intimidated into surrender even if their blood be shed.'[36] Zionism had come in many forms; there had been 'spiritual', 'cultural', 'political' or 'practical' Zionism. But the MacDonald White Paper marked the official beginning—as the Israeli deputy Uri Avneri was to dub it many years later—of 'gun Zionism'.[37]

THE REVISIONISTS ABANDON 'SELF-RESTRAINT'

The ideological roots of 'gun Zionism' reach back, as we have seen, to Theodor Herzl himself. It was inevitable, as he foresaw, that armed force would eventually come into its own as the principal instrument of a movement which, in its earlier and weaker phase, could only rely on the protection of an imperial sponsor. That phase was now drawing to a close. But long before it had done so, the proponents and strategists of armed force were preparing the way, in moral, political and practical terms, for its eventual use. The spirit of Vladimir Jabotinsky, founder of the Jewish Legion during World War I and later of the underground *Haganah* army, was permeating the *Yishuv*. It has become fashionable, particularly among Zionist historians, to play down the significance of Jabotinsky, who early broke away from the mainstream Zionist leadership. Revisionism, as his rebellious heresy came to be known, has been described as 'the lunatic fringe of Zionism as the various *Ikhwan* movements represent the lunatic fringe of Arab nationalism, or the Fifth Monarchy Men represent the lunatic fringe of English Puritanism, or the Irish Republican Army represent the lunatic fringe of Sinn Fein'.[38] But the man Weizmann called 'our d'Annunzio'[39] played a key role in that militarization of Zionism which everyone subsequently endorsed. If he was repudiated by his contemporaries it was largely because he was ahead of his time. He represented an embarrassingly aggressive militancy when Weizmann-style pragmatism and equivocation were still necessary as means of securing support for Zionism from the imperial sponsor and the assimilationist Jewry of the Diaspora. It was feared that he would give the world the 'notion that we Zionists intend to dominate the Arabs of Palestine by force of arms, thus offering our enemies a weapon against us'.[40] Although Zionists might frown on his visionary enthusiasms, and oppose him officially, some of them admired him in private. Bengurion saw him as the 'Zionist Trotsky',[41] whose purist fervour doomed him to failure. But each had a sneaking affection for the other. What divided them—and that only for the time being—was style and method rather than aim. Thus it has been truly said that 'the struggle for Palestine was fundamentally Jabotinskian. For Jabotinsky represents the most uninhibited expression of Zionism as a political movement, and in this regard he symbolized an ideological norm toward which much of Zionism's latent disposition naturally gravitated.'[42]

There is no better example of that disposition than the confidential letter which Chaim Arlosoroff, the Director of the Political Department of the Jewish Agency, wrote to Weizmann as early as 1932. Arlosoroff—it now seems hard to believe—was actually one of the most conciliatory of Zionist leaders. His very appointment was designed to allay Arab fears, for he was apparently serious, unlike others, in his attempts at Arab-Israeli understanding. Indeed, that may have been the motive for his mysterious assassination in 1933. His letter is a revolutionary adaptation of the great diplomat's own concept of dynamic stages. While he decries Revisionism as a 'madness' which merely excites the Arabs, this mild and scholarly theoretician ends up with a plan of action which, so dry and reassuringly moderate in presentation, is fundamentally Jabotinskian in spirit. In his view, the evolutionary policy of immigration and colonization, of 'goat by goat and dunum by dunum', was the only right one in the past. But it would not work for much longer. Future strategy should be developed in the light of 'the relationship of forces of the two peoples contending in the country'.

> The present stage, which we have attained by means of gradual development, may be defined approximately as follows: The Arabs are no longer strong enough to destroy our position but still consider themselves strong enough to establish an Arab state in Palestine without taking into consideration Jewish political demands, whereas the Jews are strong enough to preserve their present positions without possessing sufficient strength to assure the constant growth of the Jewish community through immigration, colonization, and the maintenance of peace and order in the country in the course of this development.
>
> The next 'stage' will be attained when the relationship of the real forces will be such as to preclude any possibility of the establishment of an Arab state in Palestine, i.e., when the Jews will acquire such additional strength as will automatically block the road for Arab domination. This will be followed by another 'stage' during which the Arabs will be unable to frustrate the constant growth of the Jewish community through immigration and constructive economic activity. The constantly growing strength of the Jews will influence the Arabs in the direction of seeking a negotiated accord. This will be followed by a 'stage' during which the equilibrium between the two peoples will be based on real forces and an agreed solution to the problem. The test of the evolutionary practices of Zionist policy within the framework of the British mandate consists in whether it will be possible to attain the next 'stage' by means of this policy. . . . Should that prove impossible . . . it would no longer be feasible to cling to the evolutionary practices of Zionist policy or to base on it the strength and endurance of the Zionist movement. I am inclined to think that it is not possible.

One reason for this, he goes on to explain, is the limits of the Mandatory Administration; it would be too much to expect the British government to assume such a burden for the sake of the colonizing enterprise of a 'foreign' people. He therefore concludes:

> Under present circumstances Zionism cannot be realized
> without a transition period during which the Jewish minority
> would exercise organized revolutionary rule . . . during which the
> state apparatus, the administration, and the military establishment
> would be in the hands of the minority, in order to eliminate the
> danger of domination by the non-Jewish majority and suppress
> rebellion against us. . . . Such a conception of the problem might
> shake the foundations of many beliefs which we have cherished
> for a great many years. It might even resemble dangerously certain
> political states of mind which we have always rejected. At first it
> might even appear as impractical, visionary, and contrary to the
> conditions in which we live under the British Mandate . . . But
> there is one thing about which I feel very strongly—I will never
> become reconciled to the failure of Zionism before an attempt is
> made whose seriousness corresponds to the seriousness of the
> struggle for the revival of our national life and the sanctity of the
> mission entrusted to us by the Jewish people.
>
> I hope I do not have to stress the fact that my way of thinking is
> as alien today as it always has been to that which is called Revision-
> ism. Now, too, I consider that the activities, the policies, and the
> educational principles of Revisionism are madness.[43]

Rarely can a man have so brilliantly advocated a thesis which
he simultaneously condemns. At any rate, it is hardly surprising
that less fastidious people than himself did indeed develop the
dangerous states of mind that he deplores. Ideas of coexistence
with the Arabs, of bi-nationalism, were increasingly dismissed as
the utopian illusions of an unrepresentative minority; the 'safeguard' clauses of the Balfour Declaration were becoming a forgotten irrelevance. Along with the rise of Hitler and the darken-
ing situation in Europe, the Arab rebellion—an event forecast by
Arlosoroff—did not engender, but simply accelerated, the process of militarization that was inevitable from the outset. If 'gun
Zionism' emerged, open and proclaimed, only after the rebellion,
it was very much in the making during it.

When the disturbances broke out, the *Yishuv* was officially
wedded to *Havlaga*—'self-restraint'—a concept rooted in traditional Jewish ethics. The Jews should not respond to Arab
terrorism with their own. In a rather vague way it was argued
that there were methods—whether useful or not—which had to
be abjured if the Jewish community's feeling of moral superiority

over its enemies was to be preserved. *Havlaga* also earned credit abroad. Weizmann described it as 'one of the great moral political acts of modern times', which had 'won the admiration of liberal opinion all over the world'.[44] The London *Times* once contrasted Jewish discipline with what it called attempts by the Arab leaders to give proof of Arab nobility by releasing three Jewish children—adding that this had not prevented Jews and Christians alike from asking pertinently what had happened to the children's parents.[45]

Havlaga may have been a Jewish virtue, but—Zionism being in large measure a revolt against Jewish tradition—it was certainly not a Zionist one. As Arab violence grew, it came under increasing strain until, in spring 1938, three young Revisionists fired at an Arab bus on the Acre-Safad highway. It was a hopelessly bungled and amateurish operation by teenage novices, a naïve and impulsive response to constant Arab raids on Safad, in the course of which several Jews had been killed and one girl stabbed to death in a ditch. Perhaps it is true, as the Jews claimed, that if he had been an Arab the ringleader might have been spared; perhaps his ill-directed volley did come as an opportunity for the administration, which had already executed dozens of Arabs, to demonstrate its impartiality. At all events in June of that year the young Polish Jew, Shlomo ben Yussif, became the first, and last, Jew to go to the gallows during the 'disturbances'—and Jabotinsky, who numbered him among 'the heroes of Israel',[46] abandoned *Havlaga*.

In the single month of July at least 100 Arabs died in the public places of Haifa, Jaffa and Jerusalem—more people, in some six incidents, than Arabs had killed Jews in the whole of that year so far.[47] The Arab Melon Market in Haifa saw the last and worst of the series. There a bomb, placed a mere ten metres from where another one had killed eighteen Arabs three weeks before, went off at seven in the morning of 26 July. The detonation was 'accompanied by the hurling of bodies, killed, maimed and injured, in all directions . . . among the blood-spattered human remains were the mangled bodies of three horses, several mules and donkeys which had brought the villagers' produce to the crowded market.'[48] Fifty-three Arabs died, and one Jew.

The official Zionist response was ambiguous. There was, to be

sure, outright condemnation. The newspaper *Davar* said that any
deviation from *Havlaga* was a 'disgrace, because the pure Jewish
colours have been stained by the blood of innocent people';
Haaretz found it 'incredible . . . that these crimes can be part of
a political system, unthinkable that by such means anyone can
hope to attain a desirable political end'.[49] But the condemnation
was very general; indeed, if an accusing finger was pointed at all,
it was liable to be in the direction of Arab quite as much as
Jewish extremists. 'Is there a Jew so insane', asked the *Palestine
Post*, 'even if cunning-minded, as to venture to deposit or throw
a bomb among the usually large crowds coming out of the
Mosque? What surer way of spreading the seed of inter-racial
war . . . than by manufacturing the type of crime which, in its
sacrifice and resultant panic, makes the credulous Arab point to
the Jew as its author?'[50] None of the perpetrators was ever caught.
The Jewish police were just as much in collusion with their own
community as the Arab police were with theirs. The outside
world had precious little doubt that the culprits were Jewish, but
there was much readiness to find extenuating circumstances. The
Manchester Guardian concluded that continual terrorism 'organized from outside' had caused a breakdown in Jewish self-
restraint, but this was 'slight . . . natural, and indeed inevitable'.
'Certainly not one of the turbulent peoples of these Islands
would have endured without violent retaliation a hundredth part
of what the Palestinian Jews have suffered for over two years.'[51]

The bombs *were* Jewish, of course, though no one claimed
them at the time, and more specifically they were Revisionist.
The denunciations of the official leadership which impressed
outsiders seemed so much hypocrisy to the Arabs who, though
right in their general intuitions, were apt to jump to some naïve
conclusions; after the Haifa explosion a deputation of veiled
women protested to the High Commissioner, and one of them
told him that Dr Weizmann, whose fame as a scientist had
apparently reached their uninstructed ears, was manufacturing
the bombs in his laboratory at Rehovoth.

According to his biographer and disciple, Joseph Schechtman,
Jabotinsky long struggled with his conscience over the morality
of terrorism. He saw what he thought to be the political justification for retaliation but, at the same time, he was a 'typical nineteenth-century liberal who considered human life as sacrosanct'.

He once told a colleague: 'I can't see much heroism and public good in shooting from the rear an Arab peasant on a donkey, carrying vegetables for sale in Tel Aviv.'[52] In time, however, he openly and fully endorsed the policy of wholesale retaliation. Everybody, he wrote, likes retaliations, provided they are immediately and exclusively directed against the bandits and not against the Arab population, however hostile. 'But it must be realized that the choice is not between retaliating against the bandits or retaliating against the hostile population. The choice is between . . . retaliating against the hostile population or not retaliating at all . . . To the spilling of *ha'dam hamutar*, the permitted blood, on which there is no prohibition and for which nobody has to pay, an end had been put in Palestine. Amen.' By June 1939 he had come to the conclusion that 'it was not only difficult to punish only the guilty ones, in most cases it was impossible'.[53]

The Arabs had begun the 1936-9 'disturbances', but—as an Israeli historian was to concede many years later—the Jews later imitated and, with their much improved techniques, quite outdid them.[54] If, in their preference for hit-and-run guerilla tactics, the Arabs were spurred by folk-memories of the 'assassins' or the tribal *ghazzia*, the Jews introduced an urban, and far more effective, terrorism that was more in the tradition of Russian Nihilists or the Anarchists of Spain.[55] It had indeed been proved possible—*pace Haaretz*—that such methods could 'be used to attain a desirable political end'. As Schechtman put it, they had been of 'inestimable political and education value. They freed the *Yishuv* from the humiliating status of British *Schutzjuden*; they taught the Arab terrorist bands a healthy lesson; and they generated a new spirit of militancy and self-sacrifice in the Jewish youth.'[56]

Yet it was in the maintenance of *Havlaga*, rather than in its breach, that the Zionists profited most from the 'disturbances'. While the British were breaking Arab military power, demoralizing the population and further emasculating an already low-calibre leadership, they were enabling the high-calibre Jewish leadership to mould the eager *Yishuv* into a formidable fighting force. *Havlaga*, however genuine in some, was purely expedient in others. It was designed to win British support for the establishment of a Jewish militia. And it succeeded. In 1936, the administration authorized the recruitment of a first batch of 1,240 Jewish supernumerary police; later that year, it informed the Zionist leadership that a special force of constables would be permitted to remain in being, with their arms, provided the already existing *Haganah* was disbanded and its illegal weapons handed over. With the growth of Arab violence, however, it tacitly dropped this condition. And in the following two years the force was further expanded until, by 1939, it totalled some 14,500 men, 5 per cent of the *Yishuv*. Its training, transferred from the police to the regular army, had continually grown in scope and sophistication. The lessons learned had been passed on to thousands of others in secret. The British civil authorities objected, on political grounds, to this rapid development of Jewish military capability, but the army command, interested only in crushing the Arab rebellion, supported Jewish demands for increased enrolment and training.

It was in the guise of the Special Night Squads that the Jews benefited most from the collaboration with the British, and, in particular, from the military genius of one eccentric captain, Orde Wingate, who, with the Old Testament as his inspiration, adopted the Zionist cause heart and soul. He it was who first inculcated those principles of offensive daring, of surprise, deep penetration and high mobility which the Israeli army subsequently developed to the full. It was under him that some of Israel's best officers had their first taste of battle with the Arabs—among them Moshe Dayan.

The British journalist Leonard Mosley describes the climax of the first raid in which Wingate took a party of young pioneers right into the enemy camp.

By three o'clock in the morning, at the conclusion of the most strenuous thirty-mile walk even these earthy, hardened Jews had ever experienced, Wingate brought his column to the edge of the Arab village. . . . He went off into the darkness (to reconnoitre), and they waited for his signal. Soon they heard a shot, and they moved into the positions Wingate had mapped out for them. From the outskirts of the village there was another shot; after which there was a fusillade of fire, obviously from the Arabs, a firefly spray of lights in the distance, shouts, screams and wails. And then, straight into the trap which Wingate had laid for them, came the Arabs. Dayan and Brenna, nearest the village, let the Arabs pass;

they had instructions to hold their fire until the Arabs could be surrounded. Only when the Jews farthest away opened fire did Brenna and Dayan begin to pick off their victims. They killed five and captured four.

Wingate came back, carrying a Turkish rifle over his shoulder. He looked calm and serene. 'Good work. You are fine boys and will make good soldiers,' he said.

He went up to the four Arab prisoners. He said in Arabic: 'You have arms in this village. Where have you hidden them?'

The Arabs shook their heads, and protested ignorance. Wingate reached down and took sand and grit from the ground; he thrust it into the mouth of the first Arab and pushed it down his throat until he choked and puked.

'Now,' he said, 'where have you hidden the arms?'

Still they shook their heads.

Wingate turned to one of the Jews and, pointing to the coughing and spluttering Arab, said, 'Shoot this man.'

The Jew looked at him questioningly and hesitated.

Wingate said, in a tense voice, 'Did you hear? Shoot him.'

The Jew shot the Arab. The others stared for a moment, in stupefaction, at the dead body at their feet. The boys from Hanita were watching in silence.

'Now speak', said Wingate. They spoke.[57]

In 1939, after the MacDonald White Paper, the Jewish community was preparing to fight the Mandate with the weapons the Mandate had given it. British rule had served its evolutionary purpose; it no longer helped, it held back, the Zionists' inexorably unfolding design. The new, self-reliant stage of 'organized revolutionary rule' by the Jewish minority had been reached. The Mandate had to go. But great events elsewhere gave it new life. With the outbreak of world war the *Yishuv* rallied to the democracies and anti-British violence all but ceased. As Weizmann foresaw,[58] the second cataclysm of the twentieth century was to furnish opportunities as sensational as the first. Those opportunities, of which he again took full advantage, were primarily international and diplomatic. But this time they were supplemented, and eventually quite overshadowed, by other opportunities, local and military, furnished by the new balance of power in Palestine itself. Zionism's centre of gravity was shifting from the Diaspora to the *Yishuv*. Weizmann, the intimate of Western statesmen, still shaped the higher strategies.

But the real striking-force, the real instrument of 'gun Zionism', was in the hands of David Bengurion, the rugged pioneer. And the seeds of the real, essentially Jabotinskian triumph—the swift, sharp transition to Jewish statehood in a land without Arabs— had already been sown in the British defeat of the Great Rebellion.

NOTES

1. Warriner, Doreen, *Land and Poverty in the Middle East*, Royal Institute of International Affairs, London, 1948, pp. 61-2.
2. *Ibid.*, p. 63.
3. Barbour, *Nisi Dominus*, *op. cit.*, p. 133.
4. Warriner, *op. cit.*, p. 126.
5. Weinstock, Nathan, *Le Zionisme contre Israel*, François Maspero, Paris, 1969, p. 168.
6. Allush, Naji, *Arab Resistance in Palestine* (Arabic), *op. cit.*, p. 91.
7. Darwaza, Muhammad Izzat, *On the Modern Arab Movement*, (Arabic) The Modern Press, Sidon and Beirut, p. 59.
8. *Palestine Royal Commission Report* (the Peel Commission), H.M.S.O., London, 1937, Cmd. 5479, p. 80.
9. See p. 63.
10. Al-Kayyali, *A History of Modern Palestine* (Arabic), *op. cit.*, p. 296.
11. *Ibid.*, p. 306.
12. Marlowe, John, *The Seat of Pilate*, Cresset Press, London, 1959, pp. 137-8.
13. Newton, Frances, *Fifty Years in Palestine*, *op. cit.*, p. 275.
14. Peel Commission, *op. cit.*, pp. 93-4.
15. Al-Kayyali, *op. cit.*, p. 311.
16. Darwaza, Muhammad Izzat, *The Palestine Cause* (Arabic), The Modern Press, Sidon and Beirut, Vol. I, p. 131.
17. Barbour, *op. cit.*, p. 192.
18. Al-Kayyali, *op. cit.*, p. 313.
19. *Ibid.*, p. 315.
20. Shaw Commission, *op. cit.*, p. 126.
21. Peel Commission, *op. cit.*, p. 391.
22. Al-Kayyali, *op. cit.*, p. 333.
23. 6 September 1938.
24. 3 October 1938.
25. *The Times*, 4 October 1938.
26. 17 September 1938.
27. Kirkbride, Sir Alec, *A Crackle of Thorns*, John Murray, London, 1956, p. 56.
28. Newton, Frances, E. *Searchlight on Palestine: Fair Play or Terrorist Methods?* The Arab Centre, London, 1938, pp. 16-18.

29. Khalidi, Walid, *From Heaven to Conquest*, *op. cit.*, pp. 846-9.
30. *The Times*, 21 July 1938; *A Survey of Palestine*, Jerusalem, 1946, pp. 38-49.
31. See, for example, Sharabi, Hisham, *Palestine and Israel*, *The Lethal Dilemma*, Pegasus, New York, 1969, pp. 184-92.
32. *The Times*, 9 September 1938.
33. John, Robert and Hadawi Sami, *The Palestine Diary*, The Palestine Research Centre, Beirut, Vol. I, p. 279.
34. Al-Kayyali, *op. cit.*, p. 350.
35. See pp. 33-4.
36. The ESCO Foundation, *Palestine: A Study of Jewish, Arab and British Policies*, Vol. II, p. 910.
37. Avneri, *Israel Without Zionists: A Plea for Peace in the Middle East*, *op. cit.*, p. 88.
38. Marlow, *op. cit.*, p. 133.
39. See p. 36.
40. Taylor, Alan R., *The Zionist Mind, the Origins and Development of Zionist Thought*, *op. cit.*, p. 89.
41. *Ibid.*, p. 89.
42. *Ibid.*, p. 91.
43. *Jewish Frontier*, October 1948, pp. 7-8.
44. Weizmann, *Trial and Error*, *op. cit.*, pp. 484, 488.
45. 15 September 1938.
46. Schechtman, *Fighter and Prophet, the Vladimir Jabotinsky Story*, *op. cit.*, p. 474.
47. *The Times*, 21 July 1938.
48. *Palestine Post*, 26 July 1938.
49. 5 July 1938.
50. 17 July 1938.
51. 15 July 1938.
52. Schechtman, *op. cit.*, pp. 449, 453.
53. *Ibid.*, p. 485.
54. Bauer, Yehuda, *New Outlook*, July-August, Vol. IX, No. 7, p. 26.
55. Marlowe, John, *Rebellion in Palestine*, Cresset Press, London 1946, p. 244.
56. Schechtman, *op. cit.*, p. 483.
57. Mosley, Leonard, *Gideon Goes to War*, Arthur Barker, London, 1955, pp. 57-8.
58. Meinertzhagen, Richard, *Middle East Diary: 1917-1956*, Cresset Press, London, 1959, pp. 191-2.

Four

Gun Zionism

DRIVING OUT THE BRITISH

IN 1946, the King David was something more, in the eyes of the *Yishuv*, than Jerusalem's most famous hotel. An entire wing of it, housing both military and civilian headquarters, had become the nexus of British power in Palestine. Every conceivable human and technical device protected this fortress in the heart of the city. Soldiers continuously patrolled around it; others manned machine-gun nests on its roof. Its front was covered by wire netting to prevent the casual throwing of explosives. You approached it through a barbed-wire alley flanked by armed guards. When you finally reached the outer door it was barred by steel shutters which could only be opened by an electrically operated switch from inside. And only when you passed through yet another electrically operated door had you penetrated to the inner sanctum itself.

This was the nut which one Menachim Begin resolved to crack. Jabotinsky had died in 1940, and it was Begin who, as the leader of the underground terrorist organization *Irgun Zwei Leumi*, emerged as a worthy successor to the founder of Revisionism. Begin had emigrated to Palestine from Poland during the war. 'A smallish man in his late thirties, looking older because of his heavy glasses', he 'appeared to be the typical Jew engaged in a small way in business in any town east of the Elbe. There was nothing military about him, nothing commanding, nothing exceptionally impressive.'[1] Yet he became a legendary figure in Palestine. Begin had one outstanding quality. He was a planner, albeit on a small scale, and meticulous down to the tiniest detail. This was the quality which he had used to the full when, in spring of 1946, he put before the *Haganah* and the official Zionist leadership Operation Malonchik—a plan for blowing up the King David Hotel. They eventually approved it, and on 22 July,

shortly before noon, a truck drew up at the hotel's kitchen entrance, which lay at the opposite end to the government wing,
and men dressed as Arabs got out. No one took any notice as they
began to unload a cargo of milk churns and rolled them into the
Regence Café next to the kitchen. No one guessed that those
innocent milk churns were packed with high explosives or that
these Arabs were the Assault Unit of the *Irgun*. In the basement,
Begin's scouts had discovered, there was a broad passageway
running the entire length of the building, and despite all the re-
finements of security deployed above ground, there was almost
none below it. The 'Arabs' held up the staff of the Regence Café,
clashed with two British officers, left the milk churns in their
appointed place and set them to explode in half an hour. As the
Assault Unit made its getaway, it released the café staff, who were
told to run for their lives. The government workers above got no
such warning—or at least none, in spite of Begin's claims to the
contrary, on which they had any time to act.

> It was now twelve fifteen. Gideon [the commander of the
> Assault Unit] was counting the minutes. So far, everything had
> gone according to plan, except for the casualties we had suffered
> in the unexpected clash. . . . Only one question bothered him:
> would the explosives go off? Might not some error have been made
> in the mechanism? Would the building really go up? Would the
> documents be destroyed?
> Each minute seemed like a day. Twelve thirty-one, thirty-two.
> Zero hour drew near. Gideon grew restless. The half-hour was
> almost up. Twelve thirty-seven. . . . Suddenly the whole town
> seemed to shudder. There had been no mistake. The force of the
> explosion was greater than had been expected. Yitsak Sadeh, of
> the *Haganah*, had doubted whether it would reach the third or
> even the second floor. Giddy had claimed that, though only about
> 500 lbs of explosives—a compound of T.N.T. and gelignite—
> had been put into the milk-cans, the confined space of the base-
> ment would heighten the force of the escaping gases, and the
> explosion would reach the roof. The milk-cans 'reached' the
> whole height of the building, from basement to roof, six storeys
> of stone, concrete and steel. As the B.B.C. put it—the entire
> wing of a huge building was cut off as with a knife.[2]

More than eighty-eight people perished in the rubble: British,
Arab—and fifteen Jews.

The blowing up of the King David carried a message for the whole world. A new nation had arisen in Palestine; conceived in the Balfour Declaration, nurtured in the Mandatory womb, it was delivered in the just violence that historic events always engender. Many, including faint-hearted Jews, had thought it would be crushed in embryo. How little they understood the innate resources of the human spirit. In his book *The Revolt*, Menachim Begin initiates his readers into the metaphysics of Jewish national redemption.

> The revolt sprang from the earth. The ancient Greek story of Antaeus and the strength he drew from contact with Mother Earth is a legend. The renewed strength which came to us, and especially to our youth, from contact with the soil of our ancient land, is no legend but a fact. The officials of the British Foreign Office had no conception of this when they made their plans. What could they foresee of those hidden forces which Herzl used to speak of as the 'imponderables'? Their error was not mathematical; they were not wrong about the number of Jews wanting to come to Eretz Israel. They assumed that in Eretz Israel, too, the Jews would continue to be timid suppliants for protection. The conduct of the Jews—or rather the attitude of their official leaders, expressed in the well-known policy of self-restraint (Havlaga)—seemed to justify and confirm this assumption. But those unseen forces, which have ever saved the Jewish people from obliteration, demolished the British assumption. . . . A new generation grew up which turned its back on fear. It began to fight instead of to plead. For nearly two thousand years, the Jews, as Jews, had not borne arms, and it was on this complete disarmament, as much psychological as physical, that our oppressors calculated. They did not realize that the two phenomena were interdependent; we gave up our arms when we were exiled from our country. With our return to the land of our fathers our strength was restored. . . . [3]

When Descartes said: 'I think, therefore I am', he uttered a very profound thought. But there are times in the history of peoples when thought alone does not prove their existence. A people may 'think' and yet its sons, with their thoughts and in spite of them, may be turned into a herd of slaves—or into soap. There are times when everything in you cries out: your very self-respect as a human being lies in your resistance to evil.

We fight, therefore we are. [4]

'Gun Zionism' had truly come into its own. Like the Arab Rebellion a decade earlier, it was directed against the British rulers of Palestine. With the outbreak of World War II, the official Zionist leadership, stifling their anger at the 1939 White Paper, had decided to offer their services to the Allies. The further development of their own military capability, through the enrolment of Jews in British forces, was the reward they expected and secured. The *Irgun* respected this truce too; only an *Irgun* splinter, the *Stern Gang*, refused to relent.

With the end of the war, and the defeat of Fascism, the Zionists immediately began to clamour for that Jewish statehood which now revealed itself as the manifest purpose, the only true fulfilment, of all their strivings. In May 1942, some 600 delegates from Palestine, Europe and America had assembled for a kind of extraordinary World Zionist Congress in New York. Weizmann, the elder statesman, was there, but it was David Bengurion who infused the conference with the pugnacious new spirit of Palestine Jewry. The Jewish Commonwealth which the so-called Biltmore Programme demanded was, in all but name, a Jewish State; the *Yishuv* should have its own army, fighting under its own flag; the gates of Palestine should be opened to unrestricted immigration under the control of the Jewish Agency, which should also be granted the authority to build up the country and develop its unoccupied and uncultivated lands. Biltmore captured almost the whole Zionist movement. It was a moral triumph for the Revisionists. Bengurion and the moderate majority had caught up with Begin and the extremist minority. After Biltmore, the jurists duly reinterpreted the Balfour Declaration. 'The Jewish people is to have not only a home in Palestine but a national home. "National" means pertaining to a nation. . . . Logically, therefore, a national home appears to be an equivalent for State.'[5] Only a tiny, nonconformist few, moralists in the tradition of Ahad Aham, refused to be carried away. Moshe Smilansky, a veteran immigrant of the 1890s, complained that

> . . . a certain royal atmosphere has begun to impose itself upon the *Yishuv*. The first in the Zionist camp to proclaim the state as a fundamental tenet were the Revisionists—they who until the Biltmore days were, rightly, like pariahs in the Zionist movement. Formerly only the Revisionist youth were brought up in the spirit of chauvinism and militarism, which crass ignorance and

short-sightedness considered 'nationalism'. Today, however, most of our youth are brought up in this spirit. . . . The *Haganah* was a pure creation in the beginning, clean of purpose and pure of motive. But the promulgation of a 'state' and the preparations that led to it have turned the *Haganah*'s dish upside down, putting that organization in the same rank as the murderers of the *Irgun Zvai Leumi* and the *Stern* Group. Since the Biltmore days, freedom of thought and speech have been banned. Scribes have turned into 'shofars' [horns] trumpeting the slogans dictated from above. Anyone who dares to have an opinion of his own is considered a traitor. Writers of any independence have been forced to remain dumb . . .[6]

A fortnight after the end of the war in Europe, the Zionists, with Biltmore as their new canon, demanded from Churchill's coalition cabinet an immediate decision to proclaim Palestine, 'undiminished and undivided', as a Jewish State. They were told that any Palestine settlement must await a general peace conference. Two months later the Labour Party defeated Churchill and the Conservatives in a landslide victory at the polls. The Zionists naturally felt that this augured well for them, because Labour's record of devotion to their cause was a long and unblemished one. Their hopes were quickly shattered. The responsibilities of office brought the Archimedean discovery that all the theoretical, Zionist-inspired formulations of successive party congresses were completely incompatible with the Arab-dominated realities of the land to which they were supposed to be applied. To Ernest Bevin, the Foreign Secretary, fell the unhappy task of giving the discovery practical expression; he was soon to be vilified for his pains as the anti-Semite which, judging by his past record,[7] he certainly was not.

Bevin tried, in the spirit of the 1939 White Paper, to win acceptance for an independent state of Palestine that was neither Jewish nor Arab, but a marriage, in conditions of mutual respect and equality, of both. For nearly two years he refused to bow to the *diktat* of either side. It was an attempt at impartiality to which the Zionists took furious exception, for it was they, rather than the Arabs, who were now on the offensive. Bevin rejected Biltmore—and he also rejected lesser, interim demands, departures from the White Paper, whose acceptance would have blasted his credit in Arab eyes. Chief of these was the immediate admission of 100,000 refugees from war-ravaged Europe. He despatched yet another Commission of Inquiry to Palestine. This time America, now leader of the West, was invited to join in the investigations. The Commission recommended the formation, after a prolonged period of UN trusteeship, of some kind of bi-national state. This was broadly in keeping with the White Paper: the Zionists consequently rejected the proposal. It also endorsed the admission of 100,000 Jews. The Arabs would have none of that—but since, at the same time, the Zionists were called upon to disband their illegal militias, neither would they. A little later they sabotaged a proposal for Arab-Jewish provincial autonomy put forward by an Anglo-American team of experts. Bevin finally gave up the struggle. In April 1947, Britain threw the whole desperate muddle into the lap of the UN. Thereafter, the final dishonourable scuttle, behind a sanctimonious façade of reluctant compliance with international will, was only a matter of time.

It was bound to come to this. The world had changed since 1939, and Britain, victorious but enfeebled, no longer had the will or the resources to sustain the burden which Palestine had become. Of this the Zionists were well aware, and when Bevin emerged as an obstacle in their path, they determined to sweep him aside. They would enforce the end of the Mandate in their own way.

The way they chose was the quintessentially Revisionist one of violence. And just as, at Biltmore, moderates had joined extremists in proposing a common goal, so the entire Zionist movement, faced with British opposition, came together in achieving it. Violence was not, of course, the only way. Diplomacy, the speciality of Weizmann and the official leadership, was still crucial. The emergence of the American super-power was one of the new realities of the post-war world, and from now on it was in the United States rather than in Britain, the old imperial power in rapid decline, that the Zionists exerted their main leverage. Weizmann achieved his apotheosis with a demonstration that he was just as much a master of his diplomatic art on one side of the Atlantic as he was on the other. America's Jewish community, electorally pivotal and far more numerous than Britain's, had finally rallied *en masse* to the cause. The Zionists now converted this leverage, via the American ad-

ministration, into a pressure on Britain that supplemented and
far outweighed that which they exerted from their local British
constituency itself. President Truman played shamelessly for
the Jewish vote. He told American ambassadors to the Arab
world: 'I am sorry, gentlemen, but I have to answer to hundreds
of thousands who are anxious for the success of Zionism; I do not
have hundreds of thousands of Arabs among my constituents.'[8]
Time and again, he threw an obliging spanner into the delicate
machinery of Arab-Jewish conciliation which Bevin was so
laboriously trying to set in motion. He pushed for the admission of the 100,000 immigrants—blithely ignoring the sugges-
tion that, in that case, he should share responsibility, through
the despatch of American troops to Palestine, for quelling the
Arab disorders it would provoke. No sooner had the Anglo-
American experts produced their painstaking plan for provincial
autonomy than, endorsing the rival Zionist scheme, Truman
drove a coach and horses through it. Nor were America's persuasions free from the taint of economic blackmail; its gallant
war-ravaged ally could only count on its portion of American
financial aid if it behaved itself in Palestine.[9]

Violence was also coordinated with propaganda. Never slow to
make a propaganda point, the Zionists now staged one of the most
successful of all time. Among the human wreckage of Hitler's
war were some 300,000 Jewish survivors of the Holocaust. Few
of them would, of free choice, have gone to Palestine rather than
the United States or Western Europe. But they did not have that
free choice. America, in particular, denied it to them. This vast
and prosperous country, this nation of immigrants, demanded of
little Palestine that it open its doors to some 100,000 deserving
refugees. Yet, at the same time, it was only with extreme reluc-
tance that Congress agreed to admit a mere 200,000 of these self-
same remnants of the Holocaust, and especially the Jews among
them; three years were needed to persuade it to accept a bill
which, in Truman's words, 'discriminates in callous fashion
against displaced persons of the Jewish faith'.[10] No one did more
to encourage the American denial than the Zionists themselves.
Truman's predecessor had sent Morris Ernst, a Jewish lawyer,
on a mission to explore the possibilities of an international effort,
with every country taking a reasonable share of the burden, to
settle the refugee problem. Ernst recalled: 'I was amazed and

even felt insulted when active Jewish leaders decried, sneered and then attacked me as if I were a traitor. At one dinner party I was openly accused of furthering this plan for freer immigration in order to undermine political Zionism.' But that did not prevent Truman or the Zionists from demanding that the gates of Palestine be thrown open to the refugees on humanitarian grounds—Palestine which, in Truman's words, had become their 'only hope of survival'. Nor did it prevent them from reviling Britain for refusing them entry—'the small impoverished island of Great Britain' which, as Ernst testified, had 'received to date more refugees than all the other nations of the world combined'.[11]

What easier way to the hearts of ordinary, decent men and women everywhere—particularly in innocent America—than this dramatization of the immigrants' struggle to reach the Promised Land? The story of the ship *Exodus*, most famous of those cargoes of human misery finding their way to the shores of Palestine, has been glorified in book and film. When, in 1947, this creaking vessel arrived in Haifa, the British authorities refused to allow the 4,500 refugees aboard to land. The Zionists knew this would happen—for by this time the British were strictly enforcing their immigration controls—and they had everything ready to make sure the world would see it. The *Exodus* sailed back to Marseilles and, after various adventures rich in heartrending spectacle, the refugees ended up in the British zone of Germany. Newspaper readers and newsreel audiences throughout the United States followed every stage of this dismal odyssey; little did they realize that it had been deliberately provoked.

The blowing up of the King David was the high point of anti-British violence in Palestine—as devastating in its symbolic as its physical impact. It was a blow deliberately aimed at the very nerve-centre of British tyranny. It was, if not a pre-ordained, at least an eminently predictable *tour de force* of 'gun Zionism'. It was the kind of deed to which all Zionists, moderate no less than extremist, had long been ineluctably gravitating. The theorists had propounded—and justified—such courses long before the men of action had carried them out. After the 1939 White Paper, Jabotinsky had come to the conclusion that 'the only way to liberate the country is by the sword'.[12] He formu-

lated a plan for a military rebellion to be staged by the *Irgun*. In
October 1939 a boatload of 'illegal' immigrants, Jabotinsky
among them, would land in the middle of the country, if possible
Tel Aviv. The *Irgun* would secure the landing, if necessary by
force. At the same time there would be an armed insurrection in
which as many official buildings as possible—including Government House in Jerusalem—would be invested. The Jewish flag
would be raised. The positions were to be held and Jabotinsky's
capture resisted, whatever the sacrifices, for at least twenty-four
hours. During the rebellion the Provisional Government of the
Jewish State would be simultaneously proclaimed in the capitals
of Western Europe and the United States; this would subsequently function as a government-in-exile, the embodiment of
Jewish sovereignty in Palestine.[13] (The Jewish *coup d'état* was
conceived in much the same madcap spirit as another enterprise
for which Jabotinsky had been trying to win United States support: the achievement of 'a Jewish majority overnight'. He had
argued that the Zionists should 'dump into Palestine about a
million lads at once'.[14]) The *coup d'état*—so Jabotinsky's thinking
ran—was bound to be suppressed, but before it was it would
have placed the Jewish and non-Jewish world before the historic
fait accompli of proclaimed Jewish statehood. The very fact that
Jews had been able, even for twenty-four hours, to occupy the
country's key administrative strongholds would have created a
political reality that could never be erased. For Jewish sovereignty—perpetuated by the symbol of the Jewish government-
in-exile—no sacrifice was too great.

At the same time, the Arlosoroff scheme for 'revolutionary
minority rule'[15] showed that the moderate mainstream Zionist
leaders, however hotly they denied it, were instinctively drawn
towards Revisionist solutions for otherwise insoluble problems;
Arlosoroff had closely studied Curzio Malaparte's book on the
theory of insurrections in the twentieth century and what he had
in mind—to put it in that plain language which, unlike the
Revisionists, the moderates characteristically eschewed—was 'a
real putsch against the British'.[16]

The official leadership had approved of the King David operation. It may be true—as the Jewish Agency later claimed—that
the *kind* of operation which they approved, designed to achieve
a maximum physical destruction with a minimum loss of life,

was very different from the one carried out, or—as Menachim
Begin claimed—it may not. But, in accordance with the theory
of 'connected struggle', they did approve the principle. This was
the theory by which the advocates of *Havlaga* in the thirties
justified a resort to violence in the forties. The violence was
supposed to be limited and selective, confined to attacks on
obstacles which stood in what they considered to be Zionism's
legitimate path. If, for example, Haifa Radar Station were interfering with immigration, then Haifa Radar Station must be
destroyed. Railway tracks carried the trains which brought the
soldiers who hunted the immigrants; it was therefore right and
proper to blow up the railway tracks. The same principle
governed the law of retaliation. *Haganah* theorists sought to
establish a kind of mathematical relationship between 'attack'
and 'reprisal'. 'The scope of the reprisal', so the equation went,
'is equal to the magnitude of the attack.'[17]

Operation Malonchik was, in their view, a fitting reprisal to a
British provocation. Troops had occupied the offices of the
Jewish Agency. This had been done in the course of a massive
security drive which mounting Jewish violence, likewise ap-
proved or condoned, had prompted. Nevertheless, the Jewish
Agency was deemed to be the 'Jewish Headquarters'. So the
Jews must repay the British in kind, and attack them in *their*
headquarters at the King David.

The official leadership, after some hesitation, denounced the
'dissident outrage'. The death toll had been far higher than they
expected. But their denunciations had little moral worth. For it
had long been their standard practice to dissociate themselves
from operations which, under the theory of 'connected struggle',
they had approved or actually sponsored. Indeed, when British
forces invaded the Jewish Agency offices, which were fondly
imagined to enjoy some kind of protected 'international status',
they were able to take out of the very typewriter a verbatim report on the speech which Moshe Sharett, the head of the
Agency's Political Department, had delivered to the Zionist
General Council (which is why, incidentally, the destruction of
incriminating documents furnished another motive for blowing
up the King David). In this speech Sharett had praised a multiple sabotage operation carried out jointly by the *Haganah*,
Irgun and *Stern*—praise which was hard to reconcile with the

Agency's repeated protest that it knew nothing of such things.[18] In fact, the Jewish Resistance Movement, a working alliance of moderates and extremists, had come into being soon after the end of World War II. Under questioning, Bengurion was forced to admit that the Agency did nothing to suppress terrorism. 'We cannot do it because, as I told you, it is futile, sir, it is futile.' Of this excuse, Richard Crossman, an influential British champion of Zionism, said that 'he seems to want to have it both ways, to remain within the letter of the law as chairman of the Agency, and to tolerate terror as a method of bringing pressure on the Administration'.[19] Weizmann himself occasionally seemed to perceive, and abhor, the aberrations of 'gun Zionism' in action: 'If you . . . wish to secure your redemption through means . . . which do not accord with Jewish morale, with Jewish ethics or Jewish history, I say to you that you are worshipping false gods. . . . Go and re-read Isaiah, Jeremiah and Ezekiel, and test that which we do and wish to do in the light of the teachings of our great prophets and wise men. They knew the nature and character of the Jewish people. Zion will be redeemed through righteousness; and not by any other means.'[20] Yet when Crossman taxed him in private on the blowing up of the King David, Weizmann said, with tears streaming down his cheeks, 'I can't help feeling proud of our boys.'[21]

Tolerance of Zionist violence was not confined to Palestine; it permeated the United States. There, public and politicians were subjected to a propaganda *blitzkrieg* which yielded nothing, in sound and fury, to the deeds it glorified. Its message was as simple as it was tendentious. The Hebrew fighters in Palestine, it said, were rising against the self-same cruel oppressor from whom, 170 years before, the American Revolutionaries had won their freedom. It was the same patriotic war that the Irish had fought, and the Boers of South Africa. Two New York Senators felt obliged to protest directly to the British Foreign Secretary. One of them called on the United States to dissociate itself from the 'crimes' and 'the brutal imperialisms' of the British. Forgotten, in this virulent campaign, were the inestimable services which, often at great cost to themselves, those British imperialists had rendered to Zionism—forgotten the three-year Arab Rebellion which they had put down on its behalf. British Tommies, it now seemed, were not much better than Hitler's

Storm Troopers. It was a climate in which the Zionists and their
American friends could openly applaud acts of violence and
solicit funds for promoting more of them. In a 'Letter to the
Terrorists of Palestine', published in the *New York Herald
Tribune*, Ben Hecht, the Hollywood scriptwriter, assured them:

> The Jews of America are for you. You are their champion.
> You are the grin they wear. You are the feather in their hats. In
> the past fifteen hundred years, every nation of Europe has taken a
> crack at the Jews. This time the British are at bat. You are the
> first answer that makes sense—to the New World. Every time you
> blow up a British arsenal, or wreck a British jail, or send a British
> railroad train sky high, or rob a British bank, or let go with your
> guns and bombs at the British betrayers and invaders of your
> homeland, the Jews of America make a little holiday in their
> hearts. . . . Brave friends, we are working to help you. We are
> raising funds for you . . .[22]

After every performance of Hecht's Zionist 'musical', *A Flag is
Born*, thousands of dollars were handed over to the *Irgun* representatives. Eleanor Roosevelt put herself in the forefront of
the fund-raising campaign. American law prohibits the private
furnishing of arms to a foreign country, but Hecht and his
friends managed to pass off the money they raised for the terrorists as tax-free contributions to charity.[23] British protests to
the State Department about what 'amounted to an incitement to
murder British officials and soldiers in the Holy Land' achieved
nothing.

America was but the most important of sixty-four countries in
which the Zionists operated. In France, for example, they commanded sympathy, as in America, through the exploitation of a
traditional strain of anti-British sentiment. Several editorial
writers on famous newspapers like *Le Figaro* and *Combat* were
members of the French League for a Free (Zionist) Palestine and
even the judicious and serious *Le Monde* was said to discern 'the
justice and strength of *Irgun*'s fight against Great Britain'.[24]

It was hardly surprising that the country which least appre-
ciated Zionist violence was Britain. Since the beginning of the
Mandate British soldiers and administrators arriving in Palestine
with neutral or pro-Zionist sentiments tended, through direct
contact with both sides, to acquire pro-Arab ones. 'Gun Zionism'
naturally accelerated and deepened such conversions. There have

been some grudging Zionist acknowledgements that, on the whole, British troops, rough and contemptuous though they often were, behaved with a discipline that few other armies would have managed in the circumstances. Nevertheless, there were disreputable episodes in which police and soldiers took private vengeance on the Jews. Mosleyite tendencies made themselves felt.[25] A court-martial was less than zealous in the prosecution of a Major Farran, acquitting him on a charge of beating to death a sixteen-year-old suspected *Stern Gang* member.

The sentiment communicated itself to the mother country. The Foreign Secretary, Ernest Bevin, had become passionately anti-Zionist. The press described Begin's 'Hebrew fighters' as terrorists and thugs. A proverbially tolerant society—wrote an American Jewish magazine[26]—was growing resentful not only of the Jews of Palestine, but also of the Jews of Britain, who were felt to be in some kind of sympathy with these foreigners who were shooting British Tommies in cold blood. There were anti-Jewish outbursts. Police had to guard synagogues. When Major Farran sailed into Liverpool a crowd of thousands thronged the docks to welcome him.

The first emotional response to Zionist violence was anger—and a natural desire to strike back. That should have been quite feasible. Britain had 100,000 troops in Palestine. The second, and eventually decisive, response was the desire to have done with the whole wretched business. 'Govern or Get Out', screamed a *Sunday Express* headline the morning after sixteen synchronized terrorist actions throughout Palestine had left a score of armoured vehicles destroyed and eighty soldiers dead and wounded. In the House of Commons, Winston Churchill, now the Leader of the Opposition, conceded that 'the claims and the desires of the Zionists latterly went beyond anything that was agreed upon by the Mandatory power', but the thing to do now was 'to lay our Mandate at the feet of the United Nations Organization and thereafter evacuate the country with which we have no connection or tradition and where we have no sovereignty as in India and no treaty as in Egypt . . .'[27] He berated the government for 'keeping one hundred thousand Englishmen away' from home in a 'squalid' war 'at a cost of £30 to £40 million a year'. Britain's diminishing resources were being squandered on a 'vast apparatus of protraction and delay'.[28] This was the impulse on which the

Zionists counted. Originating in public opinion, taken up by the
Opposition, it was bound, before long, to animate the hard-
pressed post-war Labour Government itself. The war-weary
British deeply resented the loss of yet more young lives in a
costly colonial war against an enemy as ruthless as he was ungrateful. Operation Malonchik was the Zionists' greatest coup.
But they also blew up bridges, mined roads, derailed trains and
sunk patrol boats. Day after day they attacked barracks and installations. They raided armouries and robbed pay vans. They
blew up twenty warplanes on closely guarded airfields in a single
night. They staged what the British press called the 'greatest
jail-break in history'. *Irgun* and *Stern* were ready to do anything,
anywhere. They blew up the British embassy in Rome. They
despatched letter-bombs to British ministers, and one addressed
to Major Farran killed his brother by mistake. They sent an
assassination squad into Britain, with the mission—which was
not accomplished—of executing the former commanding officer
in Palestine, General Evelyn Barker; its members included
Weizmann's own nephew, Ezer Weizmann, one of the architects
of the Israeli air force. They planned to sink a British passenger
ship in Shanghai and a destroyer in Portsmouth.[29] In Palestine
they killed soldiers in their sleep. They captured and flogged
officers; then they hanged two sergeants from a tree and booby-
trapped their dangling corpses. It was too much.

British war-weariness meant that, faced with Jewish rebellion,
the Mandatory authorities did quite the opposite of what they
had done, ten years earlier, in response to an Arab rebellion.
Field Marshal Montgomery, the Chief of the Imperial General
Staff, bitterly reproached the government for tying the hands of
his soldiers, for the 'completely gutless' tactics they were
obliged to adopt. 'The only way the army could stamp out
terrorism was to take the offensive against it, and this was not
allowed.' It had surrendered the initiative to the terrorists. He,
too, concluded that 'if we were not prepared to maintain law and
order in Palestine it would be better to get out'.[30] Thus it came
about that while, in the late thirties, 20,000 soldiers broke the
military power of a million Arabs, in the late forties 600,000
Jews, admittedly an altogether more formidable force than the
Arabs, enforced the humiliating withdrawal of 100,000 soldiers.

It was more than just fatigue, a loss of imperial will, more than

just overwhelming American pressure that generated such a
partisan spirit. This was also rooted in the pro-Zionist traditions
of the ruling establishment—traditions that were nowhere
stronger, in spite of Bevin, than in the Labour Party. Even now,
as British troops did battle with 'gun Zionism', Weizmann and
his friends continued to enjoy that easy access to the centres of
power from which they had profited so handsomely in the
twenties and thirties. One startling illustration will suffice. John
Strachey was the Under-Secretary of State for Air in the Attlee
Administration. His biographer records that

> Only on Palestine did Strachey have any serious dispute with
> the government. One day, Crossman, now in the House of
> Commons, came to see Strachey. The former was devoting his
> efforts to the Zionist cause. He had heard from his friends in the
> Jewish Agency that they were contemplating an act of sabotage,
> not only for its own purpose, but to demonstrate to the world
> their capacities. Should this be done, or should it not? Few
> would be killed. But would it help the Jews? Crossman asked
> Strachey for his advice, and Strachey, a member of the Defence
> Committee of the Cabinet, undertook to find out. The next day
> in the Smoking Room at the House of Commons, Strachey gave
> his approval to Crossman. The *Haganah* went ahead and blew up
> all the bridges over the Jordan. No one was killed, but the British
> army in Palestine were cut off from their lines of supply with
> Jordan.[31]

In the opinion of Christopher Mayhew, a former Labour MP,
this was but a particularly flagrant example of a pattern of behaviour which would normally be considered scandalous, if not
positively treasonable, and certainly inconceivable in any other
context than that of Zionism.

> At a time when the hard-pressed British army in Palestine is
> struggling to uphold the policy of the British [Labour] Govern-
> ment against attacks mounted by Zionist terrorists, a [Labour]
> Member of Parliament who supports the Zionists feels free to
> approach a Minister and ask him whether to encourage a specific
> terrorist action *against the British army in Palestine*. Most
> astonishing of all is the fact that the Minister, who is actually a
> member of the government's Defence Committee, gives his
> 'approval' for the action, which mercifully (and against the ex-
> pectations of those who had planned it, and presumably of the

MP and the Minister as well) caused no loss of life, but which did aggravate the difficult and dangerous situation of the British army in Palestine.[32]

On 2 April 1947, Sir Alexander Cadogan, the British representative at the UN, requested that the question of Palestine be put before that year's session of the General Assembly, which Britain would then ask 'to make recommendations . . . concerning the future government of Palestine'. On 29 November, the Assembly voted for the creation, within a partitioned Palestine, of a Jewish State. Britain subsequently announced that it would terminate the Mandate on 15 May 1948, by which date all its forces in Palestine would have been withdrawn.

'Gun Zionism' had driven out the British. Begin had no doubt about it: it was the hanging of Sergeants Paice and Martin in a eucalyptus grove near Natanya which gave the final push. But for 'this grim act of retaliation' which the execution of two terrorists had 'forced upon' the *Irgun*, a foreign power would be ruling in Palestine to this day. And the moral argument is reinforced by a historical aphorism which is quintessential Begin: 'When a nation re-awakens, its finest sons are prepared to give their lives for its liberation. When Empires are threatened with collapse they are prepared to sacrifice their non-commissioned officers.'[33] 'Gun Zionism' had driven out the British—but there still remained the Arabs.

DRIVING OUT THE ARABS

Kfar Sha'ul is an outer suburb of modern Jerusalem, not far from the highway that sweeps down to Tel Aviv and the coastal plain. It is the site of the Government Hospital for Mental Diseases, but, apart from that, there is nothing remarkable about Kfar Sha'ul. Yet it once had a very different appearance. Indeed, in 1948, it was an Arab, not a Jewish community, which clung to that rocky promontory. Its 400 inhabitants had a particular way of life; they were masons who worked a nearby quarry. Otherwise, however, the village was as typical, with its honey-coloured stone houses, of Arab Palestine as Kfar Sha'ul is typical of Jewish Palestine today. The story of its metamorphosis is the story of 'gun Zionism' at its cruellest. The Arab village has vanished. No

map records it. But it remains indelibly printed in a hundred
million Arab minds as the most emotive slogan of an unending
struggle. Its name was Deir Yassin.

In 1948 Deir Yassin had a particularly peaceable reputation.
For months, as Arab-Jewish clashes intensified throughout the
country, it had lived 'in a sort of agreement' with neighbouring
Jewish settlements;[34] it was practically the only village in the
Jerusalem area not to complain to the Arab authorities that it
was in danger; it had on occasion collaborated with the Jewish
Agency;[35] it was said by a Jewish newspaper to have driven out
some Arab militants.[36] On the night of 9 April 1948, the villagers
went to sleep, as usual, in the comforting knowledge that they
were among the least likely of Jewish targets. Just as a precaution,
however, and in accordance with ancient custom, the village
elders had appointed a score of night watchmen. These sported a
few old Mausers and Turkish muskets whose main function, till
then, had been the shooting of rabbits and the furnishing of a
noisy backdrop for village weddings and feasts.[37]

At 4.30 the following morning, a combined force of *Irgun* and
Stern, 132 strong, descended on the sleeping village. By noon
they had slaughtered two-thirds of the inhabitants. For this
operation, as for the blowing up of the King David, the *Irgun*
was acting in collaboration with the *Haganah* and the official
Jewish leadership.

'I wish to point out that the capture of Deir Yassin and holding
it is one stage in our general plan.' So ran the letter, quickly made
public by the *Irgun*, in which the Jerusalem commander of the
Haganah had outlined his interest in the affair. 'I have no objection to your carrying out the operation provided you are able to
hold the village . . . if foreign forces enter the place this will
upset our plans for establishing an airfield.'[38] The raiders called
it 'Operation Unity', for not only had *Irgun* and *Stern* joined
forces, *Haganah* had made its contribution too. It had furnished
weapons, and a unit of the *Palmach*, the *Haganah*'s élite commando forces, was to play some part in the actual fighting—
supplying covering fire according to its own account,[39] demolishing the Mukhtar's house with a two-inch mortar according to
the *Irgun*.[40]

Although it took place on the very edge of Palestine's biggest
city, very few people, apart from its perpetrators and surviving

victims, actually witnessed the massacre or its immediate aftermath. The perpetrators did not consider it an atrocity at all;
people who did had fallen for 'lying propaganda' designed to
besmirch their name. According to Begin, his men had fought a
clean fight against fierce resistance; they had sought 'to avoid a
single unnecessary casualty'; and, by using a loudspeaker to
warn all women, children and old men to take refuge in the hills
they had deprived themselves, in a spirit of humanity, of the
elements of complete surprise.[41]

It seems, however, that the loudspeaker was as ineffectual as
the claimed half-hour advance warning to the occupants of the
King David Hotel; the armoured car on which it was mounted
fell into a ditch well short of the first houses, and only the car's
crew could hear the message which it blared into the night.[42]
The surviving victims certainly told a very different story, although, mostly women and children, they were apparently very
reluctant to tell it at all to the British police who interrogated
them. Twelve-year-old Fahimi Zidan survived the first mass
killing of about thirty-five villagers. He recalled: 'The Jews
ordered all our family to line up against the wall and they started
shooting us. I was hit in the side, but most of us children were
saved because we hid behind our parents. The bullets hit my
sister Kadri (four) in the head, my sister Sameh (eight) in the
cheek, my brother Mohammad (seven) in the chest. But all the
others with us against the wall were killed: my father, my
mother, my grandfather and grandmother, my uncles and aunts
and some of their children.' Halim Eid saw 'a man shoot a bullet
into the neck of my sister Salhiyeh who was nine months preg-
nant'. Then he cut her stomach open with a butcher's knife. She
said that another woman, Aisha Radwan, was killed trying to
extract the unborn infant from the dead mother's womb. In
another house, Naaneh Khalil, sixteen, saw a man take 'a kind of
sword and slash my neighbour Jamil Hish from head to toe then
do the same thing on the steps to my house to my cousin Fathi'.
The attackers killed, looted, and finally they raped. They dynamited the houses; and when the dynamite ran out they systematically worked through the remaining buildings with Sten
guns and grenades. By noon they had despatched 254 people; as
for their own casualties, what Begin described as 'murderous'
fire from the old Mausers and muskets had cost them four dead.

To one of his reports, the British interrogating officer, Assistant-Inspector General Richard Catling, appended this comment:

> On 14th April at 10 a.m. I visited Silwan village accompanied by a doctor and a nurse from the Government Hospital in Jerusalem and a member of the Arab Women's Union. We visited many houses in this village in which approximately some two to three hundred people from Deir Yassin are housed. I interviewed many of the womenfolk in order to glean some information on any atrocities committed in Deir Yassin but the majority of those women are very shy and reluctant to relate their experiences especially in matters concerning sexual assault and they need great coaxing before they will divulge any information. The recording of statements is hampered also by the hysterical state of of the women who often break down many times whilst the statement is being recorded. There is, however, no doubt that many sexual atrocities were committed by the attacking Jews. Many young school girls were raped and later slaughtered. Old women were also molested. One story is current concerning a case in which a young girl was literally torn in two. Many infants were also butchered and killed. I also saw one old woman who gave her age as one hundred and four who had been severely beaten about the head with rifle butts. Women had bracelets torn from their arms and rings from their fingers, and parts of some of the women's ears were severed in order to remove earrings.[43]

One of the outsiders who did witness this terrible event waited twenty-four years before he allowed the account he made of it to see the light of day. On 9 April Meir Pa'el, then a young *Palmach* commando, had 'set down what he saw with his own eyes and what he heard with his own ears in the report which he sent at the time to Israel Galili (subsequently Minister of State), the head of the *Haganah* command'.

> It was noon when the battle ended and the shooting stopped. Things had become quiet, but the village had not surrendered. The *Etzel* [*Irgun*] and *Lehi* [*Stern*] irregulars left the places in which they had been hiding and started carrying out cleaning up operations in the houses. They fired with all the arms they had, and threw explosives into the houses. They also shot everyone they saw in the houses, including women and children—indeed the commanders made no attempt to check the disgraceful acts of slaughter. I myself and a number of inhabitants begged the commanders to give orders to their men to stop shooting, but our

efforts were unsuccessful. In the meantime some twenty-five men
had been brought out of the houses: they were loaded into a
freight truck and led in a 'victory parade', like a Roman triumph,
through to Mhaneh Yahuda and Zakhron Yosef quarters [of
Jerusalem]. At the end of the parade they were taken to a stone
quarry between Giv'at Sha'ul and Deir Yassin and shot in cold
blood. The fighters then put the women and children who were
still alive on a truck and took them to the Mandelbaum Gate.[44]

The other witness risked his life to learn the truth about
Deir Yassin. The Jewish Agency refused to render any assistance
to Jacques de Reynier, head of the International Red Cross delegation in Palestine, in his efforts to investigate the massacre.
They did not expect him, unassisted, to come back alive from
Irgun-controlled territory. But, more through good luck than any
precautions he took, this courageous man did come back—
eventually to record the grisly experience in his memoirs of the
war:

> . . . the Commander of the *Irgun* detachment did not seem willing
> to receive me. At last he arrived, young, distinguished, and per-
> fectly correct, but there was a peculiar glitter in his eyes, cold
> and cruel. According to him the *Irgun* had arrived 24 hours
> earlier and ordered the inhabitants by loudspeaker to evacuate all
> houses and surrender: the time given to obey the order was a
> quarter of an hour. Some of these miserable people had come for-
> ward and were taken prisoners, to be released later in the direction
> of the Arab lines. The rest, not having obeyed the order, had met
> the fate they deserved. But there was no point in exaggerating
> things, there were only a few dead, and they would be buried as
> soon as the 'cleaning up' of the village was over. If I found any
> bodies, I could take them, but there were certainly no wounded.
> This account made my blood run cold.
> I went back to the Jerusalem road and got an ambulance and a
> truck that I had alerted through the Red Shield. . . . I reached the
> village with my convoy, and the Arab firing stopped. The gang was
> wearing country uniforms, with helmets. All of them were young,
> some even adolescents, men and women, armed to the teeth:
> revolvers, machine-guns, hand grenades, and also cutlasses in
> their hands, most of them still blood-stained. A beautiful young
> girl, with criminal eyes, showed me hers still dripping with blood;
> she displayed it like a trophy. This was the 'cleaning up' team,
> that was obviously performing its task very conscientiously.

I tried to go into a house. A dozen soldiers surrounded me, their machine-guns aimed at my body, and their officer forbade me to move. The dead, if any, would be brought to me, he said. I then flew into one of the most towering rages of my life, telling these criminals what I thought of their conduct, threatening them with everything I could think of, and then pushed them aside and went into the house.

The first room was dark, everything was in disorder, but there was no one. In the second, amid disembowelled furniture and covers and all sorts of debris, I found some bodies cold. Here, the 'cleaning up' had been done with machine-guns, then hand grenades. It had been finished off with knives, anyone could see that. The same thing in the next room, but as I was about to leave, I heard something like a sigh. I looked everywhere, turned over all the bodies, and eventually found a little foot, still warm. It was a little girl of ten, mutilated by a hand grenade, but still alive . . . everywhere it was the same horrible sight . . . there had been 400 people in this village; about fifty of them had escaped and were still alive. All the rest had been deliberately massacred in cold blood for, as I observed for myself, this gang was admirably disciplined and only acted under orders.

After another visit to Deir Yassin I went back to my office where I was visited by two gentlemen, well-dressed in civilian clothes, who had been waiting for me for more than an hour. They were the commander of the *Irgun* detachment and his aide. They had prepared a paper that they wanted me to sign. It was a statement to the effect that I had been very courteously received by them, and obtained all the facilities I had requested, in the accomplishment of my mission, and thanking them for the help I had received. As I showed signs of hesitation and even started to argue with them, they said that if I valued my life, I had better sign immediately. The only course open to me was to convince them that I did not value my life in the least . . .[45]

The 'victory' at Deir Yassin—as the Irgunists called it at a press conference[46] had immense repercussions. Begin described them:

Arab headquarters at Ramallah broadcast a crude atrocity story, alleging indiscriminate massacre by *Irgun* troops of about 240 men, women and children in Deir Yassin. The official Zionist bodies, apprehensive of the *Irgun*'s growing strength and popular support, eagerly seized upon this Arab accusation and, without even trying to check their veracity, accepted them at their face value and bestirred themselves to denounce and smear the *Irgun*. This combined Arab-Zionist *Greuelpropaganda* produced, however, unexpected and momentous consequences. Arabs throughout the country, induced to believe wild tales of '*Irgun* butchery', were seized with limitless panic and started to flee for their lives. This mass flight soon developed into a maddened, uncontrollable stampede. Of the about 800,000 Arabs who lived on the present territory of the State of Israel, only some 165,000 are still there. The political and economic significance of this development can hardly be overestimated.[47]

It is true that, just as they did after the King David incident, the official Zionist leaders publicly denounced the 'dissidents'. They were genuinely upset. Bengurion even sent a message of apology to King Abdullah. The chief Rabbi of Jerusalem excommunicated the killers.

Yet the Jewish Agency did not go beyond condemnation. 'You are swine,' the local *Haganah* commander told the 'dissidents' as his men surrounded them in the village square. But when ordered to disarm them, he refused; 'David,' he begged his superior, 'you'll bloody your name for life. The Jewish people will never forgive you.' David Shaltiel relented.[48] Three days after the massacre, the official leadership entered into formal alliance with the *Irgun*, which, while retaining its separate military structure, would henceforward fall under overall *Haganah* command. Twelve days after that the two mounted a joint attack on Haifa.

Deir Yassin fell in with official Zionist purposes. It was Herzl himself, as we have seen, who first proposed that the problem of the Arabs should be solved by their physical removal from their homeland. This was intrinsic to the whole concept of a Jewish State in Palestine. It was not the Zionists' habit to talk about it in public—or, if they did, they tended to employ Weizmann-style rhetoric ('Palestine shall be as Jewish as England is English') which, though its ultimate significance was clear enough, fell short of a precise and incriminating formulation of intent. Indeed, in the early years of settlement, they would often insist that there was no such thing as an Arab problem at all; there was therefore no incompatibility between unfulfilled Zionist ambitions and pre-existing Arab rights. In reality, the idea of a 'population transfer' was never far from their thoughts. As early as 1911 local Zionist leaders were wondering out loud whether the Arabs of Palestine could be persuaded to settle in neighbouring countries; they could buy land on the proceeds of the land they had sold in Palestine; or the Zionists could even buy it for them.[49] Clearly, however, these were utopian notions. The Arabs would not budge. So the Zionists hardened their hearts. Theirs was an all-or-nothing creed. With time, and with the consolidation of the Jewish presence in Palestine and the sense of strength it gave, the inescapable logic of Herzl's solution began to force itself upon them. Who better qualified to judge than Joseph Weitz? As the administrator responsible for Jewish colonization, he combined a dedication to the Zionist ideal with an intensely practical understanding of how it would be realized.

> Between ourselves it must be clear that there is no room for both peoples together in this country. . . . We shall not achieve our goal of being an independent people with the Arabs in this small country. The only solution is a Palestine, at least Western Palestine (west of the Jordan river) without Arabs. . . . And there is no other way than to transfer the Arabs from here to the neighbouring countries, to transfer all of them; not one village, not one tribe, should be left. . . . Only after this transfer will the country be able to absorb the millions of our own brethren. There is no other way out.

This is what Weitz confided to his diary in 1940.[50] His views were shared not merely by the Revisionists, but by the main-stream, socialist leadership. Already, in the thirties, they had begun pressing the case for a forcible transfer of the Arabs. The Peel Partition Plan recommended an 'exchange of land and population'.[51] This was at the urging of Weizmann, who had told the Colonial Secretary, William Ormsby-Gore, that 'the whole success of the scheme depended upon whether the Government genuinely did or did not wish to carry out this recommendation. The transfer could only be carried out by the British Govern-ment and not the Jews. I explained the reason why we considered the proposal of such importance.'[52] Zionist lobbying was eventually to prove so successful that, in 1944, the National Executive of the Labour Party officially adopted the idea at its annual conference. 'Palestine', it affirmed, 'surely is a case, on

human grounds and to promote a stable settlement, for a transfer
of population. Let the Arabs be encouraged to move out, as the
Jews move in.' Indeed, the lobbying was so successful that it
embarrassed the Zionists themselves. Conscious of the effect that
such a frank and extreme espousal of what were still essentially
surreptitious aims might have on liberal opinion, Weizmann was
moved to record in his memoirs: 'I remember that my Labour
friends were, like myself, greatly concerned about this proposal.
We have never contemplated the removal of the Arabs, and the
British Labourites, in their pro-Zionist enthusiasm, went far
beyond our intentions.'[53] American Zionists, characteristically,
were less reticent about a proposal from ex-President Hoover,
who called for 'engineering' the transfer of the Palestinians to
Iraq. The American Zionist Emergency Council declared that:

> The Zionist movement has never advocated the transfer of
> Palestine's Arab population . . . nevertheless when all long-
> accepted remedies seem to fail it is time to consider new ap-
> proaches. The Hoover Plan . . . represents an important new
> approach in the realization of which Zionists would be happy to
> co-operate with the great powers and the Arabs.[54]

The late 1940s threw up precisely that 'revolutionary' situation
which Chaim Arlosoroff had foreseen.[55] The United Nations, to
which a despairing Britain had handed over the whole problem,
ruled in favour of partition. That vote was a story of violence in
itself—albeit diplomatic violence—in which the United States
went to the most extraordinary lengths of backstage manipulation
on behalf of its Zionist protégés. Partition went against the
better judgement of many of those nations which cast their vote
in favour of it. America too—at least its State Department officials who knew something about the Middle East—had grave
misgivings. But the White House, which knew a good deal less,
overruled them. It sanctioned what a deeply distressed James
Forrestal, the Secretary of Defense, described as 'coercion and
duress on other nations' which 'bordered on scandal'.[56] President
Truman warned one of his secretaries that he would demand a full
explanation if nations which normally lined up with the United
States failed to do so on Palestine. Governments which opposed
partition, governments which could not make up their minds,
were swayed by the most unorthodox arguments. The Firestone

Tyre and Rubber Company, with plantations in Liberia, brought pressure to bear on the Liberian Government. It was hinted to Latin American delegates that their vote for partition would greatly increase the chances of a pan-American road project. The Philippines, at first passionately opposed to partition, ended up ignominiously in favour of it: they had too much stake in seven bills awaiting the approval of Congress. Important Americans were persuaded to 'talk' to various governments which could not afford the loss of American good will.[57]

For the Zionists the Partition Plan ranked, as a charter of legitimacy, with the Balfour Declaration which, in their view, it superseded and fulfilled. Certainly, it was a no less partisan document. Palestine comprises some 10,000 square miles. Of this, the Arabs were to retain 4,300 square miles while the Jews, who represented one-third of the population and owned some 6 per cent of the land, were allotted 5,700 square miles. The Jews also got the better land; they were to have the fertile coastal belt while the Arabs were to make do, for the most part, with the hills. Yet it was not the size of the area allotted to the Jews which pleased them—indeed, they regarded it as the 'irreducible minimum' which they could accept—it was rather the fact of statehood itself. Conversely, it was not merely the size of the area they were to lose, it was the loss of land, sovereignty and an antique heritage that angered the Arabs. The Partition Plan legitimized what had been, on any but the most partisan interpretation of the Balfour Declaration and the Mandate, illegitimately acquired. The past was, as it were, wiped out. Overnight, the comity of nations solemnly laid the foundations of a new moral order by which the Jews, the great majority of whom had been in Palestine less than thirty years, were deemed to have claims equal, indeed superior, to those of the Arabs who had lived there from time immemorial.

The Zionists graciously acquiesced in the will of the international community. This did not mean, however, that, while they acknowledged the momentous importance of their UN triumph, they were not acutely aware of its shortcomings—and determined to remedy them. The Partition Plan not only had a very tricky birth; it was in itself, as most of its UN midwives plainly said, a very curious infant. The two states, Arab and Jewish, were a very odd shape—like fighting serpents, was the apt description of an earlier such scheme. Demographically, they were even odder, or at least the proposed Jewish State was; for, at the outset at any rate, it was to contain more Arabs—509,780 —than Jews—499,020. If the frontiers of Israel were a strategist's nightmare, this Arab majority, a ready-made fifth column, was an even greater threat. Moreover, it was an affront to fundamental dogma; could such a hybrid be called a truly Jewish State —as Jewish as England was English? The Jews were to be confined to but a part of the Land of Their Ancestors; indeed, they were to enjoy only a fettered presence, or none at all, in those places, such as Jerusalem and Hebron, to which they were most sentimentally attached.

The UN had been illogical; the creature which it brought forth was vigorous, but the conditions imposed upon it almost denied it the means of survival. The creature was bound to grow, to throw off its crippling handicaps, to achieve its full Zionist stature. Israel, more than any other nation, is the child of the UN; it is therefore ironic, though in no way surprising, that it was to prove such a delinquent child, with a unique record of censure by the organization which gave it birth.

The Zionists acquiesced in the sure knowledge that the Arabs would not. The Arabs were bound to oppose their own dispossession. Had they not mounted a full-scale rebellion against the mini-partition of Peel? Besides, they were in no sense obliged to accept what after all was only a 'recommendation' of the UN General Assembly. Yet it was this latest manifestation of the celebrated 'Arab refusal' which furnished the Zionists with the opportunity to remedy the shortcomings of the Partition Plan— and to do it without incurring the world's displeasure. For, in the eyes of the world, attempts to oppose its will by the only remaining means—force—became 'Arab aggression' while the Jewish attempts to uphold it were legitimate self-defence. Who was to hold it against them if, in the course of defending themselves, the Zionists went a little beyond the limits of what the UN had assigned them?

It did not matter if the Arab threat was a serious one or not. For propaganda purposes, it was the appearance of a threat that counted. And the actual threat, as they well knew, was far less serious than it looked. The unpreparedness of the Palestinian community was pathetic. The British had smashed their military potential in the 1930s; they had kept them disarmed ever

since. They had prevented the re-emergence of such effective
political leadership as they had ever enjoyed; only in 1946 was
the Arab Higher Committee legalized again; the Mufti was
exiled to the end. At the beginning of 1948 the Palestinians could
muster some 2,500 riflemen; not only was this derisory force
poorly trained, it lacked logistical support, and operated as a
collection of separate regional units without centralized command and subject to the vagaries of remote and often divided
politica' ontrol. In 1947 the total strength of the rural garrisons
in the key area of Jerusalem was twenty-five rifles. If there was
a threat it came from outside Palestine. The Arab Liberation
Army, hastily put together after the partition vote, mustered
3,830 volunteers under the command of Fawzi al-Kawekji—at
least 1,000 of them Palestinians—who began their gradual entry
into Palestine in January 1948. The forces which five Arab
states despatched to Palestine on 15 May 1948—after the proclamation of the State of Israel—numbered some 15,000 men;
their heaviest armour consisted of twenty-two light tanks; they
could put up ten Spitfires.[58]

By 15 May Zionist forces included some 30,000 fully mobilized
regular troops, at least 32,000 second-line troops, who, normally
confined to regional or static defence, could be attached to the
regulars as occasion arose, some 15,000 Jewish settlement police,
a home guard of 32,000—plus the well-armed and highly aggressive 'dissident' forces of *Irgun* (3,000 to 5,000 in 1946) and *Stern*
(200 to 300). Not only was this force better trained, it was far
better equipped than the combined Arab armies. If there were
any doubts about the outcome of a struggle for Palestine, they
were not shared in a quarter that was particularly well qualified
to judge. The opinions expressed as early as 1946 by the commander of the British forces in Palestine, General J. C. D'Arcy,
were soldierly, crisp and accurate.

> We discussed with him what could happen if British troops
> were withdrawn from Palestine. 'If you were to withdraw British
> troops, the *Haganah* would take over all Palestine to-morrow,'
> General D'Arcy replied flatly. 'But could the *Haganah* hold
> Palestine under such circumstances?' I asked. 'Certainly,' he
> said. 'They could hold it against the entire Arab world.'[59]

There was also the question of intent. Of course the Arab states would, if they could, have stifled the Jewish State in embryo. Indeed, much fatuous confidence was publicly expressed, though perhaps not felt, that they would do so. Musa Alami, a distinguished Palestinian, went on a tour of the Arab capitals to discover what kind of help his people were likely to get from their Arab brethren. He found that the Arab leadership, directly confronted with the ever-expanding 'Zionist peril', was no better equipped to cope with it than the Palestinian leadership had been when it was alone in the field.

His first stop, in Damascus, gave him a foretaste of what he was to find everywhere.

> 'I am happy to tell you', the Syrian President assured him, 'that our Army and its equipment are of the highest order and well able to deal with a few Jews, and I can tell you in confidence that we even have an atomic bomb'; and seeing Musa's expression of incredulity, he went on, 'yes, it was made locally; we fortunately found a very clever fellow, a tinsmith . . .' Elsewhere he found equal complacency, and ignorance which was little less crass. In Iraq he was told by the Prime Minister that all that was needed was 'a few brooms' to drive the Jews into the sea; by confidants of Ibn Saud in Cairo, that 'once we get the green light from the British we can easily throw out the Jews . . .'[60]

The Arab peoples were led to believe that their armies would have a walkover in Palestine. 'If the Arabs do not win the war against the Jews in an outright offensive you may hang all their leaders and statesmen,'[61] said Azzam Pasha, the Secretary General of the Arab League. The outside world, ignorant of the realities on the ground, was understandably none too sanguine about the chances for 600,000 Jews, pitted against 40 million Arabs. Yet the truth was that—in so far as the Arab governments, jealous, divided and incompetent, had any common policies at all—they tended towards moderation. The country with the best army, Transjordan, had made it clear that it would scrupulously observe the UN Partition Plan; it would occupy and defend that part of Palestine assigned to the Arab State, but not a foot more. As for the others they were still fundamentally thinking in terms of diplomatic solutions. This is admitted by the Zionists themselves. Thus on 19 March, *Haganah* radio broadcast that the Arab governments had reached full agreement on a plan, believed to be a moderate one, providing for the establishment of some

kind of Arab-Jewish federal system in Palestine. In the realm of
practical planning, the Arab Chiefs of Staff had their first conference only at the end of April; the decision to send in regular
armies was not taken until early May—and that was a decision
which, as late as 12 May, Egypt was still hesitating to act upon.
Thus it may have been the Arabs who cried havoc, but it was the
Zionists who, their enemies aiding, systematically wrought it.

The rise of the State of Israel—in frontiers larger than those
assigned to it under the Partition Plan—and the flight of the
native population was a cataclysm so deeply distressing to the
Arabs that to this day they call it, quite simply, *al-Nakba*,
the Catastrophe. The Zionists subsequently contended that the
Arabs brought this misfortune upon themselves, for it was they
who chose to invade the newborn state in defiance of the international community. Moreover, when it comes to the all-
important question of the Palestinian refugees, the Zionists pro-
fess that their consciences are equally clear, for it was not they
who drove them out, but their own leaders who ordered them to
flee.

The Zionist version of the Palestinian exodus is a myth manufactured after the cataclysm took place. If the Zionists could
show that the refugees had really fled without cause, at the
express instructions of their own politicians, they would greatly
erode the world's sympathy for their plight—and, in consequence, the pressure on themselves to allow them to return.
Thus in public speeches and scholarly-looking pamphlets they
peddled this myth the world over. It was not until 1959 that the
Palestinian scholar, Walid Khalidi, exposed it for what it is. His
painstaking researches were independently corroborated by an
Irish scholar, Erskine Childers, two years later. Together, they
demonstrated that the myth was not just a gross misrepresenta-
tion of accepted or even plausible facts; the very 'facts' themselves had been invented. Orders for the evacuation of the
civilian population had not simply been issued, the Zionists said,
they had been broadcast over Arab radio stations. One had come
from the Mufti himself. This was the cornerstone of the Zionist
case. Yet when these two scholars took the trouble to examine
the record—to go through the specially opened archives of
Arab governments, contemporary Arabic newspapers and the
radio monitoring reports of both the BBC and the CIA—they

found that no such orders had been issued, let alone broadcast, and that when challenged to produce chapter-and-verse evidence, the date and origin of just one such order, the Zionists, with all the apparatus of the State of Israel now at their disposal, were quite unable to do so. They found, on the contrary, that Arab and Palestinian authorities had repeatedly called on the people to stay put and that the Arab radio services had consistently belittled the true extent of Zionist atrocities. Indeed, it appears that, if anything, they expected of the civilian population, helpless before the Zionist onslaught, a much greater fortitude than they legitimately should have. Far from urging his people to flee, the Mufti was so alarmed at the incipient exodus that he sent this cable to one of his staff: 'The emigration of children and others from Palestine to Syria is detrimental to our interest. Contact the proper authorities in Damascus and Beirut to prevent it . . .'[62] Arab governments took steps forcibly to repatriate able-bodied Palestinians who had left the country, and Arab newspapers grew positively insulting about them. All this was corroborated by the Zionist radio services themselves. From time to time they carried reports of Arab efforts to prevent an exodus; when the exodus took place they duly reported it without mention of evacuation orders, and even when they came to refuting Arab claims that the Palestinians had been physically driven from their homes, they used all manner of argument except the one in question.

It was only a year later, when the refugee problem was beginning to impinge upon the world's conscience, that the Zionists began to develop their whole *post facto* thesis. Professor Khalidi traces its first elaborate appearance to two mimeographed pamphlets—almost certainly the work of Joseph Schechtman, the *Irgun*-Revisionist biographer of Jabotinsky—which were disseminated by the Israeli Information Office in New York and subsequently incorporated in a memorandum submitted by nineteen prominent Americans, including the poet Macleish and Niebuhr the theologian, to the UN. What is truly remarkable about this edifice of deceit, which has profoundly influenced Western opinion, is not merely that the Zionists were able to construct it from such unpromising materials, but that it stood solid and four-square for so long. There is no better example of the way in which Western, particularly American, opinion, pre-

judiced and ill-informed, has automatically tended to accept the
Zionist side of the story—and, it must also be said, no better
example of the ineptitude with which the Arabs have presented
their case. The edifice, though crumbling, has not yet collapsed.
For Zionist propagandists, with all the perversity of flat-earthers
but none of their innocent eccentricity, are struggling to prop it
up till this day.[63]

Deir Yassin was, as Begin rightly claims, the most spectacular
single contribution to the Catastrophe. In time, place and method
it demonstrates the absurdity of the subsequently constructed
myth. The British insisted on retaining juridical control of the
country until the termination of their Mandate on 15 May; it
was not until they left that the regular Arab armies contemplated
coming in. But not only did Deir Yassin take place more than
five weeks *before* that critical date, it also took place *outside* the
area assigned to the Jewish State. It was in no sense a retaliatory
action. There had been violence from the Palestinians, but
neither in scale nor effectiveness had it matched that of the
Zionists themselves. It was also true that the British had turned
a semi-blind eye to the infiltration of Fawzi al-Kawekji's Arab
Liberation Army, and it did score some initial successes. But by
April, overstretched and wretchedly supplied, it was already
falling back in disarray.

In reality, Deir Yassin was an integral part of *Plan Dalet*, the
master-plan for the seizure of most or all of Palestine. In the
first phase of the military campaign that followed the partition
'recommendation', the Zionists, their forces not yet fully mobilized, contented themselves with a holding operation in which
they simultaneously 'softened up' the Palestinians, engaged such
fighting men as they did possess, and undermined, through
terror, the morale of the civilian population. That was the essence
of *Plan Gimmel*. Nothing was officially disclosed about *Plan
Dalet*, *Gimmel*'s successor, when it went into effect on 1 April,
although Bengurion was certainly alluding to it in an address, six
days later, to the Zionist Executive: 'Let us resolve not to be
content with merely defensive tactics, but at the right moment to
attack all along the line and not just within the confines of the
Jewish State and the borders of Palestine, but to seek out and
crush the enemy where-ever he may be.'[64] This discretion has
persisted long after the event. Zionist histories of the 'war of

independence' abound. But most of them, especially those
written for Western consumption, hardly even mentioned *Plan
Dalet*, or, if they do, they fail to give it the central importance it
deserves. Some Hebrew accounts are franker. We learn from
them that as early as 1942—the year of the Biltmore Programme
and the espousal of Jewish statehood as the official Zionist goal—
the military planners were already working on the broad conception.[65] By 1947 they had mapped and catalogued information
about every village, its strategic character and the quality of its
inhabitants in Palestine.[66] According to *Qurvot (Battles) of 1948*,[67]
a detailed history of the *Haganah* and the *Palmach*, the aim of
Plan Dalet was 'control of the area given to us by the UN in
addition to areas occupied by us which were outside these
borders and the setting up of forces to counter the possible invasion of Arab armies'. It was also designed to 'cleanse' such
areas of their Arab inhabitants. In this way the Zionists would
expand the 'irreducible minimum' which the UN had granted
them, and make their state as large and Jewish as possible before
the Arab armies could stop them, and before it dawned on the
UN that its Partition Plan was unworkable. They went over to the
offensive because, in spite of the relentless harassments of *Plan
Gimmel* as well as the setbacks inflicted on the Arab irregulars,
the civilian population, or its great majority, was determined to
stay put; and because the United States, moving spirit behind
partition, was now going back on it in what Dr Silver of the
Jewish Agency described as 'a shocking reversal'[68] and the
American Jewish Congress as 'shameful tactics and duplicity'.[69]
It was Operation Nachson, designed to carve out a corridor con-
necting Tel Aviv with Jerusalem, which inaugurated *Plan Dalet*.
It entailed the destruction and evacuation of some twenty villages. One of them was Deir Yassin. Twelve other operations
were due to follow in quick succession, eight of them outside the
area allotted to the Jewish State. Some succeeded, some failed;
some were delayed beyond 15 May. Even so, by that date, the
Zionists were well on the way to overrunning the whole of
Palestine. Operation Nachson, as conceived by the *Haganah*
planners, did not require such a bloodbath. Yet it was not, in
method, the isolated episode that it has subsequently been made
out to have been. It was merely an extreme application of a
general policy. Twenty-four years after the event, the Israeli

historian Arie Yitzhaqi, author of a 1,200-page history of the war, wrote:

> If we assemble the facts, we realize that, to a great extent, the battle followed the familiar pattern of the occupation of an Arab village in 1948. In the first months of the 'War of Independence' *Haganah* and *Palmach* troops carried out dozens of operations of this kind, the method adopted being to raid an enemy village and blow up as many houses as possible in it. In the course of these operations many old people, women and children, were killed wherever there was resistance. In this connection I can mention several operations of this kind carried out by Pa'el's comrades in arms—the *Palmach* irregulars who were trained to be concerned for the 'purity of Hebrew arms'.[70]

It was a sophisticated combination of physical and psychological *blitz*, mounted by official and 'dissident' forces alike, which finally drove the Palestinians out. The *Haganah* and the *Irgun* would launch massive surprise attacks on towns and villages, bombarding them with mortars, rockets—and the celebrated Davidka. This was a home-made contraption that tossed 60 lb of TNT some 300 yards, very inaccurately, into densely populated areas.[71] There was also the 'barrel-bomb'. In an article entitled 'All's Fair . . .', written long after the event for the US Marine Corps professional magazine, an Israeli army reserve officer who fought in 1948 has given precise details of this device. It consisted of a barrel, cask or metal drum, filled with a mixture of explosives and petrol, and fitted with two old rubber tyres containing the detonating fuse. It was rolled down the sharply sloping alleys and stepped lanes of Arab urban quarters until it crashed into walls and doorways making 'an inferno of raging flames and endless explosions'.[72] At the same time, additional panic would be induced by Arabic broadcasts from the clandestine Zionist radio stations or loudspeakers mounted on armoured cars in the target areas. The broadcasts warned of the spread of dangerous epidemics, such as cholera and typhus, hinted at Arab collaboration with the enemy, threatened that 'innocent people' would pay the price for Palestinian attacks on Jews. But there was one particularly revealing theme, of which Harry Levin, a British Zionist author, furnishes an apt example: 'Nearby [in Jerusalem] a loudspeaker burst out in Arabic. *Haganah* broadcasting to civilian Arabs urging them to leave the

district before 5.15 a.m. "Take pity on your wives and children
and get out of this bloodbath. . . . Get out by the Jericho road,
this is still open to you. If you stay you invite disaster."[73] The
Israeli reserve-officer reveals just how deliberate this was. Amid
barrel-bombs, he wrote,

> . . . as uncontrolled panic spread through all Arab quarters, the
> Israelis brought up jeeps with loudspeakers which broadcast
> recorded 'horror sounds'. These included shrieks, wails, and
> anguished moans of Arab women, the wail of sirens and the clang
> or fire-alarm bells, interrupted by a sepulchral voice calling out
> in Arabic: 'Save your souls, all ye faithful: The Jews are using
> poison gas and atomic weapons. Run for your lives in the name of
> Allah.'[74]

A series of Arab towns—Tiberias, Haifa, Acre, Jaffa and much
of Arab Jerusalem—fell in quick succession before the irresistible
march of 'gun Zionism'. Some three or four hundred thousand
refugees, sometimes attacked and stripped of their remaining
possessions on the way, streamed towards the neighbouring
Arab countries. Those who were not driven into the desert
suffered a fate which, according to the Zionists, the Arabs have
had in store for them ever since; inhabitants of coastal towns
were literally 'driven into the sea'; many drowned in the scramble
for boats.

There is no better insight into the urgency and scope of *Plan
Dalet*, as the Mandate drew to a close, than the one furnished by
Yigal Allon, the principal hero of the 'War of Independence'. In
the *Book of the Palmach*, he recalls:

> There were left before us only five days, before the threatening
> date, the 15th of May. We saw a need to clean the inner Galilee
> and to create a Jewish territorial succession in the entire area
> of the upper Galilee. The long battles had weakened our forces,
> and before us stood great duties of blocking the routes of the
> Arab invasion [literally *plisha* or expansion]. We therefore
> looked for means which did not force us into employing force,
> in order to cause the tens of thousands of sulky Arabs who re-
> mained in Galilee to flee, for in case of an Arab invasion these
> were likely to strike us from the rear. We tried to use a tactic
> which took advantage of the impression created by the fall of
> Safed and the [Arab] defeat in the area which was cleaned by
> Operation Metateh—a tactic which worked miraculously well.

I gathered all of the Jewish Mukhtars, who have contact with Arabs in different villages, and asked them to whisper in the ears of some Arabs, that a great Jewish reinforcement has arrived in Galilee and that it is going to burn all of the villages of the Huleh. They should suggest to these Arabs, as their friends, to escape while there is still time. And the rumour spread in all the areas of the Huleh that it is time to flee. The flight numbered myriads. The tactic reached its goal completely. The building of the police station at Halsa fell into our hands without a shot. The wide areas were cleaned, the danger was taken away from the transportation routes and we could organise ourselves for the invaders along the borders, without worrying about the rear.[75]

For all the bluster, it was only the Catastrophe unfolding before the eyes of their peoples that finally induced the Arab governments, under irresistible pressure, to send in their armies and to salvage what they could. Belated and inept though it was, Allon conceded that without this intervention

. . . there would have been no stop to the expansion of the forces of *Haganah* who could have, with the same drive, reached the natural borders of western Israel, because in this stage most of the local enemy forces were paralyzed.[76]

Although, in the war that ensued, the ideal of an exclusively Jewish State in all of Palestine eluded them, the Zionists further consolidated their position. The war was marked by a series of UN-sponsored truces, but they took as much advantage of them as they did of the actual fighting. Announcing his government's acceptance of the first ceasefire on 10 June, Bengurion declared that

. . . our bounds are set wider, our forces multiply, we are administering public services and daily new multitudes arrive . . . . All that we have taken we shall hold. During the ceasefire, we shall organise administration with fiercer energy, strengthen our footing in town and country, speed up colonization and *Aliyah* [immigration] and look to the army.[77]

When the war ended, in early 1949, the Zionists, allotted 57 per cent of Palestine under the Partition Plan, had occupied 77 per cent of the country. Of the 1,300,000 Arab inhabitants, they had displaced nearly 900,000. They came into possession of entire cities, or entire quarters of them, and hundreds of villages.

All that was in them—farms and factories, animals and machinery, fine houses and furniture, carpets, clothes and works of art, all the goods and chattels, all the treasured family heirlooms of an ancient people—was theirs for the taking. Ten thousand shops, businesses and stores and most of the rich Arab citrus holdings —half the country's total—fell into their hands.

Chaim Weizmann, the revered elder statesman, became the first President of the State of Israel. It was fitting. To him, more than to anyone else, the Jewish State owed its existence. Yet if there could have been no Israel without Weizmann, assuredly there would not have been one without Bengurion and Begin, *Plan Dalet* and Deir Yassin either. Weizmann had sometimes deplored the excesses of 'gun Zionism'. 'In all humbleness', he told a UN committee of inquiry in 1947, *'thou shalt not kill* has been ingrained in us since Mount Sinai. It was inconceivable ten years ago that the Jews should break this commandment. Unfortunately, they are breaking it today, and nobody deplores it more than the vast majority of the Jews. I hang my head in shame when I have to speak of this fact before you.'[78] But now his scruples seemed to desert him. He who, just thirty years before, had assured the Arabs of Jaffa that it had never been anybody's intention 'to turn anyone out of his property' or 'to seize control of the higher policy of the province of Palestine', now returned, burdened with years and honour, to the Promised Land which 'gun Zionism' had made as Jewish, or almost, as England is English. 'It was', he piously declared, 'a miraculous clearing of the land: the miraculous simplification of Israel's task.'[79]

NOTES

1. Kimche, John, *Seven Fallen Pillars: The Middle East, 1915–1950*, Secker and Warburg, London, 1950, p. 171.
2. Begin, Menachim, *The Revolt*, W. H. Allen, London, 1951, p. 220.
3. *Ibid.*, p. 40.
4. *Ibid.*, p. 46.
5. *The Jewish Yearbook of International Law*, Jerusalem, 1949, p. 28.
6. *Commentary*, New York, July 1946.
7. See Bullock, Alan, *The Life and Times of Ernest Bevin: Trade Union Leader, 1881–1940*, Heinemann, London, 1960, pp. 455–7.

8. Eddy, William, *F.D.R. Meets Ibn Saud*, American Friends of the Middle East, New York, 1954, p. 36.

9. Mayhew, Christopher, and Adams, Michael, *Publish It Not*, Longmans, London, 1975, p. 18.

10. Divine, Robert A., *American Immigration Policy, 1924–1952*, Oxford University Press, London, 1957, p. 128.

11. Ernst, Morris L., *So Far So Good*, Harper and Brothers, New York, 1948, cited in Khalidi, *From Haven to Conquest*, *op. cit.*, p. 492.

12. Schechtman, *Fighter and Prophet, the Vladimir Jabotinsky Story*, *op. cit.*, p. 479.

13. *Ibid.*, pp. 483–4.

14. *Ibid.*, p. 364.

15. See pp. 98–100.

16. Schechtman, *op. cit.*, p. 484.

17. Begin, *op. cit.*, pp. 212–15.

18. *Ibid.*, p. 215.

19. Crossman, Richard, *Palestine Mission: A Personal Record*, Hamish Hamilton, London, n.d., p. 139.

20. *New Judea*, December 1946–January 1947, pp. 65–7.

21. Crossman, Richard, *A Nation Reborn, the Israel of Weizmann, Bevin and Ben Gurion*, Hamish Hamilton, London, 1960, p. 89.

22. 15 May 1947.

23. Zaar, Isaac, *Rescue and Liberation: America's Part in the Birth of Israel*, Bloch, New York, 1954, pp. 193–4, 200–3.

24. *Ibid.*, pp. 215–16.

25. Oswald Mosley led a small British fascist organization.

26. *Commentary*, May 1948.

27. *The Times*, 1 August 1946.

28. *Ibid.*, 19 February 1947.

29. Katz, Samuel, *Days of Fire*, Doubleday, New York, pp. 120–2, 178.

30. Montgomery, Bernard, *Memoirs*, World Publishing House Co., Cleveland and New York, 1958, pp. 340–1.

31. Thomas, Hugh, *John Strachey*, Eyre Methuen, London, pp. 228–9.

32. Mayhew, *op. cit.*, p. 33.

33. Begin, *op. cit.*, p. 290.

34. *New York Times* and *New York Herald Tribune*, 12 April 1948.

35. Kimche, *op. cit.*, p. 227.

36. *New Judea*, cited by Polk, William, Staller, David, and Asfour, Edward, *Backdrop to Tragedy*, New York, 1957, p. 29.

37. Lapierre, Dominique, and Collins, Larry, *O Jerusalem*, Simon and Schuster, New York, 1972, p. 272.

38. Ha-Mashkif (*Irgun* newspaper), 11 April, 1948; Begin, *op. cit.*, pp. 162–3.

39. *Palestine Post*, 13 April 1948; see also *New York Times*, 13 April 1948.

40. Katz, *op. cit.*, p. 215.

41. Begin, *op. cit.*, pp. 163–4.

42. Lapierre, *op. cit.*, p. 273.

43. *Report of the Criminal Investigation Division*, Palestine Government,

No. 179/110/17/GS, 13, 15, 16 April 1948. Cited in Lapierre, *op. cit.*, p. 276.

44. *Yediot Aharonot* (Israeli newspaper), 4 April 1972.
45. De Reynier, Jacques, *A Jérusalem un Drapeau Flottait sur la Ligne de Feu*, Editions de la Baconnière, Neuchâtel, 1950, pp. 71–6.
46. *Jewish Newsletter*, New York, 3 October 1960.
47. Begin, *op. cit.*, p. 164.
48. Lapierre, *op. cit.*, p. 280.
49. Laqueur, Walter, *A History of Zionism*, Weidenfeld and Nicolson, London, 1972, p. 231.
50. *Davar*, 29 September, 1967.
51. Peel Commission, *op. cit.*, p. 391.
52. *Jewish Chronicle*, 13 August 1937.
53. Weizmann, *Trial and Error*, *op. cit.*, p. 535.
54. *Palestine* (Zionist periodical), Vol. II, Nos. 9–10, November–December 1945, p. 16.
55. See pp. 98–100.
56. *The Forrestal Diaries*, ed. Millis, Walter, Viking Press, New York, 1952, p. 363.
57. Lilienthal, Alfred, *What Price Israel*, Henry Regnery, Chicago, 1953, pp. 60–6.
58. See Khalidi, *op. cit.*, pp. 858–60.
59. Crum, Bartley C., *Behind the Silken Curtain*, Simon and Schuster, New York, 1947, p. 220.
60. Furlonge, Geoffrey, *Palestine is my Country; the Story of Musa Alami*, John Murray, London, 1969, p. 152.
61. Public Statement, 14 May 1948.
62. Khalidi, *op. cit.*, p. 14.
63. See for example, Prittie, Terence, Dineen, Bernard, and Goodhart, Philip, *The Double Exodus*, Goodhart Press, London, 1975.
64. Bengurion, *Rebirth and Destiny*, *op. cit.*, p. 239.
65. Yadin, Yigal, Chief of Operations in the 1948 war, *Maariv* (Israeli newspaper), 6 May 1973.
66. Sacher, Harry, *Israel: The Establishment of a State*, William Clowes and Sons, 1952, p. 217.
67. See Khalidi, *op. cit.*, p. 39.
68. *New York Times*, 20 March 1948.
69. *Ibid.*, 21 March 1948.
70. *Yediot Aharonot*, 14 April 1972.
71. See Lorch, Natanel, *The Edge of the Sword*, G. P. Putnam's, New York, 1961, p. 103.
72. Heiman Leo, in *Marine Corps Gazette*, June 1964; cited in Childers, Erskine, *The Wordless Wish: from Citizens to Refugees*, in *The Palestinian Issue in Middle East Peace Efforts*, hearings before the Committee on International Relations, House of Representatives, September, October, November 1975, US Government Printing Office, 1976, p. 252.
73. Levin, Harry, *Jerusalem Embattled: A Diary of the City Under Siege*,

March 25th 1948, to July 18th, 1948, Gollancz, London, 1950, p. 160.
74. Childers, *op. cit.*, p. 253.
75. *Ha Sepher Ha Palmach*, Vol. 2, p. 286; cited in Khalidi, *op. cit.*, p. 42.
76. *Ibid.*, p. 43.
77. Bengurion, *op. cit.*, p. 274.
78. *Report of the UN Special Committee on Palestine* (UNSCOP) Document A/364, 1947, p. 77.
79. McDonald, James, *My Mission to Israel*, Simon and Schuster, New York, 1952, p. 176.

Five

Special Uses of Violence

THE ASSASSINATION OF COUNT BERNADOTTE

Israel was the child of the UN. So, on 14 May 1948, the day
before the British Mandate expired, the UN appointed a Mediator
to watch over Israel's birth, 'to use his good offices with the local
community and authorities in Palestine . . . to promote a peaceful
adjustment of the future situation in Palestine'.[1] The Zionists
could hardly complain of this initiative by a body which, in its
partition resolution, had already demonstrated such a bias in
their favour; nor could they complain about the person chosen
to carry it out.

Count Folke Bernadotte was a member of the Swedish royal
family, cousin to the King. He was an aristocrat in whom wealth
and high station had bred the need to serve his fellow men. So
had his deep Protestant convictions. And his sense of mission
was allied with great practical experience. He had made his
name as a representative of the International Red Cross in World
War II. It was he who had organized the first exchange of dis-
abled prisoners. Both sides had respected him for his integrity
and impartiality; they always granted him free access.

Although he came to Palestine with a rigorous conception of
his Mediator's role, determined to show neither fear nor favour,
he was in reality predisposed towards the Zionists. This was only
natural, for, appalled by the whole-scale Nazi massacres of Jews,
he had, on his own personal initiative, succeeded in rescuing a
surviving remnant of them—some 30,000—from the concentration camps.[2] Moreover, like most Europeans, he had an instinctive affinity with the Zionists, who were mainly Europeans
themselves. A cultural gulf lay between him and the Arabs,
whom he had never encountered before and who, he wrote,
expressed themselves in the 'elaborate and somewhat ceremonial
style characteristic of the east'.[3] Like many Europeans, too, he

was steeped in that Old Testament sentimentality which saw the
return of the Jews to the Land of Their Ancestors as a prophetic
fulfilment. His knowledge of the Palestine problem came largely
from Zionist sources. He was deeply impressed by the Zionist
claim to be making the desert bloom; in his diary he remarked
upon the 'amazing work the Jews had done in cultivating this
desert-like countryside . . . and the very sharp lines of demarca-
tion between the desert on the one hand and the fertile gardens
and orange groves on the other.'⁴ The entry was made during his
first visit to Palestine; apparently he was unaware, as he drove
along the coastal plain from Haifa to Tel Aviv, that this was the
most fertile part of the country, and that more than half of it was
still owned and cultivated by Arabs. Only too familiar with the
plight of European Jewry, Bernadotte seemed to know little
about the suffering which the Jews-as-Zionists were inflicting on
others. He was briefed by advisers who were apt to dismiss the
Palestinians as of little consequence. One such report, his diary
records, informed him that:

> The Palestinian Arabs had at present no will of their own. Neither
> have they ever developed any specifically Palestinian nationalism.
> The demand for a separate Arab state in Palestine is consequently
> relatively weak. It would seem as though in existing circumstances
> most of the Palestinian Arabs would be quite content to be in-
> corporated in Transjordn.⁵

Not surprisingly, Bernadotte was at first inclined to see not only
the problem, but its solution, through Zionist eyes. He imagined
that his new mission, like the one he had performed during
the war, would be more humanitarian than political, involving the
exchange of prisoners, the repatriation of refugees, helping the
sick, the needy and the homeless. Peace, he thought, would
eventually follow.

His arrival in Jerusalem must have come as a bewildering
shock to this representative of the organization to which Israel
owed its existence. Jeeps flying the banners of the 'Fighters for
the Freedom of Israel' (*Stern Gang*) careered around the city,
warning him that 'Stockholm is yours. Jerusalem is ours. You
work in vain. We are here . . . so long as there is a single enemy
of our cause, we shall have a bullet in a magazine for him.'⁶ On
17 September the *Stern Gang* killed him. But in the intervening

four months it had been the whole Zionist community, the official representatives of the infant State of Israel, who, blow by blow, shattered his vision of a Palestine at peace with itself.

The Mediator's first task was to arrange a month's truce during which he could formulate proposals for a peaceful settlement. On 11 June, after a week of gruelling effort, Bernadotte persuaded Jews and Arabs to accept an unconditional ceasefire.

On 28 June, after intensive consultations with both sides, he put forward what he called a 'possible basis for discussion'. This included specific territorial recommendations, most of them favourable to the Arabs, revising the boundaries envisaged by the UN Partition Plan. But Bernadotte's main concern was the hundreds of thousands of Arab refugees whose misery, in their makeshift camps, he had seen with his own eyes. Their plight, he later told the UN, was the greatest obstacle to peace.

> It is, however, undeniable that no settlement can be just and complete if recognition is not accorded to the rights of the Arab refugee to return to the home from which he has been dislodged by the hazards and strategy of the armed conflict between Arabs and Jews in Palestine. . . . It would be an offence against the principles of elemental justice if these innocent victims of the conflict were denied the right to return to their homes while Jewish immigrants flow into Palestine, and, indeed, at least offer the threat of permanent replacement of the Arab refugees who have been rooted in the land for centuries.[7]

On 1 July, he got word of the Israeli response from his representative in Tel Aviv, who reported that the Foreign Minister, Moshe Sharett, was ready to go to Rhodes to continue negotiations provided that the Arabs also accepted the Mediator's invitation.

A breakthrough? Bernadotte believed so, and wrote enthusiastically in his diary: 'It is perhaps not difficult to imagine my joy when I read Reedman's communication. . . . This was a wonderful piece of news. It meant that the Jews accepted my proposals in principle.'[8]

At first, the Arabs' response—collectively made through the Arab League—was less encouraging. From his sources in Cairo Bernadotte had learned that 'the Arab attitude was negative in the extreme'.[9] But on 3 July he flew to Cairo himself and came away somewhat reassured from meetings with Arab representatives. The Arabs, he realized, were not ready for direct negotiations with the Israelis in Rhodes; nevertheless, he 'did not feel in the least disappointed': he 'had a feeling that the door to further discussions was still open', that 'the confidence the Arab representatives had in me was in no way impaired' and that they 'were still willing to accept me as Mediator'.[10]

An unpleasant surprise awaited him when, on 5 July, he returned to Tel Aviv to get the official reply of the Israeli Provisional Government. Not only did this reject his specific recommendations, it challenged his authority to 'adjust' the term of the UN Partition Plan. He was 'bluntly told by Jewish circles that they were surprised that anyone who came from a Christian country could put forward such a proposal'.[11] At the same time, even as they were condemning his 'adjustments' of the UN Partition Plan, they officially proclaimed that the Jewish State would not be bound by certain of its provisions.

On 9 July the first truce collapsed. Hostilities were resumed, during which the Zionists carried out further 'adjustments' of their own; whole new areas of central Palestine were 'cleansed' of their native population.

In Amman, on 1 August, Bernadotte visited some of the uprooted victims. 'A preliminary examination which we carried out . . . in Amman showed that the refugee problem was vaster and more baffling than we had imagined. . . .'[12] The same day, the Israeli Provisional Government officially informed him that there could be no return of these, or any other, refugees. It argued that 'if we find ourselves unable to agree on their readmission to the Israeli-controlled area, it is because of over-riding considerations bearing on our immediate security, the outcome of the present war and the stability of the future peace settlement'. It went on to describe 'the Palestine Arab exodus of 1948' as 'one of those cataclysmic phenomena which, according to the experience of other countries, change the course of history'.[13]

Bernadotte tried again. Afterwards, he confided to his diary this bitter reflection on his meeting with Moshe Sharett, the man who was considered a dove to Bengurion's hawk.

Nothing that I could propose aroused any response; I got nowhere. It was significant to read later in the Jewish newspaper *Palestine Post*: 'Count Bernadotte has had a fruitless meeting with the Foreign Minister of Israel.' That was evidently regarded as a great triumph. . . . For my part I regarded the Jewish reaction as confirmation of what I had said before, namely that their military success during the ten days' war had gone to their heads.[14]

Another encounter with the refugees, this time at Ramallah, a few miles east of Jerusalem, deepened his indignation:

> I have made the acquaintance of a great many refugee camps; but never have I seen a more ghastly sight than that which met my eye here, at Ramallah. The car was literally stormed by excited masses shouting with Oriental fervour that they wanted food and wanted to return to their homes. There were plenty of frightening faces in the sea of suffering humanity. I remember not least a group of scabby and helpless old men with tangled beards who thrust their emaciated faces into the car and held out scraps of bread that would certainly have been considered uneatable by ordinary people, but was their only food.[15]

Back in Tel Aviv, in another meeting with Sharett, he appealed yet again for a change of heart over the refugees—only to incur an 'adamant refusal'. His diary entry for the day shows the radical change that was being wrought in his view of the Jewish State. At lunch with Sharett:

> I began the conversation by saying that in my opinion the international position of the government of Israel was worse than it had been only a week before. It no longer enjoyed the good will it had previously. The reason was . . . that the government had expressed itself on various occasions in such a way that people could only draw the conclusion that it was well on the way towards losing its head. It seemed as though Jewish demands would never cease.[16]

It was his impression, he went on, that the Israelis behaved as if they had 'two enemies': the Arabs were still 'enemy number one', but the UN Observers now 'ran them a close second'. He told the Foreign Minister that 'the Arabs had given the Observers every possible help, particularly during the second truce, while the Israelis had tried to put spokes in the wheel and did everything in their power to make the Observers' work more difficult'.[17] Bernadotte informed Sharett that his Observers' Corps was to be strengthened by 300 new officers; he added: 'I knew from my own experience that these officers, when they first arrived, would be very sympathetic to the Jewish cause; but I also knew that they would soon find themselves compelled by force of circumstances to revise their attitude. I could not understand . . . why the Jewish Government should adopt an attitude of such arrogance and hostility towards the United Nations representative.'

The Mediator thought he had 'made a certain impression' on Sharett, but while they were discussing certain alternatives for the future of Palestine, the Foreign Minister gave a display of that very arrogance of which he complained. One alternative, Sharett hinted, might be that 'the whole of Palestine should belong to Israel'.[18]

By 12 August, Bernadotte, '. . . had a feeling that the negotiations had reached a deadlock. The Jews had shown a blatant unwillingness for real cooperation . . .' This came as no surprise; for he had already come to the conclusion that 'with respect to the people of Palestine, the Provisional Government had had a very great opportunity. . . . It had missed that opportunity. It had shown nothing but hardness and obduracy towards the refugees . . .' Because morals, not politics, were his guide, he had at first been baffled by this attitude of 'the Jewish people, which itself had suffered so much'.[19] But before long he grasped that what he had attributed to 'arrogance' and the exultation of military victory actually flowed from deliberate policy, and he told the Israeli leaders of his surprise that

> . . . the representatives of the Jewish people in particular should look at this problem from such a narrow point of view, that they should regard it purely as a political question without taking into account the humanitarian side of the matter.[20]

In the Arab governments, by contrast, he discerned a certain flexibility. As he talked to Azzam Pasha, the Secretary-General of the Arab League, he could not help saying to himself: 'This man realizes deep down that the Arab world cannot any longer hope for a Palestine in which there will not be any independent Jewish State.'[21]

What the Arab states did insist upon was that there could be no direct negotiations with Israel until the refugees were allowed home. And to this plea Bernadotte was very sympathetic. The return of the refugees, he urged the Security Council, should take place 'at the earliest practicable date'—a date which, in his view, should not be contingent upon the conclusion of a

formal peace nor even upon the initiation of negotiations to that
end.[22] By now Bernadotte had replaced the Arabs as 'enemy
number one'.

On 17 September, the day after he submitted his report to the
UN, the Mediator flew to Jerusalem to inspect the building to
which he was thinking of transferring his headquarters. It
seemed foolish to risk his life on a mere administrative chore.
That there was indeed such a risk he was well aware. The Jerusalem front line was the scene of constant ceasefire violations; it
was infested with snipers and assorted gunmen who subjected
the UN Observers to hold-ups. Only the previous day Rhodes
radio station had picked up a report about a policeman coming
across Bernadotte's dead body in a Haifa street. As his aircraft
approached Jerusalem, the radio operator received a message,
purporting to come from Haifa, warning that all aircraft landing
at the city's Kalendia airport would be fired upon.

They landed without incident, but when General Aage Land-
ström, the Mediator's Personal Representative and Chief of Staff
of the UN Observer Corps, suggested that they take a round-
about route into the city so as to avoid the 'hot' area of the
Mandelbaum Gate, Bernadotte demurred. 'I would not do that,'
he said, 'I have to take the same risks as my Observers and,
moreover, I think no one has the right to refuse me permission
to pass through the line.'[23]

They were on their way back when the assassins struck. 'We
drove rapidly through the Jewish lines without incident,' Lundström wrote.

> The barrier was up, but when the guard saw us, he let it down
> halfway, then drew it right up, and finally let it down completely.
> This forced us to stop. The Jewish liaison officer shouted some-
> thing to the guard in Hebrew, after which he drew up the barrier
> completely and we were able to pass. It was suspected after the
> murder that this mysterious manipulation of the barrier must have
> been a signal to the murderers that we were on our way, possibly
> even indicating which car Folke Bernadotte was travelling in.
> That pre-supposes, however, that the Jewish Soldiers at the road
> barrier were accomplices in the plot. . . . In the Qatamon Quarter
> we were held up by a Jewish army-type jeep, placed in a road
> block, and filled with men in Jewish army uniforms. At the same

time I saw a man running from the jeep. I took little notice of this because I merely thought that it was another check-point. However, he put a tommy gun through the open window on my side of the car and fired point-blank at Count Bernadotte and Colonel Sérot. I also heard shots fired from other points and there was considerable confusion. . . . Colonel Sérot fell in the seat at the back of of it and I saw at once that he was dead. Count Bernadotte fell forward and I thought at the time he was trying to get cover. I asked him: 'Are you wounded?' He nodded and fell back. I helped him to lie down in the car. I now realized that he was severely wounded; there was a considerable amount of blood on his clothes mainly around the heart. . . . On reflection after the incident, I am convinced that this was a deliberate and carefully planned assassination. The spot where the cars were halted was carefully chosen, and the people who approached the cars quite obviously not only knew which car Count Bernadotte was in but also the exact position in the car which he occupied. [24]

Count Bernadotte died a few minutes after the shooting, and three days later the assassins identified themselves as *Hazit Hamoledeth* (Fatherland Front), a sub-group of the *Stern Gang*. In a letter to *Agence France Presse* in Tel Aviv, they declared that 'in our opinion all United Nations Observers in Palestine are members of foreign occupation forces which have no right to be in our territory'. They conceded, however, that the killing of Colonel Sérot was 'a fatal mistake. . . . Our men thought that the officer sitting beside Count Bernadotte was the British agent and anti-Semite General Lundström'.[25]

In a letter of protest, General Lundström described the assassinations as 'a breach of the truce of utmost gravity, and a black page in Palestine's history for which the United Nations will demand a full accounting'.[26]

There was to be no accounting, however, either to the UN or to any other authority. To the UN demand that the assassins be brought to justice, the Israelis at first replied that they could not find them. Then, after two months of international pressure, they arrested Nathan Yellin-Mor, the head of the *Stern Gang*, and Matitiahu Schmulevitz, both Polish Jews who had emigrated to Palestine a few years before.

The two were tried by military court in Acre. They claimed that there was no case against them. Their organization was not a terrorist one, nor had they themselves been party to terrorist acts, since the prosecution furnished no proof. Yellin-Mor further objected to the trial of civilians by a military court.[27] As for Bernadotte, he denounced him, in a lengthy tirade, as an enemy of Israel. Among other things 'he stood in the way of Jewish absorption of the Kingdom of Transjordan as well as the whole of Palestine'.[28] The two men were sentenced to eight and five years. They were, however, to receive special treatment as political prisoners. Then, growing even more lenient, the court ordered that they and their witness be released altogether, since they had protested their sincere desire to be law-abiding citizens . . .[29]

Twenty-seven years later, in July 1975, the perpetrators of the other famous *Stern Gang* assassination—that of Lord Moyne, the British Resident Minister in the Middle East—were accorded full military honours in Israel. Eliahu Hakim and Eliahu Bet-Zuri had been executed in Cairo in 1945. After lying in state in the Hall of Heroism, their bodies were buried in a section of Israel's military cemetery reserved for heroes and martyrs with the President, the Prime Minister and the Minister for Religious Affairs in attendance. They had been exhumed from their Cairo graves. As their flag-draped biers were conveyed from Egyptian to Israeli lines, Swedish troops of the UN forces in Sinai, unaware of their contents, furnished the honour guard.

'Cruel Zionism'—or the 'Ingathering' of Iraqi Jewry

It was the last day of Passover, April 1950. In Baghdad, the Jews had spent it strolling along the banks of the Tigris in celebration of the Sea Song. This was an old custom of the oldest Jewish community in the world; the 130,000 Jews of Iraq attributed their origins to Nebuchadnezzar, the destruction of the First Temple and the Babylonian exile. A good 50,000 of them thronged the esplanade. By nine o'clock in the evening the crowds were thinning out. But on Abu Nawwas street young Jewish intellectuals were still gathered in the Dar al-Beida coffee-shop.

Suddenly, the convivial atmosphere was shattered by an explosion. A small bomb, hurled from a passing car, had gone off on the pavement just outside. By chance no one was hurt. But the incident shook the Jewish community. They were convinced that Iraqi extremists wanted to kill them. The fainter-hearted

began to murmur 'it is better to go to Israel'. The next day there
was a rush to the offices where Jews wishing to renounce their
Iraqi citizenship had to present themselves for registration. Their
right to emigrate had been officially acknowledged by the government on the feast of Purim a month before. Its object was to
prevent emigration by illegal means. As the newspapers had
explained, 'the encounters between the police and the emigrant
groups showed that some Iraqi Jews do not want to live in this
country. Through their fleeing they give a bad name to Iraq.
Those who do not wish to live among us have no place here. Let
them go.'[30] There had been little response. Police officers had
appeared at synagogues and explained that all Jews had to do in
order to leave Iraq peacefully was to sign the necessary form.
But the Jews were afraid that this was a trap to unmask the
Zionists among them; and Zionism, under Iraqi law, was a
grievous offence.

In all, about 10,000 Jews signed up to leave after the bomb; the
big Ezra Daud synagogue had to be set aside as a registration
office; police officers and volunteer clerks worked day and night
to complete the task. A special kitchen was set up to feed them.
Most of the would-be emigrants were poor, with little to lose.
The panic did not last very long, however, and registration
tapered off. Moreover, they were to leave by air, but only one
aeroplane came to take 120 of them, via Cyprus, to Israel.

Then there was another explosion. This time it was at the US
Information Centre, where many young Jews used to come and
read. Again the theory was that an extremist Iraqi organization
had planted the bomb, which only by chance failed to hurt anyone. Once again, therefore, there was a rush on the Ezra Daud
synagogue; only this time the panic—and the number of would-
be emigrants—was less than before.

The year ended, and March 1951, the time-limit set for the
renunciation of citizenship, was approaching.

The third time there *were* victims. It happened outside the
Mas'uda Shemtov synagogue, which served as an assembly point
for emigrants. That day in January the synagogue was full of
Kurdish Jews from the northern city of Suleimaniyyah. Outside
a Jewish boy was distributing sweetmeats to curious onlookers.
When the bomb went off he was killed instantly and a man
standing behind him was badly wounded in the eyes.

And this time there was no longer any doubt in Jews' minds: an anti-Jewish organization was plotting against them. Better to leave Iraq while there was still time. The queues lengthened outside the Ezra Daud synagogue, and on the night before the time-limit expired some were paying as much as £200 to ensure that their names were on the list. A few days later the Iraqi parliament passed a law confiscating the property of all Jews who renounced their citizenship. No one was allowed to take more than £70 out of the country. The planes started arriving at a rate of three or four a day. At first the emigrants were flown to Nicosia accompanied by an Iraqi police officer. But after a while even that make-believe was dropped and they went directly to Israel's Lydda airport—the police officer returning alone in the empty plane. Before long all that was left of the 130,000 abandoning home, property and an ancient heritage was a mere 5,000 souls.

It was not long before a bombshell of a different kind hit the pathetic remnants of Iraqi Jewry. They learned that the three explosions were the work not of Arab extremists, but of the very people who sought to rescue them; of a clandestine organization called 'The Movement', whose leader, 'commander of the Jewish ghettoes in Iraq', had received this letter from Yigal Allon, chief of the *Palmach* commandos, and subsequently Foreign Minister of Israel:

> Ramadan my brother. . . . I was very satisfied in learning that you have succeeded in starting a group and that we were able to transfer at least some of the weapons intended for you. It is depressing to think that Jews may once again be slaughtered, our girls raped, that our nation's honour may again be smirched . . . should disturbances break out, you will be able to enlarge the choice of defenders and co-opt Jews who have as yet not been organized as members of the Underground. But be warned lest you do this prematurely, thereby endangering the security of your units which are, in fact, the only defence against a terrible pogrom.[31]

The astonishing truth—that the bombs which terrorized the Jewish community had been Zionist bombs—was revealed when, in the summer of 1950, an elegantly dressed man entered Uruzdi Beg, the largest general store in Baghdad. One of the salesmen, a Palestinian refugee, turned white when he saw him. He left the

counter and ran out into the street, where he told two policemen:
'I recognize the face of an Israeli.' He had been a coffee-boy in
Acre, and he knew Yehudah Tajjar from there. Arrested, Tajjar
confessed that he was indeed an Israeli, but explained that he had
come to Baghdad to marry an Iraqi Jewish girl. His revelations
led to more arrests, some fifteen in all. Shalom Salih, a youngster
in charge of *Haganah* arms caches, broke down during interroga-
tion and took the police from synagogue to synagogue, showing
them where the weapons, smuggled in since World War II, were
hidden. During the trial, the prosecution charged that the accused were members of the Zionist underground. Their primary
aim—to which the throwing of the three bombs had so devastat-
ingly contributed—was to frighten the Jews into emigrating as
soon as possible. Two were sentenced to death, the rest to long
prison terms.

It was Tajjar himself who first broke Jewish silence about this
affair. Sentenced by the Baghdad court to life imprisonment, he
was released after ten years and found his way to Israel. On 29
May 1966 the campaigning weekly magazine *Ha'olam Hazeh*
published an account of the emigration of Iraqi Jews based on
Tajjar's testimony. Then on 9 November 1972, the *Black
Panther* magazine, militant voice of Israel's Oriental Jews, published the full story. The *Black Panther* account includes the
testimony of two Israeli citizens who were in Baghdad at the
time. The first, Kaduri Salim

. . . is 49 but looks 60. He is thin, almost hunch-backed, creased-
face and with glass-eye: he lost his right eye at the door of the
Mas'uda Shemtov synagogue. He recounts: 'I was standing there
beside the synagogue door. I had already waived my Iraqi
citizenship, and wanted to know what was new. Suddenly, I
heard a sound like a gun report. Then a terrible noise. I felt a blow,
as if a wall had fallen on me. Everything went black around me.
I felt something cold running down my cheek, I touched it—it
was blood. The right eye. I closed my left eye and didn't see a
thing. The doctor told me: 'It's better to take it out.'

He remained in Iraq for three months after leaving the hospital.
Then his turn to leave for Israel arrived. The ex-clerk was sent
to an immigration camp. Since then, all his efforts to receive
compensations have been in vain. He claimed: 'I was hurt by the
bomb. The Court of Law established that the bomb was thrown

by "The Movement". The Israel Government has to give me compensations.' But the Israel Government does not recognize its responsibility for the Baghdad bombs and, anyhow, cannot recognize him as hurt in action. 'I am ready to be a victim for the State,' he said, 'but when the situation at home is bad, when my wife wants money and there isn't any, what is the self-sacrifice and goodwill worth?'

The second witness was an Iraqi lawyer, living in Tel Aviv. He told the *Black Panther* that

After the first bomb was thrown at the Dar al-Bayda coffee-house, many rumours started running around about the responsible being communists. But the day after the explosion, at 4.00 am, leaflets were already being distributed amongst the first worshippers at the synagogue. The leaflets warned of the dangers revealed by the throwing of the bomb and recommended the people to come to Israel.

Someone who saw in it something strange was Salman al-Bayyati, Investigating Judge for South Baghdad. He declared that the distribution of the leaflet at such an early hour showed prior knowledge of the bombing. He therefore instructed the police to investigate in this direction, determining at the same time that those who threw the bomb were Jews trying to quicken the emigration. Indeed, two youngsters were arrested.

Unexpectedly, the Ministry of Justice intervened. The two boys were set free. The case passed over to the hands of the Investigating Judge Kamal Shahin, from North Baghdad. In other words, at this stage, there was still a willingness not to see. For the whole emigration movement came as results of a willingness not to see—or perhaps even of a more active agreement between the Government, the Court and the Zionist representatives.

But after two more bombs and after the arrest of the Israeli envoy —it was too much. The police started acting, and it was impossible to stop the wheels. There is only one more thing to add: in the objective conditions of the issue, the trial was made according to international law. The evidence was just such that it wasn't difficult at all to pronounce such sentences.[32]

When Bengurion made his impassioned pleas for immigrants to people the new-born State of Israel he was addressing 'European' Jews (from both the New and the Old Worlds) in particular. Not only had European Jewry fathered Zionism, it was the main source of that high-quality manpower, armed with the technical

skills, the social and cultural attitudes which Israel needed. But
with the Holocaust over, the source was tending to dry up. So
the Zionists decided that 'Oriental' Jewry must be 'ingathered' as
well. It is often forgotten that the 'safeguard' clause of the Balfour Declaration—'it being clearly understood that nothing shall
be done which may prejudice the civil and religious rights of the
existing non-Jewish communities in Palestine, or the rights and
political status enjoyed by Jews in any other country'—was designed to cover Diaspora Jews as well as native Arabs. But the
uprooting of a million 'Oriental' Jews showed that, for the
Zionists, it was a clause to be ignored in both its parts. Everywhere they applied the same essential techniques, but nowhere,
perhaps, with such thoroughness as they did in Iraq. 'Cruel
Zionism', someone called it.[33]

If Zionism, as a historical phenomenon, was a reaction to anti-
Semitism, it follows that, in certain circumstances, the Zionists
had an interest in provoking the very disease which, ultimately,
they hoped to cure. Herzl himself was the first to note the useful-
ness of anti-Semitism as an incentive to Jewish immigration.
'Anti-Semitism has grown and continues to grow—and so do
I.'[34] There were dedicated Zionists who considered that it was
the duty of the Rabbinate, Jewish nationalists and community
leaders to keep the prejudice alive.[35] In the early fifties the need
for immigrants was such that a columnist in *Davar*, influential
voice of the Israel trade union movement, wrote:

> I shall not be ashamed to confess that if I had the power, as I
> have the will, I would select a score of efficient young men—
> intelligent, decent, devoted to our ideal and burning with the
> desire to help redeem Jews—and I would send them to the
> countries where Jews are absorbed in sinful self-satisfaction. The
> task of these young men would be to disguise themselves as non-
> Jews, and plague Jews with anti-Semitic slogans such as 'Bloody
> Jew', 'Jews go to Palestine' and similar intimacies. I can vouch
> that the results in terms of a considerable immigration to Israel
> from these countries would be ten thousand times larger than the
> results brought by thousands of emissaries who have been preach-
> ing for decades to deaf ears.[36]

Zionism had much less appeal to Oriental than it did to European Jews. In the pre-State period only 10·4 per cent of Jewish
immigrants came from 'Africa and Asia'.[37] In their vast majority,

the Oriental Jews were actually Arab Jews, and the reason for their indifference was simply that, historically, they had not suffered anything like the persecution and discrimination of their brethren in European Christendom. Prejudice did exist, but their lives were on the whole comfortable, and their roots were deep. They were nowhere more at home than in Iraq, and a government official conceded—tongue in cheek—that their Mesopotamian pedigree was much superior to that of the Moslem majority:

> Many of us consider the Jews to be the original inhabitants of this country. We believe, according to the Koran, they are descendants of Abraham and that goes back nearly 4,000 years. Compared to them, therefore, we Muslims are interlopers because we have been here only about 1,500 years.[38]

At one time, Baghdad numbered more Jewish than Arab residents. In this century, as an already prosperous, educated community, they were particularly well placed to benefit from the rapid development and modernization of the country. They controlled many national institutions, most of the banks and big shops. The poorest Jews were better off than the average Iraqi.[39] Under the constitution, the Jews enjoyed equality with other citizens. They were represented in parliament, worked in the civil service, and from 1920 to 1925 a Jew was Minister of Finance.

On the rare occasions in Arab history when Moslems—or Christians, for that matter—turned against the Jews in their midst, it was not anti-Semitism, in its traditional European sense, that drove them, but fanaticism bred of a not unjustified resentment. For, like other minorities, the Jews had a tendency to associate themselves with, indeed to profit from, what the majority regarded as an alien and oppressive rule. In recent times, this meant that from Iraq to Morocco the local Jewish communities found varying degrees of special favour with the French or British masters of the Arab world. If Arab Jews must themselves take some of the blame for the prejudice which this behaviour generated against them, they deserve much less blame for that other cause of Arab hostility—Zionism—which was ultimately to prove infinitely more disruptive of their lives.

Zionist activities in Iraq and other Arab countries date from

the beginning of the century. They were barely noticed at first.
There was actually a time, in the early twenties, when the Iraqi
government granted the local Zionist society an official licence,
and even when the licence was not renewed, it continued to
function, unofficially, for several years. At first it was the
British, rather than local Jews, who bore the brunt of Arab
animosity. In 1928, there were riots when the British Zionist Sir
Alfred Mond visited Baghdad. The following year demonstrations in mosques and streets, a two-minute silence in Parliament,
black-edged newspapers and telegrams to London marked 'Iraqi
disapproval of the pro-Jewish policy of Great Britain'.[40] It was
not until the mid-thirties, when the troubles of Palestine were
reverberating round the world, that Arab Jews began to excite
suspicion and resentment. In Iraq these emotions came to a head
in 1941 when, in a two-day rampage, the mob killed some 170 to
180 Jews and injured several hundred more.[41] It was terrible. But
it was the first pogrom in Iraqi history. Moreover, it occurred at
a time of political chaos; the short-lived pro-Nazi revolt of
Rashid Ali Kailani was collapsing, and most members of his
administration had taken flight as a British expeditionary force
arrived at the gates of the city.

There was no more such violence. On account of this, and
their economic prosperity, the Jews felt a renewed sense of
security.[42] Nevertheless, the Zionists were still active in their
midst. In the mid-forties, they disseminated booklets entitled
'Don't Buy from the Moslems'. However, they did not have the
field to themselves. Left-wing Jews, who considered themselves
'Jewish and Arab at the same time', set up the League for
Combating Zionism.[43]

By the end of Israel's 'War of Independence', there were still
130,000 Jews in Iraq. The Movement organized the 'Persian
underground railway' to smuggle Jews to Israel via Iran. There
were occasional clashes between the police and the caravan
guides. It was these which prompted the government to legalize
Jewish emigration. But, whether by legal or illegal means, very
few actually left. As the Chief Rabbi of Iraq, Sassoon Khedduri,
explained a few years later:

> The Jews—and the Muslims—in Iraq just took it for granted
> that Judaism is a religion and Iraqi Jews are Iraqis. The Palestine

problem was remote and there was no question about the Jews of Iraq following the Arab position . . .[44]

But Bengurion and the Zionists would not give in so easily. Israel desperately needed manpower. Iraqi Jews must be 'ingathered'. As Khedduri recalled:

By mid-1949 the big propaganda guns were already going off in the United States. American dollars were going to save the Iraqi Jews—whether Iraqi Jews needed saving or not. There were daily 'pogroms'—in the New York *Times* and under datelines which few noticed were from Tel Aviv. Why didn't someone come to see *us* instead of negotiating with Israel to take in Iraqi Jews? Why didn't someone point out that the solid, responsible leadership of Iraqi Jews believed this to be their country—in good times and bad—and we were convinced the trouble would pass.[45]

But it did not. Neither the Iraqi Jews themselves, nor the government of what, by Western standards, was still a backward country, could cope with the kind of pressures the Zionists brought to bear:

Zionist agents began to appear in Iraq—among the youth—playing on a *general* uneasiness and indicating that American Jews were putting up large amounts of money to take them to Israel, where everything would be in applepie order. The emigration of children began to tear at the loyalties of families and as the adults in a family reluctantly decided to follow their children, the stress and strain of loyalties spread to brothers and sisters.

Then a new technique was developed:

Instead of the quiet individualized emigration, there began to appear public demands to legalize the emigration of Jews—*en masse* . . . in the United States the 'pogroms' were already underway and the Iraqi government was being accused of holding the Jews against their will . . . campaigning among Jews increased . . . The government was whip-sawed . . . accused of pogroms and violent action against Jews . . . But if the government attempted to suppress Zionist agitation attempting to stampede the Iraqui Jews, it was again accused of discrimination.[46]

Finally there came the bombs.

'Ingathered' for what? The Iraqi Jews soon learned; those of them, that is, who actually went to Israel, or, having gone, re-

mained there. For by no means all of uprooted Oriental Jewry
did so. A great many of them—particularly the ones with money,
connections, education and initiative—succeeded in making their
way to Europe or America. But what the irretrievably 'ingathered'
learned was the cruellest and most enduring irony of all: Oriental
Jewry was no more than despised cannon-fodder for the European creed of Zionism.

> What did you do, Bengurion?
> You smuggled in all of us!
> Because of the past, we waived our citizenship
> And came to Israel.
> Would that we had come riding on a donkey and we
> Hadn't arrived here yet!
> Woe, what a black hour it was!
> To hell with the plane that brought us here![47]

This was the song which the Iraqi Jews used to sing. Nothing
the rulers of Israel could do quelled the bitterness which the
newcomers nurtured against them. They were lectured, in their
transit camps, by teams of Zionist educators. But, long after they
left the camps, they continued to sing that song, even at weddings and festive occasions. It remained popular throughout the
fifties. Then it eventually disappeared, but it can hardly be said
that nostalgia for the 'old country' disappeared with it. For the
contrast between what they once were, 'in exile', and what they
became, and remain, in the Promised Land is too great. One of
the 'most splendid and rich communities was destroyed, its
members reduced to indigents'; a community that 'ruled over
most of the resources of Iraq . . . was turned into a ruled group,
discriminated against and oppressed in every aspect'. A community that prided itself on its scholarship subsequently produced fewer academics, in Israeli universities, than it brought
with it from Iraq. A community sure of its own moral values and
cultural integrity became in Israel a breeding ground 'for delin-
quents of all kinds'. A community which 'used to produce
splendid sons could raise only "handicapped" sons in Israel'.[48]

THE LAVON AFFAIR

In July 1954 Egypt was plagued by a series of bomb outrages

directed mainly against American and British property in Cairo and Alexandria. It was generally assumed that they were the work of the Moslem Brothers, then the most dangerous challenge to the still uncertain authority of Colonel (later President) Nasser and his two-year-old revolution. Nasser was negotiating with Britain over the evacuation of its giant military bases in the Suez Canal Zone, and the Moslem Brothers, as zealous nationalists, were vigorously opposed to any Egyptian compromises.

It therefore came as a shock to world, and particularly Jewish, opinion, when on 5 October the Egyptian Minister of the Interior, Zakaria Muhieddin, announced the break-up of a thirteen-man Israeli sabotage network. An 'anti-Semitic' frame-up was suspected.

Indignation increased when, on 11 December, the group was brought to trial. In the Israeli parliament, Prime Minister Moshe Sharett denounced the 'wicked plot hatched in Alexandria . . . the show trial which is being organized there against a group of Jews who have fallen victims to false accusations and from whom it seems attempts are being made to extract confessions of imaginary crimes, by threats and torture . . .'[49] The trade union newspaper *Davar* observed that the Egyptian régime 'seems to take its inspiration from the Nazis' and lamented the 'deterioration in the status of Egyptian Jews in general'.[50] For *Haaretz* the trial 'proved that the Egyptian rulers do not hesitate to invent the most fantastic accusations if it suits them'; it added that 'in the present state of affairs in Egypt the Junta certainly needs some diversion'.[51] And the next day the *Jerusalem Post* carried this headline: 'Egypt Show Trial Arouses Israel, Sharett Tells House. Sees Inquisition Practices Revived.'

The trial established that the bombings had indeed been carried out by an Israeli espionage and terrorist network. This was headed by Colonel Avraham Dar—alias John Darling—and a core of professionals who had set themselves up in Egypt under various guises. They had recruited a number of Egyptian Jews; one of them was a young woman, Marcelle Ninio, who worked in the offices of a British company. Naturally, the eventual exposure of such an organization was not going to improve the lot of the vast majority of Egyptian Jews who wanted nothing to do with Zionism. There were still at least 50,000 Jews in Egypt; there had been something over 60,000 in 1947, more than half of whom were actually foreign nationals. During the first Arab-Israeli war of 1948, the populace had sometimes vented its frustration against them, and some were killed in mob violence or by terrorist bombs. In spite of this, and of the revolutionary upheaval which followed four years later, few Jews—including the foreign nationals—left the country, and fewer still went to Israel. A Jewish journalist insisted: 'We, Egyptian Jews, feel secure in our homeland, Egypt.'[52]

The welfare of Oriental Jewry in their various homelands was, as we have seen, Israel's last concern. And in July 1954 it had other worries. It was feeling isolated and insecure. Its Western friends—let alone the rest of the world—were unhappy about its aggressive behaviour. The US Assistant Secretary of State advised it to 'drop the attitude of the conqueror'.[53] More alarming was the rapprochement under way between Egypt, on the one hand, and the United States and Britain on the other. President Eisenhower had urged Britain to give up her giant military base in the Suez Canal Zone; Bengurion had failed to dissuade her. It was to sabotage this rapprochement that the head of Israeli intelligence, Colonel Benyamin Givli, ordered his Egyptian intelligence ring to strike.

Givli's boss, Defence Minister Pinhas Lavon, and the Prime Minister, Moshe Sharett, knew nothing of the operation. For Givli was a member of a powerful Defence Ministry clique which often acted independently, or in outright defiance, of the cabinet. They were protégés of Bengurion and, although 'The Old Man' had left the Premiership for Sde Boker, his Negev desert retreat, a few months before, he was able, through them, to perpetuate the hardline 'activist' policies in which he believed. On Givli's instructions, the Egyptian network was to plant bombs in American and British cultural centres, British-owned cinemas and Egyptian public buildings. The Western powers, it was hoped, would conclude that there was fierce internal opposition to the rapprochement and that Nasser's young régime, faced with this challenge, was not one in which they could place much confidence.[54] Mysterious violence might therefore persuade both London and Washington that British troops should remain astride the Canal; the world had not forgotten Black Saturday, 28 January 1951, in the last year of King Farouk's reign, when mobs rampaged through downtown Cairo, setting fire to foreign-owned hotels and shops, in which scores of people, including thirteen Britons, died.

The first bomb went off, on 2 July, in the Alexandria post office. On 11 July, the Anglo-Egyptian Suez negotiations, which had been blocked for nine months, got under way again. The next day the Israeli embassy in London was assured that, upon the British evacuation from Suez, stock-piled arms would not be handed over to the Egyptians. But the Defence Ministry activists were unconvinced. On 14 July their agents, in clandestine radio contact with Tel Aviv, fire-bombed US Information Service libraries in Cairo and Alexandria. That same day, a phosphorous bomb exploded prematurely in the pocket of one Philip Natanson, nearly burning him alive, as he was about to enter the British-owned Rio cinema in Alexandria. His arrest and subsequent confession led to the break-up of the whole ring—but not before the completion of another cycle of clandestine action and diplomatic failure. On 15 July President Eisenhower assured the Egyptians that 'simultaneously' with the signing of a Suez agreement the United States would enter into 'firm commitments' for economic aid to strengthen their armed forces.[55] On 23 July—anniversary of the 1952 revolution—the Israeli agents still at large had a final fling; they started fires in two Cairo cinemas, in the central post office and the railway station. On the same day, Britain announced that the War Secretary, Antony Head, was going to Cairo. And on 27 July he and the Egyptians initialled the 'Heads of Agreement' on the terms of Britain's evacuation.

The trial lasted from 11 December to 3 January. Not all the culprits were there, because Colonel Dar and an Israeli colleague managed to escape, and the third Israeli, Hungarian-born Max Bennett, committed suicide; but those who were present all pleaded guilty. Most of them, including Marcelle Ninio, were sentenced to various terms of imprisonment. But Dr Musa Lieto Marzuk, a Tunisian-born citizen of France who was a surgeon at the Jewish Hospital in Cairo, and Samuel Azar, an engineering professor from Alexandria, were condemned to death. In spite of representations from France, Britain and the United States the two men were hanged. Politically, it would have been very difficult for Nasser to spare them, for only seven weeks before six

Moslem Brothers had been executed for complicity in an attempt on his life. Nevertheless Israel reacted with grief and anger. So did some Western Jews. Marzuk and Azar 'died the death of martyrs', said Sharett on the same day in the Knesset, whose members stood in silent tribute. Israel went into official mourning the following day. Beersheba and Ramat Gan named streets after the executed men. Israeli delegates to the Egyptian-Israeli Mixed Armistice Commission refused to attend its meeting, declaring that they would not sit down with representatives of the Cairo junta. In New York there were bomb threats against the Egyptian consulate and a sniper fired four shots into its fourth-floor window.[56]

This whole episode, which was to poison Israeli political life for a decade and more, came to be known as the 'Lavon Affair', for it had been established in the Cairo trial that Lavon, as Minister of Defence, had approved the campaign of sabotage. At least so the available evidence made it appear. But in Israel, Lavon had asked Moshe Sharett for a secret inquiry into a matter about which the cabinet knew nothing. Benyamin Givli, the intelligence chief, claimed that the so-called 'security operation' had been authorized by Lavon himself. Two other Bengurion protégés, Moshe Dayan and Shimon Peres, testified against Lavon. Lavon denounced Givli's papers as forgeries and demanded the resignation of all three men. Instead, Sharett ordered Lavon himself to resign and invited Bengurion to come out of retirement and take over the Defence Ministry. It was a triumphant comeback for the 'activist' philosophy whose excesses both Sharett and Lavon had tried to modify. It was consummated, a week later, by an unprovoked raid on Gaza, which left thirty-nine Egyptians dead and led to the Suez War of 1956.[57]

When the truth about the Lavon Affair came to light, six years after the event, it confirmed that there had been a frame-up—not, however, by the Egyptians, but by Bengurion and his young protégés. Exposure was fortuitous. Giving evidence in a forgery trial in September 1960, a witness divulged *en passant* that he had seen the faked signature of Lavon on a document relating to a 1954 'security mishap'.[58] Bengurion immediately announced that the three-year statute of limitations prohibited the opening of the case. But Lavon, now head of the powerful Histradut Trade Union Federation, seized upon this opportunity to demand an inquiry. Bengurion did everything in his power to stop it, but his cabinet overruled him. The investigation revealed that the 'security operation' had been planned behind Lavon's back. His signature *had* been forged, and the bombing had actually begun long before his approval—which he withheld—had been sought. He was a scapegoat pure and simple. On Christmas Day 1960, the Israeli cabinet unanimously exonerated him of all guilt in the 'disastrous security adventure in Egypt'; the Attorney General had, in the meantime, found 'conclusive evidence of forgeries as well as false testimony in an earlier inquiry'.[59] Bengurion was enraged. He issued an ultimatum to the ruling Labour party to remove Lavon, stormed out of a cabinet meeting and resigned. In what one trade unionist described as 'an immoral and unjust submission to dictatorship', his diehard supporters in the Histradut swung the vote in favour of accepting Lavon's resignation. Lavon, however, won a moral victory over the man who twice forced him from office. In the streets of Tel Aviv and Jerusalem, students demonstrated in his favour. They carried placards reading: 'Bengurion Go to Sde Boker. Take Dayan and Peres with You. We do Not Accept Leaders with Elastic Consciences.'[60] The affair rocked the ruling establishment, split public opinion, forced new elections and contributed largely to Bengurion's eventual disappearance from public life.

But Lavon was not the only real victim. There were also those misguided Egyptian Jews who paid with their lives or long terms of imprisonment. It is true that when, in 1968, Marcelle Ninio and her colleagues were exchanged for Egyptian prisoners in Israel, they received a heroes' welcome. True, too, that when Miss Ninio got married Prime Minister Golda Meir, Defençe Minister Dayan and Chief of Staff General Bar Lev all attended the wedding and Dayan told the bride 'the Six-Day War was success enough that it led to your freedom'.[61] However, after spending fourteen years in an Egyptian prison, the former terrorists did not share the leadership's enthusiasm. When Ninio and two of her colleagues appeared on Israel television a few years later, they all expressed the belief that the reason why they were not released earlier was because Israel made little effort to get them out. 'Maybe they didn't want us to come back,' said Robert Dassa. 'There was so much intrigue in Israel. We were instruments in the hands of the Egyptians and of others . . . and what is more painful after all that we went through is that this continues to be so.' In Ninio's opinion, 'the government didn't want to spoil its relations with the United States and didn't want the embarrassment of admitting it was behind our action'.[62]

But the real victims were the great mass of Egyptian Jewry. Episodes like the Lavon Affair tended to identify them, in the mind of ordinary Egyptians, with the Zionist movement. When, in 1956, Israeli invaded and occupied Sinai, feeling ran high against them. The government, playing into the Zionist hands, began ordering Jews to leave the country. Belatedly, reluctantly, 21,000 left in the following year; more were expelled later, and others, their livelihood gone, had nothing to stay for. But precious few went to Israel.

NOTES

1. Resolution 186 (S2), 14 May 1948.
2. Menuhin, Moshe, *The Decadence of Judaism in Our Time*, Institute for Palestine Studies, Beirut, 1968, p. 512.
3. Bernadotte, Folke, *To Jerusalem*, Hodder and Stoughton, London 1951, p. 42.
4. *Ibid.*, p. 37.
5. *Ibid.*, p. 113.
6. Menuhin, *op. cit.*, p. 513.
7. *Progress Report of the UN Mediator on Palestine*, General Assembly, *Official Records*, Third Session, Supplement No. 11 (A/648) Paris, 1948, p. 14.
8. Bernadotte, *op. cit.*, p. 137.
9. *Ibid.*, p. 143.
10. *Ibid.*, p. 145.
11. *Ibid.*, p. 145.
12. *Ibid.*, pp. 196–7.
13. *Progress Report of the UN Mediator on Palestine*, *op. cit.*, p. 28.
14. Bernadotte, *op. cit.*, p. 199.
15. *Ibid.*, p. 200.
16. *Ibid.*, p. 208.
17. *Ibid.*, p. 208.
18. *Ibid.*, p. 210.
19. *Ibid.*, p. 209.
20. *Ibid.*, p. 190.
21. *Ibid.*, p. 186.
22. *Progress Report of the UN Mediator on Palestine*, *op. cit.*, p. 13.
23. *Death of a Mediator*, The Institute for Palestine Studies, Beirut, 1968, p. 25.

24. *Ibid.*, pp. 19–26.
25. *Ibid.*, p. 22.
26. *Ibid.*, p. 33.
27. *Palestine Post*, 14 December 1948.
28. Menuhin, *op. cit.*, p. 516.
29. *Palestine Post*, 23 January 1948.
30. *Black Panther* (Hebrew journal), 9 November 1972, see *Documents from Israel*, Ithaca Press, London, 1975, p. 127.
31. Allon, Yigal, *The Making of Israel's Army*, Valentine, Mitchell and Co., London, 1970, pp. 233–4.
32. *Black Panther*, *op. cit.*, pp. 130–2.
33. *Ibid.*, p. 131.
34. Herzl, *The Complete Diaries*, *op. cit.*, Vol. I, p. 7.
35. Lilienthal, Alfred, *The Other Side of the Coin*, Devin-Adair, New York, p. 184.
36. *Ibid.*, p. 47.
37. Central Bureau of Statistics, *Statistical Abstract of Israel*, No. 16, p. 96.
38. Berger, Elmer, *Who Knows Better Must Say So*, Institute for Palestine Studies, Beirut, p. 34.
39. *Black Panther*, *op. cit.*, p. 132.
40. Longrigg, Stephen Helmsley, *Iraq, 1900 to 1950*, Oxford University Press, London, 1953, pp. 19–23.
41. Cohen, Hayyim, J., *The Jews of the Middle East 1860–1972*, John Wiley and Sons, New York and Toronto, 1973, p. 30.
42. *Ibid.*, p. 30.
43. 'The League for Combating Zionism in Iraq', *Palestine Affairs*, (Arabic, monthly), Beirut, November 1972, p. 162.
44. Berger, *op. cit.*, p. 30.
45. *Ibid.*, p. 30.
46. *Ibid.*, pp. 32–3.
47. *Black Panther*, *op. cit.*, p. 132.
48. *Ibid.*, p. 133.
49. *Jerusalem Post*, 12 December 1954.
50. 13 December 1954.
51. 13 December 1954.
52. Berger, *op. cit.*, p. 14.
53. Love, Kennett, *Suez: The Twice-Fought War*, McGraw-Hill, New York, 1969, p. 71.
54. *Ibid.*, p. 73.
55. *Ibid.*, p. 74.
56. Love, *op. cit.*, p. 77.
57. See p. 198.
58. *New York Times*, 10 February 1961.
59. *Ibid.*
60. *Jewish Chronicle*, London, 17 February 1971.
61. *Ha'olam Hazeh*, 1 December 1971
62. Associated Press, 16 March 1975.

Six

The Arab-Fighters

A Colonial Society in a Post-Colonial Age

> Let us not today fling accusations at the murderers. Who are we
> that we should argue against their hatred? For eight years now
> they sit in their refugee camps in Gaza, and before their very
> eyes, we turn into our homestead the land and the villages in
> which they and their forefathers have lived. We are a generation
> of settlers, and without the steel helmet and the cannon we cannot
> plant a tree and build a home. Let us not shrink back when we
> see the hatred fermenting and filling the lives of hundreds of
> thousands of Arabs, who sit all around us. Let us not avert our
> gaze, so that our hand shall not slip. This is the fate of our
> generation, the choice of our life—to be prepared and armed,
> strong and tough—or otherwise, the sword will slip from our
> fist, and our life will be snuffed out.[1]

We have met the speaker before. Moshe Dayan was one of
those rugged young farmer-soldiers whom, during the Arab
Rebellion, Orde Wingate took on a daring night raid against an
Arab village.[2] Here, in 1953, he is delivering the funeral oration
of a young pioneer killed by Arab marauders as he was harvesting
grain near the Egyptian frontier. For Israeli deputy Uri Avneri—
to whom we owe the expression 'gun Zionism'—the speech epi-
tomizes the stark philosophy of the 'Arab-fighter'; that is to say,
the Israeli equivalent of what the Americans used to call an
Indian-fighter, a type common to the second generation of
settlers in a land where the newcomers are forced into conflict
with the native population. It was the towering figure of Bengurion who guided the Jewish State through its early years, but
in time, from the shadow of the master his disciple, Moshe Dayan
the 'Arab-fighter', gradually emerged to become the most
typical and celebrated embodiment of the forces which shaped
its first quarter-century.

It had been through an extraordinary combination of chance and blind devotion, political skulduggery and ruthless coercion, that the Zionists realized Herzl's dream. It was, naturally enough, in an exalted and resolute frame of mind that they set about 'up-building' the new State. There was, in Weizmann's phrase, a whole new empty framework to be filled in, a whole new stage to be completed in the emerging grand design. No more urgent task faced the builders than the peopling of the Promised Land, than the furnishing of manpower for its farms, its factories—and its army. With the interfering British gone, and the Arab enemy vanquished, they could throw open the gates of Palestine to unrestricted immigration. Under the Law of Return, every Jew, wherever he might be, automatically acquired the right to full and immediate Israel citizenship. Indeed, in Bengurion's view, it was not merely the Jews' right, it was their duty, to avail themselves of this privilege. 'A state of seven hundred, eight hundred thousand Jews cannot be the climax of a vigil kept unbroken through generations and down the patient centuries; nor could it last for long . . . the Arabs too will arm themselves in the course of time; they will not always lack learning and technical skill. . . . No! So empty a State would be little justified, for it would not change the destiny of Jewry, or fulfil our historic covenant. The duty of the State is to end Galut [Jewish dispersion] at last.'[3] Zionists everywhere had 'to see to it that the Zionist flag which has begun to fly over the State of Israel is hoisted over the entire Jewish people until we achieve the completion of the ingathering of the exiles'.[4] They should have a 'collective obligation' to aid Israel 'under all circumstances and conditions even if such an attitude clashes with their respective national authorities'.[5]

It was not enough to build the new State—it had to be protected too. And that was destined, from the outset, to be a daunting task. There were two basic courses open to the policy-makers. One was to win the acceptance of their Arab and Palestinian neighbours; the other was to fight them. A peaceful settlement or permanent hostility—there was never really much doubt which course Bengurion and his successors would take. They chose war. That is not to say, of course, that they did not offer peace. Indeed, they did so with monotonous regularity. But it was to be a peace on Israel's terms, a victor's peace. And it was completely at variance with the UN recommendation which the Arabs had rejected but which the Israelis had acclaimed as the founding charter of their very existence. It was simple enough; there were, in essence, two things which Israel required of the Arabs. First, there was to be no return of the refugees. As 'aggressors' they forfeited that right. Accordingly, only a month after Bengurion, announcing Israel's establishment to the world, had called on the Arabs to 'play their part in the development of the State' and even as his government was claiming that the Arab exodus had been neither desired nor expected, he resorted to this remarkable line of argument: 'We did not want the war. Tel Aviv did not attack Jaffa. It was Jaffa which attacked Tel Aviv and this should not occur again. Jaffa will be a Jewish town. The repatriation of the Arabs to Jaffa is not justice, but folly. Those who declared war on us have to bear the result after they have been defeated.'[6] And if the Arabs' own folly was not reason enough, others were easily found. By 1 August, the Israel government had come to the conclusion that, on economic grounds, 'the reintegration of the returning Arabs into normal life, and even their mere sustenance, would present an insuperable problem'.[7] As Bengurion spoke, Zionist emissaries were streaming into the Diaspora to 'ingather the exiles', so many of whom had to be cajoled, shamed or frightened into 'coming home'. But reasons thus advanced were necessary cant, for, as Bengurion said elsewhere, 'we must do everything to ensure that they never do return'.[8] Secondly, there was to be no return of territory. The principle which he had so succinctly enunciated at the first cease-fire—'all that we have taken we shall hold'—informed all Israel's subsequent dealings, via third parties, with its neighbours. 'Security' became the great shibboleth; Israel would not participate in its own 'destruction'. All that Israel asked, Foreign Minister Moshe Sharett disarmingly explained, was that the Arabs accept it 'as we are, with our territory, our population and our unrestricted sovereignty'.[9] As for the UN Partition Plan, that recommendation, pronounced 'unassailable' on 15 May, was dead and buried, in the words of Bengurion, by 16 June.[10]

The choice which the Zionists made was hardly a voluntary, or even a conscious, one. It grew out of their predicament. Israel was *doomed* to everlasting conflict with its neighbours. This is what Dayan, the 'Arab-fighter', instinctively understood; it has been the one consistent strain of his often mercurial temperament. That which came into being by violent and unnatural means could only survive and prosper by violent and unnatural means. The nation born by the sword must live by it. The National Home had been conceived as the answer to anti-Semitism and the ghetto, but anything more closely resembling a massive, armed ghetto than the fortress state of Israel it would be hard to find. The implacable logic of Zionism in action, held partially in check by the Mandate, now came completely into its own. There was no third party—unless one counted the fickle and ineffectual will of the international community—to hold the ring. If the Arabs had rejected the lesser Israel of the UN, with its Palestinian majority and its built-in constitutional guarantees, they naturally took even less kindly to this larger Israel, which had expelled most of the Palestinians and torn up those parts of its founding charter which it did not like. The Arabs resolved that sooner or later they would 'liberate' Palestine, and the Israelis, with enemies on all sides, were impelled further down the road they had already taken. In security's name they found justification for military exploits which only deepened the encircling hatred—hatred which, in turn, engendered still more such exploits, and necessitated more and more arms to carry them out.

There can be no question about Israel's military prowess, the skill and daring of its commanders, the courage of its soldiers. In twenty-five years it has waged four 'big wars'—all-out struggles with one or a combination of its neighbours—and an endless succession of 'little wars', those trans-frontier raids and counter-raids, by land, sea or air, which, in the absence of a peaceful settlement, inexorably lead on to the big ones. Its performance on the battlefield has already assured it of an honoured niche in history. Israel came into being in 1948, with the defeat of five Arab armies. In October 1956, with French and British assistance, it reached the Suez Canal in a five-day *blitzkrieg* against Nasser's Egypt. In June 1967 it required only six days singlehandedly to defeat three Arab countries, Egypt, Syria and Jordan, and capture the whole of Sinai, the Golan Heights and that part of Palestine—East Jerusalem and the West Bank—which it had failed to take in 1948. In October 1973 it was the turn of the Arabs—Egypt and Syria, to be precise—to strike the first, devastating blow; stunned and reeling, Israel fought back and, after a fierce eighteen-day struggle, it threw back the Syrian army beyond the 1967 ceasefire lines, and crossed the Suez Canal into 'Africa'; some military experts found this recovery even more impressive than the pulverizing victories of 1956 and 1967.

The Western public watched Israel choose war, and then ceaselessly wage it, with remarkable complaisance, not to say admiration. It was not merely because sheer military, like sporting, prowess, became its own justification, although that had much to do with it. It was also because, Hitler and the Holocaust aiding, the Zionists continued to enjoy that special favour and influence among the powerful, which had brought Israel into being in the first place. Israel also benefited from a certain cultural and historical prejudice, reinforced by European colonial experience, against the Arabs. Nor, on the face of it, did Israel fit the Western experience of a militarist society. On the contrary, nothing seemed less regimented, less Prussian in appearance than its citizens' army, rakish and debonair, which went to war in taxis, ice-cream wagons, with long hair and wearing the most eccentric attire. Above all, perhaps, the Israelis found it all too easy to persuade Western opinion, impressed by misleading disparities in size, that here was a clear-cut struggle between the weak and the strong, in which an Israeli David always won a heartwarming victory against the Arab Goliath. 1948 set the pattern. In that war, as we have seen, the Zionists were unquestionably the real aggressors, yet they had a remarkable success in portraying the Arabs in that role. Having established this travesty of history—this extraordinary distortion of cause and effect—they built on it. The Arabs helped them do it, not only because they were as incompetent in propaganda as they were in war, but because, as losers, it was they who now had to take the initiative, to undo the *fait accompli* which the Zionists had achieved at their expense. All the Israelis had to do was to stand still, to 'hold what they had taken'. They called their army the Israeli Defence Forces, and all its actions were ostensibly defensive in nature. Its 'little wars' were to punish and deter; its 'big wars' were 'wars of survival'.

In outward manner Israel may not be a militarist society, but, to the very depth of its being, it is a military one. It may not be a totalitarian society, but, in their attitude to the Arabs and the rest of the world, its people, in their overwhelming majority, slavishly approve official deeds and dogma. The army *is* the people. The Israelis made of armed might not merely the instrument of their own preservation, but of Zionism's still unfinished mission as well. Force was not merely 'punitive', it was 'purposive' too. For Israel did not really intend to stand still. That was just a façade. Israel was an aggressive colonizing power in a post-colonial era. It is true that, for Jewish and other reasons, and unique among anachronisms of its kind, it operated in a climate of extraordinary Western tolerance. But it could not tax that tolerance beyond all limits, and wherever possible—for sometimes it simply was not possible—it virtuously subscribed to the anti-colonial and other moralities of the age. Meanwhile, behind the façade, it exploited Arab violence—or the Arab counter-violence which, in historical perspective, it really was— as the pretext for an opportunistic and far more effective violence of its own, disguising offence as defence, the 'purposive' as the 'punitive'. And for twenty-five years, under Moshe Dayan, the Arab-fighter, it achieved an astonishing success.

FRONTIER RAIDS AND REPRISALS

From 1948 onwards, of course, the Israelis had as enemies not just the Palestinians, but the entire Arab world as well. It is often hard to draw a clear distinction between the two, although for our present purposes we shall do so. We can also, again a little arbitrarily, make a further sub-distinction among the Palestinians themselves, and assume that, for the Israelis, these now fell into two kinds: the 'outsiders' and the 'insiders', the immense majority who had left and those, something less than 200,000, who had managed to stay behind, unwanted Arab citizens of the Jewish State.

It was in their dealings with the 'outsiders' that Dayan and the Arab-fighters truly came into their own. Their aim was not simply to keep the outsiders out. It went deeper than that. It was to eradicate the very idea that, one day, they would return for good. The Palestinians did of course entertain that idea, and eventually, the Israelis feared, they might act upon it. They might organize their own irridentist movement, or, more im-

portant, as a powerful and disruptive force in Arab politics, they
might induce the Arab régimes to take up their cause in earnest.
Thus it was that the Israelis reacted to any attempt at Palestinian
self-assertion, however trivial or pathetic, with extreme, indeed
neurotic, severity. The reaction was entirely punitive not purposive in nature, for the outsiders, driven from land and property,
no longer represented a physical obstacle, *in situ*, to Zionism's
long-term purposes.

What the outsiders could do was to make raids across the
frontiers; indeed, as Moshe Dayan acknowledged, it was entirely
natural that they should. The Palestinian 'infiltrators'—as they
were called—came mostly from that part of Palestine, the West
Bank, which had been absorbed by the Hashemite Kingdom of
Jordan. For political and geographical reasons, incursions were
easier from there than they were from Egypt, Syria or Lebanon,
which also had refugee populations. To begin with, the infiltrators usually had little hostile intention at all. They were
going back, many of them, simply to rescue some of their belongings, sneaking by night into deserted villages to recover the
valuables they had buried before their flight. Some would go
searching for missing relatives. Others might cross to pick a few
oranges from their own orchards or even to plough a part of their
fields which, though they might not know it, had suddenly become enemy territory. For such was the caprice of the armistice
line that more than a hundred villages were cut off from the land
their inhabitants had tilled with asses and yoked oxen for generations; there it lay before their very eyes, but strangers were tilling
it with tractors and modern machinery in their stead. The plight
of these border villagers was particularly distressing because,
though cut off from their livelihood, they did not qualify for
refugee assistance—a refugee, in the UN definition, being one
who has lost both land *and* house. Moreover, it was in a mean and
pettifogging spirit that the strangers insisted on their territorial
'rights'. In his memoirs, Commander Hutchison, a UN observer
from America, recalled how a group of families working a patch
of rocky soil on their side of the line depended, for irrigation, on
a cistern that lay on the other side. The nearest Israeli settlement was a mile away, and the cistern was no use to it. When he
asked if the Arabs could continue to take their water from there,
Commander Hutchison was told that 'if they cross they will be

shot'.[11] In fact border patrols, consisting mostly of locally recruited vigilantes, frequently did shoot on sight.[12] Infiltration fell off. But naturally there remained a determined few who kept it up, and by now some of those were bent not simply on recovering what they had lost, but on wreaking a private, if useless, vengeance on the people who had taken it from them. They would steal: horses, cows, goats, agricultural implements. And then they would kill.

Yet it was not until the summer of 1953 that organized terrorism, under the auspices of the ex-Mufti and various Arab régimes, began in earnest, and then only on a small scale. Moreover, the Israelis were getting the better of it: they were killing far more Arabs than Arabs were killing Israelis. It may have been natural, as Dayan said, for the refugees to raid, but it was equally natural, according to his uncompromising credo, that those who had displaced them should hit back a hundred-fold. The Israelis spurned peaceable alternatives. These were available. Most Arab governments would probably have tried to 'liberate' Palestine, if they thought they had a serious chance. But they knew they did not, and whatever their declared policies, their actual ones were generally restrained. At all events, they were not going to let a handful of Palestinian irregulars drag them into the full-scale war they did not want—or for which they were not prepared. Jordan, the most dangerously exposed of Israel's neighbours, strained every nerve on Israel's behalf. Legislation was introduced which made a mere crossing of the line punishable by six months' imprisonment, and at one time at least half the prisoners on the West Bank were serving terms for this offence. The Jordanians even went so far, in defiance of Arab public opinion, as to seek Israeli cooperation in tracking down offenders, and on one occasion they proposed a so-called Local Commanders' Agreement providing for joint Israeli-Jordanian patrols, direct telephone communications and frequent meetings between officers. The Israelis would have none of it and even when, under pressure from the UN peacekeeping forces, they acquiesced in one or other such measure they were denouncing it within two or three weeks. They insisted on blaming Jordan. Everybody who crossed the line—the real terrorist, the orange-stealer or just the man on a visit to his relatives—belonged to the 'paramilitary forces of Jordan'.[13]

Spurning peace, they needed a war machine equal, in spirit and technique, to the task that confronted them. During their 'little war' along the Jordanian frontier they developed one. The *Haganah* and *Palmach*, the official forces of the Jewish state-in-the-making, had subscribed to the military ethic they called 'purity of arms'; during the 'War of Independence', they proved themselves ruthless enough, but, on the whole, their methods were distinguishable from the uninhibited brutality of *Irgun* and the 'dissidents'. They would not cold-bloodedly plan a Deir Yassin. After independence *Haganah* and *Palmach* furnished the backbone of the Israeli Defence Forces, but before long, it was the spirit of the *Irgun* that animated their crack units. With Zionism, as we have seen, extremism has almost always won in the end; it is the norm to which, under pressure of foreseeable circumstance, its latent forces have always gravitated. The Israelis' kill rate, across the troubled frontier, may have been far higher than the Arabs' but it was not high enough. To remedy this, the army offered money for what an Israeli newspaper, many years later, described as 'acts of revenge at so much a piece'. The practice had to be discontinued because the mercenaries so employed used to claim more killings than they had actually performed.[14] Furthermore, the army was not happy with its own reprisal raids. Indeed, according to the *Para-troopers' Book*, the semi-official history of the Israeli Airborne Corps, it was positively smarting at its failures. What 'most infuriated General Moshe Dayan—chief of operations at the time—was the scandalous defeat of the Givathi Regiment at the Jordanian village of Palma. An entire battalion, a shock battalion with a glorious name, set out to attack the village. There were only a dozen Jordanian frontier guards armed with rifles in the village. The Jordanians opened fire, the battalion halted at the village walls and retreated.'[15]

Profiting from setbacks of this kind, influential 'activists' began to agitate for the formation of a specialized reprisal unit. Their ascendancy was not achieved without a struggle. General Dayan threw his weight behind the idea, but opponents of it blocked a decision. The opposition came not merely from 'doves' on the civilian side—chief among them Foreign Minister Moshe Sharett—but from much of the military establishment, who feared the emergence of a new organization, Dayan's 'private army', liable to lead an aggressive, independent existence of its own. The activists forced the issue, and in the jingoistic atmosphere of a deliberately stepped-up violence, they succeeded in forming the celebrated Unit 101 under the command of the equally celebrated Ariel Sharon.

Unit 101 carried out its first major operation—a landmark in this history—on 14 October 1953. It was a reprisal for the killing, by a grenade, of a mother and two children in the village of Yahuda. Sharett's diary entry for 14 October records that the Mixed Armistice Commission (part of the UN peacekeeping machinery) had 'roundly condemned' the killing and 'even the Jordanian delegates voted in favour of the resolution. They took it upon themselves to prevent such atrocities in the future. Under such circumstances is it wise to retaliate? . . . If we retaliate, we only make the marauder bands' job easier and give the [Israeli] authorities an excuse to do something. I called Lavon [Defence Minister] and told him what I thought. He said he would consult B.G. [Prime Minister Bengurion].' The diary continued: 'In the afternoon, during a meeting with Lavon and others in connection with developments in the north, an army representative brought Lavon a note from the UNTSO Chief of Staff, Gen. Vagn Bennike, saying that the Commander of the Jordan Legion, Glubb Pasha, had asked for police bloodhounds to cross over from Israel to track down the Yahud murderers.' After Lavon had read the note, Sharett records, the army man asked: 'Any change in plans?' Lavon replied: 'No change.'[16]

'No change', after Jordan had asked for Israeli bloodhounds to track down acknowledged Jordanian criminals, no change in the plans to massacre that night the sleeping inhabitants of the village of Qibya. As the *Paratroopers' Book* described it: 'The operation at Qibya was to be distinguished from other operations by its purposes and its effects. The dynamiting of dozens of houses in Qibya was an ambitious undertaking surpassing anything in the past. Once and for all, it washed away the stain of the defeats that Zahal [the Israel army] had suffered in its reprisal operations.'[17] As the UN military observers, who reached the village two hours after the soot-smeared Israeli commandos had left, described it: 'Bullet-riddled bodies near the doorways and multiple bullet hits on the doors of the demolished houses indicated that the inhabitants had been forced to remain inside until their homes

were blown up over them. . . . Witnesses were uniform in describing their experience as a night of horror, during which
Israeli soldiers moved about in their village blowing up buildings,
firing into doorways and windows with automatic weapons and
throwing hand grenades.'[18] Sixty-six men, women and children
died in an operation which reminded even pro-Israeli newspapers
like the *New York Post* of Lidice.[19]

The Israeli government did not admit responsibility for the
reprisal raid. Public opinion still lagged behind the Arab-fighters;
there were still too many people who could not reconcile such
methods with 'purity of arms'. Bengurion announced in a special
broadcast that 'the government of Israel emphatically denies the
false and fantastic tale according to which 600 Zahal soldiers
participated in an operation against the village of Qibya. We have
examined the facts in detail, and we can state without hesitation
that not a single unit, not even the smallest, was absent from its
barracks on the night of the attack on Qibya.' It was frontier
settlers who had done it, the Prime Minister insisted, 'mostly
Jewish refugees from Arab countries or survivors of Nazi concentration camps'; it had been their impulsive response to the
murder of a mother and her two children. Such became the
official explanation for all the exploits of Unit 101.

In time, however, public opinion did catch up, and by March
1955 the government all but officially announced to the world
that 'there has been nothing reckless or impulsive about the
lethal raids across the borders. On the contrary, the policy of
reprisals is the fruit of cold, unemotional political and psychological reasoning.'[20] Unit 101 was never a large force, and it was
composed entirely of volunteers, but its example was to be lasting
and profound. Established as an antidote to the *Palmach*, the
virus it carried did meet with some resistance. Of one squeamish
recruit the *Paratroopers' Book* records, 'As an ex-Palmach who
believed in the purity of arms he refused to participate in an expedition directed not against enemy soldiers but against the
civilian population. Arik [Sharon's nickname] did not force him
to take part. In a heated discussion, Shlomo Baum [Sharon's
adjutant] hurled a remark at him: "There are no pure or impure
arms; there are only clean weapons that work when you need
them and dirty weapons that jam the moment you fire." '[21] In
spite of resistance, the virus quickly spread. Three months after

Qibya, at Dayan's initiative, Unit 101 was merged with the newly formed paratroop corps. According to Sharon, who assumed command of the combined force, Dayan 'was aware of the decisive influence the small unit would have on the Airborne (paratroopers) and, later, on the whole Zahal. . . . One might say that the ideology of reprisal operations was, in all respects, crystallized among the Airborne units.'[22] The army did in fact fall increasingly under the influence and command of men of the 101 and the Airborne. The spirit and methods of the *Palmach*—and the *Palmach* was hardly gentle—gave way to the spirit and methods of the *Irgun*. Meanwhile, in the country as a whole, there developed around Unit 101 the aura of heroic legend. Its centrepiece was the Arab-fighter extraordinary, Meir Har-Zion. Two or three nights a week, for months on end, this young commando took part in reprisal raids, 'laconically killing Arab soldiers, peasants, and townspeople in a kind of fury without hatred'.[23] He would introduce variations into a monotonous routine. Once, he and his comrades crossed the frontier, seized six Arabs, killed five of them with a knife as the others watched, and left the sixth alive so that he could tell.[24] His private exploits revealed the same natural bent. On leave, and bored, he once made a daredevil foray deep into enemy territory; on his way back to Jerusalem he shot an Arab soldier on the main highway. Later his sister was killed by a bedouin on one of her own sorties into enemy territory. Har-Zion revenged her by killing two bedouins whom he deemed to be connected with her death. Eventually he was critically wounded in action; his life was saved by a battlefield tracheotomy performed with a penknife. His memoirs and numerous press interviews are the story of a man who can describe, with dry relish, what it is like to stab an Arab shepherd in the back—and who recommends that anyone who wishes for the 'marvellous, sublime feeling' of 'knowing that you are a male' should kill with a knife rather than a gun.[25]

The cult which surrounded Har-Zion was both official and popular. Ministers and generals would glorify him as a 'model' for Israeli youth, the 'fighting symbol' of the entire Israeli army. He was placed above the law; when he killed the two bedouins, he was arrested and could have been charged with murder, but, on Bengurion's personal intervention, he was released without trial.[26] Half-crippled and forced into retirement, he was pre-

sented with a large piece of confiscated Arab land on Mount
Kaoukab high above Lake Galilee. In this desolate spot, not far
from his old *kibbutz*, he set up his private cattle ranch and played
host to the soldiers who came, as pilgrims, to see and admire him.
'A whole ceremony developed around Kaoukab,' he recalls in his
memoirs; 'they arrived after a long march that lasted a day and
a night. At the end of the march, the Unit's insignia were
distributed to the soldiers. The goal of the march was the
ranch. To ascend it has become a tradition; it is a summit one
must reach.'[27]

THE ARABS WHO STAYED BEHIND

Keeping out the outsiders was almost exclusively punitive;
keeping down the insiders was both punitive and purposive. For
the Palestinians who stayed behind were not merely a security
problem; their very presence stood in the way of Zionism's historic mission.

The military governed the lives of Israel's Arab minority. Outright armed violence, though by no means absent, was not its
characteristic method; force and coercion sufficed. Nevertheless,
there was a grave difficulty. Israel described itself as an outpost
of the 'free world' on which it so heavily depended, a 'bastion of
democracy' in an area which lacked such a thing It was a nation
ostentatiously founded on law, justice and humanity. Racial and
religious persecution, the bitter cup from which the Jews had
drunk so deep, could have no place in the Jewish State. In the
Declaration of Independence it promised 'complete equality of
social and political rights for all its citizens, without distinction
of creed, race or sex'. So it looked on the surface. In practice,
however, some citizens were more equal than others. The words
Arab and Jew never actually appeared in the statute books, but
in the enforcement of the law there was one set of principles for
one kind of Israeli and another set of principles for the other.
Among those who looked beneath the surface and then defended
what they saw it generated a 'double-speak' and 'double-think'
which an Israeli civil rights campaigner has called 'the Orwellian
tax that Israel pays to the concept of democracy'.[28]

The legal foundations of the military rule under which the
insiders fell were the Defence Regulations of 1945. It was the

British who introduced them and the Jewish community, then in revolt against the Mandate, which first bore the brunt of them. Their introduction had raised a storm of protest. Dr Yaacov Shimson Shapira, a future Israeli Minister of Justice, described them as 'unparalleled in any civilized country; there were no such laws even in Nazi Germany. . . . There is indeed only one form of government which resembles the system in force here now—the case of an occupied country. They try to pacify us by saying that these laws are only directed against malefactors, not against honest citizens. But the Nazi Governor of Occupied Oslo also announced that no harm would come to citizens who minded their own business. It is our duty to tell the whole world that the Defence Laws passed by the British Mandatory Government of Palestine destroy the very foundations of justice in this land.'[29] After 1948 Israel did not abolish this system of 'officially licensed terrorism', as another future Justice Minister called the Defence Regulations. It enforced them with greater severity—against the Arabs. Under these laws, the army could uproot whole communities at will, deporting them or transferring them from one place to another; it could impose indefinite curfews and establish security zones which no Arab could enter without permission; seize land and destroy or requisition property; enter and search any place; imprison a man without trial or confine him to his home, quarter or village; prohibit or restrict his movement inside or outside Israel, or expel him without explanation from his native land. The only means of redress, through a military court, was wholly futile.

Armed with such Draconian powers, the military authorities lost no time in exploiting them. Outright violence, entirely punitive in intent, may not have been their characteristic method, but there is no more revealing example of the Arabs' plight than one notorious occasion when they did use it. The Arabs remember Kafr Qasem as the Deir Yassin of the established State. Less revealing, perhaps, than the event itself was the reaction it generated. On 29 October 1956, on the eve of Israel's invasion of Egypt, a detachment of Frontier Guards imposed a curfew on villages near the Jordanian frontier. Among them was Kafr Qasem. The Mukhtar was informed of the curfew just half an hour before it was due to go into effect. It was therefore quite impossible for him to pass the message on to the villagers who would be returning, as dusk fell, from their various places of work. Major Shmuel Melinki, the detachment commander, had foreseen this eventuality, and he asked his superior, Brigadier Yshishkhar Shadmi, what should be done about anyone coming home in ignorance of the curfew. The Brigadier had replied: 'I don't want any sentimentality . . . that's just too bad for him.'[30] And there was no sentimentality. In the first hour of the curfew, between five and six o'clock, the Frontier Guards killed forty-seven villagers. They had returned home individually or in batches. A few came on foot, but most travelled by bicycle, mule cart or lorry. They included women and children. But all the Frontier Guards wanted to know was whether they were from Kafr Qasem. For if they were, they were curfew-breakers, and once they had ascertained that they were, they shot them down at close range with automatic weapons. 'Of every group of returning workers, some were killed and others wounded; very few succeeded in escaping unhurt. The proportion of those killed increased, until, of the last group, which consisted of 14 women, a boy and 4 men, all were killed, except one girl, who was seriously wounded.'[31] The slaughter might have gone on like this had not Lieutenant Gavriel Dahan, the officer on the spot

> . . . informed the command several times over the radio apparatus in the jeep of the number killed. Opinions differ as to the figure he gave in his reports, but all are agreed that in his first report he said: 'one less', and in the next two reports: 'fifteen less' and 'many less—it is difficult to count them'. The last two reports, which followed each other in quick succession, were picked up by Captain Levy, who passed them on to Melinki. When he was informed that there were 'fifteen less' in Kafr Qasem, Melinki gave orders which he was unable to transmit to Dahan before the report arrived of 'many less—it is difficult to count them', for the firing to stop and for a more moderate procedure to be adopted in the whole area. . . . This order finally ended the bloodshed at Kafr Qasem.[32]

All this was established in the trial which, as the scandal slowly leaked out, the government was obliged to hold. The trail was a *pro forma* affair. There was little moral outrage in the courtroom, and, apart from a few lone voices, very little outside it. During the proceedings the leading newspaper *Haaretz* reported that 'the eleven officers and soldiers who are on trial for the massacre in Kafr Qasem have all received a fifty per cent increase in their salaries. A special messenger was sent to Jerusalem to bring the cheques to the accused in time for Passover. A number of the accused had been given a vacation for the holiday. . . . The accused mingle freely with the spectators; the officers smile at them and pat them on the back; some of them shake hands with them. It is obvious, that these people, whether they will be found innocent or guilty, are not treated as criminals, but as heroes.'[33] One Private David Goldfield reportedly resigned from the Security Police in protest against the trial. According to the *Jewish Newsletter*, his testimony merely reflected what most Israelis thought: 'I feel that the Arabs are the enemies of our State. . . . When I went to Kafr Qasem, I felt that I went against the enemy and I made no distinction between the Arabs in Israel and those outside its frontiers.' Asked what he would do if he met an Arab woman, in no sense a security threat, who was trying to reach her home, he replied: 'I would shoot her down, I would harbour no sentiments, because I received an order and I had to carry it out.'[34] The sentences were *pro forma* too. Melinki and Dahan got gaol terms of seventeen and fifteen years respectively, but it was a foregone conclusion that they would only serve a fraction of them. In response to appeals for a pardon, the Supreme Military Court decided to reduce the 'harsh' sentence; and, following this generous example, the Chief of Staff, then the Head of State, and finally a Committee for the Release of Prisoners all made contributions, so that within a year of their sentence Melinki and Dahan were free men. As for Brigadier Shadmi—the 'no sentimentality' senior officer—a Special Military Court found him guilty of a 'merely technical' error, reprimanded him and fined him one piastre. But the twist in the tail was yet to come. Nine months after his release from prison, Dahan, convicted of killing forty-three Arabs in an hour, was appointed 'officer responsible for Arab affairs' in the town of Ramleh.[35] And the last that has been heard of Major Melinki was that, through his influential connections in the army, he had secured a coveted permit, sought after by many an entrepreneur, to set up a tourist centre in southern Israel.[36]

Let us now turn to those other, more characteristic, uses to which the military authorities—aided and abetted by the civil administration—put their Draconian powers. Zionism's basic im-

pulse has always been to take possession of the land. It goes
without saying that the new state appropriated all the land
which the outsiders left behind; but it also appropriated the
insiders' land too—about a million dunums of it.[37] In 1948 perhaps 5 per cent of Israeli-controlled territory was still in Arab
hands. By 1967—and the war which brought the remaining 20
per cent of Palestine under Israeli control—it had fallen to about
1 per cent.[38] It was here, perhaps, in the systematic harassment
of the hapless vestige of a community they had destroyed and
dispersed that the Zionists showed how far, in serving their own
people, they could harden their hearts against others.

In the early years, with wartime techniques still fresh in their
memories, the authorities would frequently 'cleanse' the land in
the quick and easy way. They would send in the army to drive
the inhabitants out—over the frontier or to other parts of Israel.
Thus, as late as the summer of 1950, the village of Ashkelon was
still Arab—at least it was until one morning when the soldiers
arrived, put all the inhabitants on trucks, took them to the Gaza
frontier and, with the help of some shooting in the air, told them
to go and join the refugees who had passed that way two years
before.[39] Under the Defence Regulations this kind of procedure
was legal. However, it was not good for Israel's reputation; the
world was sensitive about the refugee problem, and the Arab
states were exploiting it. So, being a country where the rule of
law prevailed, Israel enacted legislation to furnish a sound juridical basis for expropriations which had already taken place and
for those which were still to come. The first of a series of enact-
ments—the 1950 Law for the Acquisition of Absentee Property
—was a very ingenious, retroactive device. The absentees in
question were for the most part the outsiders who could not
return. Their property was acquired by a Custodian of Absentee
Property, whose ostensible task was to look after it pending a
solution of the whole refugee problem, his real one being to hand
it over to the appropriate authorities for Jewish settlement in
perpetuity. But insiders could become absentees too. They are
known as 'absent-presents'; the precise number of these Orwellian beings is a well-kept military secret, but they run into tens of
thousands.[40] It was very easy for the Custodian to classify a man
as 'absent-present'. For under the new law any person who left
his usual place of residence between 29 November 1947 and 1

September 1948 for any place outside Palestine, or any place inside Palestine but outside Jewish control, was considered to be an absentee—and never mind if he was actually present in Israel, a fully-fledged citizen of this 'bastion of democracy'. The simple villager of Galilee had not been vouchsafed the power to tell the future, and little did he realize that for this 'offence' committed two years before it actually became one, all his worldly possessions—his homes and fields—could be taken away from him and given to somebody else, a total stranger who came from across the seas. It did not matter how long he had been away; it could have been for one day only. No matter where he had gone; it could have been to the next village. No matter why he left; perhaps it was to buy some sheep. Moreover it was so much easier for the Custodian in that he was not expected to furnish proof of absence. His own investigations sufficed. When, on the strength of them, he 'declared' a man an absentee, he became an absentee and no one could gainsay him; for 'he may not be questioned about the information sources which led him to issue a decision by virtue of this law'. And just in case the Custodian, by his own admission, did make a mistake, the law took care of that too: 'No deal concluded spontaneously between the Custodian and another person in connection with property which the Custodian believes to be absentee property at the moment the deal is concluded may be invalidated, but shall remain in force even if it is later proved that such property was not absentee property at that time.'[41]

Thus it came about that whole communities of insiders, citizens of Israel, were no less refugees than their brethren beyond the borders. For during the nine months in question—an arbitrary time-span, dating from the UN Partition recommendation, well suited to Israel's purposes—a great many Palestinians had indeed left their normal places of residence, not simply for business or pleasure, but because they thought it was dangerous to remain where they were. They planned to return home when the fighting ended. But their new masters had other ideas. If they ever saw their homes again, it was with strangers living in them; if they ever tilled their fields again, it was in the service of those strangers. Townspeople were no better off. A frightened family might have moved for a few days to another quarter, or just across the street.[42] The Custodian declared them 'absent-presents' none the

less. He was a man of principle. What was the difference between
town and country, between ten metres or ten miles? It might
seem hard, and he was sorry. But what could he do about it? The
law, after all, was the law.

Another typical enactment—the Emergency Articles for the
Exploitation of Uncultivated Areas—was particularly useful
because it dovetailed so nicely with the Defence Regulations: a
happy blend of the purposive and the punitive. On the face of it,
this law had an entirely laudable purpose. It empowered the
Minister of Agriculture to take possession of uncultivated land to
ensure that it is cultivated when he 'is not satisfied that the
owner of the land has begun, or is about to begin, to cultivate it,
or is going to continue to cultivate it'.[43] However, it could also be
turned to another purpose. The procedure was quite simple. The
Minister of Defence, with laws of his own to draw upon, would
declare some choice farmland a 'closed area', thereby making it
a grave offence to enter the area without written permission from
the Military Governor. The Military Governor finds himself unable, for security reasons, to grant such permits to farmers. Their
fields quickly become 'uncultivated land'. Noting this, the
Minister of Agriculture takes prompt action 'to ensure that it is
cultivated'. He has this done either 'by labourers engaged by
him' or by 'handing it over to another party to cultivate it'. This
other party, of course, is always the neighbouring Jewish colony.

Clearly, in the enforcement of Israeli law, some people were
more equal than others. Indeed, some people seemed to be above
it altogether. At least that is what the inhabitants of Ghabisiya,
Kafr Bar'am and Iqrit—to name only three villages—could legitimately conclude after they appealed to the Supreme Court. The
Military Government had declared Ghabisiya a 'closed area' and
expelled its inhabitants. The Supreme Court ruled that the
Military Governor had been entitled to take this step, but that
his decision was invalid because it had not been published in the
Official Gazette. The Military Government found this ruling
very hard to accept, and a few days later, while continuing to
keep the villagers out, the necessary order was published in the
gazette. The villagers went back to the Supreme Court. This time
it ruled that since they had failed to return before publication of
the order they could not do so after it. The inhabitants of the
Christian, and notably docile, village of Kafr Bar'am which had

become a 'closed area' too, applied to the Supreme Court in their
turn. It ruled in their favour: they should be permitted to return.
The authorities were extremely angry. Aircraft of the Israeli
Defence Forces attacked the village. The bombardment went on
until Kafr Bar'am was reduced to rubble, whereupon the aircraft
returned safely to their bases.[44] In July 1951 the Supreme Court
ruled in favour of another Christian village, Iqrit, whose inhabitants had been ordered, three years earlier, to leave their
homes 'for two weeks' until 'military operations in the area were
concluded'. After this judgement the Military Government found
another justification to prevent them from returning. The villagers once more appealed to the Supreme Court, which decided
to consider the case on 6 February 1952. But a month and a half
before that date, on Christmas Day to be precise, the Israeli
Defence Forces took the Mukhtar of this Christian community to
the top of a nearby hill and forced him to watch the show—the
blowing up of every house in the village—which they had laid
on for his benefit.[45]

It hardly needs to be demonstrated that, however democratic
Israel was for the Jews, it was in every sense a tyranny for the
Arabs. Tyranny, like freedom, is indivisible, and it was not to be
expected that a government which could so persecute its citizens
in one way—by plundering their land and property—should
treat them any better in others. Israel has always claimed that it
cares for its Arab as much as its Jewish citizens, indeed that they
are far better off than they would have been under Arab rule. But
the fact that Israel made this claim—and above all the fact that
none but a 'lunatic fringe' of its freedom-loving Jewish citizens
ever challenged it—merely confirmed a natural law: Orwellian
'double-think' will always be as pervasive as the evil it seeks to
hide. Just what did happen, for example, to those dispossessed
Arab farmers? Merely to ask the question is to open a Pandora's
Box of ramifying iniquities, for the truth is that the Arabs were
deliberately reduced to the *lumpenproletariat* of Israeli society or
—in the biblical parlance which Zionists so often affect—they
became the 'hewers of wood and the drawers of water'. If the
Arabs continued to work what little land was left to them, they
did so in the face of a whole series of obstructionist measures,
designed to consolidate Jewish agriculture at their expense,
which forced them to sell their produce at uneconomic prices

and starved them of financial assistance, modern machinery and
the benefits of irrigation projects. If they gave up the struggle and
worked for Jewish masters, they had to offer their services on a
black market which grossly exploited them. And even that was
eventually denied them. For by the sixties thousands of Arab
farmers found themselves working what was once their own land
on behalf of a new class of Jewish *effendis* whom time, and the
weakening of the Zionist ideal, had brought into being. So in 1967,
parliament passed a law which in reality—though not, God forbid, in appearance—was designed to prevent Israel's Arab citizens from working the 'Land of the Nation'—even if they worked
it for Jews.[46] Not until 1962, and even then on a small scale,
would the trade union federation accept Arabs in its ranks. The
exclusivist dogmas of Hebrew Labour—or 'organized labour' as
Orwellian 'double-think' renamed it—still held sway. Arab unemployment was rife. But Arabs who did find work were liable,
not being 'organized', to dismissal at any time. They were
usually reserved for the most menial and dirty jobs. Where they
managed to rise above that, there was no such thing as equal pay
for equal work. If, as an increasing number did, they found jobs
in the cities, they could not—thanks to the Defence Regulations
—live there. They became itinerant labourers, forced to travel
huge distances every day to and from their villages—although, as
a special favour, construction workers would be permitted to
spend the night in unfinished buildings or makeshift accommodation of the kind. The Arab minority could not seek collective
redress through Israel's democratic system, because there was no
place in the system for representative Arab political parties, no
opportunity for Arabs to achieve positions of real influence in
government and administration; the 'Arab Department' of every
institution was headed by a Jew. The Arabs could only vote as
appendages of Jewish parties, and what the Israelis paraded in
the outside world as the proof of their own enlightenment they
occasionally admitted to themselves was a farce, 'a struggle in the
name of the Arabs between the Jews themselves, for the sake of
the Jews'.[47] Arab writers, intellectuals or community leaders who
showed the least independence of spirit would be placed in
'administrative detention', confined to their place of residence,
or exiled to some remote corner of the country. Nor could
parents, miserable though their own plight might be, look for-

ward to a brighter future for their children. The deliberate
stunting of Arab education meant that there were about nine
Jewish university graduates, *per capita*, for every one Arab.

Zionist apartheid, whatever one might think of its original
motivation, quickly proved itself as harsh as South Africa's. It
was rather strange therefore that whereas enlightened Western
opinion condemned racial discrimination in one place it was apt
to condone or even praise it in another. One key reason, of course,
was the extraordinary built-in favour which the Zionist movement had always enjoyed. Another was that while South Africa's
apartheid was open, even flaunted, Israel's was disguised. Moreover, Israel's was much *easier* to disguise; for the citizens it persecuted were a small minority, not a large majority. That in turn
was because, in 1948 and after, the Arab-fighters simply drove
the Arabs out. Ironically, therefore, it was the very extremism of
that original and massive act of violence which subsequently
helped Israel seem less extreme, less oppressive, in its treatment
of the few who stayed behind. The Arab-fighters' most dazzling
triumph still lay ahead—but this time it was destined to make
Israeli apartheid much harder to hide.

WARS OF EXPANSION

For Bengurion and his lieutenants, the 1948 'War of Independence' had left unfinished business. There is no need to exaggerate
Zionism's inherent expansionist tendencies. Inevitably, being an
exalted creed by any standards, it spawned its share of fantastic
conceits. But, however seriously entertained at the time, visions
of a Hebrew Kingdom stretching from the Nile to the Euphrates,
or other far-flung boundaries of biblical inspiration, belonged
essentially to the romantic early days of the movement. When an
unlikely configuration of international circumstances suddenly
brought Zionism into the realm of the possible, the politicians
who exploited this opportunity had to set what they deemed to be
realistic limits on Zionist ambitions. Although—to any but
themselves—those ambitions must have seemed overweening
enough, they were always distressed at any enforced curtailment
of them. The politicians had seriously envisaged full-scale
Jewish settlement on the East Bank of the River Jordan, and
when, one afternoon in 1921, Winston Churchill, the Colonial

Secretary, conferred British-protected but independent state-hood on the Amirate of Transjordan, thereby severing the East Bank from Palestine, the Zionists considered this to be a grievous blow to the territorial integrity of the 'National Home'. In 1948, Bengurion proclaimed that the new state had only been estab-lished in 'a portion of the land of Israel' and there were subse-quent expressions of regret that even fuller advantage had not been taken of the revolutionary opportunities, perhaps never to be repeated, which had then presented themselves. 'Israeli terri-tory might have been greater', said Bengurion, 'if Moshe Dayan had been chief of staff during the war of 1948 against the Arabs in Palestine.'[48] On the other hand, Dayan's rival, Yigal Allon, commander of the *Palmach*, thought that Bengurion himself (bowing to international pressures) had been mainly to blame. When Bengurion 'ordered a halt in our army's advance, we had been on the crest of victory . . . from the Litani [a Lebanese river which, in Zionist thinking, would always have made an ideal frontier] in the north to the Sinai desert in the southwest. A few more days' fighting would have enabled us . . . to liberate the entire country.'[49] For Bengurion, it soon became clear, expansion followed as naturally on the 'War of Independence' as growth is a consequence of birth. 'To maintain the status quo', he de-clared, 'will not do. We have to set up a dynamic state bent upon expansion.'[50] Nor was it just a question of territorial aggrandize-ment. Military conquest would stimulate other forms of growth —in manpower and wealth, in prestige, self-confidence and ideological conviction. Growth, dynamism, the maintaining of a permanent sense of emergency, were all the more important, in Bengurion's view, because the Arabs would not make peace with Israel. The Arabs would not always remain as weak as they were; Israel must therefore either pre-empt their strength, and/or strengthen itself against the day when they felt able to fulfil their promise to 'liberate' Palestine.

For all his theatrical 'peace offers', which as often as not co-incided with a bloody reprisal raid, peace was low in Bengurion's priorities, as his franker asides revealed: 'And if we cannot get real peace for ten years or twenty years, we can stand it, and there will be some blessing in it too.'[51] What those blessings were an Israeli scholar and diplomat has disclosed at greater length.

Seen in retrospect, peace with the Arabs in the early stages of the
State could have had disastrous effects. The half-million Jews
from the Arab countries would not have been forced to immigrate
to Israel. Had peace come say in 1952 or 1953, these immigrants,
having arrived impoverished and despoiled in an unfamiliar,
even hostile culture and facing hard social, economic and dietary
adjustments, would in all probability either have gone back to
their former homes, or, under the impact of free and peaceful
association with the Arabs, maintained their old culture, which
is incompatible with a modern, strong, and homogenous Israeli
nation capable of survival. There might be no-one speaking
Hebrew today in Beersheba—perhaps not even in Jerusalem.
The people would have lost their sense of crisis and purpose. We
were fighting in those days, as we still are, for survival and the
creation of one homogenous nation—one culture, one language.
Everything was subordinated to this.[52]

If Zionism's still unfinished business led to the kind of behaviour which, by contemporary civilized standards, represented
a more or less permanent violation of international law and order,
that troubled few consciences in Israel. The Israeli establishment
constructed a morality of its own to which, characteristically, the
highly politicized religious hierarchy contributed quite as much
as the politicians, the press and the intelligentsia in general.
Truculence, heavily tinged with self-righteousness, inevitably
put down deep roots in a nation whose official conscience encouraged it. Only a few voices cried in the wilderness against
rabbis who 'rave about the army and the military spirit, applaud
the ways of armed violence' and 'certify that the doings of the
Israeli army are in conformity with the teachings of the Jewish
religion'.[53] For an impartial verdict, as to which side in the
Middle East conflict has always been the more aggressive, there
is surely no better place to look than the UN. Israel has been
taken to task by the General Assembly and the Security Council
more often than any other nation. Unabashed, it has long since
had the answer to that: it simply denies the body which gave
it birth any moral authority whatsoever. More impressive, however, than formal condemnations, so often spawned by an automatic bloc vote, have been the experiences of the UN's own
devoted servants. We have already dealt with those of Count
Bernadotte. Three soldiers who came after him also record theirs

in books which they wrote on completing their tour of duty. Commander Hutchison, an American, General Burns, a Canadian, and General von Horn, a Swede, cover twelve consecutive years of UN peace-keeping from 1951 to 1963. Their task was to police the armistice agreements which marked the end of the 'War of Independence'. The territorial lines the agreements laid down were not supposed to be the definitive frontiers of the State of Israel, even if, with the passage of time, that is how the world tended increasingly to regard them. The observers' brief was a narrow legalistic one; they were to forget how they had come into being, that they represented in themselves a pure Israeli gain against a pure Arab loss, a status quo built on force of arms. If any verdict, therefore, can be taken as a cautious one, it is theirs. The verdict all three convey, on almost every page, is essentially the same; it amounts to a withering indictment of Israel—an Israel which, not content with what it had achieved by force of arms, ceaselessly, deliberately violated the new legality to which it had committed itself. Contrasting Arabs and Israelis, General von Horn said that from time to time his staff would incur a certain degree of animosity from the Arabs but never 'in the same implacable and frenetic way' that they did from the Israelis. 'The Arabs', he said, 'could be difficult, intolerant and indeed often impossible, but their code of behaviour was on an infinitely higher and more civilized level.' He said that everybody came to this conclusion, which was 'strange, because there was hardly a man among us who had not originally arrived in the Holy Land without the most positive and sympathetic attitude towards the Israelis and their ambitions for their country. . . . After two or three years in daily contact with officials, soldiers and private individuals on *both* sides, there had been a remarkable change in their attitude.' Whenever he asked them what they had liked least about their service, he almost always got the same reply: 'the consistent cheating and deception of the Israelis'.[54]

Israel has fought two 'big wars' for growth—a recourse to all-out 'purposive' violence which it presented as wars of survival, or wars for peace. Twice it scored devastating military victories. But the first war—against Egypt in 1956—yielded only minor long-term gains; Israel was forced to yield up all the territory it had captured. For opportunity was all, and Bengurion had misjudged the diplomatic circumstances. Although he had planned the whole adventure in collusion with Britain and France, which also attacked Egypt, he went beyond the limits of Western—in this case American—tolerance. But the long-term gains of Israel's next 'big war'—in June 1967—were to prove commensurate with its military victory. For the diplomatic circumstances were as ideal as they ever could be; this time Israel had waited for the perfect opportunity. Western public opinion overwhelmingly applauded the single-handed Israeli *blitzkrieg* against Egypt, Syria and Jordan; the American government did not hide its satisfaction. To this day Israel remains in possession of the Golan Heights, the West Bank and the vast bulk of Sinai, where, with expropriation and settlement, it is pressing on with the great Zionist enterprise.

SUEZ, 1956

In early 1955 Bengurion put war with Egypt on his agenda. This was a deliberate act of policy. 'It is today frankly admitted', according to the *Paratroopers' Book*, 'that if it had been up to David Bengurion, the Sinai war would have taken place a year earlier' than it did.[55] Bengurion deliberately sought a showdown with the country which, as the great power of the Arab world, could bring the most decisive influence to bear for war or peace in the Middle East. He did this at a time when the young President Nasser of Egypt, for all his revolutionary idealism, was manifestly doing his best to preserve the peace. What Bengurion needed was a pretext, for, as Dayan subsequently admitted, he and his friends had decided 'not to miss any politically favourable opportunity to strike at Egypt'.[56] He coolly set about manufacturing one. It grew naturally out of a 'little war', ceaseless reprisal raids Qibya-style, which had a far broader purpose than the discouragement of marauding Palestinians. In his article on 'Israel's Policy of Reprisals' Moshe Brilliant explained that the rationale behind them was deeply rooted in the Zionist experience. In British Mandate days, the Jews had won great praise with their *Havlaga*, their 'self-restraint', but they had courted disaster. They then turned to 'gunpowder and dynamite' and discovered that, although it earned them international censure, it also 'earned them . . . ultimately the coveted prize' of statehood. The Israelis had never forgotten that lesson. These bloody 'border incidents' were seldom accidental . . . they were 'part of a deliberate plan to force the Arabs to the peace table'. Since 1948 'each reluctant step the Arabs took from hot war toward peace was taken when they were held by the throat'.[57]

In February 1955, the Israeli army attacked Egyptian military outposts in Gaza. Thirty-nine Egyptians died. Until then this had been Israel's least troublesome frontier. That was no accident. Just as, in earlier days, the Zionists accused the Palestinian *zaims* and *effendis* of stirring up hatred against them, so now they levelled the same charge against the Arab leaders. President Nasser, the emergent pan-Arab champion, became the obvious candidate for Israeli bogeyman. The reputation was thoroughly undeserved: the real Arab militancy was to be found, as always, among the people rather than the politicians. For six years, in the last days of Farouk and the early ones of the revolution, Egyptian rulers studiously avoided militant attitudes. Israel, it was felt, should not distract them from problems nearer home. President Nasser persuaded Western visitors, even passionately pro-Israeli ones like British politician Richard Crossman, that he really was as pacific as he sounded. 'Driving back to Cairo that night, I could not help thinking that not only Egypt, but the whole Middle East, must pray that Nasser survives the assassin's bullet. I am certain that he is a man who means what he says; and that so long as he is in power directing his middle-class revolution, Egypt will remain a factor for peace and social development.'[58] One motive for that revolution had been the humiliation of Egypt's defeat in 1948; Egyptian officers, Nasser among them, attributed it in part to the poor and malfunctioning arms with which, owing to the corruptions of the old order, they had been sent into battle. Yet he made no serious attempt to narrow Israel's rapidly lengthening lead in armaments. He preferred to spend Egypt's meagre reserves of hard currency on the welfare of his backward and overpopulated country.

Not surprisingly perhaps, but disingenuously, Israeli leaders such as Bengurion and Dayan do not even mention the Gaza raid in their accounts of the period. Nasser called it a 'turning point' and all independent authorities agree with him. The raid brought him under intensified pressure not merely from the Arabs in general, but from quarters most directly involved—his own army and the refugees in the Gaza Strip. As a soldier,

General Burns, the Chief of Staff of the UN forces, had a sympathetic grasp of Nasser's problem with the army.

> Shortly before the raid, he had visited Gaza and told the troops that there was no danger of war; that the Gaza Armistice Demarcation Line was not going to be a battlefront. After that many of them had been shot in their beds. Never again could he risk telling the troops they had no attack to fear; never again could he let them believe they could relax their vigilance. It was for this reason that he could not issue and enforce strict orders against the opening of fire on the Israel patrols which marched along the demarcation line, a hundred metres or less from the Egyptian positions. These positions were held by the friends and perhaps the relatives of the men who had perished in the Israeli ambush of that bloody night.[59]

There was only one way to still his commanders' clamour for arms: to furnish them. He took that decision during the confused and sleepless night of the raid, even before the last explosions had died away.[60] At first he sought Western, especially American, arms, and in such small quantities that when President Eisenhower saw his shopping list he exclaimed: 'Why, this is peanuts.'[61] Western intelligence was convinced that he had no intention of attacking—even if he were sure of quick and easy victory. Nor was this conviction shaken when, rebuffed by the blundering and short-sighted Americans, he negotiated the famous Czech arms deal which marked the Soviet Union's first great breakthrough in the struggle to undermine Western influence in the Middle East.[62]

As for the refugees, there were more than 300,000 of them, living in poverty, idleness and a festering hatred for Israel, who shared the temptation of their brethren in Jordan. Hemmed in upon themselves by the sea, the desert and the armistice lines, they only had to look east to see the broad fields, once theirs, which the Israelis cultivated from a chain of *kibbutzim* guarding the heights of the area beyond. They too were 'infiltrators'; and so were the 7,000 bedouins whom the Israelis had driven across the border since 1948.[63] They too had crossed the lines in defiance of the official policy of the Arab country in whose territory they had found themselves. For years they had been demanding arms and the establishment of a militia. The Egyptians had done no more than make encouraging noises. The Gaza raid changed

all that. For three days the Palestinians vented their indignation
in riots and demonstrations which threatened the stability of a
still young and none-too-secure régime. As the sun rose over the
battered town of Gaza, two hundred youths stormed Egyptian
and UN installations, smashing windows, burning vehicles and
trampling on flags. The next day mob violence spread to Khan
Yunis and Rafah, where refugees burned down the warehouse
for the UN rations off which they lived. They greeted truckloads
of Egyptian soldiers with stones and shouted abuse. 'Arms,' was
the universal cry, 'give us arms, we shall defend ourselves.'[64]

The other decision which Nasser took in the wake of the Gaza
raid was to turn the hitherto discouraged, freelance 'infiltration'
into an instrument of Egyptian policy. It was in August 1955
that the world first heard of the word *fedayeen*—'those who
sacrifice themselves'—applied to Palestinians sent on raids into
Israel. On their first raid—which began on the same day that
Nasser finally committed himself to the purchase of Soviet arms
—they penetrated as far as twenty-seven miles inside enemy
territory on a week-long spree of ambushes, mine-laying and
assaults on persons, vehicles and buildings in which five soldiers
and ten civilians died.[65] But even then, and subsequently, Nasser
had only unleashed the *fedayeen* under pressure from his own
public opinion in the wake of further provocations from Israel—
provocations which he had at first met with conciliatory gestures
such as the pull-back of front-line soldiers.[66]

The raids, and Russian weapons for Egypt, were just what
Bengurion needed. The 'hosts of Amalek' were re-arming in
Egypt, he said;[67] the 'grave and dangerous' Czech arms deal
which he had virtually forced on Nasser had been concluded for
'one reason and one reason only—to destroy the State of Israel
and the people of Israel.'[68] The least sign of Egyptian activism,
at a time when border skirmishing was costing five times as many
Arab as Israelis lives,[69] was 'a vile and nefarious conspiracy . . .
which would encounter a Jewish force capable of . . . striking any
aggressor or enemy so that they shall not rise again, as in Operation Joab [against Egypt] in 1948 and the Gaza operation a month
ago.'[70] In outright defiance of all the evidence he forecast that, if
there were no peaceful settlement, Egypt would attack Israel
within five or six months.[71]

The road from the 'hidden war' of border skirmishing to the

'open war' of Suez was, as the *Paratroopers' Book* later said, a short one.[72] In October 1955, Bengurion ordered his Chief of Staff, General Dayan, to prepare for the capture of the Straits of Tiran. Shortly afterwards, in the Knesset, he denounced Egypt's violations of the armistice agreements. He named three forms which these took; *fedayeen* marauding certainly was a violation, but there was nothing in the armistice which specifically forbade Egypt from blocking the Straits or closing the Suez Canal to Israel shipping. 'This one-sided war will have to stop', he declared, 'for it cannot remain one-sided for ever.'[73] According to the faithful Dayan, this was an appeal for war within a short time; he himself urged action within a month. 'It may be, of course, that one of these days a situation will be created which makes military action possible. But this will be the fruit of chance and not the planned result of postponing it to a specific "time" and "place".'[74] Nevertheless, Bengurion had still not overcome the resistance of the 'doves' within the government who, apprised of the war plans, decided that 'the moment was not propitious'.[75]

In June 1956, after a long and bitter dispute, Foreign Minister Moshe Sharett, the leading 'dove', was driven from office. He was replaced by Golda Meir and, in the words of the *Paratroopers' Book*, 'Israeli foreign policy was adjusted to the hard and energetic line of the Minister of Defence.'[76] A month later came the final, fortuitous bonus, the event which persuaded two Western powers, Britain and France, to throw in their lot with the Israelis. 'On July 27', recorded the *Paratroopers' Book*, 'Nasser announced the nationalization of the Suez Canal before an enthusiastic crowd in Alexandria. Without knowing it, he thereby kicked off the Suez campaign.'[77] On 29 October, with the secret backing of Anglo-French accomplices, the Israeli army invaded Sinai and captured the whole of it, including the island of Tiran in the Gulf of Aqaba, in four days. The British and French governments issued a hypocritical ultimatum to both sides, calling on them to withdraw from the banks of the Canal, and then sent in their own forces, ostensibly to occupy and secure the waterway for international shipping, but really in the hope of overthrowing the man who had nationalized it. If, in laying the diplomatic groundwork for his all-out assault on Egypt, Bengurion had implicitly confined his aims to the ending of Egypt's armistice 'violations' and the achievement of peace, Menachim

Begin and his rightwing *Herut* (ex-*Irgun*) opposition, a hotbed of extremist pressures, had no such inhibitions. More than a year before Begin had urged on parliament a 'preventive war against the Arab states without further hesitation. By doing so we will achieve two targets: firstly the annihilation of Arab power and secondly the expansion of our territory.'[78] After such an overwhelming victory, however, Bengurion and his ruling Labour party lost no time, characteristically, in 'catching up' with the extremists, whose leader now said that he supported the government 'with all my heart and soul'.[79] Even the most 'dovish' parties, such as the left-wing *Mapam*, were not far behind either. All, in greater or lesser degree, developed expansionist appetites. And when the United States called on Israel to withdraw, Bengurion was outraged. 'Up to the middle of the sixth century Jewish independence was maintained on the island of Yotvan [as the victors promptly renamed Tiran] south of the Gulf of Eilat, which was liberated yesterday by the Israeli army. . . . Israel terms the Gaza Strip an integral part of the nation. No force, whatever it is called, was going to make Israel evacuate Sinai. And the words of Isaiah the Prophet were fulfilled.'[80]

Unfortunately for Bengurion, the pretext he had so carefully manufactured was simply not good enough for the Americans. President Eisenhower quickly secured the withdrawal of the chastened British and French by withholding oil supplies from them, but it took six months to prise Israel out of all Egyptian territory. It was only by raising the threat of economic sanctions, to be applied by all members of the UN, that he managed it. 'Should a nation', he asked in a special television broadcast, 'which attacks and occupies foreign territory in the face of UN disapproval be allowed to impose conditions on its own withdrawal? If we agree that armed attack can properly achieve the purpose of the assailant, then I fear we will have turned back the clock of international order. . . .'

One condition, of sorts, Israel did get away with, the lifting of the Egyptian blockade on Israeli shipping in the Straits of Tiran, and this was to furnish the Arab-fighters with the pretext for the next 'big war'.

NOTES

1. Avneri, *Israel Without Zionists: A Plea for Peace in the Middle East*, *op. cit.*, p. 134.
2. See pp. 104–5.
3. Bengurion, *Rebirth and Destiny*, *op. cit.*, pp. 276–7.
4. Lilienthal, Alfred, *What Price Israel*, *op. cit.*, pp. 210–11.
5. *Ibid.*, p. 210.
6. Gabbay, Rony, *A Political History of the Arab-Jewish Conflict, The Arab Refugee Problem*, Droz, Geneva, 1959, p. 109.
7. Israeli Foreign Minister Moshe Sharett to the UN.
8. See Bar-Zohar, Michael, *The Armed Prophet*, Prentice-Hall, London, 1967, p. 157.
9. See Weinstock, *Le Zionisme contre Israel*, *op. cit.*, p. 411.
10. Gabbay, *op. cit.*, p. 109.
11. Hutchison, E. H., *Violent Truce*, Devin-Adair, New York, 1956, pp. 120–1.
12. Glubb, Sir John Bagot, *A Soldier with the Arabs*, Hodder and Stoughton, London, 1957, p. 245.
13. *Ibid.*, p. 304.
14. *Haaretz*, 22 September 1968; see Ben-Yosa, Amitay, *Arab American University Graduate Bulletin* No. 2, reproduced in The Arab Women's Information Committee, Beirut, Supplement, June 1971.
15. *The Paratroopers' Book* (Hebrew), Tel Aviv, 1969, p. 60; cited in *The Other Israel*, Doubleday, ed. Bober, Arie, New York, 1972, p. 68.
16. *Jerusalem Post*, 31 October 1965.
17. See *The Other Israel*, *op. cit.*, p. 77.
18. Hutchison, *op. cit.*, pp. 152–8.
19. Love, *Suez: The Twice-Fought War*, *op. cit.*, p. 54.
20. In an article in *Harper's* magazine entitled 'Israel's policy of Reprisals' by Moshe Brilliant, an American resident of Israel and a correspondent of both the *New York Times* and the *Jerusalem Post*, the English-language mouthpiece of Bengurion's ruling Labour party. The article which amounted to an official and public apologia for reprisals had been cleared by the military censor.
21. See *The Other Israel*, *op. cit.*, p. 72.
22. Sharon, Ariel, 'Introduction' to Meir Har-Zion, *Chapters from a Diary*, Tel Aviv, 1969, p. 16, cited in *The Other Israel*, *op. cit.*, p. 68.
23. Elon, *The Israelis, Founders and Sons*, *op. cit.*, p. 241.
24. Diary of Moshe Sharett, *Maariv*, 28 June 1974; see Shahak, Israel, *Middle East International*, January 1975.
25. *Haaretz*, 9 November 1965; see Shahak, Israel, and Davis, Uri, *Journal of Palestine Studies*, Vol. IV, No. 2, 1975, p. 155.
26. Elon, *op. cit.*, p. 242.
27. *The Other Israel*, *op. cit.*, p. 72.

28. Ben-Yosa, Amitay, *op. cit.*, p. 2.
29. Jiryis Sabri, *The Arabs in Israel*, Institute for Palestine Studies, Beirut, 1968, p. 4.
30. Judgements of the District Court attached to the Israeli Defence Army Military Court; see Jiryis, *op. cit.*, p. 98.
31. *Ibid.*, p. 102.
32. *Ibid.*
33. 11 April 1957.
34. *Jewish Newsletter*, 8 July 1957.
35. Jiryis, *op. cit.*, p. 111.
36. *Ha'olam Hazeh*, 11 February 1970.
37. Jiryis, *op. cit.*, p. 81.
38. Cattan, Henry, *Palestine, the Arabs and Israel*, Longmans, Green and Co., London, 1969, p. 85; see *Le Monde*, 3 March 1976.
39. Ben-Yosa, Amitay, *op. cit.*, p. 3.
40. *Ibid.*, p. 1.
41. Jiryis, *op. cit.*, p. 61.
42. Ben-Yosa, Amitay, *op. cit.*, p. 2.
43. Jiryis, *op. cit.*, p. 72.
44. *Ibid.*, p. 67.
45. *Ibid.*, p. 70.
46. Jiryis, Sabri, 'Recent Knesset Legislation and the Arabs in Israel', *Journal of Palestine Studies*, Beirut, Vol. I, No. 1, 1971.
47. *Haaretz*, 14 January 1966.
48. Bengurion, *op. cit.*, p. 466.
49. *New York Times*, 9 March 1964.
50. Bengurion, *op. cit.*, p. 419.
51. Alsop, Joseph, *San Jose Mercury*, 16 June 1956.
52. Love, *op. cit.*, p. 52.
53. *Ner*, January 1956, cited in Ibrahim al-Abid, *Violence et Paix*, Palestine Research Centre, Beirut, 1970, p. 34.
54. Horn, General Karl von, *Soldiering for Peace*, Cassell, London, 1966, pp. 282-3.
55. See *The Other Israel*, *op. cit.*, p. 70.
56. Dayan, Moshe, *Diary of the Sinai Campaign*, Weidenfeld and Nicolson, London, 1966, p. 37.
57. *Harper's* magazine, March 1955, see pp. 180-2.
58. *The New Statesman and Nation*, London, 22 January 1955.
59. Burns, General E. L. N., *Between Arab and Israeli*, Harrap, London, 1962, p. 18.
60. Love, *op. cit.*, p. 20.
61. *Ibid.*, p. 88.
62. *Ibid.*, p. 100.
63. *Ibid.*, p. 61.
64. *Ibid.*, p. 83.
65. *Ibid.*, p. 95.
66. *Ibid.*, pp. 99, 107.
67. *Ibid.*, p. 121.

68. *Ibid.*, p. 102.
69. *Ibid.*, p. 68.
70. *Ibid.*, p. 89.
71. *Ibid.*, p. 115.
72. See *The Other Israel*, *op. cit.*, p. 71.
73. Love, *op. cit.*, p. 106.
74. Dayan, *op. cit.*, p. 14.
75. Love, *op. cit.*, p. 106.
76. See *The Other Israel*, *op. cit.*, p. 71.
77. *Ibid.*, p. 71.
78. 12 October 1955.
79. Menuhin, *The Decadence of Judaism in Our Time*, *op. cit.*, p. 181.
80. *Ibid.*, p. 180.

Seven

Greater Israel

THE SIX-DAY WAR, 1967

THE 'Arab-fighters' were bound to try again. According to Kennett Love, the former *New York Times* correspondent who has written the definitive history of the Suez War,

> ... from the moment Israel realized that she would have to withdraw, Sinai was recognized as a campaign that would sooner or later be refought. Plans for the new war were drawn up immediately after the old ... the 1956 war served as a rehearsal for 1967. The plans for the earlier war were only a year old when they were tested in action. Long before 1967 they had matured to near perfection, and, as in 1956, required only favourable circumstances and a political decision to be put into action.[1]

In early 1967 Israel's congenital militancy was pushing it towards such a decision. In a sense it needed the war. It was suffering the severest economic crisis of its existence; unemployment stood at 10 per cent; the growth rate had plummeted; subventions from the Diaspora were drying up; worst of all, emigration was beginning to exceed immigration—a yardstick which of course indicated, more than any other, that the economic crisis was a crisis of Zionism itself. What this portended General Burns, a soldier whose shrewd judgements ranged far beyond the arts of war, forecast in 1962. 'Israel's leaders have the habit of putting down her economic difficulties to the boycott of all trade and economic relations maintained by the Arab states, and the pressure they exercise on other countries to limit trade with Israel. In such circumstances there seems to me to be a great temptation to find some excuse to go to war and thus to break out of the blockade and boycott—to force peace on Israel's terms.'[2] He believed that if Israel should ever feel a need to expand beyond its present borders, 'the Israeli armed forces, supremely confident of their ability to defeat any and all of the Arab countries surrounding Israel with ease and speed, would take on such a task with alacrity'.[3]

As the *Paratroopers' Book* explained, the Israeli fighting man had matured:

> The reprisal actions of 1965–66 differed from those which preceded the Sinai campaign. . . . The operations were no longer acts of vengeance, savage and nervous, of a small state fighting for its independence. Rather they were blows struck by a state strong and sure of itself, and which did not fear the army it confronted.[4]

The ideal held up to the youth was not hatred of the enemy, but contempt. The flyer, particularly the bombardier, took the place of the paratrooper or the infantryman. It was typical that the bedside reading of Israeli officers in the 1950s included books like Alexander Beck's *The Men of Panfilov*, a Soviet work of World War II, which recounts the training of an assault unit, while in the 1960s their reading turned to the exploits of bombardiers 'for whom war became a hobby, something secondary that one calmly accepted'.[5]

All that was needed for the unleashing of the Israeli war machine was the 'favourable circumstances', and on 23 May they presented themselves. It was at four o'clock in the morning of that day that the Israeli Chief of Staff, General Yitzhak Rabin, woke up Prime Minister Levi Eshkol to tell him that President Nasser had decided to reimpose the Aqaba blockade. A few hours later the cabinet went into emergency session. In Israeli eyes Nasser had in effect declared war.

The challenge was indeed an intolerable one. This was not because Israel faced economic strangulation. Economically, the closure of the Straits of Tiran to all Israeli ships, and ships of other nations bound for Eilat with strategic materials, would have had little immediate impact. Only 5 per cent of Israel's foreign trade went through Eilat; oil from Iran was the main strategic material, but Israel could easily get that through Haifa. What damage the closure might have done would have been offset by President Johnson's reported offer—designed to stay Israel's hand—to maintain its economic viability. The long-term implications were certainly serious, for it was through Eilat that Israel intended to take advantage of new or expanding markets

in Africa and Asia. But the really intolerable thing lay elsewhere.
For the first time the Arabs were turning the tables on Israel.
For the first time it was they who were administering the *fait
accompli*. (Although the precise scope and strictness of the
blockade are a matter of controversy. What the Egyptian leaders
were saying in public was very different from what they were
doing in private. Field Marshal Abdul Hakim Amer apparently
instructed his troops not to interfere with any Israeli ships, or any
naval vessels or ships escorted by naval vessels.[6]) If they could
get away with one they could get away with another, and the
Jewish State, that accumulation of a thousand such accomplished facts, would begin to wither away. It would be the beginning of Zionism in reverse. The Israelis did not need Nasser to
tell them that. But he did so all the same. It was no more a
question of the Gulf of Aqaba or the Straits of Tiran; it was a
'question of the Arabs having been driven from Palestine and
robbed of their rights and their possessions . . . of the neglect of
all UN resolutions in favour of the people of Palestine'. The
whole Palestine cause had been resurrected, the confidence of
every Arab revived; and 'just as we have been able to restore the
pre-1956 situation, we shall certainly, with God's help, be able
to restore the pre-1948 situation'.[7]

The re-imposition of the blockade was at the same time, however, the perfect opportunity. The Egyptian *fait accompli*,
though arbitrary, was not illegal. After 1956, the Egyptians had
continued to insist that the Straits fell in Egyptian territorial
waters. The Israelis' claim to right of passage through those
territorial waters was indeed an exceedingly dubious one; it was
based on possession of a thin sliver of coastline, and this itself
had been secured, on the Israelis' own admission, by 'one of those
calculated violations [of the ceasefire] which we had to carefully
weigh against the political risks'.[8] That was in 1949, during the
final stages of the War of Independence', when, in defiance of a
UN-sponsored ceasefire, an Israeli patrol thrust southward to
the Arab hamlet and police post of Um Rashrash, expelling its
inhabitants and founding the port of Eilat in its place.

The trouble was, however, that, while asserting a legal right,
the Egyptians had acquiesced in Israel's political *fait accompli*;
Israeli ships were allowed through under the symbolic protection
of a handful of UN forces which had replaced the Egyptians at

the garrison of Sharm al-Shaikh. True, the Americans had insisted that the Israeli withdrawal should be an unconditional one, but the Israelis had put up such a fierce resistance that Washington was obliged to affirm its belief that, once this ostensibly unconditional withdrawal was complete, Israeli ships would enjoy 'free and innocent passage' through straits which, in its view, 'comprehend international waters'.[9] This was less than a cast-iron guarantee that America would keep the Straits open. But it turned out, in the changed international circumstances of a decade later, to be quite enough to ensure that next time the Egyptians closed them the Americans would not object if Israel went to war to reopen them. Under President Johnson, who, as a Senator, had led Democratic congressional opposition to Eisenhower's threat of sanctions, the pro-Israeli bias of American policy was flagrant; dislike of President Nasser, and other Soviet-oriented 'revolutionary' régimes in the Arab world, was scarcely less so.

DAVID VERSUS GOLIATH

Western public opinion was no less partisan, particularly when, in the wake of Nasser's *fait accompli*, Arab armies began, or so it appeared, to converge on Israel from all sides amid a terrible clamour of boastful rhetoric. Genocide, Munich, the Arab Nazis, Nasser-the-new-Hitler—these, the most emotive and virulent slogans in Western political vocabulary, rang round Europe and America in late May and early June of 1967. Never in history had the passions of so many people been engaged by a conflict in which they had no part—and engaged with such unanimity on behalf of one of the combatants. The war in Vietnam, then becoming one of the great moral issues of the sixties, was drowned in the tidal wave of emotion which swept the Western world on Israel's behalf. Vietnam divided, the Middle East united. It was the Arab threat to annihilate their enemy, or what seemed to be their threat to do so, which really turned the world against them. Nor was their enemy just a people like any other. They were Jews. What the Arabs were setting out to do was all the more 'wicked, mad and insupportable'—as one British intellectual described it—in that their intended victims belonged to the same people who, a generation earlier, had lost six million in the Nazi

Holocaust.[10] A crime against the Jews was worse than a crime against anyone else. Hitler's gas chambers still haunted the conscience of the West.

Great, then, were the fears of the outside world for little Israel on the eve of war. So they were, too, among the general public in Israel itself. It was only to be expected that the Israeli government, Zionists and sympathizers everywhere, should foster the world's alarm. None of them, at the time, would have challenged the Israeli Premier when he told the Knesset just after the war that 'the existence of the Israeli state hung on a thread, but the hopes of the Arab leaders to exterminate Israel were brought to nought'.[11] But there were those, the generals, who knew that the real situation was the exact reverse of the apparent one, that David was not merely a match for Goliath, but hopelessly outclassed him. They knew that, whatever the politicians might say and the people believe, Israel's survival was never at stake, that even if Nasser actually intended to go to war he had no chance of winning it. General Mordecai Hod had a profound confidence in the air force which he commanded. He and its real architect, General Ezer Weizmann, unruly nephew of Chaim Weizmann, had for a decade or more been perfecting their master-plan for the destruction of Arab air power. Their men were trained for every eventuality. They had pored over scale models of every possible target; it was with astonishing precision that in the first few hours of the 1967 War the pilot of a Mirage fighter machine-gunned, at close range, what he knew to be King Hussein's study at the Basman Palace in Amman. . . .[12] It was not until five years had passed, when the Israelis were basking in an unprecedented sense of their own strength, security and achievement, that General Matitiahu Peled, one of the architects of the Israeli victory, committed what, to an outraged public, seemed nothing less than blasphemy. But in the so-called 'annihilation controversy' which followed, and in spite of pleas to keep silent for the sake of Israel's reputation in the world, none of his military colleagues seriously contested his central thesis. 'There is no reason', he said, 'to hide the fact that since 1949 no one dared, or more precisely, no one was able, to threaten the very existence of Israel. In spite of that, we have continued to foster a sense of our own inferiority, as if we were a weak and insignificant people, which, in the midst of an anguished struggle for its existence, could be exterminated at any moment.' 'True,' General Peled went on, Arab leaders may have sounded menacing, 'but it is notorious that the Arab leaders themselves, thoroughly aware of their own impotence, did not believe in their own threats. . . . I am sure that our General Staff never told the government that the Egyptian military threat represented any danger to Israel or that we were unable to crush Nasser's army, which, with unheard-of foolishness, had exposed itself to the devastating might of our army. . . . To claim that the Egyptian forces concentrated on our borders were capable of threatening Israel's existence not only insults the intelligence of anyone capable of analysing this kind of situation, but is an insult to Zahal [the Israeli army].'[13] Not only did Nasser lack the means to take on Israel, he did not have the intention either. The generals were well aware of that too. Yitzhak Rabin, the Chief of Staff, was frank about it: 'I do not believe that Nasser wanted war. The two divisions he sent into Sinai on May 14 would not have been enough to unleash an offensive against Israel. He knew it and we knew it.'[14]

THE MYTH OF THE GOLAN HEIGHTS

The seeds of the Six-Day War were sown on the Syrian front. This is universally accepted. It is also more or less taken for granted that the Syrians sowed those seeds. The Golan Heights appear to sum up, in a peculiarly stark and affecting way, the image of David versus Goliath. But it would be nearer the truth to say that the Golan Heights represent one of the most success-ful of Zionist myths. A post-war visit to the windswept, battle-scarred plateau was a moving experience—at least it was for those of this writer's fellow-tourists, probably all of them, who ac-cepted what our guide told us. He told us, of course, about the Syrian guns which used to rain destruction on the farmers peace-fully tilling their fields in the valley below and how finally, on the last day of the war, some of Israel's finest troops had given their lives scaling those mine-infested heights to silence the guns for ever. It was a partisan account. That was to be expected. It also included one or two untruths, not unexpected either, like the allegation that the Arabs, in trying to divert the headwaters of the Jordan, intended to send them to waste in the Mediter-ranean. However, the guide did, with an air of complicity, tell one unexpected truth. 'We are now entering what used to be the demilitarized zone,' he said, 'regular soldiers were forbidden to enter it. Of course, we got round that by sending them in disguised as police. But that's another story.' It *is* another story, a long one, and naturally he did not tell it.

Among the many complications of the 1949 armistice agreements were the demilitarized zones. They were sources of conflict everywhere, but particularly on the Syrian frontier, where, strips of fertile soil ranging from a few hundred to a few kilometres wide, they ran nearly half its length. They represented bits of Palestinian territory which the Syrian army managed to hold during the fighting of 1948 and from which it only agreed to withdraw, behind the old frontier, under the provisions of the armistice agreements. These laid down that neither side should send military forces into any part of them; Arab and Israeli villages and settlements in the zones should each recruit their own police forces on a local basis. Neither side showed a scrupulous regard for these provisions, but it was the Israelis who, from the outset, showed less. They began by staking an illegal claim to sovereignty over the zone and then proceeded, as opportunity offered, to encroach on all the specific provisions against introducing armed forces and fortifications. They repeatedly obstructed the operations of the UN observers, on one occasion even threatening to kill them.[15] They refused to cooperate with the Mixed Armistice Commission, and when it suited them they simply rejected the rulings and requests of the observers.[16] They expelled, or otherwise forced out, Arab inhabitants, and razed their villages to the ground.[17] They transplanted trees as a strategem to advance the frontier to their own advantage.[18] They built roads against the advice of the UN.[19] They carried out excavations on Arab land for their own drainage schemes.[20] But most serious of all was what General von Horn described as 'part of a premeditated Israeli policy to edge east through the Demilitarized Zone towards the old Palestine border (as shown on their maps) and to get all the Arabs out of the way by fair means or foul.' 'The Jews', he explained, 'developed a habit of irrigating and ploughing in stretches of Arab-owned land nearby, for the ground was so fertile that every square foot was a gold mine in grain. Gradually, beneath the glowering eyes of the Syrians, who held the high ground overlooking the Zone, the area had become

a network of Israeli canals and irrigation channels edging up
against and always encroaching on Arab-owned property.'[21] It is
unlikely, in his opinion, that those Syrian guns on the Golan
Heights would ever have gone into action but for Israeli provocations.[22]

There was always tension on the frontier, and incidents without number, but it flared into the dimensions of a 'little war' only
when the Israelis, apparently for reasons of higher strategy, decided to visit upon the Syrians their familiar technique of massive
punishment to fit a menial crime. They did that in the build-up
to the Suez War. In December 1955, as part of the aggressive
strategy which had begun with the Gaza raid ten months before,
they attacked positions on the north-eastern shore of Lake
Tiberias, killing more than fifty soldiers and civilians. The
alleged pretext—that the Syrians had opened fire on fishing and
police boats—was a singularly inadequate one, even if it had been
an authentic one. But in the opinion of two UN observers who
subsequently recorded their experience it was not even that. The
most charitable interpretation was that, although the Syrians
may have opened fire, the Israelis had done their best to provoke
them into doing so. 'It was', said one of them, 'a premeditated
raid of intimidation motivated by Israel's desire . . . to bait the
Arab states into some overt act of aggression that would offer
them the opportunity to overrun additional territory without
censor . . .'[23] Eleven months later Israel did overrun the whole
of Sinai, but not, as we have seen, without censure. They were
to be more successful next time.

Every year brought its shooting season; naturally enough, it
began, in a fertile valley like this, with the ploughing, and went
on through the sowing and harvesting.[24] It was then that the
Israeli farmers ventured forth with their armour-plated tractors
to plough a few more furrows of Arab-owned land. On 3 April
1967 it was reported in the Israeli press that the government had
decided to cultivate all areas of the demilitarized zone, specifically lots 51 and 52, which, the Syrians insisted, belonged to
Arab farmers.[25] At eight o'clock on the morning of 7 April a
tractor began work on a little strip of Arab land south of Tiberias.
The Israelis waited for the Syrians to open up with mortars as
they knew they would—and then struck back with artillery, tanks
and aircraft. Seventy jet fighters pounded the enemy with

napalm and high explosives. The Syrians took a bloody nose: six planes shot down, one over Damascus, some thirty fortified positions hit and perhaps a hundred people killed. The Israelis, for their part, lost one tank commander; he had got down to observe the results of his shooting. Chief of Staff Rabin expressed the hope that the Syrians had learned their lesson.

In reality, the 'lesson' was the curtain-raiser to the June War. Nasser could not afford to stand idly by again. Syria, he could see, was now the target of the kind of military activism to which Egypt had been exposed before Suez. For the 'Arab-fighters' it represented just the kind of plausible external peril they needed. After all, Syria *did* bombard settlements from the Golan Heights. It *was* apparently going ahead with its part of a scheme to divert the headwaters of the river Jordan and thereby sabotage Israel's own scheme, unilaterally undertaken, to channel water south to the Negev desert. It *was* giving aid and comfort to *Fatah*, the Palestinian guerilla organization which, since January 1965, had been sending its men into enemy territory to lay mines and blow up installations. And since February 1966, when an extreme faction of the ruling Baath party seized power, Syria had officially adopted, with bellicose rhetoric to match, the *Fatah* doctrine of a 'popular liberation war'. Obviously, the Arab-fighters did not shout their intentions from the roof-tops, but it was none the less apparent, from the indiscretions which did escape them, that what Dayan and his men had in mind was to engineer a general preventive war—to deliver a crippling blow at the Arabs' growing military strength, to do as soon as possible, at lesser cost, what they would be forced to do, probably at much greater cost, some time in the future. It was this search for a pretext which the Chief of Staff was getting at, in a duly circumspect way, when he told the army magazine *Bamahane* in May 1965 that the Israelis could upset any Arab military timetable at a moment's notice if they knew 'how to exploit the moment when the Arabs are preparing to reach a certain level of military strength'.[36]

For anyone who cared to look closely the external peril was plausible in the extreme. Of course it must have been uncomfortable and sometimes dangerous living in a frontier *kibbutz* under the shadow of Syrian guns, but how many people actually got killed? Between January and June 1967, apparently not one.

In the same period, how many Israelis died at the hands of the *Fatah* guerrillas? One. As for the Jordan diversion scheme, this was a vain enterprise, whatever Arab propaganda might proclaim, and the Israelis knew it. Even if the Arabs had the means and the will to carry out their plans to the full—and this was doubted in official Israeli quarters—they would have deprived the Israelis of a mere 5 or 6 per cent of the share which they were taking for themselves.[27] As for the 'popular liberation war', the Israelis knew more than anyone else about the gulf between the Baathist words and Baathist deeds.

Unfortunately not many people did look very closely, and President Nasser was very afraid that, Syrian verbal excesses and irresponsible brinkmanship aiding, the Arab-fighters would lead him into a trap. Replying to the taunts of his Arab opponents, he told a Palestinian audience as early as 1965: 'They say "drive out UNEF". Suppose that we do. Is it not essential to have a plan? If Israeli aggression takes place against Syria, do I attack Israel? That would mean that Israel is the one to determine the battle for me. It hits a tractor or two to force me to move, is this a wise way? It is we who must determine the battle.'[28]

NASSER FALLS INTO THE TRAP

But withdraw UNEF he eventually did. When, on 8 May 1967, two highly agitated Syrian emissaries arrived secretly in Cairo to announce that Israel was about to attack their country, Nasser could look back on at least two years of growing Israeli pugnacity, and what he felt to be American connivance with it, as good reason for taking the news very seriously indeed. He sought confirmation from other sources, including the Russians, and they provided it. Forces had indeed been concentrating on the front. The Israelis hotly denied it at the time, and, unchallenged by any impartial arbiter such as the UN observers, their denial was convincing enough; it has served since as vital evidence for their contention that, in the build-up to the June War, the real provocations came from the Arabs, not from them. But five years later, during the 'annihilation controversy', General Ezer Weizmann, one of Israel's bluntest soldiers, conceded: 'Don't forget that we did move tanks to the north after the downing of the aircraft.'[29] UN observers also saw them, but for various reasons

their observations were—and remain to this day—a closely
guarded secret. (This is one of the conclusions of what is probably the most accurate account of the origins of the June War.
By Godfrey Jansen, an Indian journalist, it argues that from
early in 1967 the small inner group of politicians and generals
who are the real rulers of Israel felt the need for another attack
on the Arabs.[30]) The tank concentrations were followed by a
verbal threat and a taunt which were almost guaranteed to make
Nasser react the way he did. The threat, an officially enunciated
one, portended a full-scale invasion of Syria and the overthrow
of the regime. The taunt was a prediction that, when that happened, Nasser would not go to Syria's aid. Both were made in
such a way as to reach their target, but without being officially
recorded so that Israel could not be called to account later. And
just as all the pro-Israeli, and indeed the relatively impartial,
accounts of the June War dismiss the allegation of Israeli tank
concentrations, so they make out that there was no real threat
either. Thus in his widely read book *The Road to War* Walter
Laqueur says: 'There had been, to repeat again, no Israeli
threat to overthrow the Damascus government.'[31] But there had
been. On 11 May, General Yitzhak Rabin said on Israel Radio:
'The moment is coming when we will march on Damascus to
overthrow the Syrian Government, because it seems that only
military operations can discourage the plans for a people's war
with which they threaten us.'[32] This crude provocation was
picked up by Arab listening posts but not one word of it was
printed in the Israeli press. Somehow a monitoring report does
not carry the same weight as a printed statement, and it can be
that much more easily denied. The taunt came the very next day.
General Aharon Yariv, Director of Military Intelligence, gave a
background briefing for forty foreign correspondents in which,
after repeating Rabin's threats against Syria, he harped on one
insistent theme: Egypt was weak, and Nasser, 'the all-Arab
leader', would not intervene. 'I would say that as long as there is
not an Israeli invasion into Syria extended in area and time, I
think the Egyptians will not come in seriously . . . they will do so
only if there is no other alternative. And to my eyes no alternative means that we are creating such a situation that it is impossible for the Egyptians not to act because the strain on their
prestige will be unbearable.'[33] By saying these words he deli-

berately put that very strain on the prestige of the 'all-Arab leader', who was already the butt of similarly exasperating jibes from his Arab adversaries.

Israel's 'impertinence', Nasser said later, was such that 'every Arab had to react'.[34] He sent his army into Sinai. At the same time he ordered the removal of UN forces. He had to do that to lend his move conviction. UNEF's role was a purely symbolic one. It was in Sinai strictly by Egypt's consent; Israel had stead-fastly rejected any UN presence on its side of the frontier; what it symbolized was Nasser's self-imposed restraint. Its removal would therefore symbolize the end of that restraint. That was the last thing Nasser wanted; he therefore aimed at a partial with-drawal. The Egyptian Chief of Staff sent a cryptic message to the UNEF commander; he asked him to withdraw his men from the Israeli-Egyptian frontier to their bases in Gaza, but not from Sharm al-Shaikh, the lonely outpost at the mouth of the Gulf of Aqaba, which furnished symbolic protection for the passage of Israeli ships. The stratagem backfired. The UN Secretary General clumsily insisted that it had to be all or nothing. Nasser had no way out; he made it all. But of course that was not enough either. Logic—and the taunts of both Arab and Jew—required that he complete what he had begun. He imposed the blockade. He did not *really* impose it, as we have seen,[35] since he had no intention of fighting, but that did not deprive the Israelis of the ostensible *casus belli* they needed.

There would now be a war, which Israel felt certain of winning, against Egypt and Syria. Could the Israelis also exploit this unique opportunity to lay their hands on the rest of Palestine— East Jerusalem and the West Bank—which had eluded them in 1948? One wonders whether the open letter which the celebrated columnist, Ephraim Kishon, addressed to King Hussein is quite as ironic as it sounds:

> Frankly, you were not the only one to fall for our little trick. Veteran statesmen of world calibre stepped dazedly into the fiendish trap we prepared over the years in order to fool both our enemies and our friends. . . . Or did you imagine even for a second that all this was not planned? You silly man! Today it can be told, poor Hussi! Six or seven years ago we decided to take the Old City. But, we said to ourselves, we won't be able to pull it off unless the Arabs attack us first. Yes, but how could they be coaxed

into doing that? As long as the Old Man [Bengurion] was at the helm, it was to be assumed that they would have cold feet. The Old Man therefore had to be removed. So we invented the Lavon Affair. We had a few spins on the Committee of Seven, published the brief of the Legal Adviser and played around with other odd-ball gimmicks. I hardly remember what, then we started building up Eshkol as a compromiser and waverer. It came off beautifully. He cooperated, so did Abba Eban. In short within a few years we succeeded in implanting in Gamal's mind that the time was ripe to attack us. The only thing that hampered our plans was the UN force in the Strip. How to get rid of it, how? In this matter we put our trust in U Thant and he did not let us down. Gamal innocently moved into Sinai and closed the Straits of Tiran. All this was exactly according to our plans. When would they at last conclude a pact, we asked ourselves anxiously, when? For long days we waited tensely—nothing, you wouldn't budge. We shamelessly tempted you, begged the naval powers to defend us, asked the Prime Minister to make a radio speech (a stammering performance which did anything but boost Israeli morale), pressed de Gaulle to drop us, what didn't we do to bring you nearer to Nasser? In the end our efforts were successful, you flew to Cairo and signed a mutual defence agreement. We sighed, relieved. Next day we brought in Dayan, and the rest is history. Sorry, Hussi, maybe they didn't teach you such tricks at Harrow but we had no choice, we wanted all of Jerusalem so badly.[36]

ISRAEL ACQUIRES AN EMPIRE

'The triumph of the civilized'—that was how one leading Western newspaper described the Israeli victory. It was indeed an extra-ordinary feat of arms. Israel had destroyed three Arab armies and acquired territory several times its own size in the space of six days. But history will perhaps record that greater than the mili-tary was the public relations triumph. Here was a people which had conquered another's land and expelled its inhabitants—here it was winning ecstatic international approval for yet more con-quests and more expulsions. In 1917, Lord Balfour had pro-claimed that nothing should be done to prejudice the civil and religious rights of the non-Jewish inhabitants of Palestine; if anyone had prophesied that exactly fifty years later the Arabs would attempt to restore by force merely a portion of those rights which had been taken away by force and then be universally

condemned for doing so—such a prophet would surely have been
dismissed as mad. Of course, not everyone went as far as the
London *Daily Telegraph*, whose pro-Zionist enthusiasms were
always extravagant, but very few questioned whether, in this
case, might had indeed been right.[37] But the 'civilization' of
which Israel is the foster-child had its reasons, not the least of
which was eloquently summed up in the Paris newspaper *Le
Monde*:

> In the past few days Europe has in a sense rid itself of the guilt it
> incurred in the drama of the Second World War and, before that,
> in the persecutions which, from the Russian pogroms to the
> Dreyfus Affair, accompanied the birth of Zionism. In the con-
> tinent of Europe the Jews were at last avenged—but alas, on the
> backs of the Arabs—for the tragic and stupid accusation: 'they
> went like sheep to the slaughter.'[38]

It was immensely valuable, this international goodwill which
Israel had accumulated—a rich fund of credit upon which it
drew as it launched into the next stage of the great Zionist
enterprise. For, historically speaking, this was a third great
breakthrough. Like the Balfour Declaration and the 'War of
Independence' it created a whole new empty 'framework' to be
filled in. Zionism had been reborn; their pre-war depression behind them, the modern Israelis rediscovered overnight something
of the zeal and vision which had moved the early pioneers. It all
gushed forth, this Zionist renewal, in a torrent of biblico-
strategic, clerico-military antics and imagery. It was atheists
talking about the 'God of the armies'. It was paratroopers taking
their oaths of allegiance, a Bible in one hand and a rifle in the
other, at the Wailing Wall. It was a spate of biblical poems and
hymns set to jazz on the weekly hit parade. It was the indefatig-
able parachuting warrior-priest, Rabbi Shlomo Goren, resplen-
dent in all his military decorations, planting the Israeli flag on
Mount Sinai. It was all, of course, at the expense of the Arabs.

The Zionists needed, as before, to hold the land they had acquired, to people and develop it, and to expel, or otherwise keep
down, the Arabs who might oppose them. It was first a question
of how much land should be held. There were those who, from
the outset, insisted that Israel should annex all the occupied
territory. Typically, the Rabbinate was to the forefront. Accord-

ing to the Chief Rabbi, the occupied territories belonged to
Israel anyway. The land had been promised to the Jews by the
Almighty and all the prophets foretold its return to them. Therefore, 'it is forbidden by the Torah for all Jews, including the
Israeli government, to return even one inch of the territory of
Eretz [Greater] Israel in our hands'.[39] Another member of the
Supreme Rabbinical Council argued that, since Israel's conquest
meant the liberation of the Holy Land from Satan's possession,
any withdrawal would increase Satan's power.[40] Greater Israel
movements proliferated. They cut across party lines. Enthusiastic meetings were held up and down the country. Generals
and cabinet ministers addressed them. Menachim Begin's Revisionists—or the *Gahal* as the party was now known—furnished
expansionism with its organized political backbone. *Gahal's* basic
position was 'no evacuation—even with peace'. The Israelis
should settle the occupied territories, not just with colonies in
uninhabited or rural areas but with 'suburbs' in all its towns—
'Ramallah, Jenin, Nablus, Tulkaram, Qalqilia, Gaza, Rafah and
elsewhere'.[41] It would not countenance the return of 'one inch of
the Land of Israel to any foreign government', nor any official
declaration, helpful to the peace-making process, which suggested that Israel might make such territorial concessions.

General Dayan the Arab-fighter, appointed Defence Minister
on the eve of the war, was the most famous and typical embodiment of Israel's post-1967 expansionism. In essence he shared
the opinion of *Gahal*; he professed the same basic drive and
vision. But he was more subtle, more politic than they. For him,
the June War was not just another victory against the enemy. It
woke in him new and unexpected feelings:

> For twenty years, from the War of Liberation to the Six-Day War
> we had the feeling we were living at the summit, breathing pure
> air. We had fought to reach the summit; we were content with
> what we had achieved . . . but in our heart of hearts, deep down,
> we were not really happy and content. We made ourselves accept
> Eilat as our southern frontier, a State of Israel which from Qalqilia
> to the sea was less than fifteen kilometres broad. Old Jerusalem
> stood outside its frontiers—this was Israel. In our daily life we
> made our own private peace with all this. The source of the great
> disturbance we feel today lies in our understanding of the fact
> that we were wrong. We have to acknowledge this. We thought

we had reached the summit, but it became clear to us that we were still on the way up the mountain. The summit is higher up.[42]

What, in practice, would Zionist self-renewal mean? Dayan felt it necessary to remind his compatriots of what they perhaps forgot—or what some of them, the younger generation, never really knew:

Jewish villages were built in the place of Arab villages. You don't even know the names of these Arab villages, and I don't blame you, because these geography books no longer exist. Not only do the books not exist, the Arab villages are not there either. Nahalal [Dayan's own village] arose in the place of Mahlul, Gvat [a *kibbutz*] in the place of Jibta, Sarid [another *kibbutz*] in the place of Haneifa, and Kfar-Yehoshua in the place of Tel-Shaman. There is not one single place built in this country that did not have a former Arab population.[43]

Given this unflinching perception of the past, Dayan paints this grim picture of the future:

We are doomed to live in a constant state of war with the Arabs and there is no escape from sacrifice and bloodshed. This is perhaps an undesirable situation, but it is a fact. If we are to proceed with our work against the wishes of the Arabs we shall have to expect such sacrifices.

And in Dayan's view, they must continue their work:

This is what used to be called 'Jew after Jew', *Aliyah* (wave of immigration) after *Aliyah*, or 'acre by acre', 'goat by goat'. It meant expansion, more Jews, more villages, more settlement. Twenty years ago we were 600,000; today we are near three million. There should be no Jew who says 'that's enough', no-one who says 'we are nearing the end of the road'. . . . It is the same with the land. There are no complaints against my generation that we did not begin the process . . . but there will be complaints against you [Dayan is addressing the Kibbutz Youth Federation on the Golan Heights] if you come and say: 'up to here.' Your duty is not to stop; it is to keep your sword unsheathed, to have faith, to keep the flag flying. You must not call a halt—heaven forbid—and say 'that's all; up to here, up to Degania, to Mufallasim, to Nahal Oz!' For that is not all.[44]

It was therefore not only as a devout Zionist, but as a hard-headed strategist, that Dayan believed in expansionism. In Dayan the strategist there was a heavy streak of fatalism. Israel was 'doomed' by its own past to perpetual conflict with the Arabs—doomed, therefore, to expand the better to prosecute the conflict. But Dayan was also, some of the time at least, a politician. As a politician he sometimes assumed the plumage of a dove. He did not resign from the government, like *Gahal*, over Israel's acceptance of the 1970 peace proposals of US Secretary of State William Rogers. Yet in his true, his hawk's plumage, he had previously insisted, like *Gahal*, that he 'strongly opposed' the Security Council resolution 242 on which the Rogers proposals were based.[45] He was only waiting for a telephone call from King Hussein to begin negotiations. Yet, in his real self, he did not want them. 'It is perhaps possible to conclude peace treaties between ourselves and our Arab neighbours, but the Arabs are asking too high a price and I pray heaven that the day never comes.'[46] And in fact, he could be very confident that it never would. As a politician, and a clever one, he knew that he could rely on the mechanisms of the conflict to ensure that, in practice, the Israelis would never be called upon to make the territorial concessions which the *Gahal* super-hawks found it necessary to reject in advance. He was waiting for his telephone call from Hussein—but it would be 'the surprise of [his] life' if the King were to accept the kind of terms he would be offered.[47] Why therefore, like *Gahal*, flaunt an insatiable expansionism before a potentially disapproving world? He knew that the Arabs were bound to reject such terms as even the Israeli doves proposed, and he knew that, spurned, the doves would join the hawks in insisting that, until the final peace settlement, the Israelis should hold what they had.

It was the apogee of the ideology of force. In earlier, weaker days, the Zionists, while never losing sight of their long-term goal, had tempered force with a certain political realism, a readiness for tactical compromise. But now the conviction took root that the existence and defence of Israel depended exclusively on its own strong right arm, that Israel was master not merely of its own destiny but of that of the entire Middle East. The ideology of force broke down into a number of axioms which, by dint of almost unchallenged repetition, acquired a sacrosanct character. Amnon Kapeliouk, a brilliant critic of Zionist orthodoxy, has

listed them: 'We shall maintain the status quo in the region for
as long as we like; security frontiers deter the Arabs from
attacking; the Bar Lev Line (along the east bank of the Suez
Canal) is impregnable; our intelligence services are infallible; the
Arabs only understand the language of force; war is not for the
Arabs; the Arab world is divided and without military options;
the oil weapon is a mere propaganda tool; the Palestinians of the
occupied territories will resign themselves to their fate; time is on
our side; it does not matter what the Gentiles say, but what the
Jews do.'[48] The vast majority of Israelis saw in this, and its
principal exponent, the incarnation of political wisdom. From
there to the massive settlement of Greater Israel was only a short
step. It was quickly taken, and Dayan the 'Arab-fighter' acquired
a new title, 'emperor of the occupied territories'.

'Come and build Jerusalem.' 'Send your son to Jerusalem.'
'Have a second home and a first child in Jerusalem.' The slogans
were addressed not to the Arabs who might once have lived there,
and would like to return, not to the Israelis who had already been
'ingathered', but to the five-sixths of the world's Jews who lived
outside the frontiers of Israel, above all to the prosperous Jews
of the West who, bringing with them money and skills, would
make desirable inhabitants of the Holy City. Immigration, a fresh
wave of *Aliyah*, was one of the first things the Israelis thought of
in the wake of their victory. There had to be a reversal of the
disastrous pre-war situation when more people were 'going down'
than 'coming up'. Not surprisingly, the Israelis exploited their
possession of Jerusalem, unified and whole, to revive it—Jerusalem, the symbolic prize and strategic fulcrum of an implacable
conflict. But not only Jerusalem, for the rest of occupied territories were also part of the Jewish heritage. Israel did not
formally annex them, in defiance of world opinion, as it did
Jerusalem. From the very outset, however, the message went out
to world Jewry, to the would-be immigrants, that it intended to
hold these too. It is unmistakably, if furtively, embodied in this
grandiloquent appeal, put out by the Israeli government and the
World Zionist Executive to 'arise, come up and build the land'.
In a language reminiscent—according to the *Jerusalem Post*—of
a proclamation issued in the time of Ezra and Nehemiah, it
declares:

The Israeli army, a people's army, daringly overcame and vanquished vast hostile forces, who had gathered to exterminate Israel. The enemy siege was broken, our ancestral heritage liberated and Jerusalem redeemed to become once more a city that is one. In the hour of deliverance . . . new vistas have been opened and immense challenges present themselves. A sacred duty to up-build the country speedily and to ensure the future of the Jewish state now faces the Jewish people. The inevitable call of the hour is for Aliyah—the Aliyah of the entire people, young and old; a return to Zion of the House of Israel. In its homeland the Jewish people has risen to full stature.[49]

TWICE IN A LIFETIME: ANOTHER ARAB EXODUS

The immigrants did come—though in nothing like the numbers expected—and, once again, bringing in the Jews meant driving the Arabs out. The immediate aftermath of the war, with its fast-changing confusion, and especially a war in which the whole world applauds the victory, was an ideal opportunity which the Israelis had no scruples about taking. Jerusalem ranked first in their ambitions; they immediately began the process of turning it into what one minister subsequently described as 'an emphatically Jewish city'.[50] The main, and only substantial, relic of Jerusalem's Jewishness is the Wailing Wall. For Zionists everywhere, God-fearing or not, there could be no more fitting way of commemorating the deliverance of the Holy City than to dignify the remnants of the Temple with a proper, spacious foreground, making them into a national-religious shrine worthy of the name. Thus would they celebrate, with a monument, the gratification of their age-old yearning for 'Next Year in Jerusalem'. 'Jerusalem has been the Jewish capital for 3,000 years since King David. Jerusalem is more Jewish than Paris is French or London English,' said David Bengurion.[51] This is historical nonsense. But to the devout Zionist it makes bedrock emotional sense. As another Israeli leader explained it, less fancifully, to the city's Moslems: 'For the Jewish people there is only Jerusalem. Other religions have places in the city which we deeply respect, but they also have other places in the world.'[52] Only through Jerusalem does Israel feel itself a nation. And no one, neither Mandatory Power nor United Nations, was now going to stop Israel

from bringing the physical appearance of the city into harmony
with this spiritual reality. What, nearly fifty years before, Weizmann had called the 'doubtful Maghreb community'[53] would
have to go. And, in a single night of bulldozing, go it did. On 11
June, the inhabitants of the quarter, beneficiaries of an endow-
ment which Saladin's son had founded seven hundred years
before, were turned out of their homes at a few minutes' notice.
Of their possessions many rescued only what they could carry.
A thousand people, or 129 families, were scattered in the adjacent lanes and streets, in a nearby market, an unfinished
school or any other spot they could find.

The Israelis could not hide what they had begun to do in
Jerusalem. They could only count it as a drawing, the first of
many, on their immense new fund of international goodwill. Nor
could they hide for very long what they were doing in less
accessible parts of their newly conquered territory. But they
could, and did, try. As they were driving bulldozers through the
Magharibah quarter of Jerusalem, they were simultaneously
wiping whole villages off the face of the earth. Among the first to
go were Beit Nuba, Imwas and Yalu, situated close to the 1967
frontier in the strategic Latroun salient north of Jerusalem. Their
10,000 inhabitants were scattered to the four winds. In 1967
other villages, such as Beit Marsam, Beit Awa, Habla and Jifliq,
met a similar fate.

There were not many foreign observers about with the determination and local knowledge to discover and document these
acts, and the authorities tried hard to impede the few there were.
Among them was Sister Marie-Thérèse, a French nun, who recorded in her diary that, after meeting all sorts of official ob-
structions, she and others from the order of Companions of Jesus
decided to fight to get to Latroun. They succeeded . . . 'and there
was what the Israelis did not want us to see: three villages systematically destroyed by dynamite and bulldozer. Alone in a
deathly silence donkeys wandered about in the ruins. Here and
there a crushed piece of furniture, or a torn pillow stuck out of
the mass of plaster, stones and concrete. A cooking pan and its
lid abandoned in the middle of the road. They were not given
enough time to take anything away.'[54]

Amos Kenan, an Israeli journalist who participated in the war,
tells the story of Beit Nuba:

We were ordered to block the entrances of the village and prevent inhabitants returning to the village from their hideouts after they had heard Israeli broadcasts urging them to go back to their homes. The order was to shoot over their heads and tell them not to enter the village. Beit Nuba is built of fine quarry stones; some of the houses are magnificent. Every house is surrounded by an orchard, olive trees, apricots, vines and presses. They are well kept. Among the trees there are carefully tended vegetable beds. In the houses we found one wounded Egyptian commando officer and some very old people. At noon the first bulldozer arrived and pulled down the first house at the edge of the village. Within ten minutes the house was turned into rubble, including its entire contents; the olive trees, cypresses were all uprooted. . . . After the destruction of three houses the first column arrived from the direction of Ramallah. We did not fire into the air but took cover, some Arabic-speaking soldiers went over to notify them of the warning. There were old people who could hardly walk, murmuring old women, mothers carrying babies, small children. The children wept and asked for water. They all carried white flags.

We told them to go to Beit Sura. They told us that they were driven out everywhere, forbidden to enter any village, that they were wandering like this for four days, without food, without water, some dying on the road. They asked to return to the village, and said we had better kill them.

Some had a goat, a lamb, a donkey or camel. A father ground wheat by hand to feed his four children. On the horizon we could see the next group arriving. A man carrying 100 lbs of flour in a sack—he had walked like that, mile after mile. More old people, more women, more babies. They dropped down exhausted where we told them to sit. Some had a cow or two, a calf; all their property on earth. We did not allow them to enter the village and take anything.

The children cried. Some of our soldiers started crying too. We went to fetch the Arabs some water. We stopped a car with a major, two captains and a woman. We took a jerrican of water and distributed it to the refugees. We also handed out cigarettes and candy. More soldiers burst into tears. We asked the officers why those refugees were sent from one place to another and driven out of everywhere. They told us that this was good for them, they should go. 'Moreover', said the officers, 'why do we care about the Arabs anyway . . .?'

More and more columns of refugees arrived, until there were

hundreds of them. They failed to understand why they had been asked to return, yet not permitted to enter. We could not stand their pleading. One asked why we destroyed their houses instead of taking them over ourselves.

The platoon commander decided to go to headquarters and find out if there were any orders about what to do with them, where to send them, and whether it was possible to arrange transport for the women and food for the children. He returned saying that there were no orders in writing, simply that they were to be driven out.

We drove them out. They go on wandering in the south like lost cattle. The weak die. In the evening we found that they had been taken in, for in Beit Sura too bulldozers had begun to destroy the place and they were not allowed to enter. We found out that not only in our sector was the border straightened out for security reasons but in all other sectors too. The promise on the radio was not kept; the declared policy was never carried out.[55]

How magnanimous the Israeli victors must have seemed, if one judged by their radio alone, with its announcers calling on enemy civilians to return to their homes without fear. But how Machiavellian they must have seemed to anyone, like Sister Marie-Thérèse, who saw Israeli soldiers driving round Bethlehem with loudspeakers to warn the populace: 'You have two hours to leave your homes and flee to Jericho and Amman. If you don't, your houses will be shelled.' The razed villages and the loudspeakers spoke for themselves. But the general behaviour of the victorious soldiery also contributed to the same end. 'It is necessary', she writes,

To state unambiguously that the first wave of Israeli soldiers were decent, humane, and courageous, doing as little damage as possible, the second wave was made up of thieves, looters and sometimes killers, and the third was more disturbing still since it seemed to act from a resolute desire for systematic destruction.

She recorded a distressing encounter:

An Israeli addressed Father Paul who could not recognize him for the look of anguish that appeared on his face: 'But I am your friend from Haifa.' 'Oh, but you look so tired,' replied Father Paul. 'No, disheartened by these Jewish bandits, who have robbed and sacked like vandals. In the region of G—— our soldiers killed two women to steal their jewels. I have so much to tell you, but

I have to go with these disgusting characters.' He pointed to his
road companions. 'They do not understand French. Good-bye,
come and see me. I want to tell you . . .' Their car started; one
of them had time to ask in Hebrew: 'Have all the Arabs left yet?'[56]

They had not. But in that first great post-war exodus, about a
fifth of the population of the West Bank, something over 200,000,
crossed the Jordan river. For some it was for the second time in
a lifetime. The Israelis could not be directly blamed for all the
things that made the Arabs go, but, as Sister Marie-Thérèse
discovered when she went down to the Allenby bridge, they were
very pleased when they did.

> It was there that the fleeing refugees had to go, most of them
> once before refugees from that other war. With their children and
> their parcels they had to clamber down the smashed bridge and
> wade through the water with the help of ropes. The Israeli
> soldiers, seated in armchairs, had been watching them pass for a
> fortnight. If it had been necessary for tanks to cross during the
> war, the bridge would have been rebuilt in a few hours. Why
> should human beings be so humiliated? From below, glances of
> hatred, from above, glances of contempt; but it is the glances of
> the frightened children in front of the broken bridge that hurt
> most. A woman carrying her sewing machine moaned and
> mumbled something. Another replied to her groans: 'May their
> houses collapse upon them.' As we were leaving, a weeping
> woman approached me; she told me that she had just crossed
> the river to help some relatives who were leaving, but that she
> herself had to return to Bethlehem where her children were;
> for the soldiers had said that, according to the law, she had to go
> to Amman since she had crossed the bridge. We thought this
> little business could easily be settled by speaking to the officer.
> The officer, who remained seated in his armchair, said: 'This
> woman has signed at the first station and they all know that once
> they have signed they never go back . . .'[57]

The Arabs then had to be *kept* out too. The Israelis had two
ways of doing that. They made it illegal for anyone to return
without authorization from themselves, an authorization which
(with very few exceptions) they then withheld, and they shot
those who tried to return illegally. Under Order No. 125, issued
by the Commander of the Israeli Defence Forces in the West
Bank, any person who was absent from the West Bank or any

other occupied territory as of 7 June 1967 and attempted to
return without Israeli permission was to be considered an 'infiltrator' and, as such, liable to anything up to life imprisonment.
This could make infiltrators not merely of the refugees who had
fled from the fighting and Israeli intimidation, but of the many
thousands who, say, had their places of work on the East Bank or
Kuwait, who simply happened to be away, on business or on
holiday, when the war broke out. It was 1948 all over again.[58]

The 'infiltrators' would try to wade across the Jordan under
cover of darkness. At one time as many as 300 to 500 were crossing every night. But the risks were considerable, and they were
the same whether the infiltrator was an armed guerilla or a
woman rejoining her family—just as they had been the same,
after 1948, for anyone who crossed the armistice line, whether
he was in search of missing relatives or picking some oranges
from his own orchard. The Israelis laid ambushes and shot
everything that moved. The result—according to the exile
publication *Imperial News*—was that 'every morning bodies
litter the Jordan, men, women, children, whole families, massacred during their attempt to return home without the coveted
Israeli permit'.[59]

THE NEW JERUSALEM

With the war, and its unique opportunities, passed, the Israelis
proceeded with greater caution—but an undiminished sense of
long-term purpose. In Jerusalem, under the urgings of the
powerful Rabbinate, they pressed on with the Judaization of the
holy places which the demolition of the 'doubtful Maghreb community' had begun. Immediate post-war fantasies about the construction of a synagogue between the mosques of al-Aqsa and
Dome of the Rock, or even the restoration of the Temple itself,
subsided, but the men of God regularly proclaimed no less an
ambition than to expose two full sides of the Haram al-Sharif,
the great platform on which the two mosques stand, from the
south-west corner, near the existing Wailing Wall, all the way to
the Gate of the Tribes in the north-east. Along this entire three-
quarters of a kilometre length are the religious endowments,
schools, courts, hospices—not to mention hundreds of Arabs
living in them—which any great place of worship and pilgrimage

gathers about itself. They are the accretions of centuries, an
organic growth, one with the Noble Sanctuary itself. To remove
them is a maiming, a severance of the mosques from their natural
environment. No sooner had the authorities inserted an item in
the *Jerusalem Post* about the need to 'clear' 82 metres of Wailing
Wall, than, ignoring all the protests of the Moslem Council, they
began archaeological excavations to investigate the Wall's
southern reaches. Cracks appeared in historic buildings—the
Fakhriyah Hospice, ancient residence of the Mufti of the Shafi
sect, and an adjoining mosque—together with fourteen houses
traditionally reserved for Haram officials. The inhabitants were
ordered out, and the Fakhriyah went the way of the Magharibah
two months before. Shortly afterwards, the Israelis turned their
attention northwards. They used the pretext of bombs discovered in the vicinity of the Chain Gate—bombs which, local
Arabs believe, the Israelis planted themselves—to confiscate all
the property, including the ancient al-Tankiziyah School, on the
northern side of the Wailing Wall compound.

Meanwhile, the Ministry of Religious Affairs was burrowing
northwards under Arab buildings, tracing the extension of the
Wailing Wall. Their ultimate and undisguised purpose—and
that of the anything-but-religious nationalist extremists who
joined forces with them—was not archaeological. They were at
work on a two-fold undermining—of the buildings themselves
and the resistance of the 'moderates' in the Municipality and the
Ministry of Foreign Affairs, who were worried about Israel's
reputation in the world and even (a few of them, and in a
strictly limited sense) about the welfare of their Arab citizens.
By May 1972, after they had covered about 180 metres, leaving
another 160 to reach the north-west corner, what the extremists
really wanted began to happen. Just beyond the Iron Gate a
Mamluk structure, rent by great fissures, threatened to collapse
and its inhabitants were evacuated. The Municipality buttressed
it with a temporary scaffolding and began making four small
holes in the Haram Wall, exposed at this point, as sockets for
permanent props. Outraged religious leaders rushed to stop this
desecration; they collected the chippings, wrapped them in silk,
and, with the Minister of Religious Affairs at their head, paraded
round the town with them. The government was obliged to issue
a decree affirming that the Wall could not be defiled to support

the threatened building. But the resistance of the 'moderates' was not yet undermined. The Municipality did not go along with this pretext for demolition, as it had with the Fakhriyah; it devised awkward and expensive means for preserving the building instead.

But in Israel extremists usually win in the end. Devout Jews went and prayed there among the rubble and scaffolding. Menachim Begin's right-wing expansionists supported them. And the Chief Rabbi of the Sephardi Sect, Itzhak Nissim, issued a bigoted, an un-Judaic, proclamation from there:

> City contractors . . . where are your bulldozers and machines which went to work as they should on the first night to clear the ground before the Wailing Wall [i.e. to demolish the Magharibah Quarter] . . . the Municipality decided to do away with the slums and ruins and the decision must be carried out without fear or shame . . . the hundreds of people living in them must be given their marching orders . . . we shall not cease our clamour, nor desist from the struggle, until the Wall is exposed, from summit to base, from its southern extremity to its northern one near the Gate of the Tribes.[60]

The Israelis did not, of course, confine themselves to creating religious facts, although it was with quasi-religious fervour that they set about creating the secular ones that were destined to make Jerusalem, in its daily living fabric, 'more Jewish than Paris is French, more Jewish than London is English'. The first secular *fait accompli* was the formal annexation of the city. The enlargement of the Israeli Municipality—under the Interior Minister's Ordinance No. 5727 of 28 June 1967—brought it up to, and where that suited him, a little beyond the boundaries of the Jordanian Municipality. A whole series of supporting laws followed in rapid succession. They Judaized the Jerusalem administration. On 29 June the Assistant Military Commander of Jerusalem had 'the honour to inform' the Mayor of East Jerusalem, Ruhi Khatib, that his municipal council was dissolved. Municipal property and records were seized, and all government departments were brought under Israeli jurisdiction. They Judaized the Jerusalem economy. Arab banks were closed down and their funds appropriated, the Israeli taxation system was introduced along with the Israeli currency, and West Bank

products were banished from the city, which Israeli suppliers had
largely to themselves. They Judaized the Jerusalem citizens. All
businessmen, craftsmen and professional men had to obtain
Israeli licences, state schools had to follow the Israeli curricula,
civil courts had to work under the Israeli judiciary, and the
ordinary citizen was expected to vote in Israeli municipal elections. They Judaized Arab land and property.

'We take the land first and the law comes after.' With remarkable candour Yehoshafat Palmon, adviser to the Mayor on Arab
affairs, thus put in a nutshell for me his government's strategy for
taking what did not belong to it. Taking the land has always been
Zionism's basic impulse. Taking it in Jerusalem was a sacred
compulsion. The Israelis applied to the Holy City essentially the
same methods they had learned in the pioneering frontier days.
It was the tower-and-stockade technique adapted to a unique
urban environment. In a frantic programme of expropriation and
construction, immigration and settlement, they sought to obli-
terate, as quickly as possible and by sheer physical presence, the
remaining Arab claim to Jerusalem, which was built not only on
sentiment and centuries of sovereignty, but on the abstract
legality of immemorial possession of the land. During the Mandate, as a result of Zionist efforts to pack the city, the Jews had re-
tained their majority in the city proper; however, if Jerusalem
had been internationalized—as a UN General Assembly resolution of November 1947 recommended—the boundaries pre-
scribed by the UN plan would have incorporated 100,000 Jews
as against 105,000 Arabs and others.[61] As for the land, only about
5,000 dunums, or some 18 per cent of the area of Jerusalem, had
been Jewish-owned.[62] On the eastern, subsequently Jordanian,
side the Jews had represented a much smaller proportion of the
population and they had owned the merest fraction—perhaps
0·6 per cent[63]—of the land.

'We take the land . . .' Between 1948 and 1967, the Israelis
had used their Absentees' Property Law to take some 20,000
dunums of it,[64] along with a rich haul of movable and immovable property, belonging to the Arabs on the western side of
the city. Since 1967 they have taken more than 15,000 dunums
on the eastern side.[65] This included, of course, the tiny particle
of Jewish land abandoned in 1948. To their surprise, it seems,
the Israelis found it juridically intact. For there was a Jordanian

Custodian of Absentees' Property too, and he—said Israeli lawyer Chaim Aron Valero—had been 'quite fair. . . . I don't know about all the properties, but I know quite a number of properties remained registered to this day in Jewish names as in Mandate times. They were not expropriated and their ownership did not pass to the Jordanian government.'[66] It goes without saying that it was a one-way process. The Arabs of unified Jerusalem who put in a claim for property they had abandoned on the Israeli side in 1948 got short shrift. For the job of the Israeli Custodian, unlike his Jordanian counterpart, was not to preserve property for its rightful owner, but to deprive him of it.

'The law comes after . . .' In fact, for most Arabs it did not come at all. There might have been a few exceptions—propaganda exceptions—but they knew that it was futile to take their cases to the courts. 'When your enemy is your judge, to whom do you complain?' goes an Arab saying, much in vogue in Jerusalem. Besides, it was for the higher good of the whole community that they were forfeiting their land. For this time it was not its own Absentees' Property Law, but another of those British laws—the Land Acquisition for Public Purposes Ordinance of 1943—which the Israeli government resurrected for the occasion. How useful that much-maligned, but never quite abandoned, British legislation was continuing to prove! The beauty of this law—though not, of course, its framers' intention—was that it could be put to any 'purpose' the Israelis saw fit, such as turning Jerusalem into an 'emphatically Jewish city'. The British had decreed that there should be compensation for the owner of the expropriated land or property—and the Israelis duly offered it. But they practically never paid it. As they well knew, the Arabs could not take their money anyway; that would be 'selling Palestine'. But in any case what was the point of taking their money when all they were offered, as the Arabs scornfully put it, was 'the ear of a camel'?

By 1972, land values in fashionable parts of the city, such as Qatamon, were reaching £30,000 a dunum and more. Few of the 15,000 dunums could have been worth less than £3,000 a dunum. But almost every Arab would tell you that, in so far as the Israelis talked business at all, they were offering a tenth, twentieth or thirtieth of that. The Israelis have always been extremely reticent about the whole subject, but their offer to compensate

Jerusalemites—the minority of them who could still reside there
—for property they lost anywhere in Israel after 1948 was a
measure of their intentions. The Custodian of Absentees' Property had of course irrevocably deprived them of every good and
chattel they owned, but in 1971 the Ministry of Justice suddenly
decided that justice of sorts should be done. The sum of
$150,000,000 was set aside for the purpose. The compensation
was to be paid at 1948 prices, plus 25 per cent in Israeli bonds,
over a period of twenty years. What this meant in practice was
explained by a leading businessman who, taking me on a sentimental journey round West Jerusalem, and showing me the
house in which he and his father were born, came finally to a
commercial property which his family had bought in 1944. 'If it
were mine now,' he said, 'I wouldn't sell it for £450,000. But I
reckon that if I accepted Israeli compensation I would get about
£6,000 for it.' That is to say, he would receive less than one
seventy-fifth of its true value.

Although the municipal booklets—which seem to be designed
for readers who never ask questions—asserted that the Arabs
were compensated, officials, when confronted by the unaccustomed questioners with evidence to the contrary, admitted that
they were not, and took refuge in the alternative argument
that the Arabs, insisting on retaining their rights of ownership,
refused to come forward to take the compensation they were due.
'We have not yet reached the stage of talking about the price of
land,' Mr Palmon conceded. It was difficult to measure these
things in terms of cold cash but did he mean, assuming—on a
conservative estimate—an average value of £3,000 per dunum,
that the Israelis were in the process of acquiring land in East
Jerusalem to the value of £45,000,000 for almost nothing? 'Yes,'
he replied, 'it's not very much. It may seem strange to you coming from Beirut. But everything is done according to the law, a
detailed law, the law for the public benefit. The law is greater
than me, greater than Golda Meir. We can't leave Jerusalem a
desert, with donkeys in the streets.'

The lack of charity in Mr Palmon's words was even more forcefully reflected in the acts of his Municipality. Israel's smallest
single expropriation—the 116 dunums of the Jewish Quarter—
became a poignant paradigm of them all. For nowhere more than
here, a stone's throw from the most sacred of Jewish shrines, was

true religion, a true spirit of reconciliation, more strikingly
absent. Here Yigal Allon, the Deputy Prime Minister, was quick
to move into a fine new house. It has a magnificent view to the
front, high above the plunging Kidron Valley, but for a long
while it had an unsightly one to the rear, where Arab house-
holders, refusing to leave, clung to islands of habitation amid the
desolation wrought by the bulldozers and demolition squads.
Before 1948, the Jewish Quarter was not more than 20 per cent
Jewish-owned.[67] After 1967, the Israelis took over the lot. They
relentlessly forced out the 5,500 inhabitants who lived there.[68]
They described them as 'squatters'. A few squatters—that is to
say, Israeli-created refugees—had found makeshift homes in the
quarter. But most of the inhabitants were old Jerusalem families
who had lived there from generation to generation.[69]

Ostensibly, the 5,500 left of their own free will with what the
municipal booklets described as 'handsome' compensation. When
I suggested to an official responsible for 'reconstruction' that this
was untrue, he came close to losing his temper. 'Do we shoot
them?' he asked. 'Do we drive them across the river, do we deny
them work?' They didn't. What they did, when they could not
persuade some obstinate tenant (the property is mostly *Waqf*
religious endowments leased to tenants who did not feel, in taking
money, that they were 'selling Palestine') to accept the inadequate
compensation they offered, was to make his life unbearable by
demolishing everything around him, even part of the house itself,
the entrance steps or an outside lavatory. The walls cracked, the
roof leaked, water got cut off, the rooms were choked with dust.
They used intimidation. The hatchet man for the higher authorities, Ezra ben Simon—plain Ezra as the Arabs called him—decorated his room in a rather unusual way for a municipal office:
beneath a full-colour picture of General Dayan were shelves
bearing an array of upright bullets of different sizes, a grenade
and what appeared to be a bayonet. Municipal regulations were
cynically exploited. A housewife showed me the order she had
received to evacuate her house for her own safety's sake. If her
house was unsafe, it was, of course, because the Municipality,
bulldozing all round it, had made it so. They used ignoble subter-
fuges. One girl recounted how, when a squad of soldiers and
workmen came to her family's house with orders to demolish it,
they told her father, in answer to his protests, to go and see

Mayor, Teddy Kollek. He left them carrying out the furniture, but by the time he got back, bearing a stay of execution from Kollek, they had already pulled the house down, with a chain attached to a bulldozer, before his family's eyes.

It was the same with the much larger areas outside the Old City walls: the women from the village of Lifta, a twice-expropriated community, who told me they spent an unpleasant night in prison, one of them in a cell with prostitutes, after trying to resist the tractors ploughing up their land; the orphan boy from Aisawia village who showed me where his uncle gathered thirty members of his family to rebuild his humble home each time the Israelis knocked it down, only giving up after the third attempt; the woman who took me to a large patch of rubble near the Mount of Olives, the remains of a fine, uninhabited house, owned by an absentee Palestinian American, which the Israelis bulldozed with a subsequent explanation to the inquiring American consul that the house had never existed. These were just a few individual instances of the systematic spoliation which the Israelis tried to hide from prying eyes, just a few indications of what it really meant when an Israeli newspaper carried a report like this: 'The security forces yesterday sealed off the entrance to the village of Nabi Samuel and demolished some old buildings which were a danger to the public. . . . Journalists, including foreign correspondents and television crews, were denied access to the area.[70]

'Never forcibly evicted', 'handsomely compensated', the Arabs —the municipal booklet went on—were 'assured of alternative accommodation'. And officials told me brightly about the new housing estate at Wadi Joz. That sounded encouraging. Arabs building for Arabs, I learned from contractors, was at a very low ebb; costs had nearly quadrupled since the 1967 War; the risk of expropriation was ever-present; the Israelis were in no hurry to issue building licences. But perhaps, after all, I would find clinching rebuttal of Arab complaints at Wadi Joz. What I found was twenty-eight diminutive apartments. Twenty-six of them were shuttered and bolted. Only two were occupied. Salim Namari, the first to move in to one of the two, told me his story.

> I used to live in the Jewish Quarter. They knocked down so much of my house that I was all but living in the open air. I refused to

move till I found another house. I couldn't find one. So they
offered me one at Wadi Joz. First they said they wanted £1,500
down payment, then £2,300. I could not find the difference.
I went to the Municipality about four days a week for six months.
I was turned away every time. I only got them down to £1,500
again when I contacted a journalist on the *Jerusalem Post*, known
for his opposition to the Municipality, and he threatened to
write about me. Then it was the same business getting credit
instalments. Only when I barged my way into the manager's
office did I get what I wanted. It is going to cost me £7,000 all
told. It took me twenty months to get here. The Israelis never
lose a chance to make propaganda. They had the nerve at the
end of it to hold a ceremony on my account. I was on television
and in the papers.

And he showed me a picture of himself being presented with a
bouquet of flowers before a seated audience of Arabs and Jews.
'I had certain advantages, I speak fluent Hebrew. My wife is
Jewish. I have a lawyer friend in Tel Aviv. Imagine what it's
like for the others.'

Taking the land was the main thing, but it was inseparable from
a host of other unlawful actions which, by eroding Palestinian
society, facilitated the taking. The severest of these—more
severe, in fact, than expropriation itself—was the permanent
exiling of Jerusalem's Arabs. The former Mayor, Ruhi Khatib,
estimated at 100,000 the number of people, Jerusalemites by
birth, background or property rights, who could not return to
their city. A few, like himself, were banished for their anti-
Israeli activities; but the vast majority were simply absentees
who were not allowed back. They included 60,000 Jerusalemites
who left Palestine in 1948, the 5,000 who happened to be away in
1967—because they fled, because they were studying abroad,
taking a holiday, travelling on business or simply because they
were taxi-drivers on errands to Amman or Damascus—and the
35,000 children born and bred in exile.[71] The Israelis never made
any secret of it: they were bent on 'thinning out' the population
of Jerusalem more effectively than anywhere else. After the 1967
War, there were many Jerusalemites who, unable to face the
rigours and uncertainties of occupation, helped them by taking
the emigrant's way out. The Christian Arabs, more educated and

adaptable than their Muslim compatriots, were in the forefront of this 'distressing stampede without hope or joy',[72] as Archbishop Raya of Galilee described it. And in the words of another prelate, the Archbishop of Anchorage, emigration threatened to reduce the role of Christians in the Holy Land to 'no more than keepers of museums and curators of shrines'.[73]

It was the more vigorous elements of Palestinian society—the economic, cultural and intellectual élite—who fared worst in Jerusalem. The young, the students, faced the most serious problems. After 1967, they fell under the same disabilities that Israeli Arabs had suffered since 1948. In Israel's Arab schools, children have always had to see their own Arab culture, history and religion through Israeli eyes; they saw it deliberately mocked and falsified. Arab history became little more than a series of revolutions, murders, feuds and plunderings, while everything in the Jewish past was ennobled and glorified. It was always the Arabs in decline they learned about, never in their greatness; the heroes of the past, the Prophet, the Caliph Harun al-Rashid and Saladin, got perfunctory mention. In four years of secondary education Arab children had 384 periods of Jewish history as against only 32 of their own. The study of the Old Testament was compulsory, while the Muslim and Christian religions were not taught at all. The overall quality of education was extremely low; so much so that in 1966, the Arabs, who represented one-tenth of the population, boasted 171 university students compared with 14,000 Jews.[74] When, therefore, the Israelis extended their own syllabus to the Arab public schools of East Jerusalem, the result was immediate and dramatic. It meant that students had to forego their hopes of a university education. Places for Arabs at the Hebrew University—if not actually regulated by quota—were in practice extremely limited, and only the most brilliant of students, suddenly plunged into an alien language, culture and educational system could hope to pass the Israeli metriculation or *bagrut*, in order to qualify for one of them; but in making the attempt students would be denying themselves the chance of passing the Arab equivalent, or *taujihi*, to secure a place in an Arab university. Several well-known schools became ghosts of their former selves. The Rashidiya College, which had thrived since Ottoman times, boasted 800 students before the Six-Day War. By 1972 it had fourteen. Pupils and teachers transferred to private schools, and even to orphanages, which remained unaffected by Israeli legislation. But the invasion caused standards to fall sharply. There was a dramatic slump in the number of British General Certificate passes. There was only a slight improvement in the situation when the Israelis came up with an inspired compromise; public school pupils could work for the *bagrut* and *taujihi* at the same time.

Something else which the Israelis applied wholesale to East Jerusalem was their taxation system. They did not bother to ascertain whether it was truly applicable or not. And of course it was not. Israel, unlike Jordan, has a high-taxation economy—high wages with a high rate of fiscal recovery. Were the librarian in Saladin Street, the little grocer in the Old City, the civil servant from Shaikh Jarrah really the same, for tax purposes, as their counterparts in Western Jerusalem? Could the Arab citizen who had no assistance for educating his children or building his house on an instalment plan be put on the same footing as the Israeli who enjoyed welfare services from the cradle to the grave? Similarly, if municipal rates were assessed largely on the surface area a property occupied, should a prime residential or commercial quarter in East Jerusalem, where properties are spacious, be assessed on the same basis as its equivalent in the West, where they are cramped? The choice facing the Jerusalem property-owner was to submit to the new order, a burden which it was difficult, and sometimes impossible, to bear, or to cut his losses and leave. And imagine the feelings of the Jerusalemite, a non-citizen liable to expulsion at any time, when, in addition to the regular taxes, he had to make his contribution to periodic 'Defence Loans'—in other words, to the purchase of Phantoms for bombing his fellow-Arabs.

The Israelis also blessed the Arabs with what, in the Western world, is often hailed as their main achievement in an area which lacks such a thing—their democracy. The Arabs of Jerusalem were privileged to vote in municipal elections. The first time they were held some 4,000 out of 37,000 potential voters went to the polls. One official described this as an 'embarrassment' to Arab leaders. Indeed, not only did they go to the polls, they showed great enthusiasm to exercise their democratic rights; the booths were crowded with hundreds of Arabs pushing, shoving and literally begging to vote. They went there in buses decorated with slogans like 'We Want Teddy Kollek', and Arabs whose names were not on the electoral rolls would not leave without written confirmation that they had come to vote. It quickly turned out, however, that the whole operation had been organized, like a military campaign, by Kollek's own supporters, who violently drove out activists of other parties trying to corner the Arab vote for themselves. What made the Arabs so enthusiastic was the fear, deliberately inculcated, that if they did not vote for him they would lose their jobs. All this was exposed in the Israeli press, not out of any concern for democracy, but because rival parties were jealous. A Dr Rosenberg summed it up in *Yediot Aharonot*: 'the circumstances in which they voted are well known, but we shall not deal with them here—for patriotic reasons'.[75]

Into the cruder fabric of obvious discrimination was woven the finer texture of subtle irritations that a conquered people, in daily contact with their conquerors, inevitably experience. It might be arrogant policemen or discourteous bureaucrats, unpleasant anywhere, but doubly so as the agents of an occupying power. It might be the partisan verdict of authority: if there was a traffic accident involving an Arab and a Jew, who was to prevent the law from taking the Jew's side? It might be the pedantic application of municipal regulations: an East Jerusalem school was told that its windows were six inches smaller than they should be; but one has only to go to schools in the slum areas of West Jerusalem to see—even if the windows are the regulation size—how unhygienic they are. It might be some trivial but maddening experience; Arabs often failed their driving tests for silly, petty reasons; one was asked what he would do if a woman with a dog asked him for a lift and he replied, 'I would take her if she was pretty.' 'Failed; you check to see if she has a dog licence first.' It might be Hebrew memorials to the Jewish dead in the battle for Jerusalem, as against the virtual absence of Arab ones; and one in English which records that 'on this spot, seventy-eight nurses, researchers and doctors were ambushed and massacred by Arab marauders on their way to work at the Hadassa Hospital one morning in 1948.' The Land of Israel Movement which went around expunging Arabic wall signs. The changing of street names—from Suleiman the Magnificent Street to Paratroop Street and Allenby Square to Zahal (Israeli Defence Forces) Square. The coming of prostitution to East Jerusalem with

teenage girls assembling in droves at Jaffa Gate or bargaining
with their customers outside the newly established bars of al-
Zahra Street. The growing number of burglaries . . . the hooli-
gans. . . . In themselves these things were often petty or accidental enough but, taken together, they made up, in a hundred little
ways, the climate of the New Jerusalem.

Of all the occupied territories, only Jerusalem was formally
annexed. Nevertheless throughout the new domains, the West
Bank, the Golan Heights, Gaza and Sinai, no time was lost with
the 'creation of facts'—facts which, in the expansionist tradition,
could never be undone. The old slogans were revived: where the
Jews settled, there they would remain. The 'emperor of the occupied territories' never ceased to affirm that the new colonies were
not mere flowerpots that could be moved from one place to another, but trees rooted in the soil. By the October 1973 War,
some forty-two settlements dotted the face of Greater Israel, and
many more were planned. Some lay well within the biblically
defined frontiers of the Promised Land—like those on the West
Bank, a third of which, under the so-called Allon Plan, was all
but officially earmarked for annexation. Others lay beyond them
—like those on the Golan Heights, or at Sharm al-Shaikh, renamed Ophir, deep inside Egyptian territory at the southernmost
tip of the Gulf of Aqaba. The settlements were industrial as well
as agricultural; and one, called Yamit, in north-east Sinai, was
eventually destined to grow into a coastal township of some
250,000 people. Vast tracts of land went with them. Almost all of
Golan, cleared of its Syrian inhabitants, was the victors' for the
taking. On the West Bank, the Land Administration appropriated nearly a million and a half dunums of Jordanian state
domain, as well as abandoned or absentee property. It helped
itself to almost a third—some 120,000 dunums—of the entire
Gaza Strip.[76] Ostensibly—and to make the colonization more
acceptable to world opinion—the settlements had military as
well as other purposes; they were portrayed as vital new assets in
Israel's unending struggle for survival. But the officials concerned
were not always too discreet about the real motives: 'We have to
use the pretext of security needs and the authority of the military
governor as there is no way of driving out the Arabs from their
land so long as they refuse to go and accept our compensation.'[77]

Sometimes it was necessary to uproot an entire village—though
not necessarily all at once. For years the impoverished inhabitants of Beit Askariyah watched in impotent dismay as the great
cantonments of the Kfar Etzion settlement went up around them,
relentlessly encroaching on their agricultural and grazing lands
before swallowing up their homes too.[78] In January 1972, the
army expelled 6,000 bedouins from Rafah in north-east Sinai. It
demolished their houses, poisoned their wells, and kept them at
bay with a barbed-wire fence. The bedouins were eventually
employed as night watchmen or labourers—on their own property and in the service of those who had taken it from them. But
it was the villagers of Akraba who were taught the most original
lesson. The military government had requisitioned some of their
land for use as a shooting range. They objected. So their fields
were sprayed from the air with a poisonous chemical which
destroyed the entire harvest. In due course the fields were handed
over to the nearby settlement of Nahal Gitit.[79]

APARTHEID ISRAELI-STYLE

Expulsions and expropriations notwithstanding, most of the
Palestinians managed to stay behind. The Israelis were not as
thorough, in driving them out, as they had been in 1948. There
were, after all, limits to Western tolerance. It remained, however,
a frequently expressed desire that the Palestinians would eventually be persuaded to leave. Meanwhile, here they were, some
2,800,000 Jews, ruling over nearly 1,500,000 Arabs, composed of
Israel's own rapidly growing minority, plus the newly conquered
inhabitants of Greater Israel.

It was a new situation, and it troubled the Zionist soul, torn as
it was between the two primal impulses of expansionism and exclusivism. The ruling élite were anxious to absorb as much
territory as possible; but at the same time they were afraid, many
of them, of having to absorb the Palestinians along with it. Not
merely would that run counter to the whole idea of the Jewish
State, it threatened to turn Israel into a typical colonial power in
which the Jews would be to their Palestinians as the whites of
South Africa are to their blacks. The most pungent expression of
this fear came, as so often, from the Prime Minister, Golda Meir,
herself. The Palestinians' birth-rate was so much higher than the

Jews' that her sleep was often disturbed, she would say, at the thought of how many Arab babies had been born in the night. It was during her administration that the Israeli parliament passed a law which deputy Uri Avneri described as 'infamous, shameful and scandalous' in its discriminatory intent. It was designed— beneath its Orwellian disguise—to encourage child-bearing among Israeli Jews, but to discourage it among Israeli Arabs, 'to pay grants to the hungry children of one part of the population and withhold them from the hungry children of another part, the distinction—it is obscure but quite obvious to anyone who knows the facts—being an ethnic one . . .'[80]

For all their anxieties, however, the leadership quickly adapted themselves to the new realities. The threat to the integrity of Zionism was a long-term one. Meanwhile, there were alluring opportunities to be seized. General Dayan, the hard-headed pragmatist, did his best to ensure that they were. For him the occupied territories were a market for Israeli products and a source of cheap labour; they should therefore be 'integrated' into the Israeli economy. By 1973, they had in fact become Israel's largest market (except for polished diamonds) after the United States. The exports were mainly manufactured goods —commodities which the Palestinians were not allowed to acquire from any other quarter. It was Dayan's hope that, via the West Bank and its 'open bridges' across the Jordan, Israel would eventually penetrate those vast 'natural' markets which, because of the rigorous Arab quarantine, it had been denied since its foundation. By 1973, some 70,000 workers from the West Bank and Gaza were employed in Israel. That meant that Israel was furnishing jobs for about half the employed men of the West Bank; their wages accounted for about a third of its gross product. Some twenty employment bureaux opened in the West Bank with the sole purpose of channelling workers into the Israeli economy. Like the Israeli Arabs before them, the West Bankers and Gazans were concentrated in construction and agriculture. Altogether, Arabs now accounted for about one-third of the jobs in these two sectors.[81]

Economic 'integration' injected a new strain into Zionist attitudes towards the natives, or rather it intensified one which had always been there, among the less doctrinaire, from the beginning. The exclusivist dogma of Hebrew Labour and its ruthless

denial of jobs to Arabs, which had held sway since the early
years of the century, was now being challenged by the notion that
Arabs were particularly suited to work that was inappropriate for
the Jews. In a letter to *Haaretz*, which supported Dayan's policies, a reader told Mrs Meir that if she wanted to see 'Hebrew
workers sweating away on hot summer days, if it gives her
pleasure, this is her own business. But it cannot be a national
criterion on which to convince the public that we should not
integrate the economy of the West Bank. . . . I would like to say
that in many countries with developed national sensitivity there
are millions of foreign workers carrying out most of the dirty
work, and no one cares or is frightened about it.'[82] Joseph Chuba,
a farmer, was more explicit: 'If Arabs exist, let them work. Why
shouldn't Jews be the bosses? The Arab workers are naturally
built for it. I have one who is fifty years old and works bent
double for eight hours a day. Show me a Jew like him!'[83]

Although Dayan's pragmatism won the day, it never ceased to
worry the keepers of the Zionist conscience. The Secretary
General of the Trade Union Federation shocked an audience
when he declared: 'I do not know whether the territories that we
are holding are bargaining cards or perhaps embers burning
away our foundations. . . . I must say it is very sweet building
Zionism with Arab labour, to build cities of the economy and
enjoy it. We shall soon hear that anyone who says he does not
want to get rich on the work of the Arabs from the territories
questions the realization of Zionism and holds back redemption
and development.'[84] For the wife of a cooperative farmer, the old
pre-war days of honest toil had obviously become an Arcadian
memory:

> Until the Six-Day War we had lived in peace, we worked hard
> but were relatively prosperous. But since then the situation has
> changed. My husband, who is an able man, became a contractor
> for agricultural labour. We had the advantages of cheap sources
> of labour and a big market. Today we have five Arab workers and
> a situation where we do nothing for ourselves on our farm. My
> eldest son now even refuses to cut the grass saying: 'Let Muham-
> mad do it.' And of course it is no good talking of any real hard
> work. All the children of the *Moshav* as well as my own children
> are changing in front of my eyes into the kind of rich children
> who have everything done for them by their servants. Nobody

knows how to drive the tractor which stands in the yard or is interested in agriculture. Until about a week ago the Arab workers lived in the citrus warehouses where they were working but now it seems more labour has been brought in to work in the hothouses and the citrus warehouses are full. Therefore my husband has built them a hut in the yard. When I protested he sent me to look around the village and I realized that any man with ability had become a contractor. The village is full of hothouses in which only Arab workers are employed. The Arabs live mostly in mud houses some distance from the improved villas of the Jewish farmers who have adopted the style of *effendi*. Another point: the attitude towards our workers and the conditions in which they live are even worse than for the *Fatah* prisoners in jail.[85]

And for the Minister of Agriculture the phenomenon was obviously quite as repugnant as the 'painful leprosy' which so upset a Zionist pioneer more than half a century before.[86] 'The domination of Jewish agriculture by Arab workers', he lamented, 'is a cancer in our body.'[87] *Plus ça change. . . .*

Dayan's answer, in effect, was that such pragmatism does not, or should not, endanger the Zionist ideal. It was possible to have both expansionism *and* exclusivism. If there were a threat to the national fibre, to the traditional Zionist ethic of hard work and self-reliance, the Israelis should depend on their 'inner force' to meet it.[88] But there were also certain practical measures that could be taken to keep the Palestinians in their place. For it was not as if the inhabitants of the occupied territories had any political or civil rights. They might live under Israeli military rule; but juridically they were Jordanians, like the West Bankers, or just refugees, like the Gazans. It was really quite straightforward. 'When they are not Israeli citizens, they do not vote in parliamentary elections. The whole question of our demographic character, in the sense that the inhabitants of the territories would affect our way of life, *does not exist.*'[89] If the Palestinians did not like this, Dayan insinuated, then all they had to do was to leave for places where they felt more at home.[90] Thus it was that an 'Apartheid Israeli-style'—as Israeli civil libertarian Shulamit Aloni called it[91]—came quite openly into being. No longer was it the surreptitious thing it had to be for those, Israel's own Arab minority, who were supposed to be equal in the eyes of the law. The West Bankers and the Gazans could work in

Israel, but there was no question of their living there. Some would try. So inspection teams went around preventing them from squatting near their places of work. For the squatters were liable to bring their wives and families along, and before you knew where you were you had a whole Arab village on your hands.[92] Of course, there were always exceptions; it might require a bribe from an employer or a middleman, but the authorities could often be induced to turn a blind eye to the squalid tents or hutments that went up on building sites on the outskirts of cities.[93] The Palestinians went automatically into the most menial of jobs. Their wages averaged about 40 per cent of those of their Israeli counterparts.[94] They could be dismissed overnight. There were thousands of 'illegal' workers too; they were favoured by employers seeking to evade the tax that was supposed to be paid on every immigrant worker; their conditions were even worse. Workers who had no regular employment had to present themselves at the 'open markets' in various towns. Israel's Arabic-language Communist Party newspaper describes the one at Jaffa:

> In this market foremen get rich by exploiting the labour of children and young men from the occupied areas. Every morning at 4.a.m. cars from Gaza and the Strip start arriving there, bringing dozens of Arab workers who line up in the street in a long queue. A little later at 4.30.a.m. Arab boys who work in restaurants in the town begin to arrive. These boys work in restaurants for a month on end, including Saturdays.... Dozens, indeed hundreds, of boys who should be at school come from Gaza to work in Israel. The cars can be seen coming and going from earliest dawn. At about 6.a.m. Israeli labour brokers start arriving to choose 'working donkeys' as they call them. They take great care over their choice, actually feeling the 'donkeys'' muscles (though fortunately they do not examine their teeth!). Those who are unlucky and do not get work await 'God's mercy' under the trees in a neighbouring garden.[95]

UNDER THE HEEL OF THE CONQUEROR

It hardly needs to be said that the upbuilding of Greater Israel could only be accomplished through the permanent, institutional use of violence to which Zionism was irretrievably wedded. There was the systematic torture of prisoners. This has been docu-

mented by the Israeli lawyer Felicia Langer, one of the very few
who tried to secure real justice for the Palestinians before Israeli
courts, in her book *With My Own Eyes*.[96] Earlier, a UN Investigating Committee, denied access to the occupied territories,
heard what it considered to be convincing evidence of the
vicious and occasionally lethal agonies which Palestinians suffered
at the hands of skilled Israel torturers. It found the testimony of
one Ahmad Khalifa 'particularly impressive' because 'he did not
give the impression that he was moved by rancour towards his
former captors'. More hurtful to his fellow-prisoners than the
physical torture, Khalifa said, was the abuse and insults to which
they were subjected as individuals or members of the Palestinian
resistance movement. He tried to reason with his captors.

I knew, I said, that the Israelis tortured prisoners brutally, and I
could say a great deal about conditions even there, in the Russian
Compound Prison. But I wanted to tell him something else.
Physical torture was not important; sooner or later physical scars
heal but psychological scars never heal. There had been intelligence services that had tried to destroy the self-respect and
humanity of their enemies, and believed that they had succeeded.
But in fact they had turned their victims into extremists full of
hatred. 'What concerns us,' I said, 'is not the question of information and security; it is the question of the relations between
two peoples. We are fighting now, and it may well be that we shall
fight for a long time. But if you are concerned for the future of
your children and ours, you should behave in such a way as to
prevent extremism and hatred. This is your opportunity.'

I stopped and the officer was silent, while Ghuwaili (a particularly brutal torturer) spoke. I shall never forget his words. He
said: 'You Arabs are cowards. You wanted to annihilate us and
you were "——" in the war. Now you must accept the facts.
We shall not return Golan, nor the West Bank, nor the Gaza
Strip. We want to live. If you don't like it, fight us if you are
men, and may the best man win.'

After what I had said, these words came as a shock, and all I
could find to say was: 'You are right; we shall see.' The officer
then spoke a few words to him in Hebrew, then rose and, putting
his hand on my shoulder, said: 'Ahmad, I understand you very
well. Believe me, we shall not try to break you.' Then with a
greeting he left the room. I never saw him again, but I am sorry
to say that his promise was not kept.[97]

There was the 'administrative detention'. This imprisonment of politically-minded intellectuals, who were the natural leaders of Israel's Arab minority, had been a time-honoured practice. It found a much harsher, less selective application in the occupied territories. At its worst it meant the establishment of veritable concentration camps buried in remote corners of the Sinai desert. Nakhl, Abu Zu'aiman, Kusseimah were the names of places where whole families were confined in total isolation from the outside world. They were there because relatives of theirs were suspected, no more, of working for the resistance. Crowded into tents surrounded by barbed wire, they were denied radios, newspapers or the most basic amenities from their homes, which were frequently destroyed during their captivity. Women and children would be put in one camp, male relatives of 'wanted persons'—brother, nephews, cousins—in another. It was decreed that at least one man must be confined along with the rest of the family, 'so that it might not be said that we desecrate the honour of Arab women'.[98]

There were the 'collective punishments', which at one time were an almost daily routine. Curfews, often imposed on the slightest pretext, could last for days. There was a standard procedure with local variations. The whole male population of a village or refugee camp, from fourteen to seventy years of age, would be driven to some deserted spot or herded into a stockade. There they would be divided into two groups, the young and the less young, so that fathers and children should not be together. Both groups would be made to kneel, squat on their haunches or adopt some humiliating posture. Thus they would remain for two or three days, and the soldiers who guarded them would keep firing in the air above their heads. Meanwhile the womenfolk would be confined to their houses, which frequently lacked water or sanitation. Mothers with small children would often be reduced to a state of hysteria. The women could go out for half an hour or so to bring food and water. The public latrines in refugee camps were not built for mass utilization in a half-hour period, and, occasionally, among the women killed or wounded were those who, being unable to contain themselves, made a dash for the lavatories.[99] The village of Beit Sahur, from which Katiusha rockets were fired on Jerusalem, held the record: a month-long, twenty-two-hour-a-day curfew during which the inhabitants,

half-starved, could not open their doors, go out into the garden
or even open the windows and stand beside them.[100]

Curfews and 'searches' were often carried out with great
brutality and violence. In the middle of the night people had to
leave their homes until the searches were completed. To spread
panic soldiers would fire their machine-guns as they went.
Sometimes people were killed or wounded; later the Israel press
would report that they were 'shot while attempting to run
away'.[101] It was a regular practice, during night-time raids, to
carry men off to prison without any good reason, beat them up
and torture them. The Israelis sometimes called in the notorious
Green Berets, the Druze troops who seemed to take a special
pleasure in hurting their fellow-Arabs. These might go into
action with clubs and whips. They beat their victims savagely,
in order to scare them. Bones would be broken. They stripped
women naked in the streets, stealing their jewellery and smashing
their pathetic belongings.[102] Some Israeli soldiers privately expressed the opinion that 'the best way to combat terrorism was to
bind suspects tightly with electric wire on arms and legs, and
leave them in the sun . . .'[103]

There was the demolition of houses. More than 7,000 had been
blown up within two years of the 1967 War. This happened
mainly—and in the immediate aftermath of the fighting—for
strategic, Zionist purposes. There was no pretence of punishment or reprisal. But when there was it was often of the flimsiest
kind. Suspicion, not proof, was all the occupying power required.
The suspects might be released—for lack of evidence—but there
was no redress for their demolished homes. An unsuspecting
hotelier who happened to let a room to a guerilla would have his
hotel wrecked.[104] And often a house, in Israeli parlance, meant a
multi-storey apartment building, or a whole row of adjacent
dwellings. Thirty-one houses might be blown up in this way,
and they might turn out to contain 200 families, as they did in the
village of Uga, near Jericho, half of which was reduced to
rubble.[105] General Dayan made no bones about it: it was collective or, as he put it, 'neighbourhood' punishment in which the
whole community was made to suffer for the hostile activities of
one of its members. That is how he described the destruction
of some seventy houses in the village of Halhul in the wake of a
guerilla attack on Israeli soldiers. He told the villagers 'today we

demolished twenty homes [sic]. If this is not enough we will demolish the whole town, and if you don't like this policy, the bridges are open before you for departure.'[106]

There were the deportations, which took both a public and a surreptitious form. The number of public deportees, a couple of hundred or so, has been relatively small; but their prominent position as the civic, religious or intellectual leaders of Palestinian society, made up for the small number. 'Non-cooperation'—a form of protest authorized by the Geneva Conventions—brought the expulsion of those who led it. It was a cheap and effective policy leaving no middle ground between resigned acceptance of Israeli rule or the total opposition of armed resistance. Ruhi Khatib, the Mayor of Jordanian Jerusalem, who opposed the illegal annexation of his city, and Shaikh Abdul Hamid Sayigh, head of the Supreme Moslem Council, who opposed the blatant interference in self-governing religious institutions, were two leading citizens who suffered this fate. Surreptitious deportation, by contrast, befell thousands of ordinary Palestinians. There developed a familiar sequence of which deportation would be the final stage. A bomb might go off near a man's house or land; he would be arrested in the curfew, search or campaign of intimidation that ensued; in prison he would be beaten up or tortured, but, manifestly innocent, or yielding no worthwhile information, he would be despatched across the Jordan. Thus deportation came as a kind of escape—provided the deportee survived this last and most hazardous stage in the sequence. Here is how one deportee concluded his story:

> They took us out of prison to the King Hussein Bridge. They made us sign some blank papers, hit us and said: 'get out of here to the East Bank'. Then they started shooting at us, and we made for the East Bank as fast as we could. As soon as I had crossed the bridge I fell into a faint, and when I came to myself some time later I saw the face of a public security soldier looking down at me. When I saw him I thought my time had come, for I didn't realize that I was in Arab territory, and I said: 'Don't kill me, sir.' He replied: 'Don't be frightened; I'm an Arab like you.'[107]

It was not enough, of course, to break the spirit of the Arabs within the frontiers of Greater Israel. They had to be cowed, along with the countries that gave them refuge, beyond those

frontiers too. Palestinians, 'insiders' or 'outsiders', had to be kept
down at all costs. So beyond the occupied territories, where the
outsiders, recruited to the ranks of the guerilla movement,
carried on the struggle, lay the Israelis' 'free-fire zones', those areas
where, like the Americans in Vietnam, they deployed all their
modern know-how, all their sophisticated weaponry, to pul-
verize an opposition which, in skill and fire power, was still
rudimentary in comparison. Here the concept of 'neighbourhood
punishment' took on an altogether more murderous form. For
the Israelis directed their artillery and their all-conquering airforce not only against the guerillas themselves, but against the
refugee camps which spawned them, the villages in w! ose
vicinity they operated and the vital economic installations of the
countries which, willy-nilly, backed them. They threw a *cordon
sanitaire* of devastation round their new perimeter. And, in addition to the Palestinian refugees, they created Syrian, Jordanian,
Egyptian and Lebanese refugees too.

It was during the 1967 War itself that the Israelis drove more
than 100,000 Syrians from the Golan Heights—they have joined
Palestinians in refugee camps near Damascus—and razed the
towns and villages they left behind. After the war, they made
periodic air raids over Syria. When Palestinian terrorists killed
eleven Israeli athletes at the Munich Olympics of 1972, Syria bore
the brunt of Israel's eye-for-eye reprisals. It was, of course, more
like twenty eyes for one. For at least 200 people,[108] many of them
women and children, and possibly as many as 500,[109] died in
simultaneous air attacks on nine separate targets. The Phantoms
and Skyhawks swooped on the suburban Damascus resort of
al-Hama; the bombs fell indiscriminately on Palestinians in their
hillside dwellings and on Syrians, in their cars or strolling by the
river Barada on their weekend outing. Survivors recounted how
they were machine-gunned as they ran for cover.[110]

Jordan took heavy punishment, for there the Palestinian
guerillas, who emerged in strength after the defeat of the regular
Arab armies, were at their most active. King Hussein had done
his best to thwart them, just as he had tried to stop 'infiltrators' of
the earlier post-1948 vintage. But he could not cope. So the
Israelis did it for him in their own uninhibited way. Thus one
afternoon in November 1967, as children from the Karameh
refugee camp down in the Jordan Valley were coming out of

school, they were caught in the splintering fire of Israeli mortars.
'Right down the main street, hitting the police post, the ration
centre, the girls' school, came heavyweight high-fragmentation
anti-personnel bombs. Western military attachés attest to this and
to the scientific accuracy of the attack.'[111] Some miles up the
river a Jordanian army post had given covering fire for returning
guerillas. The Israelis knew that for every one given cover
several others were prevented from crossing at all; but it was not
good enough, and the children died as punishment for this
failure. The Israelis went on to devastate frontier towns like
North Shuneh with air and artillery bombardments; they shelled
Jordan's second city of Irbid. Many more civilians died.
Favourite among their economic targets was the East Ghor
Canal, the newly constructed waterway, serving 80,000 farmers
in the Jordan Valley, which has done so much for Jordanian
agriculture. They knocked it out, and no sooner was it repaired
than they knocked it out again. The bananas died off, and the
fruit trees began to wither away. Snipers took random potshots at
labourers driving tractors or harvesters too close to the river or
surreptitiously trying to water their groves. Some 70,000
Jordanians took refuge in the hills.

On their Western front, the Israelis countered the Egyptian
'war of attrition' with massive retribution. They reduced the
Canal Zone cities—Port Said, Suez and Ismailia—to a ghostly
shambles, blitzed and rubble-strewn. Hundreds of civilians died,
before they were almost all evacuated, a million of them, and
absorbed at great economic and social cost into the teeming cities
of the Delta. The canal silted up, and the longer it remained
closed the less chance it was to have, with the coming of the
supertanker, of regaining its old glory. In early 1970, with their
newly acquired Phantom bombers, the Israelis reached out
beyond the canal to strike at the Egyptian heartland; seventy
workers died in a direct hit on a scrap-metal plant at Abu Zaabal
twelve miles north of Cairo. According to General Dayan, there
had been a 'technical error'. A few weeks later, forty-six children
died in a primary school at Bahr al-Baqr. This time the Phantoms
had hit only 'military targets'.

As for Lebanon, least warlike of countries, Dayan warned in
1970 that if it failed to stop guerilla operations from its territory
the same destruction that befell towns along the Suez Canal and

the East Bank of the River Jordan would also befall the other side
of the Lebanese border. Sure enough, in the month that followed, some 50,000 inhabitants of southern towns and villages
fled northward as Dayan's soldiers began to put his threat into
practice. Many ventured back, in periods of calm, only to flee
again at the next raid. The Israelis went deeper into Lebanon
than any other country. For what resistance could this little
country, dedicated to money-making and the good life, offer? It
was against Lebanon that the Israelis mounted one of those
spectacular *tours de force* for which, in a Western world still
fascinated by the bizarre and heroic exploits of two world wars,
they are not surprisingly famous. In December 1968 two Palestinians, one of whom (like 300,000 others) happened to live in
Lebanon, machine-gunned an Israeli Boeing 707 at Athens airport, killing a marine engineer; two nights later helicopter-borne
Israeli commandos landed at Beirut airport and coolly, clinically,
in the sure knowledge that the Lebanese would not resist, blew
up thirteen passenger jets worth about £11 million.

The military parade marking Israel's twenty-fifth anniversary
on 15 May 1973 was the most grandiose ever staged. A few weeks
before it Dayan opened his heart to an assembly of parachuters:
'Until very recently, I was not sure of it, but now it seems to me
that we are nearing the apogee of the return to Zion.'[112] Israeli
leaders imbued their people with an extraordinary sense of
power and achievement. Resistance in the occupied territories
was at its lowest ebb. Calm reigned along the frontiers. Peace was
assured for another decade, or even a generation. No one should
take President Sadat's threats seriously. He surely was not mad
enough to attempt the impossible, a crossing of the Suez Canal
which, fortified by the Bar Lev line, was the 'best line of defence
any King or president has ever had in the history of the Jewish
people'. At all events, if he did, the Egyptians 'would take such a
trouncing, inside Egypt proper, in their own homes, that the
Six-Day War would seem like an agreeable memory in comparison'. Those were the words of General Ezer Weizmann,
former airforce commander.[113] Soldiers and politicians vied with
one another in eulogies of Israel's might and invincibility. Dayan
said that for Egypt another war would be 'suicide'.[114] As for
General Sharon, it was his opinion that it would entail Egypt's

'final destruction'. This was because Israel was 'today a power equal to France and Great Britain'; he did not think there was 'any military or civilian objective between Baghdad and Khartoum, including Libyan territory, which the Israeli army cannot conquer'.[115] The jokes people told exuded the same boundless arrogance. 'What does the Israeli army need to occupy Damascus, Moscow and Vladivostok?' 'To receive the order.' Generals Dayan and Elazar, very bored, are having their morning coffee. 'There is nothing to do,' said Dayan, with a sigh. 'How about invading another Arab country?' asked Elazar. 'What do you think?' 'Oh! that's no good', Dayan replied, 'what would we do in the afternoon?'[116]

Rare were the voices raised against this self-deluding folly and those that were went unheeded. Arie Eliav, deputy, writer and well-known 'dove', summed it up in a brief allegory. A ship is sailing on a perfectly calm sea; the captain and his officers are on the bridge, drunk with glory, bursting with self-confidence. Overhead a gull is circling. It sees the reef on which the ship is bearing down. It careers about, alights on the bridge, uttering ceaseless, piercing cries in an attempt to warn the men of the danger that faces them. But 'its language is not their language, its eyes not theirs, its horizon not theirs'. The night falls, the ship's passengers prepare for the great banquet to be held that evening, while the gull, impotent, continues to sound its incomprehensible cries of alarm.[117]

Davar, the newspaper for which the allegory was written, declined to publish it.

NOTES

1. Love, *Suez: The Twice-Fought War*, *op. cit.*, p. 677.
2. Burns, *Between Arab and Israeli*, *op. cit.*, p. 290.
3. *Ibid.*, p. 283.
4. *The Other Israel*, *op. cit.*, p. 74.
5. *Ibid.*, p. 74.
6. See Jansen, Godfrey, 'New Light on the 1967 War', *Daily Star*, Beirut, 15, 22, 26 November 1973.
7. 29 May 1967.
8. Kirk, George E., 'The Middle East 1945–1950', *Survey of International Affairs, 1939–1946*, Oxford University Press, 1954, p. 29.
9. Aide-memoire handed to Israeli ambassador Abba Eban by Secretary of State Foster Dulles, 11 February 1957.

10. Toynbee, Philip, *The Times*, 8 June 1967.
11. Kapeliouk, Amnon, *Le Monde*, 3 June 1972.
12. Vance, Vick, and Lauer, Pierre, *Hussein de Jordanie: Ma Guerre avec Israel*, Editions Albin Michel, Paris, 1968, p. 85.
13. *Maariv*, 24 March 1972.
14. *Le Monde*, 29 February 1968.
15. Report by Colonel de Ridder, Acting Chief of Staff, UN Document S/2084, 10 April 1951.
16. Horn, *Soldiering for Peace*, *op. cit.*, pp. 123–4.
17. Burns, *op. cit.*, p. 114.
18. Horn, *op. cit.*, p. 79.
19. Khouri, Fred. J., 'The Policy of Retaliations in Arab-Israeli Relations', *Middle East Journal*, Washington, Vol. 20, No. 4, 1966. p. 447.
20. Burns, *op. cit.*, p. 113.
21. Horn, *op. cit.*, p. 78.
22. *Ibid.*, p. 117.
23. Hutchison, *Violent Truce*, *op. cit.*, p. 110.
24. Horn, *op. cit.*, p. 69.
25. Syrian Complaint to Security Council, S/7845, 9 April 1967.
26. 2 May 1965.
27. Nimrod, Yoram, 'L'Eau, l'Atome et le Conflit', *Les Temps Modernes*, Paris, 1967, p. 893.
28. *Al-Ahram*, 1 June 1965.
29. *Ot* (Israeli weekly), 1 June 1972.
30. See *Daily Star*, Beirut, 15, 22 and 26 November 1973.
31. Laqueur, Walter, *The Road to War*, Weidenfeld and Nicolson, London, 1968, p. 75.
32. Jansen, *op. cit.*
33. *Ibid.*
34. *Ibid.*
35. See p. 208.
36. *Jerusalem Post*, 16 June 1967.
37. *Daily Telegraph*, 12 June 1967.
38. Vidal-Naquet, P., *Le Monde*, 11–12 June 1967.
39. Menuhin, *The Decadence of Judaism in Our Time*, *op. cit.*, p. 500.
40. *Noam* (annual publication of Jewish religious law), 1968, pp. 183–4.
41. Begin, Tel Aviv, 16 June 1967.
42. *Publications of the Israeli Ministry of Defence*, No. 204, January 1970, p. 23.
43. *Haaretz*, 4 April 1969.
44. *Ha'olam Hazeh*, 8 July 1968.
45. *Maariv*, 19 June 1968.
46. *Maariv*, 30 April 1968.
47. *Le Monde*, 6–7 July 1969.
48. Kapeliouk, Amnon, *Israel: La Fin Des Mythes*, Editions Albin Michel, Paris, 1975, pp. 28, 183–222.
49. *Jerusalem Post*, 13 July 1967.
50. Zeev Sharif, Housing Minister, *Time*, 1 March 1971.

51. *Lui*, Paris, March 1972.
52. Yigal Allon, *al-Quds*, Jerusalem, 13 April 1972.
53. See p. 65.
54. *Lés Cahiers du Témoignage Chrétien*, 5 October 1967, p. 47.
55. *Israel Imperial News*, London, March, 1968.
56. *Les Cahiers du Témoignage Chrétien*, op. cit., p. 27.
57. *Ibid.*, p. 20.
58. *Ibid.*, p. 41.
59. March 1968.
60. *Maariv*, 8 February 1972.
61. UN, *Report to the General Assembly by the United Nations Special Committee on Palestine*, 31 August 1947, Chapt. VI, Part II, Justification 5.
62. Khatib, Ruhi, *The Judaization of Jerusalem*, Amman, 1971, p. 13.
63. Khalidi, Walid, Speech in the UN General Assembly, Doc. A/PV 1553, July 14 1967.
64. Khatib, *op. cit.*, p. 13.
65. *The Guardian*, 26 April 1972.
66. Israel Radio, 1 July 1971.
67. Khatib, Ruhi, *Jerusalem-Israeli Annexation*, Amman, 1968, p. 7.
68. *Al-Hamishmar*, 7 April 1971.
69. *Bulletin of the Institute for Palestine Studies* (Arabic), Beirut, Supplement, 1 June 1972.
70. *Maariv*, 23 March 1971.
71. Khatib, *The Judaization of Jerusalem, op. cit.*, p. 78.
72. Ryan, Joseph (Archbishop of Anchorage), 'Some Thoughts on Jerusalem', *The Link*, New York, September–October 1972.
73. *Ibid.*
74. Jiryis, *The Arabs in Israel, op. cit.*, pp. 151–5.
75. 31 October 1969.
76. *Jerusalem Post*, 13 April 1973.
77. *Haaretz*, 23 October 1969.
78. *The Guardian*, 28 December 1969.
79. Kapeliouk, *op. cit.*, p. 24.
80. Jiryis, 'Recent Knesset Legislation and the Arabs in Israel', *op. cit.*, p. 66.
81. See Ryan, Sheila, 'Israeli Economic Policy in the Occupied Areas: Foundations of a New Imperialism', *MERIP Reports*, No. 24, January 1974.
82. 15 May 1969.
83. *Davar*, 8 November 1972.
84. *Maariv*, 2 February 1973.
85. *Middle East International*, London, December 1972, p. 22.
86. See p. 26.
87. *Haaretz*, 13 December 1974.
88. *Middle East International*, op. cit., p. 22.
89. *Maariv*, 17 April 1969.
90. Kapeliouk, *op. cit.*, p. 31.

91. *Yediot Aharonot*, 29 September 1972.
92. *Daily Telegraph*, 31 October 1972.
93. *Al-Ittihad*, Haifa, 30 April 1973.
94. Ryan, Sheila, *op. cit.*
95. *Al-Ittihad*, 30 April 1973.
96. Ithaca Press, London, 1975.
97. *Israel's Violations of Human Rights in the Occupied Territories*, Institute for Palestine Studies, Beirut, 1970, p. 147.
98. Statement by the Israeli League for Human and Civil Rights, 23 January 1971.
99. *The Guardian*, 26 January 1968; *The Observer*, 28 January 1968; Ben-Yosa, Amitay, *Arab American University Graduate Bulletin* No. 2, *op. cit.*
100. Reuters, 25 September 1969.
101. Agency reports, 18 December 1967.
102. *Israeli League, op. cit.*
103. *Sunday Times*, 23 November 1969.
104. *Ha'olam Hazeh*, No. 54, April 1969.
105. *Haaretz*, 12 February 1970; Ben-Yosa, Amitay, *op. cit.*
106. Israel Radio Broadcast, cited by *al-Ittihad*, 31 October 1969.
107. *Israel's Violation of Human Rights in the Occupied Territories*, Institute for Palestine Studies, Beirut, April 1970.
108. *L'Orient Le Jour*, 10 September 1972.
109. *Al-Nahar Arab Report,* 18 September 1972.
110. *Daily Star*, Beirut, 10 September 1972.
111. *The Economist*, 9 September 1967.
112. *Maariv*, 30 March 1973.
113. *Maariv*, 5 June 1973.
114. *Al Hamishmar*, 10 May 1973.
115. *Maariv*, 20 July 1973; *Haaretz*, 20 September 1973.
116. Kapeliouk, *op. cit.*, p. 68.
117. *Ibid.*, p. 49.

Eight

The Arab Zionists

THE EARTHQUAKE, OCTOBER 1973

'WE shall turn your days into nights and show you the stars at high noon. We shall put your faces and noses in the mud. We shall make the enemy leaders pay dearly for this. We shall break your bones.'

In its bellicose hyperbole it sounded just like those Arab radio commentators who, in June 1967, had the Arab armies bearing down on Tel Aviv when in reality they were falling back in utter confusion before an enemy already assured of victory. It was actually an Arabic broadcast on Israeli radio in the early days of the Arab-Israeli war of October 1973.[1] 'Break their bones' was what General David Elazar, the Chief of Staff, pledged himself to do in a press conference on the third day of the war. The press took up the theme. Under the title 'Breaking Them', an editor of *Maariv* wrote: 'Our counter attack must be so fierce, so crushing, so pitiless and cruel that it causes a veritable national trauma in the collective consciousness of the Arabs; their Yom Kippur adventure must cost the Arabs so dear that the mere thought of a new adventure makes them tremble with fear. . . . We must strike a blow that exceeds all reason, so that the Arab people's instinct of self-preservation makes them accept Israel.'[2] These were violent reactions, but one could hardly expect less from a leadership which, over the past six years, had demonstrated such an overweening confidence in its own omnipotence. It was also what most of the Israeli public, who trusted their leaders, expected to hear. The Arabs had asked for it. Apparently even now they had not learned the lesson which three 'big wars' and countless little ones should have taught them. Here were two Arab countries—Egypt and Syria—mounting an all-out surprise attack, a fullscale *blitzkrieg* in the Israeli manner, and, as if to add sacrilege to brazen folly, they were doing it on the holiest day in the Jewish year.

At first, the Israelis really were persuaded that this was just a variant on 1967. On Tuesday, four days after the war began, the *Jerusalem Post* titled a report from the northern front: 'Golan Troops Hope to be Home for Sabbath'. Cartoons were similarly optimistic; one showed President Sadat rushing frantically back to the other side of the Suez Canal, shedding his shoes on the way. But as the struggle wore on, the commanders began to murmur that this was no 'express war', that no 'early and elegant victory' could be expected.[3] In the end, it was three weeks before the Israelis really got the upper hand, drove the Syrians back beyond the 1967 ceasefire lines and, crossing the Suez Canal into 'Africa', threatened Egypt's encircled Third Army with destruction. But still they had scored nothing like the kind of overwhelming victory to which they had grown accustomed. This in itself was a grievous setback to their whole security philosophy. The Arabs had not merely dared to challenge their 'invincibility' —that was bad enough—but, in breaking through the Bar Lev line, they had dealt it a shattering blow, along with the whole gamut of cocksure assumptions on which it was based. The October War was like an earthquake; it marked a fundamental shift, at Israel's expense, in the Middle East balance of power. For the first time in the history of Zionism, the Arabs had attempted, and partially succeeded in imposing a *fait accompli* by force of arms. The setback was not just military; it affected all those factors, psychological, ideological, diplomatic and economic, which make up the strength and vigour of a nation. The Israelis had paid a heavy price for merely holding their attackers to an inconclusive draw. In three weeks, according to the official count, they lost 2,523 men, two and a half times as many, proportionally speaking, as the Americans lost in the ten years of the Vietnam war. Earlier wars had produced a flood of glossy albums commemorating the victory; the first book to appear this time was entitled *Hamahdal* ('The Shortcoming'). In 1967 the Israeli generals, comrades all, lectured an admiring public on their various campaigns. Hardly had the 1973 War begun than they were exchanging accusations and the most vicious insults in the local and international press; later, bereaved mothers and wives were to greet the fallen idol, Moshe Dayan, with cries of 'assassin'. Earlier wars had been followed, on Independence Day, by grandiose military parades and the display of enemy booty; there was none this time. On the contrary, the Israelis were soon to learn that a big exhibition of captured hardware had opened in Cairo. For the first time, too, the Israelis witnessed the humiliating spectacle of Israeli prisoners, heads bowed, paraded on Arab television.

Whereas the 1967 War had reinvigorated Israel's flagging economy, this time it nearly broke it. 'We, our children, our grandchildren and our great grandchildren will have to pay for this war,' lamented the Minister of Finance,[4] and his forecast was followed by a series of savage austerity measures, drastically reducing living standards, which made an ominous contrast with the soaring revenues of the oil-rich Arabs. Israel's economic dependence on the United States, now financing it to the tune of $2,500 million a year, was complete. Its diplomatic isolation, again with America as its only real friend, was frightening too. Contrary to Israeli expectations, the Arabs really had made the oil weapon work; they had quickly discovered that when they reinforced their moral and political arguments with material threats the industrial nations of Europe and Japan lent them an altogether more sympathetic ear.

Most disturbing of all, however, the war generated deep, and no doubt enduring, anxieties about the whole future of Zionism and the Jewish State. It was mainly the young, especially the returning soldiers, who publicly aired their forebodings. Does this country really have a future, they asked? Must Israel be our only choice? Zionism was supposed to secure the existence of the Jewish people in its own homeland, but is not the existence of Jews living in Israel, literally and physically, in greater danger than anywhere else in the world? After the ceasefire a soldier wrote to *Haaretz*:

> I celebrated my birthday in the Sinai desert, alone, underground. . . . I thought of the three sons whom I am struggling to bring up—for future wars—of my wife racked by anxiety, of my deserted office . . . my head swam with the wildest thoughts. Thought number one: When will this end? Thought number two: Why? Why has this happened? Thought number three: Could this not have been prevented, *at any price*? I am trying to fathom the thoughts of all those propagandists, those bleak pessimists

for whom—what tragic purblindness—the force of arms was
the only thing that counted. Why don't *they* try to fathom the
thoughts of the enemy? Why can't they understand that he was
pushed into battle, into the slaughterhouse, because that was his
only way out, because he had no other choice . . .? What have we
seriously done, on our side, to exorcise murderous intentions from
the minds of our adversaries during the six years that have passed
since their terrible and shameful rout in the Six-Day War?[5]

A university professor went back much farther than that:

The mistake was not made in the past six years, but in the last
twenty-five, ever since the signing of the Rhodes Agreements. The
guideline of our policy has always been the idea that a permanent
situation of no peace and of a latent war is the best situation for
us, and that it must be maintained at all costs. . . . As regards
foreign and security policy, this has been that we are becoming
stronger year by year in a situation of impending conflict where
it is possible that actual fighting may break out from time to time.
Such wars will usually be short and the results guaranteed in
advance, since the gap between us and the Arabs is increasing.
In this way we shall move on from occupation to further occupation. As its authors anticipated, this criminally mischievous policy
has prevailed for twenty-five years. It has led us into the crisis we
are living through today now that all the assumptions of that
policy have collapsed. . . . We have not been seeking peace for
twenty-five years—all declarations to that effect have been no
more than coloured statements or deliberate lies. There is of
course no assurance that we could have made peace with the
Arabs if we had wanted to. However, it has to be heavily emphasized that we have not only made no attempts to seek peace, but
have deliberately and with premeditation, sabotaged every
possibility of doing so.[6]

Opinions of this kind worried the leadership. The Ministry of
Education concluded that it was necessary 'to deepen patriotic
consciousness' in schools.[7] But they remained the opinions of a
minority. The majority, where they did not veer towards Menachim Begin and his Revisionist extremism, took refuge in the
hoary old Zionist slogan of *Ein Brera*, 'No Choice'. Golda Meir,
the Prime Minister, was characteristically unrepentant: 'We have
done everything to avoid war. It is with a clear conscience that I
can say that we neglected no opportunity for peace.'[8] When an
official committee of inquiry was set up under popular pressure

it was only empowered to look into 'shortcomings' in the actual
conduct of the war. What the apprehensions of a thoughtful
few should have prompted was precisely that which the government avoided: a look into the real, the *political*, short-comings
that caused the war in the first place. But that would have been
too much to expect. For to ask what 'pushed the enemy into
battle' would have been to probe deeply into Israel's past, beyond the Six-Day War, beyond even the Rhodes Agreement,
and to raise those moral issues which a small minority of
Zionists have grappled with since Herzl's day, but which the
majority, like Golda Meir, have simply thrust into a presumably
guilty subconscious. To pose truly relevant questions about
what drove the Egyptians and the Syrians, whose countries remain essentially intact, leads inexorably to another, and far more
difficult question: what drives the Palestinians, who have lost
everything they possess?

'No Such Things as Palestinians'

The October War was not the Palestinians' war. Their military
organizations—the *fedayeen* or the Palestine Liberation Army—
played only a very minor, if enthusiastic, part in it. It was to be
followed, however, by the most remarkable upsurge in the
Palestinians' fortunes since they were driven from their homes in
the Catastrophe of 1948.

As we have seen,[9] the Israelis did everything they could, after
1948, to suppress a Palestinian sense of identity, to eradicate any
ideas of Palestinian irridentism. They oppressed their own
Palestinian citizens, the 'insiders' who had stayed behind, and,
through their policy of reprisals, they intimidated the 'outsiders'
who had taken refuge in neighbouring Arab states.

The thinking behind this strategy was quite simply that the
Palestinians would eventually cease to exist. That is to say, the
armistice agreements would eventually be superseded by a final
settlement in which the Palestinians as a people—enjoying the
attributes, historical, cultural and territorial, of peoplehood—
could have no place. For another people had taken that place.
Over the years the Israelis won increasing international support
for such a settlement. Everything hinged on the question of the
Palestinian refugees. Their return would mean their reconstitu-

tion as a people, their resettlement elsewhere, their disappearance
as a people. The history of the refugee problem, as inscribed in
the annals of the UN, is an eloquent yardstick of Israel's fortunes. As we have seen,[10] Count Bernadotte, the murdered UN
Mediator who was the first to come to grips with the problem,
had no doubts about its proper solution. It lay in the refugees'
unconditional right to return. That was a necessary part of 'any
reasonable settlement', and he was persuaded that, given 'firm
political decisions' from the UN, both sides would 'acquiesce' in
it.[11] But there were to be no such firm decisions. After his
assassination, the UN debated his proposals; during the debate,
that same American-led coalition which had railroaded Partition
through a reluctant Assembly a year before again went into battle
on Israel's behalf. True, it was decreed—in Resolution No. 194
(III) of 11 December 1948—that 'the refugees wishing to return
to their homes and live at peace with their neighbours should be
permitted to do so at the earliest practicable date'. But, compared
with what Bernadotte had sought, the resolution was weak and
imprecise; its enforcement was made contingent upon Israel's
goodwill; and it failed to specify by what agency the refugees
would return.

Ineffectual though the resolution was, Israel did, at least to
begin with, pay lip-service to it. Expediency required this. As a
creation of the UN, the only one of its kind, Israel, by definition,
was not sovereign in the sense that the United States, Britain or
Egypt is sovereign. Certain limitations on its sovereignty were
built into the very charter of its existence. When pressed, it
formally acknowledged this. Only after the new State—in the
person of Abba Eban, its UN representative—had in effect
recognized the built-in obligations of its right to exist did it win
admittance, hitherto denied, to the world body. Asked whether,
upon admission, it would cooperate with the General Assembly
in settling such outstanding problems as the refugees or whether,
on the contrary, it would invoke that article of the UN Charter
which deals with sovereign rights of independent states, Eban
said that it would cooperate with the Assembly. 'My own feeling,'
he went on, 'is that it would be a mistake for any of the governments concerned to take refuge, with regard to the refugee
problem, in their legal right to exclude people from their territories.'[12] Summing up the debate, the Cuban representative said

that Israel had given an assurance that it would regard the refugee problem as falling outside its domestic jurisdiction.

But the lip-service did not last a UN session longer than necessary. The reaffirmation of Resolution 194 became one of the hardiest of General Assembly perennials. Every year it came round, it left Israel unmoved—and jealously guarding its 'sovereignty' and 'domestic jurisdiction'. From the outset, the United States and other Western powers were hardly more respectful of Resolution 194 than Israel itself. They strove diligently to secure the integration of the refugees in their host countries. Throughout the fifties and early sixties mission after fruitless mission visited the Middle East and put forward schemes which, however diverse in some respects, all had one underlying assumption in common. This was that given the necessary material inducements—compensation, financial aid and regional development projects—the refugees could be prevailed upon to accept resettlement outside the Palestine they considered their own. In 1952, Israel achieved another important success at the UN. The 'Palestine Question'—as it had hitherto been formally inscribed on the General Assembly agenda—was downgraded into the 'Annual Report of the Commissioner-General of the United Nations Relief and Works Agency (UNRWA)'. The 'Palestine Question' lasted longer in the Security Council; everything relating to the Arab-Israeli conflict continued to be discussed under that heading. It was only in the wake of the 1967 War, the last and most spectacular of Zionism's great breakthroughs, that Israel gave the *coup de grâce* to the 'Palestine Question' there too; it thereafter became the 'Middle East Situation'. The famous British-sponsored Security Council Resolution 242 of November 1967, holy writ for the peacemakers, was in keeping with this change, reducing the 'Palestine Question' to the achieving of 'a just settlement of the refugee problem'.[13]

The extinction of the Palestinians was by now almost complete. So, at least, it seemed to an Israeli leadership intoxicated by their own triumphs. The Palestinians, some of them now asserted, never *had* existed. In 1969, Prime Minister Golda Meir actually said it in those very words. 'It was not as though there was a Palestinian people and in Palestine considering itself as a Palestinian people and we came and threw them out and took their country away from them. They did not exist.'[14] Her predecessor, Levi Eshkol, though generally regarded as a moderate, was hardly less contemptuous: 'What are Palestinians? When I came here there were 250,000 non-Jews, mainly Arabs and bedouins.'[15] Prime ministers can make impetuous, ill-judged remarks like anyone else, but these extraordinary pronouncements were far from that. They reflected the congenital Zionist need to rewrite history; they were of a piece with the guidelines which a Minister of Education, in all seriousness, could lay down for the benefit of Israeli schoolteachers: 'It is important that our youth should know that when we returned to this country we did not find any other nation here and certainly no nation which had lived here for hundreds of years. Such Arabs as we did find here arrived only a few decades before us in the 1830s and 1840s as refugees from the oppression of Muhammad Ali in Egypt.'[16]

THE VISION OF THE RETURN

The Palestinians were not extinct, of course, and the Meir-Eshkol pronouncements, in their very purblind extremism, no doubt disguised an anxious awareness of the fact—the ironic fact—that just as Zionism was reaching the zenith of its power and self-esteem it was beginning to be threatened by a Zionism in reverse. It had been a long time in gestation. But it was always foreseeable. No sooner had they left Palestine than the Palestinians resolved that they would return. That is why American-sponsored efforts to resettle the refugees were so fruitless. It is sometimes said that the mystique of The Return was artificially inculcated and sustained by unscrupulous politicians, that the refugee camps were deliberately perpetuated as hotbeds of hatred for Israel. It may be true that the Palestinians have suffered more than most people from unscrupulous politicians, their own included; but even if it is, the corollary—that, left to themselves, the ordinary people would have abandoned hopes of return—is not. It can just as well be argued that, if anything, the politicians, in exploiting The Return, debased and weakened it in the minds of the people. What was true of the Palestinian cause before the Catastrophe was equally true after it: its essential impetus came from the people, not from the politicians.

The Catastrophe left nearly a million Palestinians leaderless, fragmented, prostrate. For most of them, in those desperate first

months of exile, their immediate concern was to keep body and
soul together. Those with means and skills, mainly the urban
middle classes, tried to rebuild their lives wherever they could.
The destitute majority, mainly peasants, remained more or less
where they had fetched up in their panic flight from Palestine;
they were herded into the camps which—set up under UN
auspices, in Lebanon, Syria, Jordan and Gaza—hugged the perimeter of the new-born State. The Palestinians had not, and in
such circumstances could not have, a collective will of their own.
Not surprisingly, the politics of exile were at first negative in
character. Most of the refugees had fled their homes in the belief
that, the fighting over, they would soon go back to them. Faced
with the obduracy of a victorious Israel, they evolved a can-
tankerous counter-logic of their own. All right, they said, perhaps
we cannot go home now, but let no one get the idea that we shall
accept another. This did not mean that they elected to stay in the
camps when employment and a better life presented themselves
—which they did for about 20 per cent of Palestinian society.[17]
But it did mean fierce opposition to schemes that were trans-
parently promoted in Israel's interests; the 'Organization for
Shattering Refugee Settlement Programmes' was a typical product of this era. It also meant opposition of a more irrational kind.
Suspicious to the point of paranoia, the refugees tended automatically to reject anything, however innocuous or desirable in
itself, that smacked of permanent residence. At the slightest
provocation they found themselves staging demonstrations
against the alleviation of their own misery. As late as 1958 they
might still be protesting, say, against the planting of trees which,
they well knew, would have furnished a welcome shade against
hot summer sun.

There quickly developed a whole mystique of The Return. The
inmates of the camps, particularly, thought and spoke of little
else. They made it an obsession. Just how they would return was
not at all clear in their minds. But of one thing they were sure;
one thing was self-evident, not worthy of discussion; this was
that they could only recover by force what had been taken by
force. The Return dominated everything, but violence, a just and
necessary violence, was an inevitable sub-theme. The Return
shaped camp rituals and regalia; children were steeped in it from
birth. Schools were decorated with pictures of Palestine and of

'martyrs' who had fallen in the struggle to preserve it. Classrooms or scout groups would be named after famous Palestinian towns. A much-displayed map of the lost homeland was framed in black; it was surmounted by pictures of mosques, and refugees in their camps; and right across the Negev desert there ran a bold caption 'Verily, We are Returning', with the words superimposed on a background of infantry, tanks and planes. The refugees' schoolday would begin with the children standing to attention and taking the oath:

> Palestine is our country,
> Our aim is to return
> Death does not frighten us,
> Palestine is ours,
> We shall never forget her.
> Another homeland we shall never accept!
> Our Palestine, witness, O God and History
> We Promise to shed our blood for you![18]

The Return suffused Palestinian poetry, of which there was a prolific output. Kemal Nasr, a Christian, justified in his own way the future violence of which, as the Palestinian Liberation Organization spokesman assassinated by the Israelis, he was later to be a 'martyr'.

> The refugees are ever kindling
> In their camps, in that world of darkness,
> The embers of revolt,
> Gathering force, for the return,
> They have lost their faith in the doctrine of love,
> Even here in this land of love and peace
> Their stolen rights cry in their hearts,
> Inflamed by misery and hunger.
> Dismayed by the persistent throng,
> The enemy spreads poison and hatred abroad:
> 'They are Communists', he says, 'Their hopes are false,
> Let us kill their hopes to return!'

He explains his Christian reasoning for repudiating love and peace in a *Hymn of Hate*: 'I do so because of the present suffering of humanity in my native land.'

> If Jesus could see it now,
> He would preach 'jihad' with the sword!

The land in which he grew
Has given birth to a million slaves.
Why does not He revolt,
Settle this account, tooth for tooth and eye for eye?
In despite of all His teachings
The West's dagger is red with blood . . .
O apostle of forgiveness! In our misfortune
Neither forgiveness nor love avail!'[19]

The Return was a passionate ideal in its own right; but it was
reinforced by something else. The Arab régimes vied with one
another in their devotion to the Palestinian cause. The air waves
reverberated with their militant rhetoric. Cairo's Voice of the
Arabs began its daily Palestinian programme with the song 'We
Are Returning'. But the régimes' actions did not live up to their
words. Indeed, the Palestinians were often made to feel despised
and unwanted in lands which called them brothers. In his book
The Disinherited, Fawaz Turki describes what it was like to grow
up in a refugee camp on the outskirts of Beirut:

> The irony of my plight was that as I grew up my bogeyman was
> not the Jew (despite the incessant propaganda that Cairo radio
> subjected us to), nor was he the Zionist (if indeed I recognized
> the distinction), nor was he for that matter the imperialist or the
> Western supporters and protectors of the state of Israel, but he
> was the Arab. The Arab in the street who asked you if you'd
> ever heard the one about the Palestinian who. . . . The Arab at
> the Aliens' Section who wanted you to wait obsequiously for your
> work permit, the Arab at the police station who felt he possessed
> a carte blanche to mistreat you, the Arab who rejected you and,
> most crucially, took away from you your sense of hope and sense
> of direction. He was the bogeyman you saw every morning and
> every night and every new year of every decade tormenting you,
> reducing you, dehumanizing you, and confirming your servitude.
> To the Palestinian, the young Palestinian, living and growing up
> in Arab society, the Israeli was the enemy in the mathematical
> matrix; we never saw him, lived under his yoke, or, for many of
> us, remembered him. Living in a refugee camp and going hungry,
> we felt that the causes of our problem were abstract, the causes
> of its perpetuation were real.[20]

The squalid new tensions of exile exacerbated an old rancour,
the feeling that the Arab governments, in their bungling incom-

petence and hypocrisy, had been largely responsible for that exile
in the first place.

As the poet said about the League of Arab States:

> On foreign lands they fell
> Like stars, my brethren the refugees.
> Would that they had stayed in the battlefield
> In Palestine, unaided, for their strife.
> Had they borne their own burden,
> Disbelieved in the League of Shadows,
> They would have attained glory
> With their swords, under their own banners . . .[21]

In that first decade or more of exile, The Return found no more
purposeful expression than the masochistic obstructionism of the
camp-dwellers, solemn rituals and poetic fancy. It had precious
little political, let alone military, substance. The troubadours of
The Return sounded hopelessly unrealistic; they were flying in
the face of the facts. Yet were they really? At least, were they any
more unrealistic than the Zionists themselves when they began to
propagate their ideas in the face of some very hard facts indeed?
That was the question which the Palestinian scholar, A. L.
Tibawi, asked in 1963, when, examining the growing literature of
The Return, he concluded that such feelings were no less intense
than those of the Psalmist: 'Should I forget thee, O Jerusalem . . .'[22] It was after all from such powerful emotions, seemingly visionary at first, that great upheavals spring. For Tibawi,
an Arab Zionism was now in the making.

THE RISE OF *Fatah*

No one paid much attention to an obscure, crudely produced
magazine, published monthly in Beirut, which began to find its
way around the Arab world in late 1959. *Our Palestine* always
addressed its readers as 'The Children of the Catastrophe'. Consisting of some thirty pages, it carried no advertising, so small
was its circulation. Its contents—editorials, articles, reports,
poems, letters and slogans—were exclusively devoted to Palestinian affairs. Only in the middle of 1964 did the Israelis realize
that, behind this mysterious publication, was much more than
met the eye.[23]

Our Palestine—or, to give it its full title, *Our Palestine—the Call to Life*—was the mouthpiece of an organization which had set out to translate the dream of The Return into a reality. The organization was the Harakah al-Tahrir (al-Watani) al-Falastini, the Palestine (National) Liberation Movement; its initial letters in reverse gave the name which has now become a household word around the world: *Fatah*. It means 'Opening' or 'Conquest', but, as the title of the 48th Surah of the Koran, it is also resonant with deeper meanings to the Arabic ear. Every month *Fatah* contributed a column, 'Our Opinion', to the new publication. Though anonymous, it was usually written by Khalil al-Wazir, who, with Yasar Arafat, was one of the founder-members of the organization and who, to this day, remains one of the most elusive, but influential, of its leaders.

Our Palestine was the fruit of profound frustrations. Its language was angry, bitter, making up in impetuous uncouth vigour for what it lacked in sophistication. Its first aim—as its name indicated—was simply to 'call to life' the Palestinians, to restore their common identity and purpose. For, in effect, the Palestinians, if not dead, had been politically dormant since the Catastrophe. Ironically, they had found themselves further removed from their own struggle than other Arabs.

> Where are you, dispersed people . . . sons of the Catastrophe? Where? Are you just flotsam, just jetsam strewn around . . .? How do you live? What's become of you? Are you living with your kith and kin, or are you scattered far and wide? Have you grown rich, children of the Catastrophe, or are you still dragging out the years in the shadow of hunger and sickness? Sons of the Catastrophe, you cannot forget that terrible Catastrophe, having lived through it, whether you are rich and living a life of ease, or wretched in the camps. The loss of land and honour moulds you in the crucible of the Catastrophe . . .[24]
>
> Our destiny is being shaped, but our voice is not heard. No one asks our opinion, no one cares if anyone of us is there. Has none of you asked why . . .? We tell you that our voice, the voice of the Palestinian people, will not be heard until the sons of Palestine stand together in one rank, the rank of 'life or death', solid and compact. Then you will find the world attentive to your merest whisper . . . yes, just a whisper.[25]

Never mind that they were 'the sons of the Catastrophe, provided that they become its destroyers'.[26] And that could only mean the complete recovery of Palestine—not partition, not resettlement, not emigration—but all of Palestine, 'one and Arab'.[27]

> There is one primordial, immutable reality: our fundamental desire is for the land, the land which was ours, whose loss we deem not merely material, but, above all else, a national dishonour, a badge of ignominy and shame. Our land is therefore our freedom, the land is our honour . . . the land—that is our right . . . that our wellbeing, that our peace. We made it what it was. If that goes, if that is taken from us, then everything goes, everything is taken from us, our very being, our humanity, our name. The quest of honour is to return to our usurped earth. Right—it is everything that hastens the disappearance of Israel; the good—the only good is that which leads to the collapse of the usurper state; and peace—peace is vengeance; vengeance against the butchers of Deir Yassin, the criminals of Qibya and Nahalin.
>
> Such is the psychological state in which we live, we the children of the Catastrophe; thus do we measure morals and ideals; in this scale do we weigh events. So strong have these feelings become that we only desire life insofar as life enables us to begin the battle for our land, our earth, our freedom and our dignity.[28]

The return of Palestine 'One and Arab' seemed to mean that its present inhabitants must leave. *Our Palestine* did not adopt a clear, authoritative position on this matter. It was so preoccupied with 'liberation' that it did not devote much thought to what might come after. But its various contributors just seemed to take the removal of the Jews for granted—that was the safe, unchallenged consensus; much of the time it was merely implicit—in such constantly recurring expressions as 'uprooting the Zionist entity' or 'destroying the Jewish presence'. But occasionally it became explicit. 'What shall we do with the Jews—two million Jewish usurpers? We shall say to them what Saladin said to the Crusaders. Go back to the lands you came from. Unless you can prove that you were in Palestine before the iniquitous Balfour Declaration of 1917, in which case you are our neighbours and brethren in the country, with your land and property. And then you are welcome, truly welcome. For the crime was not yours, not the work of your hands but of wicked Zionism and imperialism.'[29]

How was The Return to be accomplished? It was no good relying on others. Not on the world community which, year after year, passed pious resolutions upon which it did not act. The world's sympathy 'goes to revolutionaries more than it does to beggars'.[30]

> We cannot just sob and wail . . . we cannot just recite our woes and reiterate our complaints. We must gird ourselves—we alone —to solve our problem in our own way. We cannot just run to the United Nations, dominated by America and the imperialist states under its influence. We cannot rely on the world conscience as represented by the UN, which speaks for the hateful pair— Zionism and imperialism.[31]

Nor was it any good relying on the Arab states, which had:

> . . . contented themselves . . . with hysterical or anaesthetizing broadcasts and rousing speeches, the contents of which we all know in advance. . . . The Arab governments have stopped the Palestinians' mouths, tied their hands, deprived them of their freedom of action in what is left of their country, resisted the idea of their regroupment, turned them into a theatrical claque which applauds this and reviles that. . . .[32]

> You went with many parties, and fought for many causes . . . what was the result? Did you restore your honour? Or one inch of your land? Did any of the slogans relieve your distress? You remained scattered, without honour, or personal or collective identity. Let us raise the banner of our own unity, of revolution in Palestine, and put this aim above any other.[33]

In the first years of their diaspora, the Palestinians had, of course, relied very much on the Arab states. Lacking any organization of their own, they had given their main allegiance to a variety of Arab causes—left-wing, right-wing, Marxist, Moslem Brother—as an indirect means of promoting their own. This was a time of surging pan-Arabism, when the ideal of unity was still at its untarnished height, when 'regionalism'—the preserving of the artificial divisions in the Arab world—was held to be the outlook of reactionaries. Unity meant strength—strength to fight Israel. 'Unity', said a contemporary slogan, 'is the road to the liberation of Palestine.' President Nasser was the all-Arab champion upon whom these aspirations focused. Naturally, the Palestinians, without a 'region' they could call their own, were at first among the most fervent unionists of all. Nasser was their great hope too. Yet they were among the first to rebel against the Nasserist orthodoxy. A decade had passed, and their cause had advanced not an inch. Israel was consolidating its grip on Palestine; its population had passed the two million mark; Nasser had opened the Gulf of Aqaba to Israel shipping. Time was not on the Arabs' side; to believe so was a dangerous illusion. It was true that Arab governments had made gestures in the right direction. Both Syria and Iraq had incorporated special Palestinian units in their armed forces. In 1959 President Nasser had proposed that each host country encourage its Palestinian guests to establish a 'popular representative organization' which would be merged into a single body, the 'Palestine Entity', to be granted quasi-governmental status by the Arab League. Then, at a summit conference in January 1964, the Arab leaders agreed to set up a Palestine Liberation Organization with the object of 'organizing the Palestinian people to enable them to carry out their role in liberating their homeland and determining their destiny'. But for the Palestinian activists all such gestures were suspect. For them the PLO was not what it proclaimed itself to be at all; on the contrary, it was designed by its creators, Nasser and leaders of other Arab régimes, as a means of restoring that 'tutelage' over the Palestinian cause which, as refugee impatience grew, they were in danger of losing.

Palestinians who rebelled against Nasserist orthodoxy were accused, even by some of their compatriots, of reverting to 'regionalist' heresies. But two events helped the heresies take root. One was the break-up in 1961 of the Egyptian-Syrian union; the other was the triumph in 1962 of the Algerian uprising against the French, a source of great inspiration for the Palestinians, who believed that they should do likewise without waiting upon the uncertain patronage of the Arab world. For *Our Palestine* the great shibboleths of unity and revolutionary change had become the pretexts for endless protraction and delay. It therefore reversed the slogans. They now became: 'Liberation of Palestine is the road to unity'; 'Through loyalty to my revolution, the Palestinian revolution, the revolution of the dispersed people, I shall free Palestine and unite my Arab nation.'[34] It scorned conventional political debate; it was neither right nor left; it had no official views on the ordering of society. That was a question to

be tackled after 'liberation'. Till then the Palestinians' only concern was 'to be or not to be'.

Impatience with Arab tergivisation leapt from every page:

> The days pass; the conferences are held; the Arab military
> experts' conference, the Arab resources conference; the Arab
> Foreign Ministers' conference; the Arab Information Ministers'
> conference; the Jerusalem conference. But, for all that, the
> River Jordan is being diverted; the Negev is awaiting the com-
> ing of water, to be followed by Israel's third million of immi-
> grants, and after that by its fourth million of usurping Jews.
> If we Palestinians take a look at ourselves, we find that we are
> going round in an empty circle of inter-Arab rivalries . . . the
> situation is reminiscent of the children's story Who Will Hang
> the Bell? It concerns a family of mice plagued by a cat. They
> took counsel among themselves how to get rid of the accursed
> cat. After a long discussion, they decided that they should put
> a bell around its neck, which would ring every time it moved.
> They would thus have warning of its approach and escape
> the danger. Their great problem, however, was who would hang
> the bell. And that is our problem too. The tragi-comic thing is
> that we are thirteen cats represented in the Arab League, and not
> one of them comes forward to hang the bell on the Israeli mouse.
> Can this situation be allowed to endure . . .? No one will hang that
> bell but the Palestinian *fedayeen* . . .[35]

Fedayeen—'the men who sacrificed themselves'. Armed violence. A popular liberation war. This was the only way. 'Our
people, the people of the Catastrophe, know by instinct that
Israel will not disappear by a natural disaster, not by persuasion,
not by the decisions of Arab or international bodies, or vain and
sterile politics.'[36] Indeed, Israel itself had taught the way.
'Israel says, "I am here by the sword." We must complete the
saying—"and only by the sword shall Israel be driven out".'[37] In
becoming *fedayeen*, the young men of this generation were merely
proving themselves worthy of earlier ones:

> O heroes!
> Where are the revolutionaries of yesterday?
> Where are the companions of the *mujahideen*?
> Where the sons of Shaikh Qassam,
> The brethren of Abdul Qadir. . .?[38]

All that *Fatah* asked of the Arab governments was that they put no obstacles in the Palestinians' way—and that they throw a belt of defences around Israel's frontiers to guard against inevitable reprisals. But *Fatah* had little trust in the Arab governments, their willingness to fight, or their ability to win the kind of conventional war for which they were ostensibly preparing. It was therefore *Fatah*'s aim to draw the Arab peoples, rather than their governments, into the kind of 'popular liberation war' which they *could* win. It believed that *fedayeen* operations, of steadily increasing scale and intensity, conducted from bases inside and outside occupied territory, would win the backing of Arabs everywhere. The man in the street could not but take a simple black-and-white view of guerilla operations; he would regard it as patriotism to support them and treachery to oppose them—and judge his government accordingly. A 'supporting Arab front' would automatically spring into being; all patriots, including soldiers and government servants, would join it; so *Fatah* pledged itself not to raise arms against any Arab soldier or ruler, leaving it to the Arab peoples themselves to deal with anyone who stood in the way of armed revolution.

By 1964, Arafat and his men had gathered about themselves the nucleus of a guerilla organization. Partly for ideological reasons, but mainly in order to embarrass Nasser, the staunch opponent of military adventurism, Syria's radical Baathist régime agreed to give *Fatah* a secure base, and, in a small way, the operational support it needed to get going. The military strike force was backed by an embryonic network of collaborators and sympathizers that spanned the Palestinian diaspora. In the oil-rich shaikhdoms of the Persian Gulf, where Arafat had worked as an engineer, successful Palestinian businessmen were ready to devote some of their new wealth to the cause, or even to join it fulltime. In the more advanced and populous Arab countries, in Europe—especially West Germany—and in America, Palestinian student groups were a recruiting ground for youthful brain power and enthusiasm; the refugee camps were the main source of rank-and-file fighters. As the year passed and disillusionment with Nasser and the Arab governments grew, so did *Fatah*'s determination to act. All the leaders agreed that operations must begin as soon as possible. The question was when. To strike prematurely would be to risk hounding and suppression by Arab régimes for little in return. For *Fatah* was still a puny thing;

its training—conducted mainly in Algeria—was inadequate; it was very short of money, arms and cadres. But Arafat, who favoured immediate action, carried the majority with him. The Palestinians had had enough of talk. Had not the Algerians launched their rebellion on the eve of All Saints Day with just such a penury of means? In September 1964 *Our Palestine* wrote:

> Our people asks 'when shall we begin?'. It feels that the time has come for it to do something, to throw itself—with all the fury boiling up inside it, with all the fighting strength its sinews can muster, with all the anger that it feels to the depths of its being—to throw itself into battle . . . Our slogan today is: let the revolution begin.

Fedayeen OPERATIONS BEGIN

On New Year's Day 1965 leaflets were unobtrusively slipped into the offices of various Beirut newspapers. After a rather grandiloquent preamble, Military Communiqué No. 1 of the General Command of the *Asifah* (Storm) Forces went on: 'On the night of Friday 31 December 1964–1 January 1965, detachments of our strike forces went into action, performing all the tasks assigned to them, in the occupied territories and returning safely to their bases.' It then addressed the Israelis, warning them not to take any action against 'peaceful Arab civilians, wherever they might be, because our forces, deeming such action war crimes, will reply in kind'. It also warned all (i.e. Arab) states against interfering on the enemy's behalf in any way, 'because, whichever they are, their interests will be exposed to damaging reprisals by our forces'. If—as was certainly the case—*Asifah*'s identity was a mystery to newspaper editors that day, such was precisely the intention. For the minority opposed to immediate action had succeeded in ensuring one precaution: the first operations should be carried out under a different name so that, should they fail, *Fatah*'s prestige would not be impaired from the outset.

It is hardly surprising that *Fatah*'s inaugural exploit has been shrouded in a certain romantic obscurity. For it appears to have been an ignominious failure. Military Communiqué No. 1 described a raid which never even took place.[39] The Lebanese security services got wind of the planned operation and arrested the would-be raiders before they set out. That was to be typical of *Fatah*'s predicament; the enemies in the rear—the Arab régimes—would prove hardly less troublesome than Israel itself. In another of these earliest raids the point was even more forcefully made. The new movement suffered its first 'martyr'. But Ahmad Musa, a veteran 'infiltrator', did not fall to Israeli bullets: the Jordanian army shot him on his way out of enemy territory.[40] On the completion of one of these earliest expeditions, Yasar Arafat himself had a spell in a Lebanese gaol.

Subsequent operations were more successful. They were necessarily limited in scope—confined mainly to the sabotage of isolated installations, water conduits and the like. *Fatah* did not have the resources for more. It was not merely a question of the manpower available to an infant organization that was obliged to operate in clandestine isolation from the mass of its people. Unlike the peasants of the 1936–9 rebellion, the *fedayeen* of this generation were unfamiliar with the terrain in which they moved; they had to hire men with local knowledge—such as smugglers—to serve as guides. And according to later accounts, the first captive, Mahmud Hijazi, fell into enemy hands 'because his gun was rusty and of no use to him'.[41]

The understandable modesty of *Fatah*'s early performance was, however, hardly discernible from the communiqués which it issued at the time. On the contrary, judging by them, it proved itself from the outset a master of guerilla warfare. Its units were bold, versatile and ubiquitous. From the Negev to Galilee, they attacked Israeli patrols, mined military vehicles and blew up arms dumps, dams, pipelines and canals. Their missions were almost always a complete success. Rare, it seems, were the occasions when the *Asifah* 'strike forces', in direct clashes with enemy troops, did not inflict losses of five to twenty dead and wounded; rare the occasions when they did not 'return safely to their bases'. It is natural, and often profitable, for armies to embellish their exploits; but a boastful exaggeration that defies all probability is eventually counter-productive. The external difficulties, both Arab and Israeli, which *Fatah* faced, as it launched this latest phase of the Palestinian struggle, were certainly daunting enough; but this habit of gross exaggeration showed that, from the beginning, internal difficulties of *Fatah*'s own making were by no means absent either.

Nevertheless, exaggeration notwithstanding, *Fatah*'s activities, or perhaps what they portended, were substantial enough to provoke an Israeli response—warnings to neighbouring Arab governments, protests to the United Nations, and, eventually, massive reprisal. This Israeli response meant more, for *Fatah*'s prestige, than anything it did, or said about what it did, itself. It impressed Palestinian and Arab public opinion. That public was not a very discerning one. For years it had been fed extravagant propaganda about the coming 'battle of destiny' with Israel. Yet the battle never seemed to come. Indeed, the Arab states could not even agree on a collective strategy to deter the Israelis from going ahead with their plans to divert the headwaters of the River Jordan. In this atmosphere, anyone who actually did something against Israel, however trifling, won immense prestige. *Fatah*'s attempts to sabotage Israel's Jordan diversion project might be mere pinpricks, but at least, in contrast with the Arab states, it was making the attempt. *Fatah* therefore became the catalyst it intended to be—though not quite, judging by its theoretical texts, in the *way* it intended to be. That is to say, it did not precipitate an ever-growing Arab involvement in a 'popular liberation war' of which it deemed itself to be the vanguard. There was no significant increase in the scale and effectiveness of guerilla raids in the two and a half years that preceded the June 1967 War and the radical new circumstances it ushered in. According to the Israelis, who were predisposed to dramatize the raids for their own belligerent purposes, they caused the death of only eleven people, and the injury of sixty-two, in the same period. The Israelis also claimed to have killed a mere seven *fedayeen* and to have captured two. They put *Fatah*'s manpower in June 1967 at a mere 200. But *Fatah* did present a formidable challenge to the champions of rival formulae for the liberation of Palestine. Essentially, this meant a challenge to President Nasser and all those, including Palestinians, who subscribed to the Nasserist orthodoxy of liberation *after* Arab unity and the completion of the socialist revolution.[42]

The challenge was instantaneously recognized. On 2 January, upon receipt of that first military communiqué, the Beirut newspaper *al-Anwar*, then a leading Nasserist mouthpiece, jumped to one of the most opportunistic—and, one presumes, most embarrassing—conclusions of its opportunistic career. It denounced

Fatah as the instrument of a 'conspiracy . . . hatched by imperialist, CENTO and Zionist quarters'. *Fatah*—or *Hataf*, as
al-Anwar and others in their ignorance at first called it—was a
'very small group of Palestinians' who were embarking on 'very
small, individual' operations designed to furnish Israel with a
pretext to attack its neighbours and foil their scheme for a
counter-diversion of the Jordan waters. This was more royalist
than the king: for at first Cairo newspapers simply reported
Fatah's activities without comment. But it foreshadowed a prolonged struggle between the Nasserist and the *Fatah* schools of
thought. Declaring that 'we shall not put down our arms until
victory', *Fatah* virtuously claimed that there was no contradiction
between the two.[43] But clearly there was. For other Beirut newspapers reacted in quite the opposite way. The weekly *al-Usbu' al-
Arabi*, for example, came down wholeheartedly on *Fatah*'s side.
The Palestinians should at least be allowed to 'die standing up',
it said, and advised the Nasserists to take a leaf from the Zionists'
book:

> He who gives his blood for his country does not ask permission.
> If the Arab states do not wish to appear as aggressors then they
> can allow the *fedayeen* to provoke Israel first. Or, if they are not
> ready yet, they can dissociate themselves completely from them,
> assigning them the same role that the *Irgun* and the *Stern* played.
> The Jewish Agency condemned [terrorist action] in diplomatic
> memoranda, but blessed them—indeed coordinated with them—
> in practice.[44]

It was a rearguard action which the Nasserists were fighting.
President Nasser did not beat about the bush. He deliberately
chose a Palestinian forum to make one of the franker speeches of
his career: 'If we are today not ready for defence, how can we
talk about an offensive? . . . We must provide Arab defence and
then prepare to carry out our ultimate goal. That can only be
fulfilled by revolutionary action.'[45] But neither Nasser per-
sonally, nor the more direct forms of dissuasion he brought to
bear, could stop *Fatah*. The powerful Egyptian propaganda
machine imposed a virtual news blackout on *fedayeen* activities.
The Unified Arab Military Command (which had been set up to
cope with Israel's Jordan waters diversion scheme) instructed
Arab governments to prevent guerilla incursions into Israel.

Jordan and Lebanon certainly needed no prompting to comply.
In Lebanon would-be infiltrators were put on trial for illegal
possession of arms; one apparently died under torture. Even the
Syrians, *Fatah*'s only sponsors, did not scruple to impose un-
welcome constraints, provoking quarrels 'which sometimes
reached the point of bloody personal liquidations'.[46]

It was, of course, Palestinian Nasserists who suffered the most
agonizing conflict between heart and head. Their 'official', institutional expression was the Palestine Liberation Organization.
The PLO chairman was a deferential, if demagogic, professional
politician called Ahmad Shuqairi; well-behaved notables, more
than half of them from Jordan, dominated its legislature. It may
sound somewhat improbable today, for, as the head of the left-
wing Popular Front for the Liberation of Palestine, Dr George
Habash has come to symbolize revolutionary violence at its most
uncompromising, but in those days he was actually one of the
most influential critics of go-it-alone *fedayeen* raids. Habash was
then the head of the Arab Nationalist Movement (from which the
PFLP later grew), a radical organization with branches in many
Arab countries which saw in Nasser the instrument of Arab unity
and the liberation of Palestine through a conventional war he
would fight in his own good time. Habash had no time for
Shuqairi and his bombastic school of politics, but the two men
had a common interest in containing *Fatah*'s excess of zeal.
Shuqairi said that *Fatah* was doing very well, but that its timing
was wrong and he would try to bring it under the PLO's wing.
One of his officials reportedly told a Beirut newspaper that war
was not 'a pastime to be indulged in by certain *fedayeen* . . . to
satisfy a feeling of vengeance'.[47] The Palestinian branch of the
ANM helped found a 'Preparatory Committee for Unified
Palestinian Action'; its weekly journal *Palestine* insisted that 'to
entangle Arab forces disposing of *real* military power, with all the
risks and consequences which that entailed, is absolutely unacceptable'.[48] *Fatah* was contemptuous; the PLO 'talked but did
not act'—and collected money for holding 'demagogic rallies'.[49]
As for unified action, the only unity it ever believed in was 'unity
on the battlefield'. The battle 'must be today not tomorrow'.[50]

Neither Shuqairi nor Habash could ignore popular sentiment,
and before long these ill-matched allies, privately cursing one
another and collaborating at the same time, were hurriedly im-

provising their own guerilla movements. Apparently they had the reluctant blessing of President Nasser, who no doubt calculated that, by allowing his protégés to compete for popular favour, he stood a better chance of restoring his weakened grip on Palestinian irredentism than if he gave them no leeway at all. Essentially, 'The Heroes of the Return', which first saw action in October 1966, was the creation of the Arab Nationalist Movement, while the PLO furnished it with financial and propaganda backing. On 31 November Shuqairi, in the uniform he now regularly affected, told a mass rally in Gaza that 'bullets and blood will now be the only exchange between us and the enemy'. Still other Palestinian groupings—and this period of ferment had thrown up no less than forty of them—announced that they too were putting their fighters into the field.

But President Nasser had miscalculated. He *was* stampeded into war. And if, before the second Catastrophe of June 1967, guerilla warfare commanded great appeal, it became quite irresistible after it. For Arabs and Palestinians alike it was an indispensable balm for their terribly wounded pride. *Fatah* soon announced that it was transferring its headquarters to the newly occupied territories; Arafat and some of his lieutenants crossed the River Jordan to mastermind the bold new strategy which they had adopted. Hitherto the *fedayeen* had largely confined themselves to hit-and-run incursions across the armistice lines, but now Arafat had the opportunity to forge a self-sustaining guerilla movement out of that segment of his people, well over a million, who had fallen under direct Israeli rule. In accordance with Chairman Mao Tse-tung's famous dictum, the *fedayeen* would now be fish with a revolutionary sea in which to swim; they would be well on the way to developing a full-scale 'popular liberation war'. Young men, graduates of training courses in Syria, followed their leaders, making the hazardous Jordan crossing with the help of local guides. Arms and explosives were ferried across too, and hidden in caves, wells, and the homes of *Fatah* sympathizers. Arafat stayed in the West Bank till the end of the year. Although he sometimes moved around under the Israelis' noses, he hid out much of the time in the warren of old lanes that make up the Kasbah of Nablus. From there he recruited personnel, organized networks, laid down tactics, set targets and planned operations. His agents went into the villages

to try to arouse the peasantry. A clandestine leaflet which fell into
Israeli hands conveys something of the measure and the spirit of
Arafat's ambitions:

> To the heroes of the Arab people in the occupied land. We call
> upon you in the name of the Arab heroes Omar and Saladin to
> rise against the foreign occupation and prohibit the Zionist
> occupiers from treading on our sacred Arab land. The legendary
> resistance of Algeria, which had suffered more than a million
> casualties, will guide us on our way. . . . The Zionist occupation
> is nothing but the rise of a new Crusade. We shall continue to
> rebel until the final victory. We must boycott all economic,
> cultural and legal institutions of the Zionists. . . . We must set up
> secret resistance cells in every street, village and neighbourhood.
> For even one fighting cell, operating in any region, has the power
> to inflict great losses upon the enemy. Roll down great stones
> from the mountain slopes to block communication lines for the
> enemy's movements. If you happen to stand by an enemy's car,
> fill its gas tank with sand or sugar to put it out of action. Try to
> produce fires in the enemy's cars with oil and other means . . .[51]

After a short breathing space, *Fatah* renewed its operations on
a larger scale than before the war. It claimed ninety-two of them
before the end of the year—some of which, deep inside the pre-
1948 borders, the Israelis described as the boldest it had ever
attempted.[52]

December saw the formation of *Fatah*'s left-wing rival, Dr
Habash's Popular Front for the Liberation of Palestine, which, in
its inaugural statement, declared that 'the only language which
the enemy understands is that of revolutionary violence' and that
the 'historic task' of the hour was to open a fierce struggle against
it, 'thereby turning the occupied territories into an inferno whose
fires consume the usurpers'.[53] The Front was to put down
strongest roots in the festering, tightly-packed squalor of the
Gaza Strip.

The *fedayeen* began to draw enthusiastic applause in the Arab
world, not least from such Nasserist newspapers as *al-Anwar*
which, forgetting *Fatah*'s alleged links with 'imperialist, CENTO
and Zionist quarters', now concluded that the Palestinian resistance was a 'voice that could make itself heard in the Arab and
international fields'.[54] Inevitably, the guerillas soon felt strong
and bold enough to take over the PLO, the institution through

which the régimes had tried to keep them under control. They demanded the resignation of Shuqairi, Nasser's protégé, who was denounced by a Palestinian official in Cairo as a 'selfish, ruthless, impetuous lover of propaganda'.[55] Seven members of the Executive Committee asked Shuqairi to step down 'because of the way you run the organization'.[56] In February, the guerillas secured effective control of the National Council—and it was only a matter of time before Arafat became the PLO Chairman.

THE BATTLE OF KARAMEH

It was not, however, until the Battle of Karameh that the *fedayeen* achieved their real breakthrough. Karameh means 'dignity', and, for the Palestinians, there could be no more fitting name to commemorate the biggest 'little' battle the Israelis have ever fought against them. It had been growing increasingly clear, in the months which preceded it, that Arafat and his men were developing Jordan as the main platform for their liberation war. Syria would always remain their ultimate mainstay—but under the strictest of official controls; in Jordan, however, half of whose population was Palestinian, they were acquiring a political and military presence which quite escaped the jurisdiction of King Hussein's war-weakened government and army. He had done his best to check the alarming growth of guerilla power. The June 1967 War had not changed him. The despatch of 'so-called *fedayeen*' into enemy-held territory was still an 'unparalleled crime'.[57] In February he announced that he had taken 'firm and forceful' measures to thwart them; they had nothing to do with the Arab nation.[58] But three days later the Prime Minister, Bahjat al-Talhouni, had to dissociate himself from these policies and announce that a 'popular resistance' was to be organized. After that there was another bout of heavy exchanges, precipitated by *fedayeen* raids, in which the Israelis used tanks, artillery and aircraft against Jordanian positions. Many civilians were killed. Some 70,000 inhabitants of the Jordan Valley fled to the relative security of the hills. On 18 March an Israeli schoolbus ran over a mine, killing a doctor and wounding several children. This, said the Israelis, was the climax of some thirty-seven acts of 'sabotage and murder' in which six people had been killed and forty-four wounded. It was obvious, to the *fedayeen* in the valley, that a massive reprisal was imminent. As they watched the enemy prepare for it, they debated what to do. By all the rules of guerilla warfare, there was only one possible course; they should withdraw to the hills and harass the vastly superior attacking forces from there. This is what the diminutive PFLP contingent, some thirty-odd strong, urged. *Fatah* may have been equally well versed in their Che Guevara, their Mao Tse-tung and Ho Chi Minh, but they none the less insisted on the opposite course. The *fedayeen* would stay where they were—in and around Karameh refugee camp—and confront the enemy head-on. There were a mere three or four hundred of them altogether; this was more or less the entire guerilla strength at the time; they were armed with light and medium machine-guns, RBJ anti-tank guns and grenades.[59] *Fatah*'s reasoning was essentially political, not military. 'There is a basic fact of which all have become aware; in all our encounters with him over the years, it has been the enemy who always advanced and we who retreated. If we must retreat, let it be to Amman or Damascus. But that we refuse. The Arab nation is watching us. We must shoulder our responsibility like men, with courage and dignity. We must plant the notion of steadfastness in this nation. We must shatter the myth of the invincible army.'[60] *Fatah* turned a deaf ear to advice proffered by the Jordanians, as well as by Iraqi forces stationed in the country. They were, they said, determined to 'convince the Arab nation that there are among them people who do not retreat and run away. Let us die under the tank tracks. We shall change the course of history in this area; and no one will blame us for that.'[61]

At dawn on 21 March the Israelis struck across the Jordan River. Some 15,000 men, and an armada of tanks, took part in this biggest reprisal raid in Israel's history. Although the attack came on a wide, fifty-mile front, the main force headed up the arid slopes to Karameh, as helicopter-borne paratroopers converged on it from the rear. A parachuter said later that Karameh was like a ghost town:

> On loudspeakers we called on the inhabitants to come out with raised hands to the square in front of the mosque, but we seemed to be talking to the walls . . . We surrounded a building which we knew to be the barracks of the terrorists. Suddenly we came under heavy firing. We laid explosives under the gates and stormed the place. Inside we found about twenty guerillas in camouflage with

al-Asifah insignia. They were armed with sub-machine guns and
tried to shoot their way out, but were all shot dead.[62]

The Palestinians suffered heavy losses; anything up to half
their fighting forces were wiped out.[63] The Jordanian army,
which had joined in the fighting, put its own losses at 128 killed
and wounded. Nevertheless, from *Fatah*'s standpoint, Karameh
was a great triumph, a turning point in their fortunes. For the
first time, the Israelis, accustomed to easy, almost painless victories, got a bloody nose. They had met fierce resistance all the
way. They had suffered what for them, a small embattled country
that could ill afford them, were very heavy casualties, at least
twenty-eight killed and ninety wounded.[64] They left several
knocked-out tanks and other vehicles in the field. Moreover, they
had achieved nothing. On the contrary, *Fatah*'s romantic
'martyrdom decision' had succeeded beyond its wildest dreams.
The *fedayeen* had put on the mantle of heroism. General Mashhur
Haditha, the commander who had brought in the Jordanian
troops, paid a professional soldier's tribute: 'The *fedayeen* did
their duty in Karameh right until the final stage of hand-to-hand
fighting. Our estimate of their martyrs is 150. Having seen them,
having seen that all their wounds are chest wounds, inflicted
from the front, I must, for history's sake, record that they fought
like heroes.'[65] Foreign correspondents who visited Karameh two
days after the battle found the *fedayeen* there again in strength—
more defiant, more self-confident than before. Israel, one of them
concluded, had committed a 'massive strategic blunder'.[66] The
guerillas' precarious foothold on Israel's eastern frontier had
now become a virtual state within a state. If King Hussein had
thought to crush them, he now gave up the idea; his subjects
would not stand for it. Unable to beat them, he made as if to join
them. In a famous press conference he said that 'maybe we are all
becoming *fedayeen*'. Refugee camps throughout the Arab world
'celebrated the resurrection of the Palestinian people'.[67] There
were huge funerals for the 'martyrs'. Volunteers began to flock to
Fatah recruitment centres. They were not just Palestinians; by
May, 20,000 Egyptians had offered their services; and 1,500
Iraqis within the space of a week.[68] In Lebanon, the *fedayeen*
appeared to be a great unifying force. The press of this least
Arab of Arab countries ran riot with accounts of young men

determined to enlist—like nineteen-year-old Wahib Jawad, who, opposed by his family, held up a shop to raise money for his fare to Amman, taking only twenty-five out of a proffered 300 Lebanese pounds. A month after Karameh, Moslems and Christians turned out in their tens of thousands for the funeral of the first Lebanese 'martyr'. When the funeral procession reached the village of Kahhaleh, a stronghold of the right-wing Christian Phalangists on the main Damascus-Beirut highway, the inhabitants insisted on carrying the coffin themselves as church bells tolled; Beirut newspapers called this a 'plebiscite', the 'real face of Lebanon' carrying no 'stains of confessional fanaticism'.[69] Back in Jordan, a few months later, Wasfi al-Tal, a former Prime Minister and redoubtable scion of an influential Transjordanian family, urged the King to turn his kingdom into a latter-day 'Carthage'. The whole country should be fully mobilized behind the guerillas, who should step up their operations 'a hundred-fold' to become a real torment to the enemy. Jordan should develop its own defences to the point where it could positively welcome reprisals as a means of exhausting the enemy: the more Battles of Karameh the better.[70] It all began to look as though Fatah theory really was working out in practice, as if the revolutionary 'vanguards', through a process of spontaneous combustion, really were rallying the Arab masses behind them, bringing into being that 'supporting Arab front' which would strike down any ruler who stood in their way.

The impact of Karameh was not confined to the Arabs. The outside world began to take note of a new force emerging in the Middle East. It was apparent—The Palestine Yearbook for 1968 records—

> . . . in the enlistment into the ranks of the movement of foreign volunteers, such as the Frenchman, Roger Corday, who was martyred in June . . . in the pro-Arab demonstrations and scuffles that greeted Israeli Foreign Minister Abba Eban on his visit to Norway on 7 May, in the shouts of 'long live Fatah' hurled at him in Stockholm, and in the letters which the London Times published five days after Karameh under the signature of three British personalities, including Lady Fisher, wife of the Archbishop of Canterbury, who said that the Arabs were 'surely . . . only doing what brave men always do, whose country lies under the heel of a conqueror.'[71]

NOTES

1. *Newsweek*, 22 October 1973.
2. 9 October 1973.
3. *Newsweek*, 22 October 1973.
4. *Davar*, 8 February 1974.
5. *Haaretz*, 11 November 1973.
6. Leibovitch, Yeshayahu, 30 November 1973.
7. Kapeliouk, *La Fin Des Mythes*, *op. cit.*, p. 106.
8. Israel Radio, 1 December 1973.
9. pp. 173-93.
10. p. 149.
11. *Progress Report of the UN Mediator on Palestine*, *op. cit.*, p. 4.
12. Official Records of the 3rd Session of the General Assembly, Part II, Ad Hoc Political Committee 1949, pp. 286-7.
13. See Tomeh, George, 'When the UN Dropped the Palestine Question', *Journal of Palestine Studies*, Beirut, Vol. IV, No. 1, 1974, pp. 15-30.
14. *Sunday Times*, 15 June 1969.
15. *Newsweek*, February 1969.
16. *Haaretz*, 9 September 1974.
17. Davis, John, *The Evasive Peace*, John Murray, London, 1968, p. 62.
18. See Tibawi, 'Visions of the Return: The Palestine Arab Refugees in Arabic Poetry and Art', *Mideast Journal*, XVII, 1963, p. 523.
19. Nasr, Kemal, *Jirah Tughanni*, Beirut, 1960; see Tibawi, *op. cit.*, p. 516.
20. Turki, Fawaz, *The Disinherited*, *Journal of a Palestinian Exile*, Monthly Review Press, 1972, p. 53.
21. See Tibawi, *op. cit.* 514.
22. *Ibid.*, p. 508.
23. Yaari, Ehud, *Strike Terror, the Story of Fatah*, Sabra Books, New York, 1970, p. 49.
24. *Our Palestine* (*Falastinuna*), January 1964, p. 7.
25. *Ibid.*, January 1964, p. 3.
26. *Ibid.*, January 1964, p. 3.
27. *Ibid.*, January 1961, p. 27.
28. *Ibid.*, September 1964. p. 3.
29. *Ibid.*, November 1959, p. 30.
30. *Ibid.*, April 1964, p. 3.
31. *Ibid.*, June 1959, p. 26.
32. *Ibid.*, May 1961, p. 5.
33. *Ibid.*, March 1961, p. 5.
34. *Ibid.*, August 1963, p. 24.
35. *Ibid.*, August 1964, p. 3.
36. *Ibid.*, September 1964, p. 3.
37. *Ibid.*, September 1964, p. 3.
38. *Ibid.*, March 1961, p. 9.

39. *Al-Anwar*, 2 January 1965.
40. *Revolutionary Studies and Practices* (Arabic), *Fatah* publication, p. 42.
41. *Ibid.*, p. 42.
42. Yaari, *op. cit.*, pp. 108, 112.
43. *Torches of the Revolution on the Way of Return* (Arabic), *Fatah* publication, 1965–6, p. 10.
44. 25 January 1965.
45. Speech to Palestine National Council, 31 June 1965.
46. Al-Sharqawi, Fawwaz, *Fatah—1965–1971*, Master's Thesis (Arabic, unpublished) Cairo University, 1974, p. 169.
47. *Al-Sayyad*, 4 June 1965.
48. 24 February 1966.
49. *Al-Jaridah*, Beirut, 5 June 1965.
50. Message to the Third Arab Summit Conference, 7 September 1965.
51. Yaari, *op. cit.*, pp. 133–5.
52. *Jewish Observer*, London, 12 August 1967.
53. 11 December 1967.
54. 10 October 1967.
55. *Al-Anwar*, 21 January 1967.
56. *Al-Muharrir*, 19 December 1967.
57. Jordanian News Agency, 5 September 1967.
58. *The Guardian*, 18 February, 5 September 1967.
59. Al-Sharqawi, *op. cit.*, pp. 346–7.
60. *Four Big Battles of Asifah Forces* (Arabic), *Fatah* publication, cited in Shafiq, Munir, *Palestine Affairs*, Beirut, March 1973, p. 107.
61. Hassan, Hani, 'The Fourth Anniversary of the Karameh Battle', *Palestine Affairs*, April 1972, p. 56.
62. *The Times*, 23 March 1968.
63. Al-Sharqawi, *op. cit.*, p. 347.
64. Harkabi, Yehoshafat, *Fedayeen Action and Arab Strategy*, Adelphi Papers, No. 53, Institute for Strategic Studies, London, 1968, p. 28.
65. Abu Aswan, Hadi, 'Testimonies from the Battle of Karameh', *Palestine Affairs*, Beirut, April 1972, p. 210.
66. Morris, Joe Alex, *New York Herald Tribune*, 25 March 1968.
67. *Le Monde*, 23 March 1968.
68. *The Palestine Yearbook* (Arabic), Institute for Palestine Studies, Beirut, 1968, p. 109.
69. *Al-Anwar*, *al-Nida*, 28 April, 1968.
70. *Al-Jadid* (Beirut weekly), 16 August 1968.
71. *Op. cit.*, p. 81.

Nine

The Gun and the Olive Branch

THE DEMOCRATIC STATE OF PALESTINE

FOR all their undoubted achievements, the *fedayeen* were still a
long way from the liberation of Palestine—indeed, a good deal
further than they themselves thought—but success and recognition brought far-reaching changes of outlook, and, in particular,
a much needed attempt to define what they meant by 'liberation'.
Till then 'Shuqairism'—as it came to be known—had held
sway. The former President of PLO strenuously repudiated the
notorious declaration—'I don't expect any of them [Israelis] to
stay alive'—which news agencies attributed to him on the eve of
the 1967 War.[1] But whether he actually said this or not is not
really very important, for the ferocious rhetoric associated with
his name had already done its work. Shuqairi was certainly not
the only offender. Christopher Mayhew, the British MP, recently challenged supporters of Israel to produce any statement
by an Arab leader which could be described as 'genocidal' in
intent. He offered a £5,000 reward. No statement was produced,
even though one persistent challenger had to lose a court case
before he conceded defeat. In general, however, the language the
Arabs used was very intemperate, and the man in the street
could hardly be blamed for concluding that they really did intend
to 'drive the Jews into the sea'.

The concept of 'liberation', wrote the Syrian scholar Sadiq al-
Azm, was

> ... held in such awe and reverence that it was forbidden to dis-
> cuss it seriously, to subject it to objective criticism, or even to
> explain what it would eventually mean in actual practice. I had
> the impression that 'liberation', for the vast majority of Pales-
> tinians, meant some kind of literal and mechanical return to the
> situation which prevailed round about 1948. By which I mean
> that, in people's minds, there was a picture of conquering Arab

armies returning to Palestine; whereupon every Palestinian dusts off his documents and papers, presents himself to the Arab conqueror, shows him the title-deeds that prove his ownership of this or that piece of land, and the conqueror restores everything to its true owner, as if nothing had happened. That is to say, liberation would mean that the landowner returns to his estate, the *grand bourgeois* to his commerce and industry, the *petit bourgeois* to his shop, the worker to his toil, and the poor and destitute to his poverty and destitution.

The endless reiteration of the slogan, without any deeper analysis of it was

> ... demagogy pure and simple ... it was accompanied by a fearful official silence about the future of the Jewish masses in Palestine. The slogan of liberation, as presented, offered them no clear alternative to death and dispersal, no solid guarantee for their future as a large human community in a certain region of the Arab world. They, and world opinion, had no other criterion by which to assess the meaning of liberation than Arab information media of evil memory, our orators of Shuqairi's ilk, so much so that for the outside world (Jews and non-Jews) it became nothing but a great massacre.[2]

In the wave of official 'self-criticism' which swept the Arab world in the wake of the second Catastrophe of 1967, it was generally agreed that 'Shuqairism' and all such verbal excesses should be banished. But the Palestinians themselves went further; not only 'Shuqairism', but some of the ideas which Shuqairi— and many others—had held should be discarded too. In early 1968, *Fatah* began to formulate a new concept of 'liberation'.

Vengeance, it came to be understood, could not serve as the motive for a people's war; liberation had to be built on a vision of tomorrow, not on the nightmare of the past. It was natural, though regrettable, that in the first years of exile the Palestinians should have behaved in the way they did—that they had come to hate Jews and everything Jewish. For, although a distinction was usually made between Jews and Zionists, most refugees were either too bitter—or too simple—to take it seriously. They were inclined to accept Zionist propaganda at face value—and that propaganda insisted that all Jews were Zionists and potential Israelis. Had they not been driven out to make way for the *Jewish* National Home? Was it not *Jewish* money, *Jewish* pressure

in the United States, that was perpetuating their misery and
exile? Their hatred of Israel, and that of the Arabs in general,
took on an anti-Semitic coloration. With the Protocols of the
Elders of Zion and other classics of European racism as their
inspiration, they fitted Israel and the Catastrophe into an up-
dated demonology of their own. Indeed, there were influential,
educated Palestinians who preached that it was a matter of the
utmost importance *not* to distinguish between Zionism and
Judaism. As the head of the PFLP, and a devout Marxist-
Leninist, George Habash is now wedded to the internationalism
of 'world revolution'; but in the early years of exile, as the moving
spirit behind the Arab Nationalist Movement, he held that the
real enemy was not Western imperialism but International
Judaism, 'all Jews from the far left to the extreme right'; there
was no choice for the Arabs but to meet the Zionist challenge on
the same terms laid down by the Jews: expulsion or extermina-
tion. His slogan, which came in for a good deal of criticism even
at the time, was 'Unity, Freedom, Vengeance'.[3]

With time, however, and especially with the growth of the
fedayeen, new attitudes came into being. The distinction between
Jews and Zionists really acquired meaning:

> Revolutionary leaders engaged in a serious study and discussion
> around the topic . . . old truths emerged. Jews suffered persecu-
> tion at the hands of racist criminals under Nazism, so did 'we'
> under Zionism. Several revealing parallels were discovered. 'How
> could we hate the Jews *qua* Jews?' the revolutionaries were saying.
> How could we fall in the same racist trap? A study of Jewish
> history and thought was conducted. Jewish contributions as well
> as dilemmas were identified. The majority of those who came
> over to Palestine were fleeing German concentration camps and
> were told that they were a people without land—going to a land
> without people. Once they were there, they were told that the
> Palestinians left Palestine of their own wish, following orders
> from Arab leaders in a treacherous move to perpetrate a massacre
> of the remaining Jews.
>   Further, it was discovered, new Jewish immigrants as well as old
> settlers were told by the Zionist machine that they had to fight
> to survive, that the only alternative to a safe 'Israel' was a massacre
> or at best a little sinking boat on the Mediterranean sea. Even
> Arab Jews—called Oriental by the Zionists—who were discrimin-
> ated against in 'Israel' by the European Zionist oligarchy had to

accept the argument and fight for what they considered to be
their very survival. Fighting the Zionist revealed the strengths
and limitations of the 'Jewish' character. Jews were not monsters,
supermen or pigmies. Martin Buber, Isaac Deutscher, Elmer
Berger and Moshe Menuhin, all spiritual, human Jewish thinkers,
were read and re-read. . . .[4]

Fatah's vision of tomorrow was the 'Democratic State of
Palestine'. The Jew-as-Zionist was still the enemy, of course, and
against him and all he stood for *Fatah* would pursue its 'Revolution Till Victory'. Complete liberation was still the aim. And
complete liberation still meant 'liquidating the Zionist aggressor-
state—politically, militarily, socially and ideologically'.[5] There was
no question of accepting some kind of mini-state to be set up in
such territories as Israel, under a general settlement, might be
induced to evacuate; together, the West Bank and Gaza represented no more than 23 per cent of original Palestine; it
would, the *Fatah* theorist said, be a mere puppet—Israel's Ban-
tustan. Only through complete liberation could the Palestinians
fulfil their inalienable right to return; only thus could they assure
themselves, as a people, of a free and decent life. But it was no
longer a call for a literal and absolute justice, a restoration, pure
and simple, of the *status quo ante*. If it did not acknowledge the
Zionist *fait accompli* itself, it acknowledged the fundamental consequence of it, a physical Jewish presence in Palestine. It was a
great leap forward in their thinking; a few years ago even 'discussing this proposal would have been considered as a complete
sell-out or high treason'.[6] It happened 'because people who fight
can afford to be more tolerant'.[7] The 'Palestine of tomorrow' was
to be 'a progressive, democratic, non-sectarian Palestine in which
Christian, Moslem and Jew will worship, live peacefully and enjoy
equal rights'. The Palestine revolution stretched 'its welcoming
hand to all human beings who want to fight for, and live, in a
democratic, tolerant Palestine irrespective of race, colour or
religion'. This was 'no utopian dream or false promise, for we
have always lived in peace, Moslems, Christians and Jews in the
Holy Land. The Palestine Arabs gave refuge, a warm shelter and
a helping hand to Jews fleeing persecution in Christian Europe,
and to the Christian Armenians fleeing persecution in Moslem
Turkey; as well as to Greeks, Caucasians and Maltese among
others.' What was new, its proponents said, was that those very

Arabs who had been driven from their homes by the Jews-as-
Zionists could still—while fighting to return—call for a society
in which the ex-aggressors and persecutors, Jews as Jews once
more, would have an equal place. Just what system of government the Democratic State of Palestine would adopt, and to what
socio-economic philosophy it would subscribe, were matters to
be decided after liberation; but, as to the higher ideals of human
brotherhood on which it was based, *Fatah* would permit no
doubts. All Jews now in Palestine, not just those who were already
there before 1917, 1948, or whenever the Palestinians deemed the
'Zionist invasion' to have begun, would be entitled to stay there.
Naturally they would have to foreswear their Zionist beliefs. The
Palestine of tomorrow could not be a bi-national state, not just
another Lebanon, with its confessional system which, rather than
eroding contradictory loyalties, perpetuates them within a framework of precarious co-existence that is subject to frequent and
bloody breakdowns. That would simply encourage the Jews, like
the Maronite Christians of Lebanon, to go their own separatist
way. There would, of course, be many diehards, the Begins, the
Dayans and the Golda Meirs, who could not possibly adapt themselves to such a radical new order—they would have to leave; but
it should be remembered that what the Israelis called Oriental
Jews are, for the most part, Arab Jews, and they make up at least
half the population; for them, adjustment would not be very
difficult. Once they had made it, they would find themselves the
victims of no discrimination whatever. A Jew could even be
elected President just as well as an Arab. Reciprocal accommoda-
tions, transitional or permanent, could be made between the Arab
and Jewish components of the Democratic State. These would be
mainly cultural and linguistic; both Hebrew and Arabic would be
official languages in government schools. But they could also
embrace the higher policies of the state. Thus, in the transitional
phase, immigration would be restricted to Palestinians wishing
to return. Thereafter, however, and subject to agreed estimates
of the country's absorptive capacity, it would be open to all
without discrimination.

As *Fatah* conceived it, in fact, the Democratic State would
offer liberation not merely for the Palestinians, but for the Jews
too—for those of them, that is, whom it considered fellow-victims
of a creed which professed to help them. It offered them an open,

safe and tolerant Palestine in place of the insecurity of a Jewish
State ever threatened by its neighbours. There would eventually
come a time, it was hoped, when Jews would be fighting side by
side with Palestinians in the liberation struggle.

The Democratic State won neither immediate nor universal
acceptance from Palestinians. Some were totally opposed to the
whole idea; it was an intolerable concession to the enemy. Some
considered it no more than a tactical propaganda move designed
to impress international opinion. Some objected to the creation
of yet another Arab state; they preferred to talk of a 'democratic society' that would merge with the greater Arab world.
Some were afraid that in such a state the Palestinians would be
outnumbered by the technologically more advanced Jews, who
would exploit their position to dominate the Arab world and
destroy its unity. Some were critical of the religious classification
—Moslem, Christian, Jew—of the citizens of the future state.
Some said that the proposal was premature in that the Middle
Eastern balance of power was still tipped heavily in the Israelis'
favour. Some said that it would weaken the Palestinians' fighting
spirit. In general, however, the Palestinians came to accept the
principle, while deferring any precise definition of it, and in 1970,
it was formally endorsed by the PLO's National Council, the
'parliament' of the Palestinian people.

No Uprising in the Occupied Territories

Karameh was the Palestinians' finest hour. But their very success
contained the seeds of future failure. Indeed, the fact that
Karameh took place at all was at least in part the consequence of
an earlier failure, for which, however, it furnished a spectacular,
if ultimately unavailing, cover. *Fatah* had failed, in that first six
months after the 1967 War to set off the 'popular liberation war',
inside the occupied territories, on which it had counted. The
fedayeen failed to become fish in a revolutionary sea. True, there
was great enthusiasm, especially in the countryside, for the new
breed of fighting Palestinians and it was hoped that, inspired by
their example, West Bankers and Gazans would in due course
take to armed struggle themselves. But it became clear, during
those first six months, that this was not going to happen. Gaza

did have a considerable tradition of militancy, but in general the West Bankers were not ready for great self-sacrifice in a cause whose success they doubted. The *fedayeen* were the product of a refugee society which had lost all; but *they* still had something to lose. They were therefore more immediately interested in the evacuation of newly occupied territories than in the liberation of all Palestine, and they hoped that, by political or military means, the Arab states would achieve that for them. On the whole the local leadership—the mayors, the urban notables and the village *mukhtars*—discouraged the resort to arms. Thus, unlike those of the Great Rebellion of 1936-9, the fighters, though Palestinians, were in large measure outsiders. They found it hard to hide among the local population. It was to prove an embittering experience. The exhilaration which they felt on crossing the Jordan eventually gave way to demoralization in the inhospitable caves and hide-outs in the hills of Judea and Samaria.

Fatah itself was partly to blame, too, with its hasty and slip-shod methods of organization, undiscriminating recruitment and poor security. Israel's efficiency, and the severity of its reprisals against the local population, did the rest. In the first three months of its efforts to establish a 'secure base' in the occupied territories it put its losses at forty-six—including twenty-six officers—of its best men.[8] And by early March 1968 the Israelis were claiming that they had wrecked *Fatah*'s hopes of promoting a 'serious' resistance movement. According to General Dayan, they had killed ninety *fedayeen* since the June War, fifty of them in the previous two months, and had captured a thousand. In January Arafat himself, roused from sleep in a sympathizer's house in Ramallah, had made a hair-breadth's escape from Israeli troops[9] and crossed the River Jordan for the last time. And only a few months after it had been decided to transfer guerilla headquarters to the occupied territories, they were transferred back again—to Karameh.

Fatah MAKES POLITICAL HEADWAY

The glorious cover of Karameh held firm for a while, for who, confronted with the outward façade of *Fatah*'s rapidly growing power, paid much attention to the 'inner sickness' of which that rapid growth was itself a principal cause?[10] If the losses of

Karameh were heavy, they were before long replaced a hundred-fold.[11] New recruits flocked to the training camps which dotted the countryside west of Amman; the tranquil hills and valleys echoed to the unaccustomed sound of gunfire. Advanced and specialized training was to be had in Algeria and Egypt, China and North Vietnam. The fighting forces of *Fatah*—some 300 before Karameh—and lesser, left-wing organizations had swollen to more than 30,000 two years later. There was also the Palestinian militia, the community self-defence organization, which supplemented the fulltime guerillas. There were the *Ashbal*, the Lion Cubs, ten- to fifteen-year-old youngsters who were being moulded as the *fedayeen* of the future. Women, too, found an emancipating place in the revolution. As for funds and arms, they registered an explosive increase in the order of 300 per cent.[12] A whole range of ancillary services—clinics, hospitals, schools and orphanages for the children of 'martyrs'—sprang into being. The civil servants of the revolution moved into offices in the respectable residential or business quarters of Amman and other Arab capitals. Militant posters and slogans decorated the walls of middle-class homes in the vicinity. Guerilla vehicles, bristling with armed men, plied as casually as taxis through the streets. The sudden emergence from a persecuted obscurity to international fame engendered a string of public relations departments devoted to the publishing of guerilla literature in many languages, the reception and guidance of foreign politicians, journalists, the curious and the sympathetic. In all the leading hotels, restaurants and bars, you would find the usual clientèle of businessmen and high society; but among them, and often hardly distinguishable from them, there would usually be a sprinkling of guerilla officials entertaining their foreign visitors.[13]

As the *fedayeen* movement grew in size and in the number of its competing organizations, so did the frequency of its operations. Most of them—61·5 per cent—were mounted by *Fatah*; they increased, according to its own estimate, from a mere twelve a month in 1967 to fifty-two in 1968, 199 in 1969, and 279 in the first eight months of 1970.[14] The small-scale mine-laying and sabotaging of the embryonic pre-1967 days developed into altogether bolder and more ambitious enterprises which—in spite of the failure on the West Bank—the movement's vastly expanded manpower and resources put within its grasp.

They put bombs in supermarkets in Jerusalem and bus stops in Tel Aviv; they lobbed rockets on Kiryat Shmona in the north and Eilat in the south. They mounted frontal assaults on border outposts, sometimes several at once, and raised the Palestinian flag for a few symbolic hours on patches of territory they seized.

It was disturbing for the Israelis. 'I have never underestimated this matter from the very beginning,' said Defence Minister Moshe Dayan,[15] and Prime Minister Levi Eshkol believed that in many respects the campaign against the guerillas was more violent than the 1967 War. But the really worrying thing was the political implications of the *fedayeen*, not their military effectiveness, although the former were partly a result of the latter. Politically, the *fedayeen* continued to build on what they had achieved at Karameh. Not, of course, that their ultimate goal, the Democratic State of Palestine, looked much less utopian than hitherto. Internationally, they won a certain credit for what was seen as a more civilized, if still hopelessly unrealistic, presentation of their case. But in Israel itself few indeed were those who showed any inclination to live in Arafat's 'Palestine of tomorrow'. That was hardly surprising since, by definition, Israel was a state for the Jews; the Jews-as-Zionists had driven out the Arabs to create it in the first place and now, to consolidate it, they were multiplying *faits accomplis* in the newly occupied territories. There were, of course, 'doves' of various feathers. But they were still Zionists; they called for a return of the occupied territories —and, usually, not even all of them—in exchange for Arab recognition of Jewish statehood in all its essential Zionist attributes. Some accepted the need for a kind of 'Palestine entity'. The most 'dovish' among them, like Deputy Uri Avneri, urged a federation between a Jewish and an Arab State in Palestine. There were others who fought the occupation on moral and spiritual rather than political grounds. Men like Israel Shahak, former inmate of a Nazi concentration camp, were persuaded that Israel was now an oppressor which, in its treatment of the Arabs of the occupied territories and of Israel proper, was violating not only civilized international standards but the higher teachings of Judaism. As President of the Israeli League for Civil and Human Rights, he and a like-minded few, such as lawyer Felicia Langer, braved the abuse and hostility of fellow-citizens as they campaigned against the wrong done in Israel's name. But only outright anti-Zionists,

wedded to the dismantling of the Jewish State, could so much as
consider the Palestinians' vision of what would replace it; and
anti-Zionists, as an organized political force, were a tiny handful,
the merest *groupuscule* as the French say. *Matzpen*, or the Israeli
Socialist Organization, stood on the lunatic fringe of the Israeli
political spectrum, denounced as traitors even by those, such as
Avneri, who came anywhere near them. Unlike the conventional
'doves' they did not draw an arbitrary distinction between Israel
proper and the occupied territories; they considered that what
was wrong in Hebron or Nablus must be wrong in Tel Aviv too,
the original injustice committed in 1948 and before no less deserving of redress than a subsidiary injustice committed in 1967
and after. Only de-Zionization and the establishment of a society
in which Jews and repatriated Arabs lived together without
discrimination could bring peace to the Middle East. Socialist
revolutionaries, *Matzpen* believed that, for the Israelis, the overthrow of Zionism should take precedence over the classical proletarian struggle; Arabs and Jews, inside and outside Israel,
should join forces to bring this about. They recognized 'the right
and duty of every conquered and oppressed people to resist
occupation and struggle for its freedom . . . in our opinion resistance to occupation is natural and legitimate . . . as for the
means used in the struggle—even when we do not approve of
them—they do not constitute the main criterion by which we
determine our position'.[16] *Matzpen* leaders, some of whom lived
in exile, entered into direct communication with the *fedayeen*.
They attended Palestinian conferences. Resistance publications
disseminated their views in the Arab world. Even *Matzpen*,
however, did not go quite far enough for the Palestinians, who
tended to balk at its insistence that the Jews of Palestine, like
the Arabs, had a national identity, preserving which, within the
framework of a bi-national state, was not incompatible with the
restoration of Arab rights. 'Despite the fact that it was created by
Zionism,' *Matzpen* insisted, 'a Hebrew nation in the full sense of
the term now exists in Palestine. And as such it has the right to
self-determination, not certainly in the Zionist sense, but within
the context of a socialist federation of the Middle East.'[17]

But the great majority of Israelis accepted the official vilifica-
tion of the *fedayeen*, and the PLO under whose auspices they
operated, as no more than 'terrorist gangs', 'murderers' and

'saboteurs'. How could they have the nerve to proclaim their desire for a peaceful coexistence in the 'Palestine of tomorrow' with their victims of today? The idea of a Democratic State, or even some kind of 'Palestine entity', should be as ruthlessly combated as the terrorists themselves. This emotional rejection of Palestinian aspirations was rationalized, at its most articulate and uncompromising, by General Yehoshavat Harkabi, the former military intelligence chief, who argued that the Democratic State was no more than a propaganda device to lend respectability to a struggle which was still 'genocidal' in intent.[18] In this he was helped by the Palestinians themselves, who, as one of their leading theoreticians concedes, furnished the Zionists with a 'rare opportunity' to question their sincerity, and to present the Democratic State as a tactical manoeuvre which caught them 'saying one thing in English and another in Arabic'.[19] As a result of doctrinal quarrels over the precise nature of this state, especially its relation to the rest of the Arab world, the Palestine National Council was unable to introduce an important promised amendment in the Palestine National Charter which would have endorsed *Fatah* doctrine that all Jews, not just those who arrived in Palestine before a certain date (1917 or 1948), would be entitled to Palestinian citizenship.

For all their disappointments, however, the Palestinians had established themselves once and for all as a political force, champions of their own cause, which they promoted not only in defiance of Israel, but, where necessary, of the Arab régimes. They had made nonsense of Golda Meir's claim that they did not exist. Never again was the conflict to be just an Arab-Israeli one. In the Third World they were recognized as an authentic liberation movement; ideologically opposed at first, the Soviet bloc eventually felt obliged, on political grounds, to bestow its favours on them; in the West they continued to make steady, if modest, inroads into a public opinion that was predisposed to see Israel as an outpost of civilization and a bastion of democracy in the Middle East. 'What we have done,' said Yasar Arafat, 'is to make the world . . . realize that the Palestinian is no longer refugee number so and so, but the member of a people who hold the reins of their own destiny and are in a position to determine their own future. As long as the world saw the Palestinians as no more than a people standing in a queue for UN rations, it was not likely to respect them. Now that they carry rifles the situation has changed.'[20] They were not strong enough to impose their will on anyone. But they had acquired a considerable power of veto. The least sign that an Arab régime was ready to foist some 'surrender settlement' on them and they reacted with strident indignation. A balloon which various Western quarters regularly floated at this time was the establishment of a mini-state of Palestine, co-existent with Israel. That it was floated at all was an encouraging measure of their success, but none the less they just as regularly shot it down.

MILITARY FAILURE AND THE 'INNER SICKNESS'

Militarily, the *fedayeen* were never to be much more than a serious nuisance. They had a negative effect, certainly, in many fields. Israeli soldiers and civilians died. Counter-insurgency cost money and manpower. The less adventurous would-be immigrants, tourists and pilgrims were frightened off. But a 'popular liberation war' could not just stand still; it had to escalate. And that, beyond a rather low level, *Fatah* could not achieve. Indeed, at the height of their success, the *fedayeen* were already in decline.

Consciously or unconsciously, they sought to disguise this fact from the world and from themselves. True, the number of operations increased, but that was more than offset by the simultaneous Israeli success in driving the *fedayeen* even further east. For the increase was not to be found in operations inside Israel proper, nor even in the occupied territories. It was to be found in what can hardly be described as guerilla warfare, in the true sense, at all—in sniping and shelling across the ceasefire lines, and down in the Jordan Valley in particular. An Arab news agency reported that a mere 2·1 per cent of operations were taking place in Israel proper (excluding Upper Galilee), 3·4 per cent in Upper Galilee, 3·5 per cent in the West Bank, 7 per cent in the Negev desert, 7 per cent in the Golan Heights, 10 per cent in Gaza—as compared with a full 67 per cent in the Jordan Valley.[21] The prime yardstick of military effectiveness is casualties. The Israelis' figures were demonstrably confusing and contradictory.[22] But if they minimized their losses from *fedayeen* action—and they never admitted more than a hundred killed a year—this was not as flagrant as the way in which the *fedayeen* exaggerated them. In reality, as a Palestinian scholar later pointed out, Israel's casualties on all fronts, let alone from the *fedayeen*, never even approached the 'critical level' that might have pushed it into full-scale war.[23] Yet it was not unusual for *Fatah* to announce that, in a single operation, it had killed and wounded fifty, sixty or even seventy enemy soldiers for the most paltry losses of its own. 'Oriental fantasy,'[24] scoffed the Israelis; and clearly the spirit of Shuqairi, that contemptible symbol of a past which the Palestinians had supposedly put behind them, was far from dead. The extravagance of their claims was occasionally outdone by their efforts to prove them. Once, insisting that it had shot down six Israeli war planes over Jordan, Fatah exhibited a few twisted hunks of machinery as 'evidence'. Time and again, rival organizations would claim the same exploit. And if something quite ordinary or accidental happened—like the fatal heart attack of Premier Levi Eshkol or the injury of Moshe Dayan on an archaeological dig—they would rush in with silly assertions that nothing was beyond the long arm of the Palestinian revolution. And as if their own claims were not extravagant enough, the Arab propagandists who, before the June War, had derided the *fedayeen* now made amends with crass glorification and the raising of grandiose expectations. It frightened some of their sympathizers:

> I am afraid for the Palestinian revolution. I am afraid not from its enemies . . . but from some of its friends, dedicated to the 'true path' and committed to revolutions in the Arab world. . . . But the road is long. It is not paved with victories as the stalwarts of revolution imagine. The picture of the *fedayi* training to cross the enemy lines does not mean that he has already crossed that line and reached Haifa. It simply means that a new Arab has been born whose brother—should he perish—must follow him into the caravan of *fedayeen* and perhaps into the martyrs' grave—until one of them, crossing the enemy line, does reach Haifa, and another Askelon . . .[25]

Exaggeration, as we have noted, was from the beginning one of the symptoms of the resistance movement's 'inner sickness'. Another, partly engendered by this embarrassing gulf between the real and the proclaimed performance, was an increasing readiness to compromise the ethical code by which they professed to fight. In its communiqué of 1 January 1965, announcing the completion of its first operation, *Fatah* warned the enemy not to retaliate against 'peaceful Arab civilians'. Thereafter, *Fatah* regularly insisted that the army and 'Zionist institutions' were its target, not civilians, 'particularly women and children';[26] if it did attack them, it was essentially in reply to Israeli attacks on Arab civilians, and it was selectively done. 'Whenever a civilian target is chosen, every effort is made to minimize loss of civilian life—though one would find it hard to distinguish civilians and non-civilians in this modern Spartan militaristic society where every adult is mobilized for the war. Hitting quasi-civilian areas aims at the psychological effect of shocking the Israelis into realization that the racist-militaristic state cannot provide them with security when it is conducting genocide against the exiled and oppressed Palestinian masses.'[27] The doctrine was not rigorously implemented. True, the Israelis, with their greater means, killed far more Arab civilians than the *fedayeen* killed Israeli civilians, and that furnished the justification. But there is little doubt that, even without it, the ineffectualness of day-to-day harassment of the Israeli soldiery, the scant publicity it brought, was pushing *Fatah* into straightforward terrorism designed, by shock tactics, to achieve a maximum of impact with a minimum of resources. Besides, the doctrine, loftily enunciated, was not deeply inculcated in daily living practice. Thus in January 1968 the old, officially discredited idea of revenge seemed to win approval, as a motive for killing civilians, in the *Fatah* monthly *The Palestine Revolution* when it recounted what a captive *fedayi*, responsible for the death of a three-year-old boy, had told an Israeli court. His orders, he explained, had been to engage in patrols and sabotage everything he could. Asked whether that meant the killing of children too, he replied: 'Yes, to destroy everything, because we haven't forgotten Deir Yassin.'[28] A few months later an article in *The Palestine Revolution* dismissed the need for too much discrimination in the selection of targets:

> If military action in well-known guerilla wars concentrated on the armed forces of the enemy and spared the people whom the revolution wanted to win over, the Palestine revolution, owing to the nature of Zionist society, does not recognize this distinction

between the enemy's armed forces and people. The colonialist
Zionist society is a military society root and branch and there
can be no distinction between military and civilian . . .[29]

The great bulk of *fedayeen* operations were directed against the
military proper, but when civilians were killed, the communiqués
which announced it included few expressions of regret about
this unfortunate necessity.

HIJACKINGS AND THE POPULAR FRONT
FOR THE LIBERATION OF PALESTINE

Fatah did at least try to confine the Palestine struggle to the land
of Palestine itself. Its left-wing rival, the Popular Front for the
Liberation of Palestine, did not. A former opponent of guerilla
activism, Dr George Habash now became its most extreme
practitioner. The ideologues of the PFLP saw themselves in the
front line of a global struggle between the two great forces of the
age. For them, the enemy—in the shape of Zionists, imperialists
and local reactionaries—was one and omnipresent. Almost anything was therefore a fair target. It was legitimate to hijack not
just Israeli civil aircraft, but American, British and even Swiss
ones too. It was a contribution to the cause to blow up a pipeline
transporting Arab oil—revenues from which helped finance the
Arab war effort—because the oil was extracted by an American
company, Aramco, on behalf of a 'feudal' Arab monarchy, the
House of Saud. The planting of firebombs in Marks and
Spencer's, a British chain store and big fundraiser for Israel,
fitted without difficulty into the same Manichaean scheme of
things. As for the ethics of hijacking, and the charge that it put
the lives of uninvolved, non-Israeli civilians at risk, the PFLP
had a prompt retort to that: don't blame us, blame the wicked
Israeli crew who try to foil our irreproachable form of warfare.
When the PFLP's Leila Khalid, the world's most celebrated
aerial terrorist, was asked at a press conference what advice she
would have for an Arab pilot confronted by Israeli hijackers, her
only answer was a demure smile. The PFLP justified the
machine-gunning of an Israeli airliner at Athens airport—and the
killing and wounding of two aboard—on the ground that El Al
was an integral part of the enemy war machine. When the Israelis

replied by blowing up thirteen aircraft at Beirut airport and—for once—killing no one, the PFLP called this 'barbarous aggression' and 'unprincipled cowardly piracy'. Nor did the PFLP heed *Fatah*'s warnings about the obvious dangers to the whole guerilla movement of making unnecessary, above all Arab, enemies.

There is no doubt that 'foreign operations' of the kind that George Habash pioneered did bring publicity to the Palestinian cause, and, beneath the veneer of exalted ideology, that was one of his purposes:

> When we hijack a plane it has more effect than if we killed a hundred Israelis in battle. For decades world public opinion has been neither for nor against the Palestinians. It simply ignored us. At least the world is talking about us now.[30]

Probably, however, the underlying motive for a form of terrorism of which *Fatah* disapproved was the PFLP's military weakness, which, in the nature of things, pushed it into a series of spectacular, daring, but essentially facile exploits far removed from the real battlefield.

THE ENEMY IN THE REAR

The 'inner sickness' was more than just military. It was organizational and political. Some of its symptoms were relatively concealed, obvious only to insiders, one of whom recalls that, both in theory and practice, the movement's

> . . . bungling was beyond all imagining; from a glance at the minutes of the PLO Central Committee's sessions, for example, with their muddle, their repetition, clashes and contradictions, one would hardly guess that they came from a common organization with a common purpose; there was nothing consistent or constructive in decision-making; rarely did one decision supplement or complete an earlier one; every session started from scratch . . .[31]

Other symptoms were plain to all. The rise of the *fedayeen* had been an act of Palestinian self-assertion, against Arabs as well as Israelis, but, ironically, no sooner had one form of Arab 'tutelage' been thrown off than another took its place. Instead of opposing guerilla action altogether, the régimes now vied with

one another in their support of it. Not content with their court-
ship of the mainstream *Fatah*, or of its PFLP rival, they spawned
whole new organizations of their own. The Syrian Baathists had
their own protégé—Vanguards of the Popular Liberation War
(Saiqa)—so naturally the Iraqi Baathists, implacable rivals, had
to have theirs too—the Arab Liberation Front—and, although
both were punctilious about their own ideological *raison d'être*,
they were really no more than extensions, in Palestinian guise, of
the régimes which sponsored them. Palestinian politics were an
Arab world in microcosm; much more democratic, it is true, but
rent by the same splits, mergers and shifting alliances. No wonder
Arafat was to exclaim that, in spite of the absence of real ideological differences, 'I feel that the difficulties of working for
complete unity are greater than fighting itself.'[82]

It was gravely debilitating for the movement as a whole, however manfully *Fatah* strove to maintain its independence. It was a
travesty of that spontaneous, popular-based 'supporting Arab
front'—the scourge of aberrant governments—of which it had
dreamed. For all their initial popularity, the guerillas failed to
translate it into the organized backing which alone, in the end,
could preserve them against official machinations. Indeed, even
in their most sympathetic environment, East Jordan, where half
the population were Palestinians, they began to lose rather than
gain support, and their state-within-a-state, ever more powerful
in external appearance, was in reality being eroded from within.
Why was it that many a Jordanian village, which might once have
offered food and hospitality to nearby guerillas without being
asked, would now fire on them if they so much as entered it?
How could things go so wrong in Lebanon that the Nasserists of
Sidon engaged in street warfare against guerillas from a nearby
refugee camp; or that the Christian village of Kahhaleh, which
in 1968 paid such splendid tribute to the first Lebanese 'martyr',
in 1970 laid a murderous ambush for a Palestinian funeral
cavalcade?

The causes of the alienation were manifold. An immediately
obvious one was the hooligan fringe of pseudo-guerillas which
many people took to represent the whole. Another was the offence
to the *amour-propre* of the regular armies. These were problems
which the more responsible leaders, especially in *Fatah*, always
recognized, but only half-heartedly corrected. But there were

other problems, much more complex ones, stemming from the whole nature of the Arab environment. *Fatah*, hard though it often tried to cultivate the local population, fell into the trap one way, and its left-wing rivals in another. For *Fatah*, political pragmatism in the service of the military struggle was the supreme virtue, and it was inclined to believe that simple good behaviour and the distribution of largesse—like more guns for the tribes—would suffice. But all the Jordanian government, far more experienced in these time-honoured practices, had to do was counter with more and better. The left-wingers, on the other hand, naturally saw themselves in an educative, emancipating role. But they could take this to foolish extremes. Nayif Hawatmeh's Popular Democratic Front for the Liberation of Palestine, intoxicated by its own originality, grievously offended against those two sanctities of traditional Arab society: religion and woman's honour. The Front did what it did on a very small scale, but news of *fedayeen* paying nocturnal visits to the tents of *fedayaat*, and the broadcasting of Marxist slogans from a minaret to commemorate the 100th anniversary of Lenin's birth were the kind of things which the Hashemite régime could, and did, exploit to the full. It did not take much to shock the peasants and tribes of Jordan, but it was with the help of calculated indoctrination that they learned, some of them, to hate the *fedayeen*, as blasphemers and degenerates, in the way they did.[33]

The 'inner sickness' was not the only reason for the guerillas' military shortcomings. There were external ones too. Not the least of them was the continuing severity and efficiency of the enemy. The Israelis learned the lesson of Karameh. From then on they made relentless use of their complete aerial supremacy; the *fedayeen*, mercilessly pounded—along with a great many civilians—in their Transjordanian redoubts, bitterly complained about the absence of Arab anti-aircraft defences. At the same time the Israelis threw around their new frontiers a *cordon sanitaire*—minefields, electronic detection devices, highly mobile patrols—of formidable sophistication and complexity. As early as March 1968 they were claiming to have captured or killed thirty-five out of fifty *fedayeen* who had forged the River Jordan in the previous ten days[34]—and that was only a beginning. There were other inescapable obstacles too. The Palestinians had been greatly influenced by the Algerian struggle against the French—

but if motivation was similar, geographic and demographic conditions were not. Palestine, unlike Algeria, was not good guerilla country. Moreover, in Algeria, not only did the *indigènes* far outnumber the *colons*, they lived all amongst them. In Palestine, by contrast, Israelis not only outnumbered Arabs, but, for the most part, lived in their own segregated, easily policed areas. Without the 'inner sickness', however, the resistance movement might have triumphed over the external problems—or at least avoided the calamity of 'Black September', 1970.

CIVIL WAR IN JORDAN

The story goes that, inspecting a tank regiment in early September 1970, King Hussein spotted an incongruous pennant suspended from a radio antenna. It was a brassière, and by it his loyalist bedouin troops were signalling that they could not be expected to behave 'like women' much longer. They had had enough of these so-called freedom-fighters who, instead of 'liberating Palestine', swaggered around the streets of the royal capital, or what they chose to call the 'Arab Hanoi', and, with variants on the Bolshevik slogan of 'All Power to the People', openly proclaimed their ambition of replacing the Hashemite kingdom with their own revolutionary order. The King's patience, too, was running out. It only required the PFLP's last great *tour de force*, a multiple hijacking, to exhaust it altogether. Leila Khalid, in her second such exploit, had failed to seize control of an Israeli airliner; she had been taken into custody at London airport. But the spectacle of three other airliners—American, British and Swiss—brought down in the desert wastes of eastern Jordan, the PFLP's threats to blow them up with all aboard unless Leila and other comrades were released, camels wandering by, hectic international negotiations as deadlines came and went, the final ceremonial destruction of the aircraft—all that was exotic and riveting drama enough.

And yet a larger drama overtook it when, on 17 September, King Hussein, after long hesitation—but also long preparation—unleashed his impatient bedouins. In ten days of fratricidal struggle, they broke the back of guerilla power in Jordan. In their hour of desperate need, the *fedayeen* were betrayed by the quarter which had most loudly trumpeted its solidarity with them: Iraqi forces in Jordan left them to fight alone. The Syrian régime despatched armoured forces of the Palestine Liberation Army to their assistance, but General Hafiz al-Asad, the Defence Minister and future President, fearing Israeli or American intervention, refused to give them air cover, and they were routed. Contrary to guerilla hopes, the Jordanian army, though substantially Palestinian, failed to disintegrate in a conflict of loyalties. Within a year of 'Black September', as the *fedayeen* called this disaster, they were expelled from Jordan altogether. Prime Minister Wasfi al-Tal, the very man who, three years earlier, had urged the King to turn his kingdom into a latter-day 'Carthage', conducted the final ruthless drive against their last bases in the north of the country. It was so ruthless that scores of *fedayeen*, in the last extremities of exhaustion and despair, crossed the River Jordan rather than fall into the hands of the King's vengeful troops. One of them told his jubilant Israeli captors: 'I am ready to join the Israeli army and fight against Jordan and Syria—because these are worse enemies of the Palestinians.'[35] Arafat had lost his most important political and military base. It had been an Arab army, not the Israelis, which, in 1965, claimed the first Palestinian 'martyr'; it was the same army which, characteristically, had now dealt the whole resistance movement the hardest blow of its career. For Arafat, it was the ultimate betrayal, by the Arabs, of their most sacred cause; Jordan was but the spearhead of 'an Arab plot'[36]—a plot whose full, astonishing and treacherous dimensions only the future would reveal.

BLACK SEPTEMBER

The Jordanian civil war ushered in a whole new phase of Palestinian violence—pure, unbridled terrorism. Wasfi al-Tal was its first victim. On 28 November 1971 four young men shot him down on the steps of the Sheraton Hotel in Cairo, where he had been attending an Arab League conference. Although they belonged to something calling itself the Black September Organization, they had, they made out, acted largely on their own initiative. One said that he had sold his car to raise money for the operation; another that he had paid 300 Lebanese pounds for his false Syrian passport. They had been brought together in a common desire for revenge. One claimed to have seen King Hussein's bedouin troops rape his sister and cut her child's throat. The body of Ali Abu Iyyad, a *Fatah* commander, had—or so Palestinians believed—been dragged in triumph behind Centurion tanks. The four assassins made no attempt to resist arrest.

As grief and anger swept Jordan, or rather the loyalist Transjordanian half of the population, and as Arab kings and presidents despatched the obligatory messages of condolences, the Palestinian masses did not hide their feelings in those places—outside Jordan—where they could freely express them. In Lebanon the refugee camps reverberated with joyful salvos. The same day the Palestine Students' Union, and other popular organizations, appealed to President Sadat to release the four men 'because they did their national duty'. Three days later *Hisad al-Asifah*, mouthpiece of *Fatah*, said that 'the four heroes who executed the Palestinian people's sentence on Wasfi al-Tal are sons of the Palestinian people and represent the will of the Palestine revolution'.[37] Many Arabs shared the Palestinians' feelings, and scores of lawyers volunteered to defend the assassins when they went on trial. But they never did. They were released on bail by the Cairo State Security Court: a leading lawyer cited gun tests to prove that a fifth man, who escaped arrest, had actually fired the fatal shot, and added that 'even if they were responsible, their act is no crime but a commando action. The four were in a state of legitimate defence of themselves and their land.'[38] They eventually left Egypt scot-free.

Black September, in contrast to *Fatah*, shrouded itself in secrecy of an extreme, cloak-and-dagger kind. However, the Jordanians promptly denounced it as no more than a clandestine arm of *Fatah*, and there is no doubt that, from the outset, *Fatah* was deeply involved in the new-style violence. Discovering who, among its leaders, was the real *éminence grise* behind it became a rather futile guessing game of the international press and intelligence community. *Fatah*, or those of its leaders who were involved, could not, of course, acknowledge a connection. That would have run counter to its official policies. It had always opposed the kind of 'foreign operations' which the Popular Front had pioneered. It was the backbone of the Palestine Liberation Organization, which, aspiring to be the internationally recognized representative of the Palestinian people, had to maintain a respectable façade. Nor could it embarrass Arab and other governments whose friendship it needed. On the other hand it could no more stifle the impulse Black September represented than, in the 1940s, the Jewish Agency and *Haganah* could stop their own extremists. And it was to those that some Arabs were to liken them. 'In their struggle against Zionist colonialism', commented the Beirut daily *L'Orient-Le-Jour*, 'the Palestinians have taken 27 years to come round to the methods of *Irgun* and *Stern*. Can we blame them for seeking to avenge Deir Yassin?'[39] Twenty-seven years was felt to be a long time. Most outsiders familiar with the cause, wrote one Palestinian scholar, were given to expressing their surprise—some as a commendation, others as a reproach—at the relative absence of this kind of violence.[40]

The classic definition of Black September, at the time, was that it was less an organization than a state of mind. 'It cannot be pinpointed, tracked down or crushed. It has no name, no flag, no slogans, headquarters or base. It requires only men who have the determination to fight and succeed and the courage to die.'[41] So one ardent youth described it. An arm of *Fatah*, it was at the same time a grassroots phenomenon, spontaneous and self-generating. It was a popular response to the mistakes and declining moral authority of the official guerilla leadership. It was a compensation for the slump—from some 300 a month before the Jordanian civil war to about fifty after it[42]—in the number of conventional guerilla operations. Above all, it was a product of extreme frustration and despair, the feeling that only by shocking the world could the Palestinians get it to redress the injustice it had done, or even to consider it as such. Black September required of its adherents a readiness to take suicidal risks. Martyrdom, however, did not merely advertise the Palestinian cause to the world in the most dramatic way possible, it was intended to regalvanize the Palestinians themselves, to trigger mass emotional reflexes, which, channelled in more constructive directions, would eventually revive the struggle where *Fatah* had begun it, in Palestine itself.

MUNICH, 1972

The most famous Black September operation—public relations terrorism at its most sensational—was the one which disrupted the Olympic Games at Munich in September 1972. A Palestinian spokesman was hardly exaggerating when he claimed that:

> A bomb in the White House, a mine in the Vatican, the death of Mao Tse-Tung, an earthquake in Paris could not have echoed through the consciousness of every man in the world like the operation at Munich. . . . It was like painting the name of Palestine on the top of a mountain that can be seen from the four corners of the earth.[43]

The Munich games were covered by 6,000 newsmen and the most sophisticated electronic television set-up ever assembled. Apart from the guaranteed publicity of the world's most grandiose sporting occasion, the terrorists had another, fortuitous bonus. For the West, particularly for the German hosts, these were the Games which should, as it were, have formally buried the unsavoury past. Berlin, 1936, was the last time the Olympiad had been held on German soil. Hitler had turned it into a festival of his Nazi rule, of the militarism and racist, anti-Semitic doctrines which it exalted. Munich, by contrast, was to be remembered as the 'carefree games'; if there was a touch of the Mediterranean holiday resort about them, that was no accident; no one was forbidden to walk on the grass; *verboten* was *verboten*.

Munich, of course, was the city that set Hitler on the road to absolute power; and Dachau concentration camp had not been far away. But that, too, was forgotten—until, on the morning of the eleventh day, the camera atop the television tower, switching from the Olympic arena, zeroed in on Block No. 31 in the athletes' village, and, as if transfixed, remained on that 'shot' until the ensuing drama was over.

At 4.30 a.m. on 5 September post office engineers saw a group of men in track suits clambering over the eight-foot wire-mesh fence; they did nothing about it: that was how many athletes got home after a night on the town. Armed with Kalashnikov assault rifles and hand grenades, the group, eight Black September terrorists, entered the Israeli pavilion, in Block No. 31, through an unlocked door. They ran into Moshe Weinberg, a weightlifter, and Joseph Romano, a wrestling trainer, who attempted to resist them. Weinberg was killed, Romano wounded. In the confusion, several Israeli athletes escaped, but nine others were captured. Romano, denied medical attention, died.

Shortly after 5 a.m. the terrorists throw a list of their demands
out of a first-floor window. They want the release, by 9 a.m., of
two hundred of their comrades held in Israeli prisons. If the
demands are met, the hostages will be freed; if not, they will be
shot. At 8 a.m. the German police start preparations to rescue the
hostages by force. In negotiations with the authorities, the terrorists refuse to exchange the hostages for German volunteers
but agree to extend their deadline till midday. Sharpshooters are
summoned. At 11 a.m. the Israeli ambassador informs the Germans that his government rejects the Palestinians' ultimatum, or
any kind of negotiations with them: 'If we once give way to
blackmail, hijackings and kidnappings will multiply infernally.
Our citizens know and accept this. Every one of us has been ex-
plicitly warned: in no case can we serve as bargaining counters.
After all, we are at war. Every kidnapping, every commando
attack is regarded as a military engagement in which we Israelis,
soldiers or civilians, risk losing our lives. We do not bargain, but
we must defend ourselves. That means, in this case, that there
must be an immediate counter-attack. My government will
accept nothing else.'[44] Israeli security men, despatched from Tel
Aviv, later join the ambassador to 'advise' the German police.
They too insist: no bargaining. So the Germans have no choice
but to buy time, and to complete their plans for a showdown.
They offer the kidnappers free passage out of the country, a large
sum of money, even a night with 'beautiful Munich blondes'.[45]
Arab ambassadors, unaware of the Germans' real intentions, also
act as go-betweens. But the eight men remain unmoved. 'Money
means nothing to us,' they say, 'our lives mean nothing to us.'
All they will countenance is fresh extensions of their deadlines.
1 p.m., 3 p.m., 5 p.m., 7 p.m.—still they do not execute any
hostages; and they seem ready to walk into the trap which the
police are preparing for them. They are willing to fly to Cairo,
with their captives, aboard a German airliner. This is a trick;
contacted by Chancellor Willi Brandt, the Egyptian Prime
Minister has already turned down a proposal that, on arrival in
Cairo, the Egyptians would see to it that the hostages are sent
back to Munich, or on to Tel Aviv. The real purpose is to get the
terrorists to leave the Israeli pavilion, which does not lend itself
to armed assault. The terrorists suspect as much, but they take
the plunge, and at 10.06 p.m. they and their hostages, bound one

to another, leave Block 31. They board two helicopters which, twenty minutes later, land at Fürstenfeldbrück military airport. Five marksmen are in position; flood-lights ensure excellent visibility at thirty metres' range. They are reinforced by police with sub-machine guns, and 600 men of the Frontier Guards surround the perimeter. The two helicopter pilots jump down—and so do two terrorists, who keep them covered at point-blank range. Two other terrorists, one from each helicopter, walk over to inspect the Boeing airliner which is waiting, all lit up and apparently ready for take-off, on the tarmac 150 metres away. But there is no crew aboard, and as the two walk back, the marksmen open fire. The two men guarding the pilots slump to the ground. The other two run. One is hit. A second, probably the leader, manages to hide beneath a helicopter. His comrades, still on board, shoot back, killing one of the marksmen. At 10.50, the police, using a loudspeaker, call on the surviving terrorists to surrender. They address them in German and English; an Israeli security man addresses them in Arabic. There is no reply; just the silence of impending disaster. The end comes at 1.05 a.m. The police open fire again. A terrorist jumps from one helicopter, and lobs in a grenade. Another shoots into the other helicopter. As armoured cars close in, all the hostages and two more terrorists die.

At first, through some ghastly blunder, it was announced to the world that the ambush had been a complete success; the hostages were safe. Altogether, it had been a day of error and misjudgements. Among other things, the German authorities had underestimated the number of terrorists; their five marksmen were not nearly enough for the job. They had also under-estimated the skill and, above all, the determination of men who did not make a single tactical mistake themselves and were ready to die for their cause.

The three survivors were taken to prison; another Black September exploit secured their release a few weeks later. In their 'will', published by the Palestine News Agency in Damascus, their five dead comrades apologized to the world's sportsmen. 'But we want them to know of the existence of a people whose country has been occupied for twenty-four years, and their honour trampled underfoot. . . . There is no harm if the youth of the world understand their tragedy for a few hours . . . so let the

Games stop for a few hours.' To their own people, the Palestinians, they appealed 'not to abandon your guns, in spite of the difficulties and conspiracies that beset the struggle. Our land will be liberated by blood, and blood alone. The world only respects the strong. We shall not be strong through words alone, but only by acting on them. We care not where we are buried for, as our ancestors said, it does not hurt the goat to be skinned after it is slain. We want Arab youth to know how to die for their people and their country . . . when one martyr falls from us, he is replaced by a thousand men . . .' Their bodies were flown to Libya, where they had a heroes' funeral which the official news agency described as a 'majestic spectacle'.

Three days later the Israeli airforce made one of its massive reprisal raids, over Syria and Lebanon, in which anything between 200 and 500 people, mostly civilians, died.[46]

Munich shocked the world. And, naturally enough, no people, apart from the Israelis themselves, were more outraged than the German hosts. In its cruder forms their outrage again stirred remembrance of unpleasant things past—though this time, of course, the man the popular cartoonists gave a hooked nose, swarthy complexion and shifty eyes was not a Jew, as he used to be in Göebbels' *Völkischer Beobachter*, he was an Arab. You were unlikely to overhear the word *Untermenschen* (subhumans), but the banner carried by a crowd of demonstrators asked: 'Are These People Human?' In cafés signs went up saying 'Arabs not wanted'. In the weeks to come, hundreds of Arab residents were summarily expelled from Germany; and Arabs trying to enter the country complained of their unfriendly reception at airports and border posts. Munich was denounced, with unusual severity, throughout the Western world. Readers' letters of rare virulence appeared in leading newspapers, like this one in *Time* magazine:[47]

> For this thing that they have done in Munich the Black September mob are truly the scum of the earth. On the battlefields they are nowhere to be found, yet these 'martyrs', these degenerate 'heroes of the sewers' shriek their hysterical victories over unarmed innocents, over women and children and airborne passengers, and then scuttle back to the dungheaps from where they came.

Munich was seen as a particularly odious example of a kind of violence, barbarous, random, pointless, that was becoming a world-wide plague. The Arabian Assassins, declared another letter in *Time*, have joined the Belfast Bombers and the Pakistani Predators. This breaking of the 'Olympic peace' was in addition a kind of sacrilege, the intrusion of human conflict on one of those universal rites of modern man which, by sublimating it, supposedly helped to prevent it. Attitudes towards Munich were held to distinguish the civilized from the uncivilized. President Nixon sought UN backing for a world-wide campaign against 'international terrorism'.

Yet there was clearly a counter-current of opinion which, in spite, or perhaps because, of the barbarism of Munich, argued that desperate men must have desperate reasons for doing what they do. That was the kind of response for which the Black Septembrists hoped. It was far from being a majority view which another letter in *Time* magazine expressed,[48] but at least the letter appeared. That, for the Palestinians, was progress.

> Must retaliation always follow atrocity in the awful agony of the Middle East? Harsh retaliation has only forged patriots into terrorists and forced them out into the world to destroy peace. Oh, Israel, let these people return to the land of their fathers. Show the world your great goodness. Destroy the cause of which terror is a symptom.

The only forthright condemnation in the Arab world came from King Hussein, who described Munich as a 'crime engineered by sick minds who have nothing in common with humanity'. That was to be expected; an implacable foe of the resistance movement, he himself was very high on Black September's list of targets. In the Palestinian refugee camps, by contrast, there was cheering when the final news from Munich came through, not so much because of the death of the hostages, but because eight Black Septembrists had acquitted themselves so well, foiling the German 'double-cross'—as one of the three survivors later called it—and demonstrating so conclusively that death really did mean nothing to them. In the rest of the Arab world, it was widely acknowledged—though without much conviction—that the massacre was unfortunate. The real thrust of Arab censure was not directed against the terrorists; it was reserved for the German authorities whose 'deceit' and 'trickery' were held mainly responsible for the tragic outcome. The Arab press and radio tended to endorse Black September's arguments that its men had been more than ready to negotiate with the German authorities, that they had treated the hostages 'humanely' and repeatedly refrained from executing them as the deadlines came and went. The last thing they wanted was a massacre of innocents, or, if it occurred, it was the other party's fault—this was familiar terrorist logic. It was all the more disingenuous in that, as every Palestinian knew, Israel could not compromise. Its whole security philosophy—indeed, as the Israelis themselves saw it, its very survival—was founded on the no-compromise of its strong right arm.

It was more honest to argue, as some apologists did, that terrorism was the weapon of the weak and the oppressed, of people who had no other means of fighting. The Arabs, like Mr Nixon, thought that terrorism was bad, but it was necessary to take into account not just the acts themselves but their underlying causes; that was the case which, with Third World support, they argued at the UN. But in any case, it was not for Israel, or its Western supporters, to wax indignant about a form of warfare which Israel itself had pioneered. 'After the creation of the State of Israel, classical terrorism gave way to the outwardly more respectable terrorism, designed to cow and subjugate the Palestinians and their Arab sympathizers which the state, with all its resources, can mount. Palestinian violence, by contrast, is reactive, small-scale but more easily branded as barbaric. We may, indeed some of us do, have misgivings about this kind of terrorism but we also condemn that of an Israel which was built on terrorism and continues to glorify its terrorists to this day. Look at the former terrorist leaders who enjoy respected places in public life. Look at Marcelle Ninio.'[49]

But the more honest arguments were not those most frequently heard. The Black Septembrists wanted it both ways. On the one hand, by blaming their enemy for the unhappy endings of violent deeds which they initiated, they were paying lip-service to the conventional ethics of war: you don't slaughter unarmed civilians in cold blood. On the other hand, their operations depended, for their whole effect, on the flouting of conventional ethics, and each operation more flagrantly than the last.

Palestinian terror and Israeli counter-terror were locked into an inexorable spiral of evergrowing ruthlessness. Thus, if the Munich hostages died, it was at least in part because earlier ones had lived.

Three and a half months before, four Black Septembrists had hijacked a Belgian airliner to Israel's Lydda airport. It was the most daring operation of its kind so far, the first time hijackers—two men and two women—had ventured right into the lions' den. They demanded the release of 106 Palestinian prisoners in Israeli prisons; otherwise they would blow up the aircraft and all aboard. After twenty-one hours of tergivisation and suspense, Israeli commandos stormed the plane, killing the two men and capturing the women. Six of the hundred passengers were wounded; one of them later died. Red Cross officials had been involved in the negotiations, and, in a breach of good faith, the commandos had exploited their presence to achieve complete surprise for their assault. According to a Black September communiqué, the four hijackers had received strict instructions not to blow up the plane; they had also agreed to let food and water aboard. It was, therefore, 'humanitarian' scruples which caused the operation to fail; next time, it warned, there would be no such mistakes.

The next occasion did not involve Black September, but George Habash's Popular Front. This left-wing organization prided itself on its world revolutionary role and, through its international connections, it had enlisted the services of three young members of the Japanese 'Red Army'. On 30 May, after training in Lebanon, the trio arrived at Lydda airport on an Air France flight from Rome, and, with the other passengers, they went into the customs hall to await their luggage. As soon as it arrived they whipped out their Kalashnikovs and grenades, and opened up on the crowd. They killed twenty-five people and wounded seventy-eight, many of them Christian pilgrims from Puerto Rico. Two of the *kamikazis* apparently committed suicide while a third, Kozo Okamoto, was overwhelmed before he could do likewise. The Puerto Rican pilgrims were not the planned target; it was their misfortune to get in the way. The planned target was passengers disembarking from an El Al flight and friends and relatives who had come to greet them; over and above that, the general idea was to 'kill as many people as possible at the airport,

Israelis, of course, but anyone else who was there'.[50] The PFLP described its 'Deir Yassin Operation' as a 'revolutionary retaliation' to the 'cheap trick' by which the 'butcher' Moshe Dayan and his men had foiled the Black September hijacking three weeks before. It was a more than adequate revenge, but it did have a flaw. It was a 'struggle by proxy'[51] which naturally provoked the jibe that, when it came to the supreme self-sacrifice, the Palestinians had to enlist foreigners to make it. It tended to reinforce the belief—apparently dear to General Dayan—that an Arab's nerve usually cracks in the end.

That was the background against which the Munich terrorists, tricked by the Germans, were bound to kill their hostages and, if necessary, themselves in the process.

TERROR UNLIMITED

After Munich, nothing Black September did could achieve the same impact. The law of diminishing returns began to operate; Black September went on trying all the same. The next major operation was a fiasco; this time, apparently, the Arabs' nerve did crack. On 28 December Black Septembrists seized six diplomats at the Israeli embassy in Bangkok, demanding the release of thirty-six Palestinian prisoners. But within a few hours two Thai ministers and the Egyptian ambassador had talked them out of it; the diplomats were released and the terrorists were flown to Cairo. A Beirut newspaper reported that a 'revolutionary court' might be set up to try the men for disobeying orders.

Ignominious failure in Bangkok meant cold-blooded murder in Khartoum. The world must be taught—a Black September source told a Beirut newspaper—to 'take us seriously'.[52] On 1 March eight armed men took over the Saudi embassy in the Sudanese capital. They seized Curtis Moore, the American *chargé d'affaires*, for whom a farewell reception was being held, his ambassador, Cleo Noel, the Belgian *chargé d'affaires*, Guy Eid, the Saudi ambassador and the Jordanian *chargé d'affaires*. They demanded the release, among others, of Abu Daoud, a *Fatah* leader, and sixteen comrades under sentence of death in Jordan. Abu Daoud had been convicted for subversive activities against the régime, and on Jordanian radio was later to confess—without much exaggeration—that 'there is no such thing as

Black September'; its operations, he said, were masterminded by three men: Abu Iyyad, generally regarded as the *Fatah* second-in-command, Abu Yusuf, chief of intelligence, and Abu Hassan, his assistant. After two extensions of their deadline, the Black Septembrists took Moore, Noel and Eid into the basement of the embassy, ignoring the impassioned pleas of a 'voluntary' hostage, the Saudi ambassador's wife. There were several bursts of machine-gun fire; when the terrorists re-emerged, said the ambassador's wife, they did not 'look like men who had killed before'.

They eventually gave themselves up to the Sudanese authorities, raising their arms in victory signs as they left the building. President Numairi of the Sudan was outraged. He saw 'no heroism in seizing defenceless men, when you yourself are armed to the teeth, bargaining with their lives for impossible demands, slaughtering them like sheep, and keeping their corpses for 24 hours to rot.' Many of his people agreed with him. A wall poster at Khartoum University denounced the exploit: 'Can any sane mind justify it? Does Israel's inhumanity justify the abandonment of all human values?'[53] It was inept and ungrateful too. A Libyan-backed branch of *Fatah* was behind the killing, or so it seemed to Numairi, and he produced much evidence to support his claim. It was apparently a coded message (*al-Nahr al-Barid*—Cold River—the name of a refugee camp in north Lebanon, which the Israelis had raided a fortnight before, killing forty people, mainly women and children) broadcast from a Palestinian radio station, probably in Tripoli, which instructed the Black Septembrists to despatch their victims.[54] And there seemed to be no doubt at all that the head and deputy head of the *Fatah* bureau in Khartoum had done all the local planning. This was an intolerable abuse of Sudanese hospitality—and all the more so in that it was Numairi who, in the Jordanian civil war of Black September 1970, had gone to Amman, at considerable personal risk, and reported back to the Arab leaders that King Hussein was out to crush the guerillas.

After the killing, there came the justification. Their operation had been 'in no way aimed at bloodshed', a communiqué said, 'but only to bring about the release of our heroes', who were being 'tortured and terrorized in violation of all human values'. As a diplomat in Amman, it claimed, Curtis Moore had helped King

Hussein to make war on the Palestinians. In fact, Moore had never been in Amman. Why the Belgian diplomat, Guy Eid, deserved the same fate the communiqué did not say. When King Hussein confirmed the death sentence on Abu Daoud and his sixteen comrades, and then said that he would only reprieve them if the resistance movement would give up all subversive activity against his régime, the PLO accused him of 'blackmail'. It certainly was—but why, in that case, Black September's exploits did not also rank as blackmail of the most cruel kind is something which the PLO never cared to explain.

In Khartoum, not only did Palestinian terrorists go further, in their contempt for conventional ethics, than ever before, they did so one week after Israel, in shooting down a Libyan airliner that had strayed over Sinai, had demonstrated a capacity for the same thing. At a stroke they wiped out the debit which their enemy had incurred in the balance-sheet of world opinion. They also played into the hands of the enemy in the rear. *Fatah*, King Hussein and others could plausibly argue, was a menace to every Arab régime.

So it went on, this terrorism that fed upon itself. It was not, strictly speaking, Black September any more. It was a host of imitators. The *fedayeen* had always been faction-ridden and un-disciplined, but, with the genie out of the bottle, they surpassed themselves, all but spawning a new organization for every exploit. They grew more and more capricious in their choice of targets, ever more remote from the real, the Palestinian, battlefield, ever more incoherent, not to say incomprehensible, in what they hoped to achieve. In July the 'Sons of the Occupied Lands' took a Japanese airliner on a ninety-hour odyssey round the Middle East; as 140 exhausted passengers made their getaway it finally went up in flames at Benghazi airport. The purpose—according to a mimeographed statement slipped under the doors of Beirut newspaper offices—was to punish the Japanese government, which had paid Israel six million dollars in compensation for the Lydda airport massacre a year before. In August, two members of the 'Seventh Suicide Squad' attacked passengers in the transit lounge of Athens airport with machine-guns and grenades, killing three and wounding fifty-five. The victims were about to board a Trans World Airways flight to New York. In its communiqué, the Seventh Suicide Squad crossed a new threshold in the logic of Palestinian violence: 'We have finally come to the conclusion that in order to make you understand us and appreciate our right to live . . . we must adopt your criminal methods . . . no sooner had we reached this conviction than we mounted our operations against you, the American people, against your men, women and children. These are not our usual ways, but it is you who forced them upon us.' Hostile crowds surged round the two gunmen on their way to an Athens court; they shouted 'death to the murderers'. In September it was the turn of the 'Punishment Organization' to deal a blow at Arab 'reactionaries'; its men seized the Saudi embassy in Paris and demanded the release of Abu Daoud, who, after a reprieve by King Hussein, was serving a life sentence instead. After a hectic two-day siege of the embassy, the terrorists secured a Syrian airliner to take them to Kuwait, then a Kuwait one to Saudi Arabia; their final flourish was a threat, not carried out, to hurl their four Saudi hostages from the aeroplane as it flew over the desert. In November the 'Organization of Arab Nationalist Youth' hijacked a Dutch airliner; during a two-day peregrination round the Middle East and the Mediterranean, they landed at five different airports and were denied access to three others; they demanded, among other things, the closure of transit camps which had been set up in Holland to receive Soviet Jews emigrating to Israel. In December, five Arabs shot their way out of the Rome airport terminal, killing two people as they went; threw incendiary bombs into a Pan American Boeing 707, burning to death twenty-nine people, including four Moroccan officials; seized seven Italian policemen as hostages, forced their way aboard a nearby Lufthansa Boeing 737 and ordered the crew to fly to Athens; demanded the release, on arrival in Athens, of the two gunmen of the Seventh Suicide Squad, shot one of their hostages and threw his body from the plane; flew off, empty-handed, to Damascus and Kuwait, where they released their hostages and surrendered. Apart from two obscure statements signed by 'the Palestinian people', this, the bloodiest hijack of them all, had no claimants. But perhaps the final extravagance, the *reductio ad absurdum* of the hijackers' reasoning, was reached eleven months later when the 'Martyr Abu Mahmud Group' seized control of a British Airways VC 10 and called on the British government to 'declare its responsibility for the greatest crime in history, which was the establishment of the Zionist

entity, and foreswear the accursed Balfour Declaration, which
brought tragedies and calamities to our region'.

The British Airways hijack was the last straw for Yasar Arafat
and the mainstream *Fatah* leadership. With a fanfare of publicity,
they mounted what was described as an all-out drive against the
hijackers, the 'renegades' and 'mercenaries', in their midst. In
Beirut the PLO announced that twenty-six people had been
arrested and would face public trial. If the trial did take place, it
was certainly not held in public. However, the PLO subsequently
claimed that the British Airways hijackers had been tried and
sentenced. Journalists were shown round a 'correction centre' in
Damascus; its inmates were convicted of acting 'against the
interests of the revolution'. They were also shown the PLO's
newly amended code of criminal law; hijacking that resulted in
loss of life had been made into a capital offence.

ACCEPTERS AND REJECTIONISTS

It was far from just a routine purge. Higher policy, indeed the
very *raison d'être* of resistance movement, was ultimately at stake.

The *Fatah* leadership had, of course, always disapproved of
hijackings and 'foreign operations' of that kind. Not that they
were dogmatic about it. They did not condemn Munich or
Khartoum; indeed, if *Fatah*, or a wing of it, did not actually
sponsor those two exploits, there was an implicit blessing in the
absence of serious criticisms. Although they took place outside
the land of Palestine, their targets were at least Israeli in one case
and (if one overlooks the unfortunate Guy Eid) official representatives of the arch-villain, America, standing behind Israel in the
other. The leadership also appeared to feel that, in certain circumstances of which they themselves were the judge, such operations could, if not overdone, further the cause. However, if the
wild, anarchic excesses that followed in Munich's wake had any
public relations value it was heavily outweighed by the disgust
they also engendered. Moreover, attacks on Arab targets, such as
the Saudi embassy in Paris, were flagrant violations of the sacred
Fatah principle of non-interference in Arab affairs. Above all,
however, the hijackings were becoming a challenge from a new
quarter: from the enemy within.

This was apparent before the October 1973 War, but it came

right into the open after it. That war, as we have seen, was a
great turning point in the history of the Arab-Israeli conflict, an
earthquake which, overnight, produced a massive shift, in the
Arabs' favour, of the Middle East balance of power. The Arabs
have always been painfully aware that, politically and militarily,
their potentialities—inherent in a large population, vast and
strategically located territories and, of late, oil wealth beyond the
dreams of avarice—far outstrip their actual power. If they could
only mobilize the resources at their disposal, they would quickly
bring Israel to its knees. But they never could; internecine conflict, endless upheavals and *coups d'état* frustrated them; their
régimes were incompetent or corrupt, their societies backward
and ill-adapted to the modern world; they lacked an institutional
system of collective decision-making. And yet that potential was
indeed *so* vast that it required only a minimal community of
purpose to convert it into an awesome force. And that is what, in
the unplanned *élan* of the October War, President Sadat achieved.

The Egyptian leader decided to exploit the new balance of
power, not to pursue the struggle but to end it. This was a revolutionary step. For all Arabs, not just the Palestinians, Palestine
is as much theirs as Oxfordshire is English, Pennsylvania
American. That is axiomatic, not worthy of discussion. They had
been deprived of it, in times of weakness and division, by alien
invaders who were no more entitled to it than the Crusaders
centuries before them; like the Crusaders, the Zionists would
eventually be driven out. Yet here was President Sadat expressing
a readiness to make peace with Israel and, with the weight of
Egypt behind him, calling on the rest of the Arab world to do
likewise. Egypt, Syria, Jordan and the Palestinians—all should
now face the Israelis across the conference table in Geneva. Obviously this peace would require Israeli concessions, territorial
and of other kinds, but, in the true historical perspective, it
would be the Arabs, not the Israelis, who were making the real,
the fundamental concession: the formal renunciation of the
'liberation' of Palestine as a national aim. They would be
acknowledging Israel's existence as an independent state, con-
secrating a pure Zionist gain against a pure Arab loss; it would
be an act of historic magnanimity. To sell this peace to the Arabs,
the very least that Sadat needed in return was that Israel should
surrender all the occupied territories. And there could be no-

thing like the full 'economic peace' which the Israelis apparently wanted. The idea, Sadat once said, that Mrs Golda Meir could drive down to Cairo on a shopping expedition was a pipedream. Nor could there be Israeli embassies in Arab countries, or anything like that. Such things might come in the end, but, after decades of hatred and bitterness, the Israelis could not expect so much so soon. Future generations would decide; what he had done was to take the all-important first step in that direction.

Selling this peace to the Palestinians was naturally Sadat's most difficult task. Almost all Palestinians believed that the tide had now turned against the Zionist intruders, the menace had been contained, the endless *faits accomplis* at their expense checked. Zionism had reached its zenith in 1967. But after the October 1973 War articles with titles like 'The Beginning of the Zionist Decline' began to appear in Palestinian journals. In one, Sabri Jiryis, a respected scholar who had lived most of his life in Israel and knew the country intimately, forecast the drastic repercussions, ideological, political, economic and psychological, which the war would have on an enemy that once seemed well-nigh invincible. But Palestinians reacted differently to this new and encouraging reality. Some accepted, some rejected a peaceful settlement. Those who accepted it—or at least did not strenuously oppose it—could be said, with a good deal of over-simplification, to fall into two schools of thought. One held that the more complete the peace the better. For it was in conditions of complete security that, paradoxical as that might seem to the uninitiate, the inherent unviability of the whole Zionist enterprise would be exposed. Thus in a second article, entitled 'Israel in Danger of Peace', Jiryis argued that both in the short and the long term the Arabs, not the Israelis, would come out 'winners' from a settlement. In effect, he said, the Jewish State—or at least the one they knew, exclusivist, expansionist, aggressive—would simply wither away. A revolution would break the hold of the old-guard activists—whether from Menachim Begin's Revisionist right, the religious parties, or the ruling Labour government—on the country's political life; social conflict, particularly between European and Oriental Jews, would intensify; immigration would fall off; normal relations with the Arabs would undermine the self-segregating instincts which had put down such deep roots among the people. Jiryis even went so far as to suggest that the

Arabs would have nothing to fear from an 'economic peace' with Israel. The idea of Israeli economic domination was far-fetched. Owing to its scarcity of manpower and economic resources, Israel would have more need of the Arabs than they of it. In recent years, he pointed out, talk of a peaceful settlement had always raised the question of what guarantees the Arabs should give the Israelis in return for their withdrawal from the occupied territories. 'But now it seems that, in the event of negotiations or a peace with Israel, it is Israel which must give guarantees to the Arabs, not the other way round. . . . And if Israel were obliged to abolish all those peculiarities which perpetuate its Zionist character, would that not lead, in the end, to the disappearance of that character and the rise of a secular democratic state in its place?'[55]

The other school of thought, espoused by much of the resistance leadership, held that the Palestinians should adopt an 'interim programme', seeking what 'immediate gains' they could from a settlement without forfeiting their 'historical' rights to the whole of Palestine. Ideologically, it was impossible for the *fedayeen* to renounce their official goal of complete liberation, of Revolution Till Victory. Yet it was also exceedingly difficult for them to boycott the peace-making. True, they now felt stronger, in relation to Israel, than they ever had before; but the new strength was essentially Arab, not Palestinian, and all the more so as the *fedayeen*, after their setback in Jordan, were simultaneously weaker, in relation to other Arabs, than they had ever been before. The Arabs, as represented by the two states which had done most of the fighting, wanted to exploit that strength to achieve peace. If they succeeded, the occupied territories would have to revert to someone, and there was a grave danger, unless the PLO came forward to claim Jerusalem and the West Bank, that the someone would once again be King Hussein. That would be almost as bad as not getting them back at all. Thus it was that a man like Abu Iyyad, who, through his links with Black September, had been widely regarded as one of the most uncompromising *Fatah* leaders, began to play a key role in preparing rank and file opinion for a new strategy that seemed to have much in common with President Bourguiba's 'doctrine of stages'. When, from a Palestinian refugee camp in 1965, the Tunisian leader had first propounded that infamous doctrine, arguing that the Arabs

should recognize Israel and seek to restore their lost rights by
negotiation rather than by an eventual war which they would
probably lose, he was burned in effigy round the Arab world.
'Absolute rejection', said Abu Iyyad, 'is sometimes a form of
escapism. . . . How long can we go on saying no? . . . Is it not a
provisional gain to get back part of our land, 23 per cent of
Palestine?'[56] A 'national authority' should be established, under
PLO control, on the liberated territory. What this really seemed
to imply was a fully-fledged mini-state of Palestine, co-existent
with Israel; but 'Palestine State' were two heretical words which
Abu Iyyad, and like-minded comrades, would not utter; for they
signified permanence, finality, the abandonment of historic
rights. Even one of the most enthusiastic advocates of the interim
programme, Nayif Hawatmeh, leader of the Popular Democratic
Front for the Liberation of Palestine, insisted that the 'national
authority' would indeed be able to 'retain its guns and pursue the
struggle in all its forms'.[57] Popular support for the new strategy
was strongest in the occupied territories, especially the West
Bank, now the stronghold of Palestinian moderation. As 'insiders', the West Bankers had a greater interest than the 'outsiders', mainly refugees of 1948 vintage, in achieving the
'immediate gain' of throwing off enemy rule. For they were still
living, most of them, on their own land, in their own homes. In
the inevitable upheavals of Revolution Till Victory they would
still have a lot to lose. And, in any case, was victory assured? An
organization calling itself the National Front for the Occupied
Lands urged the PLO to join the international peace-making
because 'it is clear that under the present circumstances the
realization of our full strategic goal is impossible'.[58] What all this
amounted to was the semi-official espousal of a new, and altogether more moderate form of Zionism-in-reverse. 'Remember', said a delegate to the Palestine National Council, 'remember
what Bengurion told the 22nd Zionist Congress at Basle in 1946:
that the Zionists would accept a state in a reasonable part of
Palestine without foregoing their historic rights to it all.'[59] It was
a greater contribution towards Arab-Israeli conciliation than the
concept of the Democratic State which had emerged six years
before.

The 'rejectionists', as they came to be known, would have none of it. They were Arab as well as Palestinian. 'The Arab nation', proclaimed the Beirut newspaper *al-Muharrir*,

> . . . today stands at the crossroads. Either it acquiesces in a sur-
> render solution, which consecrates the imperialist-Zionist entity
> in its heartland, consolidates and strengthens it, enabling it to
> carry out fresh expansionist aggressions against the Arab world
> and put it at its mercy for ever. Or it rejects such proffered solu-
> tions, looks to its own devices, summons up all its resources, all
> its human, financial, economic and military capability—a
> capability which, as the October War showed, is much greater
> than we imagined—and renews the fight on all fronts, however
> much that might upset the calculations of the great powers. Let
> us have done with the play-acting at Geneva . . .'[60]

The 'rejectionists' were very disappointed when President Sadat, reluctantly followed two days later by President Asad of Syria, accepted the ceasefire that ended the October War. It was their conviction that, had Egypt and Syria gone on, they would, by a process of spontaneous combustion that was already far advanced, have forced the entire Arab world to throw ever more resources into the fray. Israel would eventually have been over-whelmed. Why 'rescue' an enemy which could now so easily be finished off? They rejected Geneva and all it stood for. If the Arab world was emerging as a powerful force on the world stage, it should act like one. It was not in the nature of the strong to forget what they lost in times of weakness; France waited forty-eight years to get back Alsace-Lorraine. They believed that the fabulous Arab oil riches should be spent on arms, and yet more arms. The most prominent of Arab 'rejectionists' was that *exalté* and *enfant terrible*, Colonel Gadafi of Libya, who fired off a mes-sage to Sadat, telling him: 'You would have been greater, Mr President, if you had led us in a war with swords only and if, during it, we had lived in mountains, jungles and barren land, without oil or electricity, without towns or night-clubs, without politics, but with honour and dignity, with religion and Arabism. Let the land and buildings fall, but not the honour.'[61] The ruling Iraqi Baathists officially adopted the same viewpoint, and in many an Arab 'accepter' there lurked a suppressed 'rejectionist'.

Among the Palestinians, it was Dr George Habash's Popular Front which led the opposition to the interim programme. There must be no deviation from Revolution Till Victory, from the

stand their fathers and grandfathers had maintained since the
Balfour Declaration of 1917—'total rejection of the Zionist presence and fighting it to the end'. Habash held that, in its refusal to
take any clear-cut position, the *Fatah* leadership was simply
'burying its head in the sand'. The 'doctrine of stages' was so
much wishful thinking, for the 'present balance of Palestinian,
Arab and international power make it impossible to create a
national, democratic state or authority which our masses could
rely upon to continue the struggle'.[62] He was saying what the
Fatah leaders were not brave or honest enough to admit, that an
integral part of any settlement would be the once-for-all suppression of Palestinian belligerency. In the wake of the October
War, Habash and the 'rejectionists' kept up a relentless harassment which threatened, if the international peace-making ever
got seriously under way, to tear the whole resistance movement
violently apart. They accused *Fatah* of pusillanimously following
in the 'capitulationist' course charted by Egypt; they hinted
darkly at secret contacts between Arafat and Dr Kissinger; the
Popular Front walked out of the Executive Committee of the
PLO amid threatened moves to set up a rival, and truly revolutionary body of its own. For the extremists among them, international terrorism was the only answer to Arafat and his interim
programme, the only way of sabotaging that respectability which
he now felt he needed. The main culprit, in *Fatah*'s view, was
less George Habash than Abu Nidal, leader of a Baghdad-based
Fatah splinter group. For his part, Abu Nidal, suspected sponsor
of the British Airways and previous hijackings, warned of a
'Palestinian civil war'.

SUICIDE MISSIONS: QIRYAT SHMONA AND MA'ALOT

The civil war did not come. For one thing, the peace-making
never did grow serious enough for a cornered Arafat to make the
critical choice—such as going to the Geneva peace conference—
which might have provoked it. For another, he had not given up
the armed struggle. He was ready for a showdown with the 'rejectionists' over international terrorism; and in fact it did decline.
But he had no objection to operations which borrowed the essential techniques of international terrorism—hostage-taking and
blackmail—provided only that they took place on the soil of

Palestine proper. The spring and summer of 1974 saw a series of spectacular 'suicide missions' staged by 'accepters' and 'rejectionists' alike. In April, three young men belonging to Ahmad Jibril's Popular Front for the Liberation of Palestine (General Command), a small but militarily competent outfit, struck for the 'rejectionists'. They and eighteen Israelis, eight of them children, died in an apartment block in the northern town of Qiryat Shmona. According to the Israelis, the three terrorists systematically killed everyone they could find before they were killed themselves. According to the Popular Front, they seized hostages and demanded the release of a hundred Palestinian prisoners; when the Israeli soldiers stormed the building, they blew themselves and their hostages up. In a posthumous letter to Arafat, they told him that 'we have given our lives in confidence that, through you, our sacrifice, and that of all our martyrs, will not be sold for surrender solutions.'

A month later it was the turn of the 'accepters'. In the forefront of these was the Popular Democratic Front for the Liberation of Palestine. Its leader, Nayif Hawatmeh, often seemed to act as Arafat's trail-blazer in post-October 'moderation'. His latest 'first' was an interview, carried in a Tel Aviv newspaper, directly addressed to the Israeli people. He assured them that what the Front wanted was 'peaceful relations between Palestinians and Israelis'; for the time being, the official Palestinian ideal, the democratic, de-Zionized state for Arab and Jew in all of Palestine, was unattainable; meanwhile, the fulfilment of certain Palestinian rights—the establishment of an 'independent national authority' in the West Bank and Gaza and the return of the refugees— would open the way to a dialogue between 'progressive and democratic' Palestinians and Israelis 'opposed to imperialism and Zionism'.[63] On the night of 13 May, seven weeks after the interview, three of Hawatmeh's men slipped across the heavily guarded Lebanese frontier; the next evening they killed two Arab women in the back of a pick-up truck; at 3 a.m. on the 15th, Israel's Independence Day, they broke into an apartment in the village of Ma'alot, shooting three of its occupants. Then they seized about ninety teenagers in a nearby school. The choice of children as hostages was apparently deliberate;[64] that they happened to be a party of Gadna—Israel's school cadets—was hardly a mitigating circumstance. The terrorists demanded the release

of twenty-six prisoners—one for each year of Israel's existence—
and, among them, two Israeli Jews convicted of working for the
fedayeen. Equally deliberate, apparently, was Israel's failure to
negotiate with the terrorists for the lives of the schoolchildren.[65]
It was the climactic collision of two implacable logics and it ended
in catastrophe. The terrorists would release their hostages upon
receipt of a codeword, transmitted from Damascus, indicating
that twenty-six prisoners had arrived in the Syrian capital. The
codeword never reached them. The Isralie government's apparent readiness, for once, to bow to terrorist blackmail was no more
than an outward show of compassion to impress an anguished
public. It planned to storm the school all along, and shortly
before night fell the assault force went in; twenty children and
three terrorists died in the carnage, and some seventy were
wounded.

At first, the Israelis thought that the same 'rejectionist' organization which had mounted the Qiryat Shmona raid a month
before was behind this one too. It therefore came as an additional
shock to learn that if, in the persons of Hawatmeh and Arafat, the
Palestinians now had 'moderate' aims, their methods were still as
'extreme' as ever. *Fatah* had indeed come a long way from the
early innocence of—officially at least—military targets only. 'It
is sad and I dislike it,' said a PLO official, 'the Israelis have
indoctrinated us and we are now fighting like them. It is the
Israelis who have taught us, by bloody experience, that there can
be no differentiation between the soldier and the civilian.'[66]

The efficacy of the 'suicide mission' seemed beyond dispute.
To put it, as some guerillas did, in cold economic terms, it was
very cost-effective. The difference between a conventional high-
risk and a *kamikaze* operation was a quantum leap in one's kill
rate. Hitherto, that had generally been in the Israelis' favour, but
in the two most 'successful' of a series of 'suicide missions'—
Qiryat Shmona and Ma'alot—it was forty-eight dead Israelis
against six dead Palestinians. Only with the bombardment of the
refugee camps did the Israelis restore the balance in their favour.
For the Israelis, the guerillas believed, such losses were hard to
bear, while their own people, who had little to lose but their
camps, could absorb death and destruction with what, by contrast, looked like fatalistic serenity. The implication of the
'suicide mission', they believed, must also be deeply disturbing to

the Israelis, who could not but see in it a measure of Palestinian determination never to give up the struggle. In fact, they did not have to look far for evidence of the 'hysteria' which—even the enemy press admitted—was permeating Israeli society. They heard about hostile crowds, in the bereaved frontier townships, mobbing General Dayan, who had to be protected by his soldiers; about an opinion poll indicating that 68·6 per cent of the Israeli people disapproved of his hard-line, 'no compromise' policies; about the demoralization of Oriental Jews who, already resentful of their second-class status, were the main victims of the new terror; about anxiety over renascent nationalism among Hebrew-speaking Israeli Arabs and their recruitment to the *fedayeen*; about the old man in Ma'alot who murmured: 'there will never be peace in this cursed land'.

ARAFAT ADDRESSES THE UNITED NATIONS

The new terror appeared, on the whole, to make the Israelis more, not less, intransigent. Israel's little band of 'doves', who had found encouragement in Hawatmeh's conciliatory overtures, now seemed to command less influence than ever. Where was his dialogue now? 'We have been set back ten years', sighed Uri Avneri, 'the left has lost all the ground it won. That Hawatmeh should play into the hands of Golda Meir and Menachim Begin is quite beyond me.'[67] Under its new Prime Minister, Yitzhak Rabin, the Israeli government found all the hard-line pretexts it needed. Ma'alot proved that, for all his humanist posturing, Arafat's aim was still as wicked as ever: to destroy Israel. There was therefore no need for Israel to change its policies either. It would not recognize that there was such a thing as a 'Palestinian people', still less that the PLO had a right to represent it. A Palestine state would be a 'time-bomb'. No less than 70·8 per cent of the Israeli people agreed with him; they were opposed to such a state even within the framework of a general peace.

There could be no doubt, however, that Israeli intransigence was increasingly unrealistic. The doves continued to point that out. Few Israelis, one said, would still contend that there was no such thing as a 'Palestine problem'. 'Yet the majority still hope that, by not thinking about it, it will simply go away, that the earth will magically open and swallow all the Palestinians.' Time, he warned, was not on Israel's side; one day it would 'wake up and find the Palestinians at the negotiating table whether it liked it or not'.[68] The outside world pointed it out too.

Indeed, it was there, in the international diplomatic arena, that Arafat was about to score a run of spectacular successes which reinforced, and quite overshadowed, the military ones—and pushed Abu Nidal's threatened civil war still further into the background. The key forum was the UN. In 1947, with the General Assembly's vote for partition, the Zionists had won a famous victory. They claimed it as the charter of Israel's legitimacy; yet, even though it was already a verdict grotesquely weighted in their favour, they systematically flouted those of its provisions which did attempt to safeguard the rights of the Palestinians. Thus, if there were any international legitimacy by which the Palestinians could buttress their cause and strengthen their hand in the peace-making, it was the UN that should furnish it. They had been seeking a definition of their rights—and making considerable headway. In 1947 the UN, a much smaller, Western-dominated body than it later became, was prejudiced in the Zionists' favour; the boot was now on the other foot; the Palestinian cause became an automatic beneficiary of Afro-Asian bloc voting. The Palestinians' main objective was to achieve recognition for themselves not merely as refugees deserving of help on humanitarian grounds, but as a people with political aspirations. Thus, in 1969, the General Assembly first affirmed the right of 'the people of Palestine' to 'self-determination'; the denial of that right, it said, was at the root of the whole refugee problem. This was reiterated, with growing emphasis, in succeeding years until, in 1973, the Assembly established a clear link between self-determination and the right of return, the latter being an 'indispensable' prerequisite of the former. Recognition of the 'rights' was accompanied by recognition of the right to 'struggle' for their attainment. Accordingly, in a resolution of 1970, the Palestinians had been classified with various peoples of Southern Africa as victims of 'colonial and alien domination', and, as such, entitled to restore their rights 'by any means at their disposal'.[69]

The climax was still to come. The UN General Assembly decided, for the first time since 1952, on a full-dress debate of the 'Palestine Question' and invited the PLO, as the representative

of the Palestinian people, to take part in it. The climax was appro-
priately ushered in. In 1947, France had voted for partition, to
become one of the staunchest friends of Israel's early years. But
when, in October 1974, her Foreign Minister Jean Sauvagnar-
gues paid an official visit to Lebanon he made a point of taking
breakfast with Yasar Arafat. Afterwards, he reportedly confided
that Arafat was acquiring 'the stature of a statesman'; he was a
'moderate' who 'represents, embodies, the aspirations of the
Palestinians.'[70] The intimate repast, in the French ambassador's
residence, began and ended to the accompaniment of loud sonic
booms from overflying Israeli warplanes—apparently a gesture
of displeasure at what amounted to the first official recognition of
the PLO by a major Western power. A few days later came 'a
wedding feast for the Palestinians.' That is how Arafat described
the Arab summit conference in Rabat. In his eyes, the Hashemite
throne ranked second only to Israel as an instrument of Palestinian misfortunes. At Rabat, King Hussein bowed to overwhelming Arab pressure and gave away half his kingdom—ceding,
juridically, to the PLO the West Bank and Jerusalem which he
had lost, physically, to the Israelis in 1967. It was a diplomatic
victory that avenged the military defeat of Black September 1970.

Arafat's apotheosis—a fortnight later on the rostrum of the
UN General Assembly—was savoured by all Palestinians, 'accepters' and 'rejectionists' alike, as a moment of truly sweet
revenge. Not only—*pace* Golda Meir—did the Palestinians exist,
here was their leader getting the kind of passionate attention, as
he addressed the world, that no visiting statesmen, however
illustrious or controversial, had ever quite commanded before
him. Arab journalists reported from New York that the man who,
ten years before, began slipping across Israel's frontiers on almost unnoticed sabotage missions, was now mounting the most
spectacular commando operation of his career. For New York,
which contained more Jews than Israel itself, was definitely
enemy territory. Arafat, said one Jewish leader, was regarded
there with the kind of hatred once reserved for Hitler; the
atmosphere, before his arrival, generated 'the same sort of solidarity as when a war breaks out'.[71] A huge demonstration preceded him. Tens of thousands gathered in Hammarskjöld Plaza
in the shadow of the UN building to hear Israeli leaders denounce the outrage that was about to be perpetrated. They were

led by Senators and Congressmen from New York and half a
dozen other states, city councillors, the mayor, state officials,
trade union leaders and most of the candidates in the forth-
coming New York elections: such is the importance of Israel in
domestic American politics. The demonstrators, Jewish and
gentile, white and black, carried placards reading: 'UN Becomes
a Forum of Terrorism'; 'PLO is Murder International'; 'We
Refuse to Shake the Bloody Hand of the PLO'. Among the
speakers, Senator Henry Jackson, champion of Soviet Jewry,
earned the warmest applause. The UN decision to recognize the
PLO, he declared, 'threatens the already pale prospect of peace.
The United Nations reeks with the smell of blackmail.' On behalf of the AFL-CIO labour federation, another speaker called
for an American embargo of 'poisoned Arab oil'. He claimed that
America's European allies had already 'surrendered' to the
Arabs. Protest took a violent turn too. Militants of Rabbi Meir
Kahane's Jewish Defence League invaded the mid-town offices
of the PLO on Park Avenue and clubbed the assistant director
with a lead pipe. Russell Kellner, the League's 'operations
officer', called a press conference, and with a pistol on the table
in front of him, announced that the PLO 'murderers' had no
place in New York and that 'trained men' would 'make sure that
Arafat and his lieutenants do not leave New York alive'.[72]

Normally, on a sunny autumn weekend, the UN building is
packed with four or five thousand visitors. New Yorkers stroll
through the gardens of its eighteen-acre premises on the East
River, enjoying the chrysanthemums or the last roses of summer.
Suburban families descend on the gift shops in the basements
and sightseers take the guided tour. But not on 11 and 12
November 1974—on that weekend the whole place was her-
metically sealed off from the outside world. For Arafat was due
to address the General Assembly on Monday, the thirteenth, and
he was being guarded by the tightest security in UN history. Two
US Army helicopters brought him and his party from the airport; as they deposited him in the compound, other helicopters
patrolled overhead, launches cruised in the East River, sharpshooters kept watch from high buildings and hundreds of
specially assigned New York police and Federal Guards manned
wooden barricades in the streets below.

Shortly before noon, Arafat entered the General Assembly to a

standing ovation. Only the American delegation remained seated.
The chamber was crammed to capacity; only two groups of seats
were empty, those of the Israelis, who could not face this
Palestinian triumph, and the South Africans, who had been
suspended from the Assembly the night before. Arafat was
escorted to the rostrum by the Chief of Protocol and seated in the
white leather chair reserved for heads of state. Under a procedure
which had been invoked only once before—and that for no less a
personage than the Pope—he became the first leader of a
'national liberation movement' to receive such an honour. But he,
in return, did little to affect the demeanour of a head of state. He
was, as always, wearing his chequered *kefiyyah* head-dress, his
baggy trousers, open-necked shirt and ill-fitting jacket. And
when, acknowledging the applause, he raised his arms in a
revolutionary salute, he exposed the holster at his side. But for
once, apparently, he had at least had a proper shave and, it was
claimed, the holster was empty.

Figuratively speaking, however, he and the people he represented had certainly not disarmed—although they were
eagerly awaiting the day when they could. 'I have come bearing
an olive branch and a freedom fighter's gun. Do not let the olive
branch fall from my hand.' With this appeal, he ended his 100-
minute address. In the course of it he had dwelt lovingly on his
'Palestine of tomorrow', on his Democratic State for Moslem,
Christian and Jew. He called it his 'dream' and invited the Jews
now living in Palestine, all of them, to turn away from Zionist
ideology, which only offered them perpetual bloodshed, and to
share his dream.

The speech—and subsequent UN resolutions in favour of the
PLO—met with much the same dark fury, among Israel and its
supporters, as partition had, among the Arabs, twenty-seven
years before. From the Israeli ambassador there came a tirade
of rare violence not merely against Arafat's band of 'murderers
and cutthroats' who had plunged the UN into a 'Sodom and
Gomorrah of ideals and values' but against the international
community which, in 'days of degradation and disgrace, of surrender and humiliation', had let them do it. For the Foreign
Minister, 'the voice of Arafat was, and remains, the voice of indiscriminate terror, the voice of the gun, with nothing in it of the
olive branch of peace'. The Minister was not to be deceived by

gracious rhetoric. Nor was the Israeli press. It was obvious, the
commentators said, that any Palestine State in the West Bank or
Gaza would be no more than a platform for renewing warfare
against an Israel conveniently reduced to its earlier, more vul-
nerable dimensions. 'No reasonable person—if there are any left
in a world thirsty for oil—can ask us to hand over these regions
to the PLO, unless it expects Israel to commit suicide.'[73]

But where the Israelis saw only the reiteration, in beguiling
form, of an intransigent orthodoxy, the Palestinians, and particularly the West Bankers, saw more of the post-October moderation. Arafat's 'dream' was the only thing the Israelis noticed; the
practical, immediate goal he put forward, the 'national authority',
was what mattered to them. The Israelis only saw the gun; the
Palestinians saw the olive branch. For most Palestinians, the
'dream' was mere lip-service to the goal of complete liberation.
It was self-evident that Arafat had to pay it, for he had to appease
those, the 'rejectionists', who believed that Revolution Till Victory, continuous armed struggle, was the only way to change the
nature of Israel, the only way to achieve that goal which the
newly 'moderate' Arafat and the unyielding George Habash still
officially had in common. In reality, however, the establishment
of a Palestine State could only mean that the struggle, if it continued at all, would be a peaceful and political one. The final
Middle East settlement would outlaw violence. Iron-clad
guarantees would have to come from all parties—and not least
from the *fedayeen*, who, for the past ten years, had fought and
died in the conviction that violence, or revolutionary counter-
violence as they considered it, was their people's only salvation.
Many Palestinians, especially West Bankers, understood and
accepted that. 'For us', said the editor of Jerusalem's militant
al-Fajr newspaper, 'the democratic Palestine is a dream too, but
we believe that only by a gradual political process can the Arab
and Jewish states in Palestine merge into one'.[74] It was also
widely understood that that might be as far as Zionism-in-
reverse would ever get, that what Arafat postulated as a transitional stage of indefinite duration would really be the final one.
'Deep down', said a professor from Bir Zeit college, '80 per cent
of us realize this. It is very difficult for us to say goodbye to what
is ours—Haifa, Jaffa and most of Jerusalem—but we are in effect
telling the Israelis that we are ready to do so. We are saying that

we no longer want to drive them out of the land from which they drove us. Some of us still want to do so, but they are not the dominant voice. But in return the Israelis must withdraw from at least all the territories occupied in 1967. Nothing less is feasible. They must grasp this.'[75]

They did not grasp it. Moreover, the professor did not really expect them to do so. If the Israelis saw no change in the Palestinians, he, like most of his compatriots, certainly saw very little change in them. In theory, Arafat was still holding his olive branch, but it quickly withered with neglect. The Israelis, the Arabs understood, were congenitally incapable of abandoning the policy of force upon which they had always relied. The more obvious the renaissance of the Palestinians became, the more obdurately they refused to recognize it. The cartoonists now portrayed Israel as the man who put his fingers in his ears and refused to listen. Its 'refusal to accept realities', its 'perseverance in the absurd' became dominant themes of the editorialists. It was a defiant posture which they found all the more remarkable in that, as they saw it, Israel simply did not command the resources to sustain it. All the signs were, they said, that, whatever the strictly military situation, the underlying balance of power was continuing to shift in the Arabs' favour. Since the October War, said one Beirut newspaper, 'the whole Zionist entity has been in a state of permanent crisis which is now all but out of control'. Israel, said another, could no more expect to live as a 'foreign body' in its region than Rhodesia or South Africa in theirs.[76] But they warned that Israel would probably try to turn the tables on the Arabs in the one field, the military one, where it still had a chance of doing so. Such an attempt would be irrational, they pointed out, in so far as the main reason for its present plight was the economic, diplomatic and psychological consequence of the last war. But then the picture of a near-hysterical enemy, of an Israel on the run, an embattled, fortress Israel girding itself to die by the sword by which it was created was also taking root in the Arab mind.

The Israelis certainly had not laid down the gun. Six days after Arafat's apotheosis at the UN, four men of Nayif Hawatmeh's Popular Democratic Front stormed an apartment building in the town of Beit Shean. They killed four and wounded twenty Israelis before they were killed themselves. A maddened crowd seized the bodies of the dead terrorists, threw them from the windows and set fire to them. So blind was their fury that they apparently mistook a dead or dying Israeli for a terrorist and finished him off too. It was a particularly gruesome 'suicide mission' which showed that Arafat, in raising an olive branch in one hand, certainly had not dropped *his* gun either.

NOTES

1. *Palestine Documents, 1967* (Arabic), Institute for Palestine Studies, Beirut, 1968, pp. 264, 1084.
2. Al-Azm, Sadiq, *Left Studies on the Palestine Problem* (Arabic), Dar al-Tali'ah, Beirut, 1970, pp. 53, 55.
3. See Kazziha, Walid, *Revolutionary Transformation in the Arab World*, Charles Knight, London, 1975, pp. 52-3.
4. Rashid, Muhammad (Nabil Shaath), *Towards a Democratic State in Palestine*, PLO Research Centre, Beirut, 1970, p. 16.
5. Al-Sharqawi, *Fatah—1965-1971, op. cit.*, p. 181.
6. Rashid, *op. cit.*, p. 15.
7. *Ibid.*, p. 48.
8. Al-Sharqawi, *op. cit.*, p. 321.
9. Yaari, *Strike Terror, The Story of Fatah, op. cit.*, p. 150.
10. Khatib, Husam, 'Whither the Palestinian Revolution?', *Palestine Affairs* (Arabic), Beirut, October 1971, pp. 5-7.
11. *Ibid.*, p. 7.
12. *Ibid.*, p. 7.
13. Al-Sharqawi, *op. cit.*, p. 318.
14. *Ibid.*, p. 317.
15. *Haaretz*, 20 October 1968.
16. Orr, A., and Machover, Moshe, *ISRAC*, March 1970.
17. *The Other Israel, op. cit.*, p. 176.
18. Harkabi, Yehoshafat, *Palestinians and Israel*, Keter Publishing House, Jerusalem, 1974, pp. 70-126.
19. Shaath, Nabil, 'Palestine of Tomorrow', *Palestine Affairs* (Arabic), Beirut, May 1971, p. 9.
20. *Al-Muharrir*, 19 November 1968.
21. Al-Sharqawi, *op. cit.*, p. 318.
22. *Ibid.*, pp. 313-15.
23. Sayigh, Yusif, *The Attrition of Israel as a Result of the Military Struggle, Palestine Affairs* (Arabic), Beirut, September 1971, p. 58.
24. Military spokesman, 8 August 1968.
25. Sulh, Alia, *al-Nahar*, 4 June 1968.
26. Yasar Arafat, to *Rose el-Youssef* (Cairo weekly), 11 November 1969.
27. Rashid, *op. cit.*, p. 33.

28. *Filastin Al-Thaurah*, January 1968, p. 25.
29. *Ibid.*, September 1968, p. 29.
30. *Der Stern*, 16 September 1970.
31. Khatib, *op. cit.*, p. 8.
32. *Al-Anwar*, 12 February 1969.
33. See *The Guardian*, 29 December 1970.
34. Yaari, *op. cit.*, p. 353.
35. *The Guardian*, 20 July 1971.
36. *Africasie*, Paris, 24 January 1972.
37. 1 December 1971.
38. *Arab Report and Record*, London, Issue No. 4, 1972, p. 104.
39. 7 September 1972.
40. Khatib, Husam, 'Thoughts on Palestinian Violence', *Palestine Affairs*, March 1972, p. 23.
41. *Observer* Foreign News Service, 15 September 1972.
42. Al-Sharqawi, *op. cit.*, p. 317.
43. *Al-Sayyad*, 13 September 1972.
44. *Le Nouvel Observateur*, 11 September 1972.
45. *Al-Nahar*, 24 November 1972.
46. See p. 251.
47. *Time*, 2 October 1972.
48. *Ibid.*
49. *The Guardian*, 3 October 1972; see pp. 164–70.
50. *Ibid.*, 1 June 1972.
51. Haikal, Muhammad, *al-Ahram*, 9 June 1972.
52. *Al-Muharrir*, 3 March 1973.
53. *The Guardian*, 22 March 1973.
54. *Sunday Times*, 29 April 1973.
55. *Al-Nahar*, 7, 8, 9 November 1973.
56. *The Guardian*, 17 January 1974.
57. *Ibid.*
58. *Ibid.*
59. *Ibid.*, 10 June 1974.
60. 5 January 1974.
61. *The Guardian*, 18 January 1974.
62. *Ibid.*
63. *Le Monde*, 23 March 1974.
64. *Sunday Times*, 19 May 1974.
65. *The Times*, 29 May 1974.
66. *Daily Star*, Beirut, 19 May 1974.
67. *Le Nouvel Observateur*, 21 May 1974.
68. *Davar*, 30 June 1974.
69. See Armanazi, Ghayth, 'The Rights of the Palestinians—the International Definition', *Journal of Palestine Studies*, Beirut, Vol. III, No. 3, 1974.
70. *The Guardian*, 22 October 1974.
71. *International Herald Tribune*, 11 November 1974.
72. *The Times*, 13 November 1974.

73. *Yediot Aharonot*, 14 November 1974.
74. *The Guardian*, 27 December 1974.
75. *Ibid.*
76. *Ibid.*, 14 November 1974.

Epilogue

YASAR ARAFAT'S United Nations address was a high point in the Palestinians' reviving fortunes; but more successes were yet to come. At its next session, a year later, the General Assembly formally branded Zionism 'a form of racism and racial discrimination'. Israel was expelled from UNESCO in protest against its Judaization of Arab Jerusalem, while the PLO was admitted as an observer to such UN bodies as the International Labour Organization, Habitat and even the International Atomic Energy Agency. What Israel and most of its Western friends thought about the Zionism-Equals-Racism resolution, and other such progeny of Third World bloc voting, was reflected in the rumbustious oratory of Daniel Moynihan, the American ambassador to the UN, who declared that the 'abomination of anti-Semitism has been given the appearance of international sanction'. But Israel and its Western friends were not always so united; indeed, in the court of Western opinion, Israel's reputation, though still high, was suffering a steady decline. For a doting American public, the 'bastion of democracy in the Middle East' was no longer quite the paragon of virtue it used to be; answering its every wish was no longer quite so pressing a necessity for American governments. Even as Moynihan was abhorring the new anti-Semitism another State Department official was telling the House of Representatives that the United States should work towards 'a reasonable definition of Palestinian interests'; the Israelis saw in the so-called 'Saunders document' the first timid American recognition of the obvious: any Middle East settlement must grant the Palestinian people the right of self-determination which they have always sought to deny them. A few days after that, to Israel's 'great distress', the US voted in favour of the PLO's participation in a Security Council debate.

Then Moynihan's successor at the UN, William Scranton, provoked an official protest against his severe criticism of Israel's
colonization policies in the occupied territories; well over sixty
settlements had been established since the June 1967 War.

Official American strictures were no longer as strenuously
contested, inside America itself, as they once were. For many
years Israel's hold over American Jewry, that most potent and
energetic of lobbies, had been all but complete. For the main
Jewish organizations, official Israeli attitudes—on the Palestinians, the Arab world and the road to peace—were theirs too.
Those who challenged them were as voices crying in the wilderness. But when the Israeli 'dove', Arie Eliav, visited America in
early 1976 he observed that the American Jewish scene was
changing. 'It's deceptive,' he said. 'It's like a frozen river: the
surface is quiet, but underneath, watch out.'[1] Ripples of dissent
were indeed beginning to splash into view. In December 1975,
Rabbi Henry Siegman, Executive Director of the Synagogue
Council of America, defined Israeli policy as one of seeking to
'avoid at all costs, or delay as long as possible, a confrontation
with the larger question of a final peace'. He expressed the fear
that such a policy 'may contain the seeds of disaster' because
neither the US nor the world would accept the 'permanent
annexation' of large slices of Arab territory.[2] Early in 1976 the
Social Action Unit of Reform Judaism adopted a formal resolution criticizing Israel's 'provocative actions' in the West Bank;
the Israeli Government had permitted the expansionist zealots
of the Gush Emunim movement to celebrate Passover with a
two-day march through the West Bank proclaiming 'the inalienable right of every Jew to every part of Eretz Israel', and it
had failed to dislodge them from the 'illegal' settlement which
they had established in the hitherto exclusively Arab neighbourhood of Nablus.

But nothing did Israel more harm than the Arab rioting which
erupted in the first half of 1976. A primary cause was renewed
manifestations of the insatiable Zionist appetite for Arab land.
These were not confined to the occupied territories. Inside pre-
1967 Israel, the government was planning to expropriate a
further 6,000 acres of what little land remained in Arab hands.
Its motives were transparent; in some districts of Galilee, the
Arabs, with their very high birth rate, now outnumbered Jews;

it was determined to halt this change in the 'demographic balance'—as the official euphemism put it—which was held to be not merely an intolerable affront to Zionist ideology but a threat to the very integrity of the state. The rioting shattered the carefully fostered illusion that Israel's Arabs, if not content with their lot, were at least resigned to it; it demonstrated that the October 1973 War, the subsequent shift, in the Arabs' favour, of the Middle East balance of power and the diplomatic successes of the PLO had deeply affected not only the West Bankers but the 'forgotten' Palestinians of Israel proper. They also caused Israel to exhibit that ugly, oppressive side of its nature which it had generally managed to hide from the world. Palestinians were now 'news'—another sign of the times—and although investigative zeal has never been the hallmark of Western newsmen based in Israel, they showed enough of it on this occasion to exasperate a government unaccustomed to such persistently unflattering scrutiny. The authorities tried to hinder journalists' work, and the Foreign Press Association was moved to protest against a campaign of slander which insinuated that the Palestinians had been bribed to stage their demonstrations by the journalists themselves.

As if the riots were not damaging enough, the Israeli Government chose this time to dramatize one of the most significant, if hitherto little publicized, of contemporary international friendships. The official visit to Israel of John Vorster, Prime Minister of South Africa, and the warm welcome he received, consecrated the deepening alliance between two states whose predicament and methods of dealing with it have long been remarkably similar. After Vorster's visit a South African cartoonist portrayed him expostulating: 'What do you mean, some of my best friends? Some of my only friends . . .'[3] In September came the embarrassing leak of the 'Koenig Memorandum'; in this top-secret document a high official of the Ministry of the Interior put forward proposals, overtly racist in tone, for 'thinning out' the Arab population of Northern Israel. By the end of 1976 well over half the Soviet Jews who had secured exit visas for Israel were heading straight for the US and other Western countries instead; American Jewish charitable organizations came under heavy Israeli pressure to cut off aid to all such undeserving 'drop-outs'; if Israel had its way, a group of emigrés protested, that would

produce a situation in which 'the Jews of the Free World help
the KGB stop Soviet Jews leaving the USSR'.[4]

These, and other, blemishes deepened the misgivings of
American Jewry, and this, in turn, could not but help President
Jimmy Carter and his new administration to screw up the necessary courage for the kind of 'even-handed' peace-seeking diplomacy which Israel has always managed to sabotage in the past.

The Palestinians could only rejoice at Israel's growing difficulties.
But they were soon in deep trouble too. It was profoundly ironic
that just as they were scoring brilliant victories, in the international diplomatic arena, against the main enemy they should
be struck with devastating force by the enemy in the rear. It was
another, scarcely credible twist in what Arafat had once called
'an Arab plot'.[5]

Disunity has always been the Arabs' curse. In the October
1973 War President Sadat spurred them to a higher degree of
collective purpose than had ever been achieved before. In the
diplomatic struggle that followed the ceasefire he did more than
anyone to destroy that purpose. Although, for reasons we have
described,[6] the war was an earthquake that shook Israel to its
foundations, its army came close, in the end, to winning it; it
thereby denied Sadat the fulfilment of what, in the initial
triumph of crossing the Suez Canal, he had proclaimed as his
war aims—the immediate evacuation of the territories which
Israel had occupied in the June 1967 War. Sadat turned to
America and Dr Kissinger for the achievement of a 'just peace'.
Desperate to prove that the much-glorified Crossing really was
the victory he claimed, he acquiesced in the two Sinai disengagement agreements negotiated by his 'friend Henry' in
prodigious feats of shuttle diplomacy. The Israelis did yield
territory, but not much, and their concessions were richly re-
warded. The first disengagement, in January 1974, was followed
five months later by a similar one on the Golan Heights, but the
second, in September 1975, drew the fierce reproaches of Sadat's
war-time Syrian partner, and charges on all hands that he had
sold out the Arab cause. To deal separately with its neighbours has
always been a guiding purpose of Israel's foreign policy. But the
second disengagement agreement actually achieved much more
than that: it consecrated the bankruptcy of a whole political order.

In February 1949, the Egypt of King Farouk had been the first of the four defeated 'front-line' states to conclude armistice agreements with the new-born State of Israel; within six months of this initial, much-condemned defection, the three others, Lebanon, Jordan and Syria, had all followed suit. The armistice agreements set off a wave of violent upheaval in the Arab world. President Nasser and the 'revolutionaries' of his generation attributed the Catastrophe to the rottenness of the old order—the monarchies, the régimes of the *beys* and the *pashas*, the great landowners and feudalists, selfish, frivolous, reactionary, subservient to the Western creators of Israel—and, ostensibly, at least, their central mission was to expunge the shame of defeat. But first they were to transform and modernize their societies. While the transformation lasted Israel would enjoy a respite; once it had been completed the 'liberation' of Palestine would come, so to speak, as crowning proof of their success. By any but the most partisan assessment, however, the 'revolutionary' order which the Catastrophe threw up has proved a failure. The Arab world enjoys—to take the most famous slogans of the past quarter-century—neither Unity, nor Freedom nor Socialism. As for Palestine, far from liberating it, the 'revolutionaries' lost more of it. President Nasser called the 1967 defeat the *Naksa*, the Setback, but in reality it was another *Nakba*, another Catastrophe— and a worse one. In October 1973, the Arabs made a partial recovery. But this was achieved in spite, as much as because of, the régimes. It meant that they had finally succeeded, and scandalously late, in achieving a minimal mobilization of that vast potential which their countries' strategic location, manpower and immense wealth had bestowed upon them. But here, eight years after the second Catastrophe, was the leader of the 'revolutionary' camp, Nasser's heir, making a deal with Israel which, in the words of a Palestinian leader, 'King Farouk would not have dared to make.'[7] It was 1949 all over again; for all his fury, President Asad of Syria was only too anxious to do likewise.

The Palestinians paid the price of Arab bankruptcy. True, the *fedayeen* organizations, racked by their own 'inner sickness',[8] shared some of the bankruptcy, but that hardly diminished the enormity of what the régimes now perpetrated against them.

The Lebanese civil war, which began in April 1975, was largely internal in origin, but after the second Sinai disengagement, it developed into an Arab civil war by proxy. In Arabic commentaries on the war, one word, *tahjim*, occurred again and again. It means 'a cutting down to size', and it furnishes a key insight into a uniquely complicated and savage conflict. All the peace-seeking Arab régimes shared the same strategic purpose; they all wanted to cut the Palestinians down to size. But, tactically divided, some of them wanted to cut each other down to size too. President Asad was striving to establish a *Greater-Syrian* power base which he could use, in the wake of Sadat's sell-out, for a counter-strategy of his own; if Egypt was to be the gateway for *Pax Americana* in the Middle East, he was determined that Syria should at least be the key that unlocked the gate. To this end he had already allied himself with King Hussein's Jordan on one flank; a few years before that would have been judged a most unnatural alliance, because Hussein—whom Asad used to describe as 'an asset to the gangster-state [of Israel]'[9]—was a miraculous survival from that 'reactionary', pre-1948 order which the 'revolutionaries' had tried to replace. Asad now sought to bring the Palestinian resistance movement—once destined, in his own words, to help 'blast the Zionist presence out of the Arab homeland'[10]—firmly under his wing in their last, Lebanese refuge on the other flank. In the first half of the war, when the Egyptians were encouraging the right-wing Christians, he threw most of his weight, albeit cautiously, behind the Palestinians and their local Moslem-leftist allies. In the second half, when the Christians were getting the worst of it, he contracted an alliance with them that was even more flagrantly unnatural than the one with King Hussein. For the Christians' other ally was Israel.

Thus it was that Syria, the so-called 'beating heart of Arabism', now connived with the devil himself against the supreme, the Palestinian embodiment of the Arab cause; thus the self-same Baathist régime which had first promoted the *fedayeen* in the fire-breathing irresponsibility of its youth now turned against them in the survivalist cynicism of its decline. Among the Palestinians, Black June, 1976—when the full dimensions of the 'Arab plot' were finally exposed—is remembered as a greater villainy than Black September, 1970; and Tal al-Zaatar, the re-

fugee camp whose grisly siege and fall marked the climax of the
civil war, as a synonym for the treachery which Arab historians
will almost certainly judge it to have been.

The Egyptian régime heaped abuse on the Syrian Baathists—
while it secretly rejoiced at their handiwork. President Asad had
incurred most of the odium of cutting the Palestinians down to
size; and he had overreached himself in the process. So Egypt—
with the help of increasingly powerful, oil-rich Saudi Arabia—
now cut Asad down to size in his turn.

Reconciled—at the Riyadh summit conference of October 1976
—in the blood of the Palestinians, the two war-time partners
swung from the extremes of mutual antipathy into yet another of
the umpteen experiments in Arab 'unity'. They set up a joint
political command to co-ordinate their peace-seeking strategy.
They began a great 'peace offensive' designed to prove their
moderation. The chances of ending the world's most dangerous
and implacable conflict had never looked better. Shortly after
his inauguration, President Carter called 1977 'the brightest hope
for peace that I can recall'. Undoubtedly the greatest asset of the
peace-seekers was the changing outlook of the Arab world;
public opinion, led by the Palestinians themselves, was readier
than ever before to accept the kind of settlement—a mini-state of
Palestine—which seemed to be in the making. The readiness
came, in its more positive form, from the feeling that, with the
underlying balance of power now shifting in their favour, the
Arabs could afford to be magnanimous. In its negative form, it
came from apathy and fatigue; the people were tired of a
struggle, which, in spite of the shifting balance of power, their
governments conducted with such incompetence.

President Carter's high regard for Israel seems to spring
largely from his Southern Baptist convictions; he has actually
said that, for him, the Jewish State is 'a fulfilment of biblical
prophesy'. At the same time, however, he has acknowledged the
Arabs' moderation and, in his first few months of office, he led
them to hope that it might earn the American response, in the
shape of real pressure on Israel, that it deserves. He began to
stake out public positions with all the boldness of his new-style
open diplomacy. He outlined his conception of the final peace;
but for 'some minor adjustments', he said, Israel should relin-

quish all the territories it had occupied in 1967; and a 'homeland'
must be found for the Palestinian refugees, 'who have suffered
for many, many years'. It was almost as encouraging to the
Palestinians as it was disturbing to the Israelis. 'If this is true,'
said Yasar Arafat, in an unprecedented tribute to an American
president, 'he has touched the core of the problem without
which there can be no settlement.'

But was it enough? The chances for peace may have looked
better than ever before—but they were not good. By the spring
of 1977 the Arab régimes were degenerating, as a result of their
moral and political bankruptcy, about as fast as the progress
towards a settlement which alone could save them. President
Sadat—mainstay of the emergent *Pax Americana*—had been
shaken by the worst riots since the Egyptian people rose against
British rule in 1919. President Asad was struggling to contain the
consequences of his Lebanese adventure. His grip was much
tighter than Sadat's, but the dangers which beset him, though
less easy to discern, were no less real. Some things could not be
hidden. His enemies resorted to acts of violence and sabotage.
In the most spectacular of them, Abu Nidal, the Iraqi-based
Fatah renegade, despatched four desperadoes to occupy the
Semiramis Hotel in the heart of Damascus; the 'Tal al-Zaatar
Operation'—Arabs seizing Arab hostages—was public-relations
terrorism at its most shocking. It was a symptom of the hatreds
and frustrations poisoning the Arab body politic—and threatening it with complete disintegration. One year after the first
Catastrophe—with the *coup d'état* which brought Husni Za'im
to power in Syria—the old order had begun to collapse; nearly
ten years after the second Catastrophe the 'revolutionary' order
which replaced it, reprieved by the October 1973 War, was still
in place—but its eventual collapse threatened to be incomparably
more dramatic.

The chances for peace were not good, either, because, although the Arabs might have changed, the Israelis had grown
more unbending than ever. As we have seen, it has always been
Israel's instinct, in Bengurion's words, 'to hold what we have',
to build its security, not on agreement with its neighbours, but on
overwhelming military superiority. In the short run—and in
spite of the parlous state of its economy—Israel now felt stronger
than at any time in its history. The then Prime Minister, Yitzhak

Rabin, said that Israel was now 'stronger than all the Arab states combined'; each year since the October 1973 War it had received $1,500 million-worth of armaments compared with a mere $300 million-worth in the three years that preceded it. For all the doubts assailing American Jewry, they were still ready to exert immense influence on their protégé's behalf. Above all, the Israelis could draw comfort from their enemies' disarray. They sensed that by 'holding what we have' they could not but deepen it. The turmoil that followed the first Catastrophe had brought them several years' respite; the greater turmoil that threatened to flow from the second would buy them another respite. To 'gain time' was, as Rabin explained, Israel's main purpose; somehow, it had to get through 'seven lean years' during which, according to his (exceedingly optimistic) estimate, America and Europe would still be dependent on Arab oil.[11]

So once again Israel dug in its heels. As American peace-seeking diplomacy gathered momentum, its leaders returned to their old, uncompromising refrain: they would never sit down with the PLO at Geneva, not at least before it had amended the Palestine National Charter which called for Israel's 'destruction', and they would never permit the rise of an 'Arafat state'. In the general elections in May, the rightwing *Likud* trounced the ruling Labour party; thus democratically did the fanatical, openly expansionist wing of the Zionist movement come triumphantly into its own; the former *Irgun* leader, and Prime Minister-designate, Menachim Begin, immediately proclaimed his attachment to Greater Israel; what he called the 'liberated' territories would not be given up in the peace settlement which, in the same breath, he urged upon the Arabs.

Intransigence has worked so far. Or at least, in spite of four wars, that is a judgement to which most Israelis still resolutely subscribe. The advocates of conciliation, who recently entered into direct contacts with PLO representatives, remain a small, if growing, minority. Perhaps the majority are right: the Arabs could no more reconcile themselves to the Israel of 1948 than the Israel of 1967. Perhaps half a loaf, half-Palestine (or, to be precise, 23 per cent of it) is the kind of half-justice they could never accept: having recovered Nablus and Bethlehem, they would demand Jaffa and Nazareth too. Perhaps. But, if one thing is certain, it is that intransigence cannot work for ever. Dr Kis-

singer perceived its ultimate consequences. 'It's tragic to see a
people dooming themselves to a course of unbelievable peril', he
told Israeli leaders in a moment of anguished failure.[12] No
friend of Israel worked harder, and more thanklessly, to save
Israel from itself. His disengagement agreements did buy it more
time. But the Arabs will not remain in such disarray for ever; a
new order will eventually emerge which is better able and—in
the absence of a peaceful settlement—more determined to
mobilize the vast potential at its disposal.

The olive branch will never replace the gun unless the outside
world does save Israel from itself, and in a much deeper sense
than Dr Kissinger even contemplated. Without that salvation the
last act of violence in the Middle East will be nuclear; the fatal
Zionist propensity for the extreme solution, which we have seen
in action at every stage of this history, all but guarantees it.
Israel has not signed the Non-proliferation Treaty, it possesses
the Bomb, and the further development of its nuclear capacity is
the only way that it can match its enemies' ever-growing conventional strength. The logic of force on which it has always
relied is ultimately a self-destroying one. But without a peaceful
settlement nothing can stand in the way of its apocalyptic appeal:

> From time to time the U.S. Administration wonders [in] all
> innocence why we're so greedy. From time to time it plays dumb
> and pretends not to know of this tragic situation where three
> million weary Jews who've just begun building their home in the
> desert are being forced to maintain a huge military force to defend
> themselves against a hundred-million millionaires building up an
> army of Nato size. The U.S. Administration acts as if it had no
> idea that nearly half our Gross National Product lies under wraps
> in our military emergency stores, and that if it weren't for this
> back-breaking burden we wouldn't be standing like beggars at
> their door.
>
> All this generous American assistance, even when it's called
> economic, goes directly or indirectly to sustain a losing arms
> race. All the parties involved have an interest in this race, each
> for his own reasons—except Israel who can never win it. To be
> sure, Israel won't be defeated in battle: it'll collapse—eco-
> nomically and socially—under the fearful load of endless arms
> purchases. . . .
>
> It's a fully planned vicious circle: when the Arabs have
> 10,000 tanks, we'll need at least 6,000; when they have 20,000—

we'll need 12,000, and so on *ad infinitum*. Interim agreements or not—the race will go on, and our total dependence on the U.S.

And this total dependence will mean total retreat to the 1967 frontiers and the sticking of a Palestinian State in our throat, *without peace*.

Of course the Americans don't intend to abandon us. They'll stand by their obligations. So their post-Yom Kippur [October 1973 War] dialogue with us runs like this: 'If you don't toe the line you won't get arms,' they tell us. 'But if you withdraw and make us the dominant power in the region we'll safeguard your existence.' 'What kind of existence is that', we say, 'where Soviet missiles sit 12 miles from Tel Aviv and only 200 yards from Jerusalem? You call that secure boundaries?' 'As long as we're here we'll protect you.' 'And what if you're not?' 'That's a calculated risk you must take, because what's your alternative?'

Our one and only alternative to our gradual destruction by arms race is to develop a nuclear deterrent of our own. It's our single chance for telling our many enemies and our one friend: that's it, we're not playing any more, we refuse to go on running for ever in the circles you've drawn for us. We want no more of your arms, we want a sophisticated educational system.

Sooner or later we'll have to say it out loud. Sooner or later we'll have to announce: if any Arab army crosses this green line we reserve the right to use atomic weapons, and if it crosses the red line we'll drop the bomb automatically, even if this whole country is blown up by nuclear retaliation. You don't believe it? Try us!

Shocking? It's exactly what an inferior West has been saying to a mighty Soviet bloc for the past 30 years. It's what has saved its skin, and it's what will keep the free world free when China and the U.S.S.R. join forces—the bloody bomb.

Israel has no better ally.

We know the arguments of the sanctimonious peace camp, who abominate any bomb that isn't in their own arsenal. We also know the Arabs will have one of their own eventually, whether we do develop ours or not. Still, for our neighbours it will mean the *novel* threat of a mass holocaust; for us it'll just be a difference in method since we have been living under the threat of annihilation from the moment this State was born.

True, the nuclear arms balance may wipe out the *entire area* or it may not—but the present arms race is going to finish *us* for certain.[13]

Notes

1. *Middle East International*, London, June 1976, p. 4.
2. *Ibid.*
3. *The New York Herald Tribune*, 15 February 1977.
4. *The Guardian*, 10 November 1976.
5. See p. 308.
6. See pp. 258 ff.
7. *The Guardian*, 12 September 1975.
8. See pp. 300 ff.
9. *Al-Thaurah* (Damascus daily), 14 February 1967.
10. *Al-Ba'ath* (Damascus daily), 21 May 1967.
11. *Haaretz*, 3 December 1974.
12. See Sheehan, Edward, 'Step by Step in the Middle East', *Foreign Policy*, March 1976.
13. Kishon, Ephraim, *The Jerusalem Post*, 25 April 1976.

Index

All Futura Books are available at your bookshop or newsagent, or can be ordered from the following address:
Futura Books, Cash Sales Department,
P.O. Box 11, Falmouth, Cornwall.

Please send cheque or postal order (no currency), and allow 45p for postage and packing for the first book plus 20p for the second book and 14p for each additional book ordered up to a maximum charge of £1.63 in U.K.

Customers in Eire and B.F.P.O. please allow 45p for the first book, 20p for the second book plus 14p per copy for the next 7 books, thereafter 8p per book.

Overseas customers please allow 75p for postage and packing for the first book and 21p per copy for each additional book.